THE GREAT CONVERSATION

THE GREAT CONVERSATION

NATURE AND THE CARE OF THE SOUL

BELDEN C. LANE

OXFORD
UNIVERSITY PRESS

OXFORD
UNIVERSITY PRESS

Oxford University Press is a department of the University of Oxford. It furthers the University's objective of excellence in research, scholarship, and education by publishing worldwide. Oxford is a registered trade mark of Oxford University Press in the UK and certain other countries.

Published in the United States of America by Oxford University Press
198 Madison Avenue, New York, NY 10016, United States of America.

CIP data is on file at the Library of Congress
ISBN 978–0–19–084267–3

1 3 5 7 9 8 6 4 2

Printed by Sheridan Books, Inc., United States of America

For Grandfather—and Elizabeth

Belden and Elizabeth in Grandfather's Side.

CONTENTS

PERMISSIONS

Excerpt from "Reverence," from *The Gift* by Daniel Ladinsky, copyright 1999. Used with permission.

Coleman Barks, lines from his translation of "The Sheikh Who Played with Children," in *The Essential Rumi*, copyright 1995 by Coleman Barks. Used with his permission.

Lines from Naomi Shihab Nye's poem "The Art of Disappearing," from her book *Words Under the Words: Selected Poems*, copyright 1995. Used with permission from Far Corner Books, Portland, Oregon.

Lines from Farid Ud-Din Attar's *The Conference of the Birds*, translated by Afkham Darbandi and Dick Davis, copyright 1984, Penguin Random House, UK. Used by permission.

Lines from David Wagoner, "The Silence of the Stars," from *Traveling Light: Collected and New Poems*, copyright 1999 by David Wagoner. Used with permission of the University of Illinois Press.

Lines from the Bennett B. Sims translation of *Lao-tzu and the Tao Te Ching*, copyright 1971, Franklin Watts.

Nathaniel M. Campbell, International Society of Hildegard von Bingen Studies, lines from his translation of Hildegard of Bingen's "O Viridissima Virga." Used with permission.

Part of chapter 3 appeared in "In Quest of the King: Image, Narrative, and Unitive Spirituality in a Twelfth-Century Sufi Classic," *Horizons* 14, no. 1 (Spring 1987): 39–48.

The excerpt from "Who Is This 'Jesus'?" in chapter 13 originally appeared in an article by that title in *Sojourners* 45, no. 4 (April 2016): 34–37.

PREFACE

"The teachers are everywhere. What is wanted is a learner."
—Wendell Berry[1]

I confess that I've always been more of a meddler than a scholar. Meddling in spheres that, strictly speaking, are none of my business. Crossing disciplinary boundaries with abandon, strolling library aisles as if they were forest paths, mixing genres in juxtaposing personal essays and scholarly articles.

If anything, it's getting worse the longer I write. In this book, I wade into the field of natural history with none of the deftness of David Quammen or Barry Lopez. I wander into explorations of cross-species communication without the depth of Celia Deane-Drummond or Peter Wohlleben. I run the risk of oversimplifying the teachings of the saints, lacking the expertise of theologians like Bernard McGinn or Elizabeth Johnson. My forays into thinking ecologically have none of the sophistication of Joanna Macy or Ilia Delio.

I have to bank on the little I know: my experience with a single tree. Yet that's no small thing. Grandfather has been a teacher and friend to me for many years. He's taught me more than I can express in these pages. Reminding me that being a meddler doesn't mean you're merely dabbling in this and that. It means you're thinking across fixed lines that others have drawn. Thinking like a mountain—like a tree. Practicing what E. O. Wilson called the consilience, the "jumping together," of knowledge.[2]

At any rate, I'm in this for the long haul. Engaged with (and dependent on) a much larger community of mentors, filtering my experience through their wisdom. Thomas Berry, Bill Plotkin, and Richard Rohr among them.

I'm grateful for each of the human and other-than-human teachers who've supported me in this work. These include two spiritual directors I've had over the past two decades: a sister in the Dominican Order of Preachers (and my friend), Joan Delaplane, and a cottonwood tree I affectionately know as Grandfather. I can't imagine living an authentic life without either of them.

I'm indebted also to a dog named Desert, a cat named Rusty, and numerous wilderness places that feed my soul. People to whom I owe much include my writing partner, Terry Minchow-Proffitt, a poet after my own heart; my extraordinary editor, Cynthia Read at Oxford University Press; and my encouraging friends—Mike Bennett, Douglas Christie, Jay Kridel, Glenn Siegel, Laura Weber, and Sherryl White, of the Congregation of Sisters of St. Joseph. In the work of Illuman.org, I'm thankful for men on four continents—including Jim Taylor and Stephen Gambill. I'm grateful to Jan Stocking, of the Religious Sisters of Mercy, and Diza Velasco of the Rockhaven Ecozoic Center for embodying Thomas Berry's vision. To John DePuy for his artistic vision and stories of Ed Abbey.

I owe much to my tree-climbing teacher, Guy Mott of AdventureTree; Sally Longley and Beth Roberton of the Australian Network of Spiritual Directors; Anna Killigrew of the Koora Retreat Centre in Boorabbin, Western Australia; Ben Verheul of Ring Lake Ranch, Dubois, Wyoming; Ken Grush of the Missouri Karst and Cave Conservancy; Sandy Cooper of the C. G. Jung Society of St. Louis; the staff of the Iain Nicolson Audubon Center at Rowe Sanctuary in Gibbon, Nebraska; the Department of Parks, Recreation, and Forestry in University City, Missouri; the Cahokia Mounds State Historic Site in Collinsville, Illinois; and the Endangered Wolf Center in Eureka, Missouri.

Kate, I'll never forget watching polar bears with you on the subarctic tundra. Or hiking with you, Jon, among the red-rock wonders of Ghost Ranch. You both make me so grateful to be a father. And then there's Patricia, a landscape of endless amazement for me, the greatest joy of my life. Thank you all.

THE GREAT CONVERSATION

INTRODUCTION

WILDERNESS AND SOUL WORK

"Books and talks and articles about Nature are little more than . . . dinner bells. Nothing can take the place of absolute contact, of seeing and feeding at God's table for oneself."

—John Muir[1]

"I frequently tramped eight or ten miles through the deepest snow to keep an appointment with a beech-tree, or a yellow birch, or an old acquaintance among the pines."

—Henry David Thoreau, *Walden*[2]

I've taken the dirt road toward the monastery, turning off before the Big Eddy takeout. Having left the car under juniper trees overlooking the Chama River, I'm hiking the bluff downstream toward Lake Abiquiu. This is Ghost Ranch land. Georgia O'Keeffe country.

The high desert landscape of northern New Mexico is a sparse terrain, bearing the trace of stories long forgotten. It's a good place to study the parlance of wind and flowing water, to ponder ravens on the wing and the play of shadows among the rocks. The land here cuts through you like a knife, enticing you to relinquish one trusted language for another—or for none at all.

I'd like that to happen, intrigued as I am by what shamans and mystics call "the secret language of nature." I've no illusion of being either a shaman or a mystic, but I've longed all my life to be able to listen as wild things speak. For years I've been a modest wilderness backpacker. Nothing very ambitious, a few days out now and then. But something happens when I'm alone on a wilderness trail. Language falls away, and I lose control. Hearing the voices of birds, insects, and trees, I'm like a child missing out on what's being said—surrounded by whispering adults, spelling out words they don't want me to understand. I'm set on edge, bewildered.

Hasidic Jews tell the story of a rebbe's son who began leaving the synagogue during morning prayers to wander in the woods. The boy loved being alone in the forest. His father was concerned—not simply because the boy neglected his prayers, but because the woods were wild and dangerous in the Carpathian Mountains where they lived. One day he asked his son, "Why do you go out there alone in the forest? I notice you've been doing it a lot lately."

The boy replied, "I go into the woods to find God." "Ah, that's wonderful," replied his dad. "I'm glad you're searching for God. But you know, you don't have to go anywhere special to find the Holy One, Blessed be his Name. God is the same everywhere!" "Yes," answered the boy, "but *I'm* not." God might be the same everywhere, but he knew there was something different about *him* out in the wilds. Stripped of things familiar, he was more vulnerable, more open and receptive.[3]

My own life as a theologian has been absorbed in language about God. But the appeal of wilderness has always made me question the effectiveness of words. Having taught with the Jesuits for thirty-five years, I've been inspired (and intimidated) by their facility with languages. Unable to match their expertise, I've gone in search of a different kind of communication. I'm a scholar-in-recovery now, spending more time on the trail, moving into a deliberate contemplative practice. This invites a gradual abandonment of words, an unnerving entry into what the desert saints called the "via negativa." What's most worth saying, they argued, can't be put into language. "*Neti, neti*" the Upanishads said of Brahman, the ultimate mystery. It's "not this, not that." You reach your heart's longing by discounting all the descriptors people use to contain it. You listen more carefully to what *isn't* being said, or only hinted at obliquely.

Things happen here in the northern New Mexican landscape for which I have no language. I was sitting by a cliff this afternoon fifty feet above the river, where a dry arroyo empties when it rains. Down below, the wind was playing havoc with a ribbon of thick green tamarisks growing along both banks of the stream. It moved with a fury, as if wild things were plunging through the underbrush, thrashing back and forth. Something more than wind was *alive* in there! The hair stood on the back of my neck as I felt its presence.

Later, just before dark, I pressed through the tall, thick branches to pump water for my Nalgene bottle and I couldn't get out of there fast enough. The rushing wind had left a memory of uncontrolled ferocity. God might be the same there as in the monastery chapel down the long dirt road behind me, but *I* sure wasn't.

We're easily deadened by familiarity. How many times have I watched wind racing through tall weeds? Emerson complained that people seldom marvel at a night sky filled with stars. If the stellar extravagance of a typical New England evening were to appear only once in a thousand years, people might really take notice, he said. The seers would "preserve for generations the remembrance of the city of God as shown to them." But when the same array of stars shows itself every night, these "envoys of beauty" are lost on us altogether.[4] The capacity for astonishment escapes us.

We have to be pushed to the edge in order to see and hear what's been talking to us all along. Some people seem inherently better than others at communicating with the natural world. Members of the Findhorn Community in northern Scotland speak of collaborating with the spirits (the devas) of the plants with whom they work. They've grown forty-pound cabbages and other vegetables that never thrive that far north. Listening to intuitions that come to them from the plants they tend, they take seriously what William Blake said about talking with angels. When Blake was nine years old, he saw "a tree filled with angels, bright angelic wings bespangling every bough like stars." On telling his father of his vision, he was threatened with a thrashing if he told a lie like that again. Sadly, there are ways of perceiving that have been beaten out of us.[5]

Out here in the Piedra Lumbre wilderness, I'm tempted to dismiss as fanciful the intimations of mystery that burst into ordinary experience. It happened again last night. I woke up around 2 a.m. with an intuition that I ought to move outside of the tent, that, in a dream I'd just had, a wolf was waiting to speak to me.

The idea was absurd, but I did as I was told. Spreading out my mummy bag between sagebrush plants, I looked up into a sky suddenly alive with shooting stars and the wide band of the Milky Way. It was as wild as Blake's angel-filled tree. Who could imagine such a thing if they'd never seen it? Orion the Hunter lying on his side just above the horizon, arms outstretched, holding Betelgeuse in his right hand. How could I believe it myself? How could I accept my own account over the next few hours of the Jeweled Face (that hexagonal cluster of stars) rising in the eastern sky? Taurus, the Pleiades, Auriga, Gemini, the bright "Dog Star" Sirius. I was blown away by their mind-stopping grandeur. Lupus (the wolf constellation) was lower on the horizon than I could see. But he was there, hiding between Scorpio and Centaurus, whispering, "I told you so."

We're surrounded by a world that talks, but we don't listen. We're part of a community engaged in a vast conversation, but we deny our role in it. We haven't the courage to acknowledge our desperate need for what we can't explain. The soul feeds on what takes us to the edge, but we don't go there willingly.

Conversely, the Earth needs *us* as well right now, given the immense threat of climate change, species loss, and environmental destruction. The planet longs for a body of wild souls who will love it intensely, acting boldly on its behalf. We're just beginning to value wild places—now that we're losing them. Yet we haven't understood how our increased attraction to wilderness is the wilderness's own intense desire for life. Our longing is an echo of its own. The Earth yearns to teach us languages we didn't even know existed. These are more than the arcane exchanges of quantum physicists and astronomers, more than the esoteric skills of medicine men and indigenous healers. They're the multilingual obligation of an extended family.

FINDING A TEACHER

The natural world is full of teachers ready to carry us into amazement. Experiencing them, however, means making ourselves vulnerable to nature's wild splendor. That's the paradox explored by this book. Only in risking ourselves to wind and fire, cave and tree, birdsong and wolf-cry can we grasp the language of glory whispered through it all. These are teachers whose lessons can't be studied from the safety of armchairs. They require "absolute contact," as Muir insisted. They demand our falling in love—crazy, self-abandoning love—in giving ourselves to wild things. Only as we're shocked by what we've not yet subdued do we have a chance of stammering a response to nature's hidden language.

4

Six themes summarize the intent of this book, each of them growing out of my experience with a single cottonwood tree over the past quarter of a century. He lives in a city park across the street from my house, but he's as untamed as any tree you'll find in the woods of an Ozark hollow. I call him Grandfather. Our conversations tend to be one-sided; he speaks with a profundity I find difficult to grasp. Yet these are the things he's taught me over our years together. I'll be developing them further in the chapters that follow.

1. *The teachers are many, but we begin with one.* In this book I'll be looking at twelve particular teachers in the natural world. For thousands of years, spiritual traditions close to the earth have studied them—from Inuit shamans in Greenland to indigenous healers in Brazil. Even the prophet Job declared: "Ask the animals, and they will teach you, or the birds in the sky, and they will tell you. Speak to the earth, and it will instruct you, let the fish in the sea inform you. Which of all these does not know what the hand of the Lord has done?" (12:7–9). The teachers are many, but our access to them comes most often through a single one we've chosen—or, more likely, has chosen *us*. One tree has introduced me to a world that's alive with wonder.

Scientists tell us that "reality is composed of neither wholes nor parts but of whole/parts, or holons." In relating to a single cottonwood tree, therefore, I'm simultaneously connected to every other piece within nature's integral system. The one offers entry into the many. As Richard Rohr says, "How you love one thing is how you love everything."[6]

2. *We communicate to the extent that we learn to love.* To enter the Great Conversation is to bring to consciousness the relationship that already exists between the parts and the whole. To "be" is to be related. Hence, the more I give myself with attentiveness to any other being, the deeper the relationship grows. To most of the people in my neighborhood, Grandfather looks like any other tree. But to one who spends time with him every night, nurturing (over the years) an increasing curiosity about his life, the ordinary becomes wrapped in mystery, even love.

He's driven me to read all I can about trees—from canopy and tree-root research to arboriculture and tree-climbing techniques. Along the way, I've found myself falling in love with what I can't understand. Love is the language by which Grandfather and I communicate best. The principle is an ancient one in the history of spirituality. "Love itself is a kind of knowing," said Gregory the Great in the sixth century. *Amor ipse notitia est.*[7] Deep exposure over time to the inner beauty and mystery of "another" generates an undeniable knowledge of the heart.

3. Suffering is the door, joining us by a mutual woundedness. Something deeper than shared time and space is necessary in fostering an intimate relationship of this sort. It was a common loss that opened Grandfather and me to each other years ago—his blowdown from a storm, my death of a parent. The door connecting us was suffering. A grief we knew in our bodies brought us together.

It's important for us as humans to recognize the common anguish that we share with the other-than-human world. The teachers in this book are facing an overwhelming threat—due to climate change, habitat destruction, the use of pesticides and herbicides. We hear increasingly of "historic" and "record-breaking" forest fires, floods, hurricanes, and loss of species diversity. These are the voices of a planet in travail. They call us to a celebration of all that still lives—and to a language of lament that gives birth to action.

4. The conversation has to engage us with all its participants. We can't pick and choose, reckoning only with daisies and loveable black labs, nature at its nicest. The entirety of a wild and wondrous world confronts us out there. Both predator and prey, things that attract and things that strike us as outrageous. The Great Conversation will have to be pursued with long sleeves and thick gloves, with beekeeper's head-net in place and snakebite kit within reach. It involves risk, a stretching of mind and body.

The dialogue demands our relating to the world with a greater evolutionary/systemic depth, as well as a deeper ethical awareness. Attending to where the Earth hurts most and where the poor hurt most with it. Those we find easy to fear and ignore: refugees fleeing drought and famine, people living near toxic waste dumps, others displaced by forest removal. Each part (human and other-than-human) is integral to the whole.

5. The journey is lifelong, moving through cycles common to the Earth itself. Learning from the others in the natural world is a process that persists throughout our lives. It subtly changes as we move through various stages of psychospiritual development. As *children*, we're drawn upward—to fly with the birds, soar with the wind, and climb into trees. As *adolescents*, we're drawn outward—to flame with the passion of fire, the brilliance of stars, the burning ache of the desert. As *adults*, we move inward—learning how to flow with the river, deepen with the canyon, or retreat to the island. As *elders*, we're taken downward—grounded in the mountain's stability, taken into the cave, recovering the wolf's wild freedom.

Through it all, we're invited to move with the cosmos toward integrating the first and second halves of life; the four elements of air, fire, water, and earth; and teachers from the twelve compass points of an integrated life.[8]

6. The connecting web is a mystery embedded in the ordinary. My falling in love with a tree has, finally, been a profound experience of the sacred. Not in spite of, but *because* of the mundane nature of the exchange. I increasingly encounter God's presence in the rough touch of bark and the sound of rustling leaves. In the ordinary.

The God I encountered growing up in the evangelical fervor of the American South was, by contrast, an *interventionist* in the natural order, seen mainly in the miraculous. There wasn't much to celebrate in a world where God appeared only in the rare interruptions of nature. The spirituality I remember was a pretty thin gruel—not much to feed the soul. The God I marvel at now has outgrown the child I was then.

Ironically, I've rediscovered the shaggy-haired Jesus of my youth by bonding with a tall, leafy cottonwood tree. I'm joined with a larger presence permeating the cosmos. Call it what you will—Teilhard's Cosmic Christ, Rumi's Beloved, our Buddha Nature, Spider Woman's web-weaving magic—it leads me to amazement and praise. I yearn (like an entire world absorbed in evolutionary change) to be drawn into an ever-deepening bond of connection, novelty, and complexity.

The mystics explain this attachment in numerous ways. "We are like lutes once held by God," said Hafiz. "Being away from his warm body fully explains this constant yearning." John Ruysbroeck spoke of a wild and divine Spirit looming beyond the borders of our knowing. "He enters the very marrow of our bones . . . He swoops upon us like a bird of prey to consume our whole life, that he may change it into His." We live in a universe that longs for ever-deepening connection, argued Teilhard. A world bending toward self-transcending fulfillment. "Come," the Beloved pleads with Rumi. "Even if you have broken your vows a thousand times. Come, yet again, come."[9] It's an old voice I hear anew in the tree I've learned to love.

Yet understanding these six insights also requires a *practice.* Not only a hands-on exposure to specific teachers in the natural world, but a commitment to time for silence and contemplation. It means learning to be still before the wisdom of those speaking an unfamiliar tongue. This can take many forms—from Aldo Leopold's "thinking like a mountain" to Douglas Christie's "contemplative ecology" (drawn from the early Desert Christians) to Joanna Macy's merging of Buddhist meditation with "the work that reconnects."[10] Whatever the discipline, the outward journey requires an equally challenging inward journey. Restoring the Great Conversation involves our learning to listen from the inside-out as well as from the outside-in.

NATURE ARCHETYPES AND THE LIFE JOURNEY

How, then, might one's life be shaped by a *lifelong* practice of learning from teachers in the natural world and the saints (or sages) who have pondered them? What if—throughout our lives—we were to embrace the risk and wonder of the wild, living in communion with a world that stretches us at every turn, submitting ourselves to a succession of powerful teachers? When we understand the spiritual life as a progression that echoes the Earth's natural patterns of seasonal change, we find instructors to whom we can apprentice ourselves along the way. We recall teachers who've already come to us at significant points in our lives.

What would happen if you were to *give yourself* to a particular mentor in the natural world, being transformed by a meticulous study of something you love? Perhaps becoming a student of the stars at a time in your life when your horizons need expanding? Studying a patch of sky every evening through a given year, learning the constellations, spending time at the local planetarium, marveling at images from the Hubble Space Telescope, adopting a discipline of meditating under the stars.

Can you imagine apprenticing yourself to the birds that gather at a feeder in your backyard? Studying their species, learning about their migration patterns, how they mate and raise families, the convoluted melodies of their songs. This could lead you to explore the hundreds of references to birds in the Bible, the Quran, or the sutras of the Buddha. Learning to fly, as it were, in your own spiritual life.

If you live in a city, you might spend time with a littered urban creek, perhaps when a flow of creative energy has slowed in your life. What might come from pondering its flow, being aware of the wildlife it supports, identifying the pollutants that clog it, discovering how those living downstream are affected, thinking of clean water as a matter of justice?

I know people who have embraced a deliberate study of desert terrain while recovering from a season of loss in their lives. Entrusting themselves to a place like the Mojave Desert, making periodic trips to explore its dunes and salt flats, spending time with its Joshua trees and creosote bushes, wandering through Badwater Basin in the depths of Death Valley. They've allowed the desert to offer the strange healing of its emptiness.

Over the years, I've attached myself to teachers like these in my own commitment to wilderness backpacking as a spiritual practice. Submitting to these spiritual guides in a penetratingly physical way is a life-changing experience. In wilderness (wherever you find it), there's always risk, but the physical challenge is the least part of it. Out on the trail, I find myself longing for an unsettling beauty, for a power I cannot control, for a wonder beyond my grasp. I can't begin to name the mystery that sings in the corners of an Ozark night. But I *can* be crazy in love with it, scribbling, in turn, whatever I'm able to mumble about the experience.

In the process, the wilderness reaches back. Carl Jung spoke of archetypal images that come to us as readily in the natural world as in our dreams and mythic tales.[11] Nature archetypes include land forms like islands, mountains, or canyons; energy conveyors like fire, wind, and water; flora and fauna like trees, wolves, and birds; even heavenly bodies like the stars and planets.

They project back to us what's going on deep inside us at various times in our lives. Learning to listen to these teachers is powerfully integrating. It's how we participate in the Great Conversation, valuing the "others" as revered teachers in their own right, whether we find them on a wilderness path or the interior life of the psyche. They're alive and well in both.

Jung insisted that there's no hard-and-fast difference between inner and outer, physical and spiritual worlds. They meet in a collective unconscious that's *shared* by the human and more-than-human world. We see "inherited patterns of behavior" in a weaver bird building its perfectly round nest *and* in human beings instinctively drawn to doing things in a circle.[12] Jung discovered mandalas in the fossils he found in the Jura Mountains, in flower petals and the patterns of dried desert mud, in the convoluted dreams of his patients.

Everything points to a longing for integrated consciousness, for perceiving all of reality as an interrelated whole.

When I speak of these nature archetypes as teachers, I'm talking about a *sensuous* reality we experience in body and soul—preferably in a situation that takes us to the edge of what's comfortable. We don't learn about trees without climbing and sleeping in them. We can't understand caves without spending time in them alone in the dark. We won't appreciate the wildness of wolves without hearing them howl in the night a few hundred yards away in a Montana wilderness.

When you give yourself to a teacher in the natural world, you won't be the same any more. An archetype occasions a "bedazzlement of consciousness," says James Hillman.[13] It engages you at every level of your being—it recurs in your dreams, drives you to study its ecology and natural history, prompts scientific investigations of its details, and stirs forays into the writers and poets enthralled by its mystery. It drives you, at last, into the silence of contemplation, into wordless wonder.

The best teachers often arrive without warning. We unconsciously seek them out at various periods of our developmental growth. In this book I've chosen twelve such teachers or archetypes that suggest themselves in the changing seasons of our lives. They form a template patterned after nature's turning seasons, the phases of the moon, the movement of the stars. Bill Plotkin plots a series of life transitions in his "soulcentric developmental wheel," building on the work of Eric Erikson and Joseph Campbell. He sees each of these life passages as marked by a different way of relating to the physical world around us.[14]

Childhood is a time of innocence and wonder, when we're incurably drawn to the magic under every rock and bush. In *adolescence* we're pulled to mystery-probing adventure. We take risks, pushing the edges. *Adulthood* hopefully carries us into a period of creativity and visionary leadership. We look to nature to spark our imagination and to find renewal. In *elderhood*, we assume a more holistic role of tending to the larger Earth community.

In the diagram (Figure I.1), I've plotted these four life stages in relation to the four classical elements of air, fire, water, and earth. A "pattern of four" repeats itself throughout the cosmos. A circle divided into four quadrants— the "squaring of the circle"—is an ancient mandala pattern. It incorporates

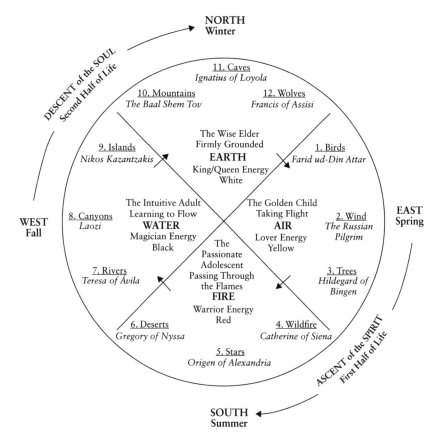

Figure I.1 The Path of Transformation: Nature Teachers and the Mystical Journey.

the insights of medieval alchemy, Jung's depth psychology, and Richard Rohr's spirituality for the two halves of life.

This developmental wheel—what I'm calling the path of transformation—plots the pattern of our spiritual lives as a two-part journey: the ascent of the *spirit* in life's first half and the descent of the *soul* in the second. The fiery, transcendent energy of youth leads to the salty reality of sweat and tears that comes with maturity. If the spirit blazes in the noonday sun, the ripened soul finds its home in the dark places, the night world, the realm of the moon.[15]

Life stages are more fluid than fixed. They vary widely from one person to another. We may find ourselves having to go back to earlier periods in our lives to finish uncompleted work. These stages are not mutually exclusive. Nor is movement from one stage to the next automatic. Individuals in our culture frequently seem to become fixated at an adolescent stage, never moving into the soulful work that maturity requires. People not uncommonly will give up on the full adventure.

My choice of these twelve particular teachers is fairly arbitrary. They are archetypes I've found meaningful, but there are many others one could use in working her way around the wheel. There are an infinite number of archetypes, says Jung.

The first two chapters of the book introduce the idea of the Great Conversation and my experience of it through Grandfather. Subsequent chapters connect each of the twelve teachers with a complementary saint or sage. These include a Sufi mystic, a Jewish rabbi, a Taoist philosopher, five Roman Catholic sisters and brothers, three Eastern Orthodox writers, and a Greek novelist who was declared a heretic. Each of them has served as a spiritual guide at one time or another in my life. They've accompanied me on backpacking trips into terrain similar to the living world that formed their own spiritual lives.

A conclusion reflects on some of the biological, philosophical, and ethical questions the book raises, asking how the notion of a communicative world (and a communicative *God*) can energize our speaking for and with the Earth. Once we begin listening to the great teachers in the natural world, we're empowered (and obliged) to act on their behalf.

RECLAIMING THE ELDERS

I write from the perspective of one moving into the last quadrant of the circle, asking what it means to be an elder at this point in his life. My primary teacher—an old Missouri cottonwood—is himself an elder. Through the years, he's survived flames racing up his trunk, wind shattering his limbs, and insects causing most of his leaves to fall. But he's stayed in one place—like Julian of Norwich confined to her anchor-hold—making the choice over and over again to thrive where he's planted. He models a passionate insistence on life.

An elder does more than move beyond the previous stages of life, passing into a new role as solitary sage. She incorporates the earlier phases in a wider perspective. The crone enters with the wolf into the mountain cave, gathering the energies of trees, stars, and canyons. She's more compassionate (more grounded) than ever, weaving together the disconnected threads of a life that's more than her own.

John Muir was one such elder, smitten with love for an Earth that sings. "As long as I live," he declared, "I'll hear waterfalls and birds and winds sing. I'll interpret the rocks, learn the language of flood, storm, and the avalanche. I'll acquaint myself with the glaciers and wild gardens, and get as near the heart of the world as I can."[16]

He knew the yearning that a storm awakens in the limbs of wind-driven trees. "A few minutes ago," he wrote, after a summer squall had swept through his Yosemite campsite, "every tree was excited, bowing to the roaring storm, waving, swirling, tossing their branches in glorious enthusiasm like worship . . . Every hidden cell is throbbing with music and life, every fiber thrilling like harp strings."[17]

The words "glory" and "glorious" echo through Muir's writings in a frantic effort to describe what he couldn't put into words. His editors urged him to refrain from all this religious language. But he couldn't help himself. Having soundly rejected his Presbyterian roots and his father's angry God, he remained overwhelmed by the wonder he found in the natural world. He didn't stop believing in God; he simply learned that God was far wilder than he'd been taught.[18]

I'm drawn to this old Scots mountaineer, as well as to a tree named Grandfather. They urge me to embrace my calling as an elder, assuming—like them—my place in the family of things. The oldest teachers among us are still in search of learners: a 150-year-old Galapagos tortoise, a 200-year-old bowhead whale, a 5,000-year-old bristlecone pine tree in northern California, 10,000-year-old glass sponges in the East China Sea, 500,000,000-year-old stromatolites in the depths of a Missouri cave. These are the true elders.

***

Stricken dumb by the unnerving beauty of the Chama River Canyon Wilderness, I've headed back upstream toward the car and the road to the monastery. The river gets its name from the Tewa word for "red," the color of the water flowing through this reddish sandstone of northern New Mexico. Coursing down the backbone of North America, it parallels the Continental Divide Trail, which passes nearby. This entire Piedra Lumbre land grant area is magical. A history strewn with stories of cattle rustlers and witches (Ghost Ranch was originally *el Rancho de los brujos*), and the scene of an effort by Chicano activists to secede from the United States in the 1960s. It's a country full of surprises, murmuring the language of the trickster and wandering fool.

Before leaving, I stop at a place up the bluff from the water where an expanse of bright blue river stones lie scattered. Cornflower blue rhyolite, glistening in the morning sun. A product of one of God's blue periods, no doubt. Taking a drunken pleasure over hundreds of years in rolling rocks down the river bed to make them smooth, he's tossed them here in a spray of reckless artistry. I sit among them, listening to what chooses to speak.

Painted layers of Jurassic sandstone adorn the mesa on the other side of the river—red, white, yellow, beige. Water laps on the rocks below. A raven flies in a tight circle overhead, sun catching its black wings in a luminous silver flash. My attention wanders to a brown, speckled stick lying on one of the blue stones nearby. It almost looks like a lizard. No, it *is* a lizard! I just saw it move. A fly tried to land on its clever disguise, and the "stick" suddenly came to life. But their exchange attracts the attention of the raven overhead and yet another scenario begins to unfold, another meal taking shape.

In this shimmering landscape where water flows toward one distant ocean or another, I can't tell whether a stick is pretending to be a lizard or a lizard is pretending to be a stick. Reality here is fluid, indeterminate. The consciousness of the fly transforms into that of a reptile, the perception of the reptile into that of a raptor. In the end, as I watch the mystery unfold, I'm haunted by the roguish language of the wild, by an evolutionary God who delights in endless transformations, a God of restless love revealed in predator and prey alike. Saying that *everything* belongs.

I shoulder my pack and hit the trail, realizing I'm being called to a memory deeper than my own, to a language my body has known all along. The desert speaks—out of lifetimes of patience and pain—with a subtle but insistent voice. My role in the Great Conversation isn't finally to understand, only to listen and to love.

PART I

BEGINNING TO LISTEN

"The first duty of love is to listen."

—Paul Tillich[1]

CHAPTER ONE

RESTORING THE GREAT CONVERSATION

"At the heart of the question of human relationship to other creatures is the use of language . . . Because animals [or trees] are mute, the prevailing opinion goes, it matters not how we treat them."

—David B. Dillard-Wright, "Thinking Across Species Boundaries"[2]

"Questioner: How are we to treat the others?
Ramana Maharshi: There *are* no others."

—*Talks with Sri Ramana Maharshi*[3]

I'm in love with a hundred-year-old eastern cottonwood in the urban park across the street from my house (see Figure 1.1). The Swedish botanist Linnaeus named him *Populus deltoides*. I call him Grandfather. He's a member of the poplar family; his leaves flutter like those of aspen trees in the slightest breeze. The Lakota people say that cottonwood trees are sacred. They pray as their leaves move in the wind.

Grandfather is a male of his species, producing flowery red catkins each spring, full of pollen. The wind carries the pollen to the green catkins of female trees nearby. When pollinated, these produce capsules of tiny seeds attached to cottony parachutes that fill the air in late May and early June. The sexual and reproductive life of my leafy mentor is a marvel of creativity and overabundance. A mature cottonwood tree can produce 25 million seeds in a single season.

For more than twenty years I've entrusted this tree with the care of my soul. In the past six years we've assumed a more formal apprenticeship, exploring deeper ways of communicating with each other. What that means is

Figure 1.1 Grandfather Cottonwood and the Park.
Photo by Jim Taylor.

that we're increasingly falling in love. Communication, in the end, is nothing more than learning to love—"letting the soft animal of your body love what it loves," as Mary Oliver says.[4]

Grandfather and I met more than two decades ago at a time of mutual crisis. My mother was in a nursing home with Alzheimer's disease and dying of cancer. He was dealing with a lightning strike and fierce windstorm that had blown down one of the two great trunks growing from his roots. A twelve-foot high wound was left in his side. That's what first drew me to him. A common hurt opened the door between us.

Grandfather is old for his species. I counted eighty rings in the tree trunk that was cut up and hauled away at the time, twenty-five years ago. Eastern cottonwoods don't live much beyond a hundred years. But Grandfather's still very much alive. He stands more than ninety feet tall, with a fifty-five-foot canopy and a sixteen-foot circumference at his base. When I lean into his hollow at night, I'm a tiny figure, almost hidden from view.

The two of us, Grandfather and I, live on the edge of the city of St. Louis. Our neighborhood is generally safe, but like many city parks, this one has its share of rowdy beer-drinkers, furtive drug dealing, and even occasional gunshots. You learn to be careful. Three years ago, a raucous bunch of partyers set a fire in Grandfather's cavity. It was put out, but his bark is scorched black on that side, twenty feet up.

* * *

He's given me plenty to worry about through the years. In winter storms, I've watched a half-inch layer of ice weighing down his branches. I've stood inside him while sixty-mile-an-hour gusts of wind twisted his frame like tensile steel. One night, after a twelve-inch snowfall, the temperature dropped to almost twenty degrees below zero. Having heard of trees exploding as their sap freezes, I feared for him.

But Grandfather's a survivor. He's withstood the threats of wind, fire, lightning, insects, and ice that bring terror to creatures of the wood. In Tolkien's universe, the treelike Ents, having survived all kinds of dangers, are an extremely patient and cautious race. Time moves slowly for them. They've learned to wait for what they need. Grandfather is like that.

For most people passing through the park, this is an old tree past its prime—scarred by fire, rotting from the inside out, soon to be marked with a large red "X" by the parks and recreation forestry crew. For me, he's a presence in my life that's hard to describe. Martin Buber, in *I and Thou*, spoke of two different ways of relating to a tree. On the one hand, he said, "I can assign it to a species and observe it as an . . . object. But it can also happen, if will and grace are joined, that as I contemplate the tree I'm drawn into a relationship, and the tree ceases to be an It." Buber and his tree were able to enter into a mystery of reciprocity.[5]

Grandfather and I do the same, communicating in a nonverbal, sensuous way. When I pass my hand over the deep furrows of his bark, he doesn't move—not in the way that a horse's flank will shiver under your touch. Trees do nothing in a hurry. Yet they "move their bodies as freely, easily, and gracefully as the most skilled animal or human," said the Austro-Hungarian biologist Raoul Francé. "The only reason we don't appreciate the fact is that plants do so at a much slower pace than humans."[6]

So I touch—and imagine being touched by Grandfather in return. The play of imagination and reverie, operating through the senses, is how we connect. I delight in his smell, pressing my nose each night into the shallow cave of his wounded place. It's the musty smell of old furniture, cinnamon bark, and wood smoke. It reminds me of my dad putting me to bed at night, remembering his smell of stale cigarette smoke (menthol Kools) and Old Spice aftershave.

I'm reliving that memory in these days as I take our grandchild, Elizabeth, over to spend time with Grandfather (see figure in frontispiece). She's two years old, so we're joined as three generations, bridging a biological as well as chronological divide. She delights in the murmuring of his smooth, waxy leaves—evincing a wide-eyed wonder that I've long since lost.

There are deep creases on the thick, gray bark of cottonwoods. Grandfather's bark and my skin are boundaries that define our separateness. Yet we connect more readily as I lean into the cavity in his side. I do that every evening, giving myself to the reverie that Gaston Bachelard says is our most important medium of contact between human consciousness and the natural world. "There are reveries so deep," he says, "reveries which help us descend so deeply within ourselves that they rid us of our history."[7]

Within that reverie, I may sense a subtle shift in consciousness—a thought or feeling that arises within me (and yet seems to be *more* than me). It's nothing I can verify. The mystery of our entire relationship is that "nothing happens" as such. I hear no voices. We share no identifiable language. And yet we connect.

RECOVERING WHAT WE'VE LOST

How do I explain my fascination with this tree? It's the mystery of recovering something basic and primeval. Thomas Berry said we've lost our ability to converse with the rest of the natural world. "We are talking only to ourselves," he complained. "We are not talking to the rivers, we are not listening to the wind and stars. *We have broken the Great Conversation.*"[8]

Researchers have been trying to correct this—probing the songs of humpback whales, studying the subsonic stomach rumblings of elephants, exploring the verbal and nonverbal language of dolphins. But Berry is concerned with more than linguistic exploration. He seeks a widening sense of interactive community, as the entire cosmos becomes conscious of its common source in the divine mystery.

My fascination with Grandfather is more than an experiment in cross-species communication. I think of him as my leafy spiritual guide. It may sound strange to speak of a tree as a mentor. But what do you look for in a good spiritual director? You want a fine listener. Not prone to talking too much—not full of himself. Someone who knows loss, who's familiar with the depths of contemplative silence. Grandfather is good at these things.

Too often spiritual guides seem to think it's their job to make people "feel good," hoping that people *like* them, become dependent on them. The indifference of trees is refreshing. They don't try to be nice. They aren't invested in whether we like them or not. They care nothing for most of the things that make us anxious. Trees are disinterested teachers drawing us out of ourselves, reminding us that we aren't in control, taking us to our knees in awe.

Carl Jung regrets that we've lost our "emotional participation" in nature's mystery. We don't talk to trees anymore. We hear thunder, and it's no longer the voice of the spirit coming on the wind. We notice raindrops glistening on a spider's web without being astonished. "[Our] immediate communication with nature is gone . . . and the emotional energy it generated has sunk into the unconscious."[9] That's a great loss, one that signals our spiritual poverty while allowing us to destroy a world we once held in reverence.

We haven't a language anymore for what once energized our myths and fired our imagination. We've stopped listening to trees. "The tree which moves some to tears of joy, is in the eyes of others only a green thing that stands in the way," said William Blake.[10] We suspect that people who are brought to tears by trees have been reading too much Tolkien. They still believe in fairy tales, reverting back to what French anthropologist Lucien Lévy-Bruhl called the participation mystique of a so-called "primitive" mindset.[11]

Our problem is that we've bought into a dualistic worldview that strictly distinguishes human rationality from the rest of an embodied creation. This dual way of thinking cuts against the conviction of indigenous peoples—and the biblical tradition as well—that creation is a seamless whole. All of it is sacred. You can't pull out a single part as superior to all the others without damaging the whole. Trees are crucial, not simply because they provide timber, a carbon sink, and oxygen in support of human life. They witness to something holy in their own majestic beauty.[12]

Carl Jung described the forest as a "place of magical happening."[13] It's more than an imaginative symbol of the unconscious. It participates in the very mystery to which it points. The forest is a place where we touch the sacred, where we're most in touch with ourselves. Jung looked to the great oaks of Europe for a charmed wisdom. In Japan, the practice of *shinrin-yoku* ("forest bathing") draws on the energy of ancient cedars and cypress trees.[14] I myself find more than enough wonder in a single cottonwood tree.

For many people household pets are their most available access to the mystery of the "others" in the natural world. Trees speak with a cleaner, more detached honesty. They lack the ingratiating solicitousness of a dog or even a cat. They don't come to you. They don't wag their tails and purr for attention. They're easily ignored, taken for granted. Yet they constitute a keystone—biologically and spiritually—in any life-sustaining system. They prevent erosion, regulate atmospheric balance, lend elegance to the world, and undergird the community of everything that lives.

Indigenous healers speak of the enormous generosity of trees. Yachaq elders in the upper Amazon learn of their medicinal value through direct communication with the trees. As *vegetalistas* (plant specialists), they know how to listen to the foliage, attending to what trees send them in dreams and visions. They talk to the standing folk when gathering medicinal substances. They're sensitive to the compassion that plants have for human beings.

A Cherokee legend says that when humans first appeared on the Earth, the insects and animals were outraged at the way they casually killed and trampled the homes of all the four-legged, six-legged, and eight-legged creatures. In reaction, the animals and insects brought diseases into the world to afflict these arrogant two-legged ones. But when they asked the plants and trees to help them punish the humans, they refused. "The human beings are our children," they said. "We have to help them even if they're foolish."

Consequently, "each tree, shrub and herb, down even to the grasses and mosses, all agreed to furnish a remedy for each one of the diseases the insects had given."[15] Twenty-five percent of prescription medicines today are drawn from the four hundred thousand known plant species on our planet. We wouldn't be here if it weren't for the trees and other plants.

EXPANDING A WIDER CONSCIOUSNESS

So how do we understand this notion of "communicating" with other species? What specifically happens between Grandfather and me? I don't possess any particular skills of "listening" to trees. I don't hear anything more than what you'd hear. Our connection isn't a paranormal exercise in altered states of consciousness. I've never heard Grandfather speaking with a deep, gravelly voice. I just spend a lot of time in silence with him. Every night I go over, leaning into his hollow, moving into a practice of contemplative stillness. I let go of thoughts and words. Sinking into the tree's heartwood, releasing what's been rummaging around inside me through the day.

Once in a while, something comes up. Is it from inside me or from inside him? I never know for sure. It may be a feeling of being unaccountably loved in that moment, feeling utterly at home in the hollow of that tree. Or it may be a thought that arises: "Just stand there," it might say. "All you really need will come to you." I hear this spoken with authority, because it's something only a tree can say with conviction. Grandfather can't go anywhere for what he needs. He has to wait for everything to come to him. When a tree says this, I listen.

Even when nothing passes between us, being together is an end in itself. That's how it is with anyone you love. I call him Grandfather not in an effort to claim him as *my* tree so much as to put myself in a posture of being *his* person. Someone who simply enjoys sitting at his feet, admiring how big he is, imagining what it's like to be a tree. Isn't that what grandchildren do?

I delight in wandering over to the park with my granddaughter Elizabeth. Imagining the tree's pleasure in our coming. The three of us fit together, as she and I stand in his hollow. That's a mysterious thing in itself.

Finding a "fit" in nature has long intrigued ecological psychologist James Gibson. His theory of affordances focuses on the way a bird or animal discovers a particular niche in the environment that offers an occasion for connection. A tree branch affords a perch for an owl. An abandoned woodpecker hole provides a nest for squirrels. The coming together of the creature's need and the niche's affordance is a dynamic process, says Gibson. The two encounter each other in a mutual exchange as both subject and object.[16]

You might think of a child as similarly drawn (with her grandfather) to the niche of a hollow tree that affords a hiding place where she (and he) can safely see without being seen. In a transaction of this sort, the human and other-than-human parties are joined in the affordance and acceptance of a mutual fit.

Having experienced such a relationship with Grandfather over a period of years, my perception of everything else in nature has changed. I've learned to expect the rest of the world to be alive as well. (As any perceptive two-year-old might do.) Thomas Berry cautions that we have to stop perceiving the world as a collection of objects. It's a communion of subjects.[17] We need to be thinking more ecologically about everything. Ecology, after all, is the study of connectedness. It focuses on the intricate bonds that pull us out of our isolation.

A huge shift in consciousness is underway in our time. A sea change from an "I and it" marketplace conception of the world to an "I and thou" sense of communal identity. Joanna Macy describes it as a "Great Turning," an ecological revolution widening our awareness of the intricate web that connects us. Teilhard de Chardin called it an evolution of consciousness, an emergence of the "planetization" of humankind. We have to think now like a planet, not like separate individuals.

We need a "psyche the size of the earth," James Hillman says, participating in a collective unconscious that includes the whole of nature. We can't think of the individual soul any more as confined to the body alone. "The greater part of the soul lies outside the body," he argues.[18] My own soul is enlarged immensely by my relationship with Grandfather.

All this forces me to think in radically different ways about how I speak of this tree. In distinguishing our separate identities, where do I make the cut between "me" and the "not-me"? Where does Grandfather begin and I end? Am I an isolated self, a psyche that stops at the boundary of my skin? Or is there a fluidity between my spiritual life and the life of this tree, to such an extent that I recognize him as involved in the care of my soul?

Sir James Frazer, in *The Golden Bough,* his classic study of magic and religion, described an ancient practice of entrusting one's soul to a tree. He said that in so-called "primitive societies," a person might take her soul out of her body and "deposit it for security in some snug spot, intending to replace it in her body when the danger was past . . . or she might leave her soul there permanently." Trees, he said, were preferred places for doing this.[19]

Trusting one's soul for safekeeping in a tree is an idea I can appreciate. A "soul friend," an *anam cara* in the Celtic tradition, suggests a more intimate relationship than what one might have with a spiritual director. It involves a bonding and connecting of souls, possibly even across species boundaries. All I know is that part of me is inescapably lodged in a tree across the street from my house.[20]

Grandfather has something invested in me as well. I regularly share ideas with him about this work, wondering at times if he's not the source of what comes to mind as I write. I think of the two of us as working together on this project. I'm intrigued, for that matter, by the number of artists, composers, and scientists who have attributed much of the power of their creative work to a teacher in the natural world, joining together in producing a common effort.

In 1829, the German composer Felix Mendelssohn made a visit to Fingal's Cave on the island of Staffa off Scotland's western coast. It's one of the largest sea caves in the world, cut by ocean waves out of black lava pillars rising from the earth. The cavern is a huge cathedral cut into stone. Years ago, I was blown away, standing inside it. But Mendelssohn wasn't simply overwhelmed by the haunting beauty of the place. He *heard* it "singing" to him. He sent a postcard back home to his sister, scribbling the opening notes of the Hebrides Overture that "came into his head" there. The idea for Jules Verne's novel *Journey to the Center of the Earth* also came to him in that cave, as did some of J. M. W. Turner's best impressionist paintings. This single cave has been extraordinarily productive in all kinds of artistic creations.

In 1972, the French composer Olivier Messiaen traveled to Bryce Canyon in Utah. He was astounded by the number of tall, red-orange hoodoos (spires) that rise from the canyon floor. Messiaen was gifted (or cursed) with a neurological condition called synesthesia, a strange mixing of the senses. When he saw colors, he heard distinct musical notes accompanying them. As he wove his entire experience into an orchestral work, *Des canyons aux étoiles* ("From the canyons to the stars"), he confessed that he was, to a large extent, simply a medium for the music that the canyon itself created.

You find a similar sensitivity among scientists. In 1983, Barbara McClintock won the Nobel prize in biology for her work on the cellular structure of corn plants. In her acceptance speech in Stockholm, she thanked the corn plants for what they had taught her. She attributed her success to having listened carefully to what the corn stalks were saying, having developed what she called a "feeling for the organism." George Washington Carver claimed the same thing about his work with peanut plants: "If you love it enough, anything will talk with you."[21]

French philosopher Maurice Merleau-Ponty argued that human perception is deeply invested in a full-bodied exchange with the rest of the world. Sitting near his home on the seacoast near Bordeaux, he writes: "As I contemplate the blue of the sky . . . I abandon myself to it and plunge into this mystery, it 'thinks itself within me.' I *am* the sky itself as it is drawn together and unified . . . my consciousness is saturated with this limitless blue."[22] The lines blur between his act of perceiving and the stunning character of what he perceives. The sky "thinks itself" within him.

In each case, these people are recognizing a wisdom and creativity that comes through them, but also from beyond them—from the earth itself. They become a channel for what's being created together. I sense something akin to this with respect to Grandfather. I hope for it, at least, wanting to listen carefully enough to be able to write out of what I hear him speak.

RECOVERING A FORGOTTEN LANGUAGE

Native peoples have been telling us for a long time that the world speaks. We just haven't been listening. We've dismissed as naïve the stories of shamanic teachers referring to the "secret languages" of nature.

A David Wagoner poem shares the story of Laurens van der Post, a South African explorer, sitting by a campfire with San Bushmen in the Kalahari Desert. They don't believe him when he says he can't hear the stars singing, as *they* can so clearly. They lead him away from the noise of the crackling fire so as to attend more carefully.

> Do you not hear them now?
> And van der Post listened, not wanting
> To disbelieve, but had to answer,
> No. They walked him slowly
> Like a sick man to the small dim
> Circle of firelight and told him
> They were terribly sorry,
> And he felt even sorrier
> For himself and blamed his ancestors
> For their strange loss of hearing,
> Which was his loss now . . . [23]

What the Bushmen perceived so readily was lost on the European sensibilities of the Afrikaner explorer: nature speaks. Poets and mystics have always acknowledged this. We don't comprehend the language of the others, yet the Psalmist says "their voice goes out through all the earth, and their words to the end of the world" (Psalm 19:3–4). Our failure to hear the "music of the spheres" is the measure of our enduring poverty as children of the Enlightenment.

Hildegard of Bingen, a twelfth-century Benedictine lover of nature, perceived the cosmos as a vast musical instrument pulsing with praise. Every tree branch and star plays its part in a symphony of vital joy (*symphonia vitae laetate*), making audible the world's praise of God's glory. She heard musical tones that others couldn't. It was part of her gift as a visionary. She spoke of receiving, by divine illumination, an "unheard music," even an "unknown language" unique to the more-than-human world. She composed a secret alphabet for this hidden language, providing new names for more than eight hundred plants—allowing her to speak to and for them.[24] She was a gifted herbalist, fascinated by the healing powers of all things green.

In the earliest biography of Francis of Assisi, Thomas of Celano wrote of the saint's remarkable ability to converse with birds, rabbits, and wolves. "In a wonderful way, unknown to others, he could discern the *secrets of the heart of creatures* like someone who has passed into the freedom of the glory of the children of God."[25] Muhammad similarly knew that animals and birds "with wings outspread" gave praise to Allah, "each one knowing its own mode of prayer" (Quran 24:41).

The Baal Shem Tov, eighteenth-century founder of the modern Hasidic movement, is said to have spoken twenty-six different languages. These were more than Hebrew, Yiddish, or Polish. He knew the tongues of birds, trees, animals, plants, and clouds as well. In the Jewish mystical tradition every creature has its own distinctive *nigun* (song or melody). Rabbi Nachman of Breslov exclaimed, "How wonderful it would be if one could only be worthy of hearing the song of the grass. Each blade of grass sings out to God without any ulterior motive and without expecting any reward." He urged people to pray in pastureland and meadows because "grass awakens the heart."[26]

In world mythology—from indigenous traditions along the Pacific Rim to the Eurasian Steppe—people have described a universal "green language" (*langue verte*), often associated with the language of the birds. In the Jerusalem Talmud, Solomon's wisdom is rooted in God's gift of understanding avian speech. Birdsong was considered a secret and perfect language, akin in Sufi thought to the language of the angels. Mircea Eliade mentions "the existence of a specific secret language [of nature]" among shamanic teachers in many cultures—from the Lapps of northern Sweden to the Yakuts of eastern Siberia.[27]

Folklore is rich with stories about the languages spoken by creatures among themselves. A medieval legend affirms that on the first Christmas Eve, at the stroke of midnight, each of the animals in the stable at Bethlehem burst into praise, singing (of course) in Latin. "*Christus natus est* (Christ is born)," crowed the rooster. "*Quando?* (when)," asked the raven. "*Hoc node* (this night)," the rook replied. The ox then murmured, "*Uuubi?* (where)?" as the sheep bleated in response, "Beh-eh-eh-le-hem!" The whole earth cries glory, declares the traditional wisdom—every creature responding in its own dialect.

So what's happening to me in my pursuit of all this? Am I reverting to a naïve world of fantasy and myth? Since retiring from half a lifetime of teaching at a Jesuit university, I've been admittedly "in recovery," letting go of my need for rational analysis and proof. As a professor, I'd cultivated an intense curiosity, a questioning mind, a search for precise language. All good things. But I wouldn't have gotten this far with Grandfather had I not released my grip on the academic's suspicion of unconventional ideas.

In one of George MacDonald's fantasy novels, a young man wanders into a dark forest, farther than others have been able to venture. "You must have fairy blood in you," says an old woman who meets him there. "You wouldn't have gotten so far into this wood if it weren't so."[28] I wonder if there isn't a bit of "fairy blood" in all of us, something we tap into as we yield to a deeper intuition, listening to a world that's more alive than we ever dreamed.

In the end it can't be one or the other: *either* scholarly research *or* the intuition of myth and dream. Our deepest encounter with the world demands both. The most creative minds have been "clinical mythologists" like C. G. Jung, "mystical paleontologists" like Teilhard de Chardin, and "astronomer novelists" like Carl Sagan. None of them fit the usual patterns; all of them thought outside of the box, weaving stories in their passionate probing of the universe.

THE TRANSFORMING POWER OF STORY

Storytelling is the most effective way to heal our rift with the others, seeing ourselves as part of a 13.8-billion-year history of exploding stars, evolving species, and emerging consciousness. The world sings in languages we're still trying to untangle as scientists, backpackers, and poets. We deal with the immensity of it all by spinning tales——connecting around the campfire, calling in the mysteries of the night, making sense of what we can't otherwise explain.

There are stories, carried by the land, that sometimes come leaping into our imagination without warning. Tales we may have heard before suddenly burst into life as they "live" themselves through us in a given moment, *insisting* on being heard. I've experienced it myself.

For years I've told a Zuni tale of a young boy's first deer hunt. It's one of those stories you can't hear often enough, knowing it holds a mystery you might finally "get" on the 103rd time of listening. I never imagined that one day I'd find myself *inside* the tale, "living" the intensity of the story.[29] First the narrative, then my experience of being plunged into its life:

***

If you were to drive a hundred miles west of Albuquerque, New Mexico, into the high desert country of Cibola National Forest toward Bluewater Lake, you'd enter the ancient hunting grounds of the Zuni Pueblo people. There you might hear a story of a young brave's first deer hunt, told in initiation ceremonies to this day.

The boy would have prepared a long time for this pivotal event in his life, learning how to follow tracks, how to walk in silence over dry leaves, how to shoot an arrow straight and true, and (most importantly) how to sing the Sacred Song of Promise and Offering that's expected of a hunter. He would have learned that one never takes the life of an animal without offering something in return. Asking the deer to give his life so that the boy and his family might live, the boy would hang red prayer streamers in a tree in the deer's honor and offer sacrifice to the Great Spirit on his behalf.

If the boy did these things well, the deer would be set free from his bone antlers and fur coat to become a spirit animal, free to roam the high plains and upper meadows of the Spirit World. This is something a deer longs for more than anything else, so much so that he could come to relish the boy's arrows—so long as he'd be sure the boy would remember what was required of him.

The young hunter set out early one morning with his friend and tutor, Coyote, following fresh tracks in a dusting of light snow leading up a long canyon. Coyote said that whenever they spotted the deer up ahead, he would cut off to the side and make his way to the head of the canyon to block the animal's escape. The boy would then begin to sing his Sacred Song of Promise and Offering, singing the deer to himself.

Before long they caught sight of the animal, an eight- or ten-point buck, a beautiful creature that (if taken) would provide meat for the boy and his family for much of the winter. Coyote did as he said he would, cutting off to the side to make his way to the head of the canyon to seal off any escape. Meanwhile the boy began to sing his sacred song: "Heya, Heya, listen deer. Thy footprints I see, I following come. Sacred favor for thee I bring as I run."

But he was nervous, stumbling over some of the words. The deer, listening up ahead, thought to himself, "Young hunters are like that! They forget the words, and they also forget to offer sacrifice." He turned then to race over the rocks toward higher ground.

The boy, filled with chagrin, gathered all of his concentration about him, anxious to fulfill everything expected of him in the ceremonial hunt. Gradually the hunter and his prey entered into a strange sort of dance, making their way in flight and pursuit up the canyon floor. The deer moved more slowly as the words of the song sank into his hearing. "I could die contentedly," he thought, as he stopped higher up the ravine. "If only I knew he'd remember to offer sacrifice. But who can be sure?" Once again, the animal turned to flee, but by this time he had reached the head of the canyon where Coyote was blocking his escape.

Suddenly this ten-point buck, filling the air with energy and the smell of musk, turned to charge at the young hunter. The boy nervously drew and shot, but his arrow missed, glancing off the antlers. Fortunately, the deer missed as well, racing past the boy. But he turned to charge a second time as the boy drew and shot once more. This time the arrow found its mark, sinking to the feathers in the breast of the great beast. The buck staggered and fell.

Filled with feelings of fear, regret, and necessity, the boy ran to the deer. He should have stayed back to shoot again; that's what Coyote was yelling at him to do. But in his excitement, he could only think of what came next in the choreographed ballet of the ceremonial hunt. The deer was still alive, struggling to get to his feet as the boy ran to embrace it and speak his holy words, "I give thanks this day, my brother, to have drunk your sacred wind of life."

The buck thrashed his antlers back and forth as the boy dodged their points to press his face to the deer's neck and speak his holy words. Caught up in this odd, tortured wrestling, the boy was close enough to breathe the deer's life breath, to be covered with his blood. Seeing at last how eager the boy was to do all that was expected of him, the deer knew that this boy would not forget to offer sacrifice. With a sigh of release, he relinquished his spirit into the boy's clutching arms. In that moment the young brave, the deer, and the ground that absorbed their common blood were caught up in a mystery the boy would never forget for the rest of his life.

He would return from time to time to that place—the sacred place, the place of first death and the promise of life. There he would remember his entry into the mystery of the Great Hoop, knowing that in the turning of all things, we take the lives of others and we offer our own in return. In doing so, the gift is offered over and over again in endless exchange.

***

I was planning on using this story three years ago as part of a men's retreat at Ghost Ranch. We'd be looking at the Desert Fathers and Mothers, attending to the "mother work" the men needed to do. The story wandered through my mind as my wife and I drove south from the ranch a few days before the retreat.

Suddenly a deer leapt off a tall bluff alongside the road, slamming into the front of our car. For a split second I saw with perfect clarity the light-brown body of that beautiful animal, her long ears, black nose and eyes, muscles taut. Then a sickening crunch, an appalling dread.

I braked the car and ran back to the animal lying beside the pavement. She was still alive—a doe with a full udder, I noticed with horror. She was unable to move, twitching her ears and racing her eyes back and forth in shock. Feeling helpless, I ran my hands over her warm coat, muttering over and over how sorry I was. Mouthing the words of the Twenty-Third Psalm, as I'd done at my own mother's dying many years earlier.

As I held the animal in my arms, I saw her eyes relax. Sensing her making the decision to accept her death at my hands. She gave up resisting and slowly stopped breathing. Allowing the one who'd caused her death to offer comfort in the end. It was as strange a gift as I've ever received.

I'd been heading that morning toward Mount Taylor where I'd hoped to camp that night with my friend Mike. He and I would be coming back for the retreat at the ranch a few days later. I reported the accident, receiving assurance from the State Game and Fish Department that someone would pick up the deer's body. Patricia and I then drove our damaged, but still drivable car to Albuquerque, where Mike and I continued on our trip to the Turquoise Mountain, one of the four sacred peaks of the Navajo.

We drove in silence, knowing somehow that we'd been meant to carry the animal's spirit to the holy mountain. A mother deer had come to us (as a circle of men), and we had a duty to honor her death. Late that afternoon just below 11,000 feet on the mountain's northern slope, we found a place with flattened grass where a deer had slept the night before. It was perfect. We knelt there, releasing the doe's spirit and much of my guilt. The next morning, we tore a bandana into red prayer streamers and tied them to a tree in the deer's memory.

On our way back to the ranch two days later, I was appalled to find the deer still lying beside the road, a raven atop her bloated body. Returning with a pick and shovel, I dug a grave and left more prayer streamers, praying for the fawn or fawns the doe had left behind. I learned later that three-month-old fawns are nearly weaned by that time in September. They would have survived.

The encounter filled me with a flood of grief and gratitude, knowing I'd received an astonishing gift in the convergence of the story and the incident on the road. It was as if the deer had sought us out, like an animal yielding itself to the hunt. Our efforts to honor her spirit and respect her body were part of an exchange we were blessed in keeping. The deer, in turn, blessed our work in the days that followed. She came (in the story I somehow managed to tell) as a spirit animal, entering with us into a conversation we hadn't expected, a Desert Mother, bringing gifts to a vulnerable community of men.

Animals come to us as we need them—leaping across the rocks, wandering into the stories we tell, drifting into the dreams that come to us in the night. The "others" are far more generous than we realize, giving themselves to us in a mystery we haven't begun to understand.

I find this in my relationship with a wounded tree named Grandfather as well. We commit each night to a ritual that joins us as one. We are both hunters, hungry for a connection we aren't able to define. Gathering each evening as a hunting party—stalking the holy, pursuing a grandeur that's more than us, waiting for what passes in the dark. "A hunting party sometimes has a greater chance of flushing love and God out into the open than a warrior all alone," says Hafiz.[30] Think of us as surreptitious trackers of the divine, watching the moon rise over the distant trees, yearning for a mystery we've glimpsed partially in each other, but that lies beyond us both.

THE DREAM

My granddaughter Elizabeth is another part of this collusion. She became party to it even before she was born, coming to me in a dream. The most insistent stories appear in our dreams, calling us deeper into soul work and offering yet another avenue into the Great Conversation. Two months before Ellie's birth, I had a powerful dream, bordering on the visionary.

In the dream I was standing in the park next to the cavity in Grandfather's side, when a little girl, maybe three years old, stepped out from inside the tree. She was incandescent—a dryad spirit in a dazzling white dress, seemingly lit from within. Blond hair, blue eyes. A striking presence. Somehow I knew she was my granddaughter, though she hadn't yet been born.

She'd emerged, not simply from the tree's hollow, but from *inside* its heartwood. I stood there in astonishment, as she asked if I'd like to go back inside the tree with her. She assured me that it wasn't frightening and led the way through Grandfather's great wound into the tree's center.

We climbed up its dark, womb-like interior, ascending higher and higher until we reached the inside tips of the highest branches. For the first time I was experiencing Grandfather from the *inside*––what I'd always dreamed of doing in our years together. I was taken into the depths of his interior life. When we reached the very top, the dream ended and I awoke.

I'd been brought into the core of Grandfather's being by a granddaughter I'd yet to meet—in a strange overlapping of generations erasing all arboreal and human differences. It was a breathtaking experience, made even more extraordinary two months later as I stood with my wife in a hospital waiting room, holding our newborn, *blond and blue-eyed* granddaughter in my arms.

Ellie is one of the most important links in my apprenticeship to this revered old cottonwood and my entry into the mystery of the Great Conversation. It's taken an old tree, a young child, and even a white-tailed doe—pushing me beyond the edge of language—to occasion an interior work I hadn't imagined possible.

My granddaughter makes me aware of the importance of doing this work for the generations to come. Renewing the Great Conversation isn't only what we do for ourselves. It assures the future of an Earth where life in all its diversity continues. It occasions a rebirth of wisdom, a community of hope. May it be so.

CHAPTER TWO

FALLING IN LOVE
WITH A TREE

"Everything want to be loved. Look at them trees. Notice how the trees do everything people do to get attention . . . except walk?"

—Shug Avery in Alice Walker's *The Color Purple*[1]

"It is a lovely language, but it takes a very long time to say anything in it, unless it is worth taking a long time to say, and to listen to."

—Tolkien's Treebeard, speaking of his Entish language[2]

Talking to trees isn't something I've always done. It began rather abruptly two and a half decades ago at a significant turning point in my life. My last parent was dying. As an only child, I was overwhelmed by an unexpected sense of cosmic loneliness. Three things happened at the time, coming together in the same month with a strange synchronicity. My mother died in the nursing home where she had lived for the past three years. A great storm took down half of the tree that I'd come to know as Grandfather. And my first conversation with trees occurred on an overnight backpacking trip down in the Ozarks.

Three weeks before my mother finally died, I'd needed to get away to sort things out for myself. On a March afternoon I hiked into Lower Rock Creek, a narrow gorge cutting through the mountainous terrain of the Ozark Plateau.[3] A week earlier there had been a twelve-inch snowfall, followed by a thaw and heavy rain that brought a flash flood careening down the gorge. As I walked in, I saw branches and debris caught in tree limbs high overhead. It was a landscape awash with the memory of rushing water.

Downstream I found a place to camp, set up my tent, and built a small fire, eating supper as the sun was setting. I rarely build a fire in the woods, but needed the comfort of one that night. Sitting beside it, I noticed a small pine tree across the fire from me, maybe two feet tall. I hadn't seen the tree before and said hello. I wasn't accustomed to talking to trees at the time. (I've learned better since.) In the reverie evoked by the flames I imagined the tree responding, asking me to tell a story. That's what kids do, after all, when you're sitting around a fire.

I'd never told a story to a tree before, but I liked the idea—especially as a Lakota tale about death and transformation came to mind. A storyteller has to adjust his narrative to his listener, of course, and there were things I had to explain that the tree might not understand. It was a challenge at first, but I sensed we were both getting into it.

Night was coming on as I took another handful of sticks to put on the fire. As the light blazed up I noticed three or four *other* little pine trees that had gathered around. I could have sworn they hadn't been there when I'd set up camp, as if they'd snuck in to listen to the story along with the other tree.

As a storyteller, I don't ever remember being listened to as carefully as I was that night by a handful of trees in an Ozark forest. I was stunned by the intensity with which I imagined them attending to the tale. I realized that they'd never heard a story before. Few people wander into this remote stretch of wilderness, mostly hunters and backpackers: people who aren't accustomed to telling stories to trees. So this was a novelty.

I also realized that the trees *knew* what I was talking about, as they listened to a tale about death and transformation. They'd just survived a flash flood rushing over them. Amazingly, they hadn't been uprooted. Moreover, they were surrounded by death, growing out of the rotted remains of grandfathers and grandmothers before them.

But there was something still *more*. At last, I caught on. They were watching the fire along with me. None of these trees had ever seen flames before. There was no sign that a forest fire had swept through the area or that a campfire had been built there during their lifetime. The hair rose on the back of my neck as I realized these trees were listening to a story about their own death and transformation as they *watched wood burn*. Seeing the stuff of their own being transformed into flickering tongues of orange, red, and yellow, then left as a light gray ash that was blown away by the wind.

This was my first experience of communicating with trees. They never spoke, but the exchange between us was as powerful as anything I'd known. What made it possible, as I look back on it now, was a mutual convergence of vulnerabilities. Hearing the story as the *trees* heard it, I was carried more deeply into my own untapped grief. I was given another way of looking at my mother's dying and offered a new sense of community, shared across a boundary bridged by mutual loss.

HEARING NEW VOICES IN A TIME OF CRISIS

Communication in its deepest form is rooted in a shared vulnerability. This is happening for the human family on a cosmic level today, inviting a richer encounter with the rest of the natural world. The Earth is threatened as never before by unnatural forces of climate change, habitat destruction, and loss of biodiversity. Human beings are beginning to acknowledge the extent to which their throwaway culture, consumerist mentality, and rampant militarism are contributing to this threat, how it's destroying *us* as well.

We and the more-than-human "others" find ourselves staring together into a fire of apocalyptic loss. Yet within that looming crisis, new opportunities emerge. New ways of listening and being heard arise. The Great Conversation is gradually being renewed *because* of our growing consciousness of being collectively at risk.

My encounter with a few pine trees in an Ozark wilderness made me open to the old cottonwood I'd soon be meeting back home, newly threatened himself by death. At a time of crisis in my life, it seemed that trees everywhere were trying to tell me something, that I wasn't alone.

Restoring the Great Conversation requires our meeting and being met by others in the natural world in the most intimate and risk-filled way. Martin Buber observed that "all real living is meeting." Loren Eiseley said that you don't really meet *yourself* until you see your reflection "in an eye other than human."[4] It's only in seeing and being seen by one who is radically different (another species, glimpsed in the wild) that you begin to know the mystery of who *you* are as well.

Looking into the eyes of a bear twenty feet away on a mountain trail, being "stared through" by a doe with two fawns in tow, gazing on the face of a horse you've learned to love, holding the head of a dying dog you've had to put down: you *know* in that moment that you've been seen. You know that something rich in mystery and spirit is looking back at you, opening you to a world full of others erupting in your dreams, interacting in ways you'd never imagined. But too often we aren't paying attention. We're blind and deaf to a world that's truly alive, responding to us at every turn, no less vulnerable to suffering than we ourselves.

MAKING CONTACT: GOING OUT AS GOING IN

How, then, do we connect more deeply with the world of sentient beings around us? It won't happen without our venturing out, exposing ourselves to the beauty and threat of nature's wild wonder, seeing where it rages, where it suffers, and bringing our own poverty with us.

We marvel at the wings of a monarch butterfly along a Wisconsin stream, knowing that the milkweed plant it feeds on is being wiped out by herbicides. We hike the Nevada desert along Lake Mead, appalled by the 130-foot drop in water level caused by a diminishing supply of water in the Colorado River—recognizing the immense dangers facing the American West. We get down on our hands and knees in our own backyard, noticing how little life and diversity are left in a weed-free lawn––discovering at firsthand the consequences of monocropping.

The world of nature once seemed invincible, threatening us by its overpowering force. Now it's ravaged by our reckless efforts to control what we used to fear. Everything is askew. Hence our "going out" must also involve a "going in," as John Muir affirmed. The "great unraveling" that endangers the fabric of our common life—ecologically, socially, and politically—puts the soul at risk as well. But it also points us to an unexpected gift in the predicament we face.

The threat to *natural* wilderness forces us into the *inner* wilderness of the human psyche where wonder, grief, and longing are storming within us as well. Every experience in the natural world invites us to a corresponding work of the soul. There we imagine a world without piping plovers and polar bears, knowing we're losing more than a few breathtaking species. We're diminishing a spiritual community that has formed us—making us what we *are*.

Mourning that loss, urges Joanna Macy, is our first and most authentic response to the ecological crisis.[5] Recovering a lost language of grief makes it possible to heal the widening divide between ourselves and the others. In my case, it was a shared sense of loss that brought Grandfather and me together. He became more than a local specimen of *Populus deltoides*, arousing my casual interest as an amateur forester. I found him participating in my inner life, in the fears we share and dreams we inhabit, in memories arising out of the place where the two of us seem to overlap.

Carl Jung became aware of this intimate interaction between nature and psyche during a volatile period of his life, at the beginning of the First World War. He was exploring the unconscious as never before, painting images of snakes and sea monsters that came to him in his dreams. Trees growing upside down, a world threatened by overwhelming floods, a fierce sun rising over a Swiss landscape. All this, pictured in his *Red Book*, was stirring within him as the Great War spread across Europe. The land, sea, and sky themselves were crying out within him. He was convinced that "there are things in the psyche which I do not produce."[6]

He knew that our fantasy world taps into a collective unconscious that includes far more than individual *human* experience. It's cosmic as well. Nature and psyche are overlapping realities that continually slide into each other. Our unconscious connections with the natural world are as real as our conscious experience. Injury felt in the one will be echoed in the other. The power of shared grief is its ability to lament what we've irretrievably lost and to love what we can't bear losing.

Stories of Grief Evoked by the Loss of Trees

- Hurricane Andrew struck Homestead, Florida, on August 24, 1992, its 170-miles-per-hour winds stripping the trees of all their leaves. Nothing symbolized the devastation so powerfully, even for people who had lost their homes, than the stark nakedness of bare limbs on every single tree.

- When an ice storm hit Omaha, Nebraska, on December 11, 2007, hundreds of trees collapsed under the weight of ice an inch thick, followed by five inches of sleet and snow. "It sounded like gun shots throughout the night," said one resident. "You could hear the branches cracking and popping and falling." For weeks people grieved the loss of the city's trees, as if family members had been shot in the street.
- Hurricane Hugo made landfall over Charleston Harbor on September 21, 1989, leveling hundreds of acres of old-growth trees in nearby Francis Marion National Forest. "I just cried," said a state forester the following day as he looked at hundred-year-old longleaf pines flattened to the ground. "Everybody I talked to, the guys that work in the forest, the timber markers, guys like that—these rough, tough guys—they all had tears in their eyes."[7]

The trees we grieve, the animals who come to us in our dreams, are more than fabrics of our imagination, Jungian psychologists insist. They're on a mission of their own. The tree that seems to be speaking out of our reverie may indeed be doing so, as we've tapped into a consciousness that includes thousands of years of tree history. The "others" continually call out to us from across the divide. When people report identical dreams of a vast flood overpowering the land, it may be the Earth saying something to the culture as a whole. James Hillman put it down as a principle: "I take all dreams as belonging first of all to the figures in them."[8]

USING, EXPLORING, CELEBRATING,
AND LOVING

As we try to tune in to what comes to us from across the chasm, it helps to designate a partner in conversation. Whether we're going out into wilderness, paying attention to our senses, or attending to inner work, exploring images that arise from within, it's important to narrow our focus.

David Quammen studied a single species—the dodo bird, the last of which died on an island in the Indian Ocean in 1681—as a way of probing the far-reaching effects of extinction.[9] Dōgen, a thirteenth-century Buddhist master, urged his disciples to concentrate on a single blade of grass in the effort to free the mind of thoughts. Any significant quest, whether in science or in the spiritual life, begins on as small a scale as possible. The way to the many is through the one. Loving all things starts with learning to love *one* thing.

In my relationship with Grandfather, I've seen myself pass through four stages of growth, four stages of falling in love with this tree. We all share distinct levels of interaction with the natural world, whether we're aware of it or not. We move from casually knowing something as an object to profoundly experiencing it as a subject. Through the years, in my relationship with Grandfather I have shifted from being a *user* to becoming an *explorer* to evolving into a *celebrant* and finally emerging as a *lover.*

Years ago I made use of his shade now and then as a good place to sit and journal. When one of his two great trunks fell during the storm––after my experience with the trees along Lower Rock Creek––my curiosity was aroused. This gradually turned to wonder as I studied his process of healing and realized how much we shared in our common experience of recovering from loss. Finally, about six years ago, I began a formal apprenticeship with the tree. I committed myself to spend time with him each night, realizing that our shared grief had been slowly transformed into love. These four stages mark my entry with Grandfather into the Great Conversation. They represent roles that all of us play in responding to the natural world.

1. Our Role as Users: Moving Beyond Exploitation

As uncomfortable as it sounds, our first and most obvious way of relating to the "others" is as *users.* We're inescapably involved in taking, consuming, and benefiting from the lives of other-than-human beings. We eat plants (if not also animals) to stay alive. We use wood in building our homes. We draw medicines from plants and trees. We depend on rocks and minerals for many of the things we make.

Life in nature's web is inexorably interdependent. The question isn't whether or not to use, but how to exercise a wise and compassionate use as opposed to reckless exploitation. I take advantage of trees like Grandfather in disturbing yet necessary ways. I do my work at an old oak desk. My office is filled with books made of the same wood pulp as the one you may be holding in your hands right now. Trees like Grandfather are cut down to support my calling as a writer. This puts the two of us in a morally ambiguous relationship, to say the least. I'm asking a cottonwood tree—whom I love—to excuse my taking the life of other trees so that I might speak and write on behalf of all trees.[10]

This is the sacramental mystery at the heart of all relationships. We take life and we offer our own in return, in a deeply invested mutuality. I turn trees like Grandfather into paper, hoping that what I write may help to turn trees like Grandfather into *spirit*—into a still greater consciousness, a stronger voice for justice in the world, a deeper ability to celebrate life.

I suspect that Grandfather may be using *me* as well! That he's been attracting me to himself—from the very beginning—in order to pass on a wisdom gained from his woundedness. Perhaps even from the collective memory of trees going back 440 million years ago when vascular plants and early trees first began to evolve. Perhaps this explains the passionate attachment I have to this tree.

For a long time our species has been trapped at this stage of "using" everything at our disposal in the natural world. We clear-cut ancient forests, strip mountaintops, and hunt whales to extinction, as if none of these have value beyond their use to us. Nature writer Derrick Jensen says we fail to listen to anything we abuse. We actively silence it. In the nineteenth century vivisectionists routinely severed the vocal cords of animals before operating on them without anesthesia. They didn't want to hear the screams. Silence is essential to the maintenance of any abusive system.

Jensen writes out of his own experience of sexual abuse as a child, knowing that human systems tend to cooperate in keeping victims silent. "The most basic commandment of our culture," he notes, is "thou shalt pretend there is nothing wrong."[11] We regularly close our eyes and ears to whatever we misuse.

But when we use *well* (and allow ourselves to be used well in return), it can become a life-giving, even Eucharistic experience. I won't forget the revulsion—and subsequently the wonder—that I experienced one night in a cabin in the Wyoming wilderness. That year the mountain lion population had increased in the Wind River Range, allowing the Game and Fish Department to offer a few tags to hunters. A bow hunter known to a friend of mine had taken a cougar and shared some of the meat with him. He invited us to dinner. I was appalled at the idea of eating the body of such a marvelous creature, but there we were—facing an evening meal of mountain lion stew.

The best we could do was to prepare a ritual for honoring the animal, blessing the territory he had roamed, and asking that his spirit be carried on (somehow) in us. As an alpha predator in the Rockies, he'd held a responsibility for the well-being of everything in the community. We vowed to do the same. Hoping that our audacity might be mitigated by the awe we felt. Our deepest desire was to *become* the food we ate. I can only hope that the spirit of that lion is still looking out through my eyes today.

2. *Our Role as Explorers: Yielding to Fascination*

We relate also to the natural world as *explorers*. Our curiosity is insatiable. This is Rachel Carson on her hands and knees in a tide pool along the Chesapeake Bay; E. O. Wilson fascinated with ants; Jane Goodall studying chimpanzees for forty-five years in Tanzania. Our capacity for attentiveness is more powerful than we think—even awakening that to which it attends.

This is my experience with Grandfather. I've become an ardent student of eastern cottonwoods, their natural history and ecology, captivated by how they heal themselves in the face of fire, wind damage, and insect attack. Their seeds germinate everywhere along Missouri streams. They harbor a host of birds and animals in their branches. Hopi artists use the thick bark of their western cousins in carving kachina masks.

I have a lot yet to learn from this tree: how he "speaks" in different kinds of wind, for example—the way the wind plays him like a musical instrument. Sadly, I move too fast to learn very much from a teacher who's incredibly slow in doing everything. Yet each night I lean into his heartwood and attend to what arises out of the silence we share. My attentiveness evokes a corresponding intrigue on his part. Nature delights in being loved. Shug Avery got that right.

Being an effective listener requires discipline. It doesn't just happen. John Burroughs tells of sitting on the front porch of a literary editor's home one afternoon. The woman was lamenting that there were never any birds in her yard. During the hour they talked, Burroughs saw and named half a dozen birds. She was astonished, declaring how much she wanted to see and hear them, too. "No," Burroughs replied with blunt honesty, "you only *want* to want to see and hear them. You must have the bird in your heart before you can find it in the bush."[12] She was charmed by the *idea* of attending to birds, but didn't have the will to give herself to its *practice*.

Grandfather longs for the kind of attentive student that the nineteenth-century naturalist Louis Agassiz cultivated in his classes at Harvard. Agassiz had a habit of testing bright new graduate students on their readiness to learn. He'd take them into a lab and show them a fish preserved in a jar of alcohol. "Study it," he said, "and tell me about it when I come back." Hours later he returned as the student said wearily, "Well, it's got two eyes, fins and scales, and it smells. What else *is* there?" "You tell me," said Agassiz. He came back the next day and by then the student had begun to push his fingers down the fish's throat to see how sharp its teeth were. He counted the rows of scales on its sides and began drawing pictures of the fish, discovering new features of it in the process. Two days later, Agassiz returned, nodding his head at the notes he'd taken.

Before long, he got excited about what he was finding. He explored the bony flap that covered the delicate, fringed gills on either side of the fish, allowing it to breathe. He noticed the way the fins rise out of its back on rigid spines. He observed how the fish was completely symmetrical on each side with paired organs along its body. When Agassiz came back a week later, he was too busy to talk. He'd fallen in love with the fish, realizing how much it could teach him. Agassiz knew he was ready for work.

This is the ravenous interest that Grandfather stirs in me. He's taught me that I won't *love* what I haven't first learned to *know* in exquisite detail. The art of exploring nature requires no extensive scientific knowledge or macho skills of hiking long distances. It simply demands an inquisitive spirit. That's how Einstein explained his success: "I have no special talents," he said. "I'm only passionately curious."[13]

3. Our Role as Celebrants: Embracing Awe and Praise

A third way we interact with the natural world is as *celebrants*. This happens when we move beyond curiosity, experiencing a sense of awe, even an urge to praise in the presence of mystery. We revert to the child's earliest natural response of wonder. Children don't hesitate to talk to trees, to think of animals as playmates, to communicate with invisible beings. The celebrant knows that our exchange with the other-than-human world is more than information gathering. It's a wanting to bless and to be blessed. It's about communication that turns into communion.[14]

I stand every night at the foot of an enormous creature towering almost a hundred feet above me. His silent immensity never fails to amaze. Through my years with this tree, wonder has turned to knowledge, knowledge to praise, and praise to love. I bless him, and he blesses me in return. I run my fingers over his waxy leaves. Touch my lips to the deep furrows of his bark. Bow to him when leaving, observing rituals that make us mutual celebrants of something grander than either of us.

Experiences in the natural world often break into celebration. It happened years ago for a student in a course I was teaching on nature and theology. The class was taking part in a micro-hike on the grass outside the classroom building. We each had a tent stake with a fifteen-inch piece of string attached. The plan was to spend the next forty-five minutes paying attention to whatever we found within the circumference of that small circle. And nothing else. The student thought this was the most boring thing he'd ever heard of. So he jabbed his stake into a patch of dead grass, lay down on his stomach, and planned to sleep the rest of the class period.

Just as he was dozing off, however, a spider climbed onto the top of his tent stake. The eight-legged creature (with eight eyes, as most spiders have) began looking around from her vantage point. She then shot out a length of web from the spinneret in her rear-end, drawing it back in again. The student had never seen such a thing and was enthralled. Lying perfectly still, he watched next as the spider shot a length of web over to his hand and began slowly walking across it toward him. On reaching his hand, the spider looked around again and eventually spun out another line, this time to the boy's forehead, walking up that as well.

By now the class was nearly over and the student was torn—not wanting to end this astonishing encounter with the spider, yet eager also to share the experience with others. So he carefully disconnected the spider and its web from his body and ran over to me. He was ecstatic. For the first time in his life he'd watched a spider spin its web, *and* he'd been still enough for it to spin its web on *him*.

Many things have the power to drive us to amazement and praise. Poet Christian Wiman remembers his grandmother walking through common weeds in her West Texas landscape—creosote, cattails, goatsbeard—and crying out, "O Law', Honey, ain't this a praiseful thing?" Rilke, in his "thing poems" (*dinggedichte*), marveled again and again at how the smallest entity— "each stone, blossom, child," every single spider—can be full of blessing.[15] The human soul delights in the alchemical transformation of knowledge into adoration.

4. Our Role as Lovers: Seeking Union

A final way of connecting with nature involves the possibility of our becoming *lovers*. Given the current ecological crisis, this is the crucial and most hoped-for completion of the entire communication process. "We will not fight to save what we haven't learned to love," says Stephen Jay Gould.[16] Many of us naturally love the animals that share our homes, but we haven't reached out beyond household pets. We haven't allowed a *river* to sweep us off our feet or spent time enough in a *desert* to join the fight for its well-being.

Before meeting Grandfather, I'd never fallen in love with a tree. Yet it proved easier than I would have thought. I realized it was love when I noticed how much I looked forward to seeing him every night, how often my eyes teared up in talking with him, how pissed off I became when those fools built a fire in his hollow. I knew it was love when my sense of wanting to "protect Grandfather" shifted into seeing myself as "a part of Grandfather wanting to protect us both."[17] I found it progressively harder to separate the two of us.

Rilke marveled at how a process of penetrating insight can occasion our deep attachment to another being in the natural world. He called it a matter of "in-seeing." This is more than looking with appreciation at another creature. It involves seeing our way *into* it, so that the lines between the two become nebulous and porous. Standing inside Grandfather's hollow some nights, I imagine myself invisible to others, indistinguishable from the tree himself. Part of this is self-protectiveness—not wanting to be seen in an urban park that can feel unsafe. But it's also a wish that the two of us were one, a sharing in the intense human longing to *become* what we love.

Rilke speaks of what it's like to in-see a dog. It's "letting [yourself] precisely into the dog's center, the point from which it begins to be a dog, the place in it where God, as it were, would have sat down for a moment when the dog was finished, in order to . . . know that it was good, that nothing was lacking, that it couldn't have been better made."[18] This profound delight in the other becomes a sharing, then, in God's pleasure, an entry into the divine enjoyment of creation. Grandfather is for me a sacrament of God's pleasure.

Falling in love with any of the "others" leads naturally to embracing a larger, ungainly community. Loving the tree, you connect with the hawk that sits in it. You're brother or sister to the moon that shines through its branches. You care about the soil that links its roots to neighboring trees. The city park and its "membership" assume a new significance: the women's rugby team on the practice field; jazz concerts; family barbeques with loud music; teenagers in trouble.

It's like a strand of yarn in a sweater—you pull out one thing to love and everything else comes with it. The vulnerability of each piece affects the well-being of every other. Where once you saw disconnected parts, you now find an organism.

Thomas Berry says that the new cosmology, along with our sad record of environmental degradation, demands a new sense of community rooted in love. Our commercial-industrial world of indiscriminate "use" has resulted in a "psychic world of no attachment, no intimacy." We lack a sense of place, any real connection with (or even awareness of) the larger sustaining web of which we're a part. We're not tied by bonds of affection to anything in the natural world.[19]

MEMBERSHIP AND COMMUNITY

The four roles of using, exploring, celebrating, and loving are four ways of honoring one's membership in a body of belonging. Wendell Berry remembers what those bonds used to be like in his fictional world of Port William, Kentucky. It's a close-knit community of townsfolk, farm animals, aging oaks, and colorful characters like Burley Coulter—all participating in the *membership* of the place. Coulter can disappear for days at a time with a favorite coon hound, wandering the woods along the headwaters of Willow Run. There he'll sit in the hollow of an old sycamore, pondering a world so intertwined that even his own being isn't his own. "We are members of each other," he exclaims. "All of us. Everything. The difference ain't in who is a member and who is not, but in who knows it and who don't."[20]

This is more than nostalgia for an idealized rural America. Port William has its share of people who choose not to belong—like Cecelia Overhold, who knows she deserves more than she gets, her unhappiness always because of someone else's fault. "Whatever she already had was no good, by virtue of the fact that she already had it."[21] Belonging, like happiness, is a choice we make over and over again, wherever we are.

Belonging to a community that includes more than its people—honoring its hemlocks, rhododendron, pileated woodpeckers, and the smell of its rich earth—is a deep part of what it means to be human. That's why Berry has always cherished the Shakers who thrived in his native Kentucky. Renowned for their skill in growing trees and making furniture, they were convinced that the spiritual dimension of any living thing persists beyond its death into what it's thoughtfully *made*. How it's used, celebrated, and loved.

Their woodworking was exquisite because they knew that wood is alive. A tree's spirit lingers in a ladderback Shaker chair with woven cane seat. Shaker "herb deacons" who tilled the soil and developed medicinal herbs taught that a "tree has its wants and wishes." If you "love the plant and take heed of what it likes," you'll not be surprised when an old cedar tree enters the community as a finely crafted trestle table or chest of drawers.[22]

The Shakers believed, like Teilhard, that "God truly waits for us in things," hiding in nature's tightly knit web, holding everything together by the power of allurement that is "the true sap of the world."[23]

Shaker communities extended beyond what their members could touch and see. A world of angels and unseen spiritual beings was as real for them as the strawberries and asparagus they cultivated. Thomas Merton observed that "the peculiar grace of a Shaker chair is due to the fact that it was made by someone capable of believing that an angel might come and sit on it."[24] They regularly moved back and forth between interconnecting worlds, one as vividly alive as the other. Hannah Cohoon, a Shaker artist in the Hancock, Massachusetts, community, received visions of trees in the Spirit Land that she painted in the 1840s and '50s. One tree appeared to her so lucidly that she feared its fiery intensity might burn her hand as she drew what she'd seen.[25]

THE COMING OF FIRE IN THE NIGHT

How do we understand the overlapping of worlds that appear in those rare "visionary" experiences of nature's wonders—when our dreams and outdoor encounters intersect?

It's more than two years ago now since that little girl, lit like the sun, came walking out of Grandfather's hollow, inviting me back inside. At the time she seemed far too real to have been only a dream. How could a granddaughter, not even born yet, come to me from inside a tree I'd learned to love? It was like fire coming in the night.

Two months after Elizabeth's birth, I had an opportunity to "test" the reality of my experience in the dream. I was babysitting her alone for the first time and took her over to the park. Holding her in my arms in the hollow of that old cottonwood, I asked if she remembered the two of us having been there before she was born.

Gazing up into the vast expanse of the hundred-year-old tree, her eyes were wide. She said nothing, of course, but something passed through the three of us in that moment A memory anchored in wood; a hope shared across generations and species. I felt that Ellie would carry my love of this tree into a wider community extending far beyond the span of my life. She was embedded now in the life of that particular neighborhood, in a multispecies, multigenerational membership, a bond not erased even by death.

All it requires is my being open in each new moment to the unexpected, to what continually breaks into the world with new possibilities.

It happens all the time as dreams, stories, and wilderness intersect. One fall last year I was backpacking in southern Missouri. I'd camped for the night at a point where the Castor River plunges through a boulder field of pink rhyolite—hardened granite rocks from volcanic explosions a billion and a half years ago. I'd tried to cross the water with my pack, but the torrent was running too fast and deep. So I had to camp on this side, facing the darker part of the wilderness instead of entering it.

Lying in my hammock under the stars, I watched the silhouette of tall pines atop the ridge on the opposite bank. I suddenly noticed a campfire in the distant trees. I hadn't seen it before and was surprised anyone would be there. Entrance to the river's conservation area is only feasible from this side of the river. Sixteen hundred acres of uninhabited wilderness extend beyond the horizon. But there it flickered, a light glimmering through the trees.

Gradually the fire climbed higher into the pines. It was obviously spreading. The whole sky behind the distant trees was glowing, as if a forest fire were making its way up the other side of the ridge. I felt more awe than fear, mesmerized by the strange play of light in the trees. But as it burst through the treetops, I knew something was terribly wrong, a light flared up, brighter than fire.

Then it struck me. After a week of overcast nights, I'd forgotten the coming of the full moon. There it was, in all its splendor. I wasn't witnessing a raging forest fire, much less a numinous apparition. Yet I sensed what primeval hunters ten thousand years ago might have made of such an event: the soul-gripping mystery of fire breaking into the night.

In Isak Dinesen's *Out of Africa*, her Kenyan houseboy awakens her one night, whispering, "Msabu, I think that you had better get up. I think that God is coming." He points out the window to a huge grass fire burning on the distant hills, rising like a towering figure. Intending to quiet his fears, she explains that it's nothing more than a fire. "It may be so," he responds, unpersuaded. "But I thought that you had better get up in case it was God coming."[26] This same possibility is what draws me again and again to backpacking in wild terrain: the prospect that God (that Fire) might be coming in the night.

Carl Jung raised the great question of our time: How do we find a way "to get everything back into connection with everything else?" In struggling to find an answer, he warned, "We must resist the vice of intellectualism, and get it understood that we cannot only understand."[27] We have to get out of our heads and into the wilds. We have to risk ourselves to mystery. We have to *love* what we're finally unable to explain. Only then will we comprehend the power of community that is already ours.

PART II

NATURE TEACHERS AND THE SPIRITUAL LIFE

AIR: The Child

"Come forth into the light of things. Let nature be your teacher."
—William Wordsworth[1]

"Praised be You, my Lord, through Brother Wind,
and through the air, cloudy and serene, and every kind of weather,
through whom You give sustenance to Your creatures."
—Francis of Assisi, "Canticle of the
Creatures"[2]

We begin exploring spiritual teachers in the natural world by turning to the element of air in the east quadrant of the diagram pictured on page XX (Figure I.1). This is the first of the four life stages, the place of the golden child. As a creature of air, the child comes newborn into a world of buoyant lightness. She reaches for the sky, longing to fly. Children delight in climbing trees, flying kites, flapping their arms like wings. They turn circles in the dancing wind; dream of living in a tree house. Mystery calls to them from every cloud and high branch.

You might think of the archetype of the *Lover* as dominant in this quadrant—sustaining the child's vision through a mentoring process that provides roots as well as wings.[3] Elemental teachers in childhood include birds, wind, and trees. They serve as instructors in the ascent of the spirit, feeding the child's longing for transcendence. This is the season of spring, the color of the yellow rising sun.

Our first intense experience of the world comes through breathing—gasping for air. For the rest of our lives this happens automatically, without conscious effort, handled by a respiratory control center at the base of the brain. We breathe an average of 28,000 times a day. But breath is more than a physiological function. It represents an interior, spiritual dimension of a life. According to the Torah, God's breathing brought the first humans into existence, filling them with the "breath of life" (*nishmat hayyim*, Genesis 2:7). Called by various names—pneuma, ruach, prana, *chi, nafas* —breath is a divine energy recognized across every religious tradition.

Air signifies verticality, reach, sweep, growth, and aspiration, says Gaston Bachelard in his study of *Air and Dreams*. "A human being in his youth, in his taking off, in his fecundity, wants to rise up from the earth. The leap is a basic form of joy."[4] Air is the most inescapable of the four classic elements, as well as the most ethereal. It is quintessentially the realm of the imagination.

Air pollution increasingly threatens our cities, however. According to the World Health Organization, carbon monoxide and sulfur oxides contribute to millions of human deaths each year. Greenhouse gases trap heat in the atmosphere, "thickening the earth's blanket" and contributing to global warming.[5]

CHAPTER THREE

BIRDS

SANDHILL CRANES, THE PLATTE RIVER, AND FARID UD-DIN ATTAR

"In Japanese mythology, the crane becomes immortal at the age of two thousand, when it is done being a crane."

—Mark Nepo, *Seven Thousand Ways to Listen*[6]

"Cranes are the stuff of magic, whose voices penetrate the atmosphere of the world's wilderness areas, from arctic tundra to the South African veld, and whose footprints have been left on the wetlands of the world for the past 60 million years or more."

—Paul Johnsgard, *Crane Music*[7]

They start circling over the Platte River as a crimson-orange sun sinks into the wetlands to the west: huge, swirling clouds of red-topped, gray-feathered birds settling onto the sandbars to roost for the night. Five hundred thousand sandhill cranes are on their way from Mexico to northern Alaska and Siberia. They stop each year for a few weeks in central Nebraska to feed along the river and in nearby cornfields. Their goal is to add a pound of body fat before tackling the next three thousand–plus miles of their trip.

I've hiked the river's north channel into the Bassway Strip Wildlife Management Area. It's closer to Interstate 80 than I'd prefer, but this is one of the few areas of wilderness left along the Platte. It's the route of the old Oregon Trail. Three inches of snow are predicted for tonight, a late March snowstorm. I've set up camp beside a gnarled cottonwood, half-chewed through by beavers. The north wind on the flat Nebraska plains has nothing to slow it down, so I've rigged an extra tarp to shield the tent, securing the guy lines.

Winter plays hard on the land here. Aside from an occasional cedar or juniper, everything's brown. It's a world of dun-drab Zen emptiness. Dried grass swept flat by previous floods. Rotting driftwood along the banks. Mud flats within the river itself, where the cranes settle for the night, safeguarded from coyotes and other predators. Flocks have been passing overhead all afternoon, the *birrrt* of their calls heard from a mile away. But their main roosting area is a protected zone several miles to the west.

The Platte divides into braided channels east of the town of Kearney, named after the army fort established nearby in 1848. The early settlers described the river as "a mile wide and a foot deep." It flows silently through the night, glittering by starlight before the clouds move in and snow begins to fall.

I've come to witness the mystery of migration, to watch enormous birds move with graceful ease, and to read once again a Sufi classic called *The Conference of the Birds*. I ponder a question that Rumi asked seven centuries ago. "And you? When will you begin that long journey into yourself?"[8]

A SIEGE OF CRANES ON PILGRIMAGE

Cranes are great teachers as well as travelers, revered as messengers of the gods in many cultures. Their fifteen different species are among the oldest of the world's birds. The ones who fly this eighty-mile-wide stretch of Nebraska farmland are lesser sandhill cranes (*Grus canadensis canadensis*). Majestic creatures standing four feet tall, they weigh up to seven pounds and have a seven-foot wingspan. Their elegant gray feathers cover an underlay of gold and tan, making them luminous as they take flight. But their distinctive mark is a bright red crown, a bald patch of skin with blood vessels close to the surface. When the birds are excited—whether sexually aroused, warding off attackers, or recognizing a familiar nesting place—the crown expands in size.

Aldo Leopold frequently watched cranes flying over a marsh near his shack on the Wisconsin River. "When we hear his call we hear no mere bird," he said of the sandhill. "We hear the trumpet in the orchestra of evolution. He is the symbol of our untamable past, of that incredible sweep of millennia which underlies and conditions the daily affairs of birds and men."[9] These avian pilgrims fly ten thousand miles a year, to and from their nesting area along the Yukon River watershed. They live for twenty-five years or more in the wild, mate for life, and communicate through thunderous vocal calls and complex dance sequences.

Their distinctive trumpeting note comes from a long-coiled trachea at the base of the sternum, resounding up through their long necks. Each bird has the vocal power if not the mellow tone of a French horn. You hear them in the distance, long before you see them overhead. But their physical stamina—their sheer *love* of flying—is what amazes you most. They soar on high thermals for 350 miles a day, usually at altitudes of 3,000 to 5,000 feet, ascending as high as 4 miles into the sky. They give new meaning to the wonder of flight. Indigenous people have long thought of cranes as psychopomps, guides who escort the souls of the dead into the afterlife, carrying them on their wings. They certainly stir *this* soul.

I watch them circle the next morning as snow melts along the river's edge. We had more freezing rain than snow last night, and the passing storm front has brought in warm air. The birds, with their hollow bones and aerodynamic wings, delight in the added lift. I marvel as more and more flocks take to the sky. Great black ribbons twisting and turning, appearing and disappearing as the sun catches their wings. Massive communities of birds in flight have long fascinated ornithologists and poets alike. They speak of a siege of cranes, a parliament of owls, a murder of crows, a conspiracy of ravens.

On the trip here the other day, driving up the Missouri River flyway from St. Joe's in Missouri, I saw murmuration after murmuration of starlings. (That's the proper term for a flock of such birds.) There were tens of thousands, wheeling and darting through the sky in tight, fluid formations. Möbius strips of birds passing through each other without ever colliding. Physicists marvel at how the individual birds manage to operate within a unified system always poised on the brink of chaos. They stay intimately attuned to each other, sharing in near-instantaneous transformations, akin to what happens at the moment of "criticality" in avalanches and crystal formation.[10] If flight itself is miraculous, how do you comprehend micro-synchronized flying done on a scale of thousands? Don't even try, says Rumi. "Sell your cleverness and buy bewilderment."[11]

Amazement increases two days later as I make my way to the Audubon Society's Rowe Sanctuary on the river's south channel. That evening at dusk, thirty of us stand in perfect silence inside a straw-covered plywood blind twenty feet from the river's bank. Cranes are gathering again to roost for the night, having spent the day feeding along the river. They circle in huge braided ribbons, moving lower and lower until they touch down gracefully with wing-flaps raised on the sandbar before us. The air fills with the intense "barking" sound with which they sing the day's end. The hair rises on the back of my neck. I'm witnessing more creatures of the wild in a single place than I've ever seen in my life. Standing in a symphony hall with twenty thousand French horns sounding off in every direction, I'm at the heart of an unexplainable ancient mystery.

Ornithologist Paul Johnsgard says that listening to sandhill cranes is like hearing "an amateur performance of Handel's *Hallelujah Chorus* chaotically sung by a vast assemblage of tone-deaf but enthusiastic lovers of fine music."[12] It would be comical if it weren't so utterly and soul-searchingly *wild*. As night comes on, the birds stand in tight groups, settling into a soft "purring" that can be heard across the water.

I'm fascinated by the instinct for migration—the impulse to "pilgrimage"—that stretches across so many species. What is it that drives us every now and then to embrace a journey to a distant place, beyond the familiar, only to return again to where we began? What compels cranes to fly ten thousand miles, year after year, simply in order to raise a family? They must absolutely *exult* in flying. They start arriving in Nebraska on Valentine's Day, reach their peak on St. Patrick's Day, and are all gone by Tax Day in April. But come September and October, they're passing through again, headed back toward Arizona and Mexico. It happens every year.

Nor are they alone. One and a half million wildebeests walk 1,800 miles each year from the Serengeti in Tanzania to the Maasai reserve in Kenya and back. One hundred and seventy thousand caribou trek eight hundred miles through the Arctic National Wildlife Refuge to their calving grounds in northern Alaska. Millions of monarch butterflies migrate two thousand miles each way between Mexico and Canada. The butterflies that return aren't even the same generation that began, yet they find their way back to the same place each year, massing together in fiery orange blankets that cover Mexican fir trees. When sandhill cranes reach the end of their journey, circling over a familiar nesting site on Alaska's western coast, their bright red crowns widen in excitement. They are home.

Arctic terns make the longest migration of any bird or animal in the world—flying south from the tundra of Greenland in autumn and north from the ice fields of Antarctica each spring. They follow the flow of wind currents, covering an average of 44,000 miles a year. A thirty-year-old tern may have flown more than a million miles in his or her life, the equivalent of two trips to the moon and back.

Something similar draws human beings on pilgrimage as well. Two hundred thousand people a year will walk at least part of the five-hundred-mile Camino de Santiago across northern Spain. They go for various reasons—as a spiritual exercise, a physical challenge, a cultural experience, even an opportunity for camaraderie over a glass of wine at the end of each day. The journey is almost always more important than the destination. Two hundred million human travelers annually visit other pilgrimage sites around the world—from the banks of the Ganges at Varanasi and the Great Mosque in Mecca to Jerusalem's Western Wall and Bodh Gaya on the Phalgu River in northeast India. Pilgrimage is a spiritual as well as biological impulse, cutting across species. It's even a *cosmic* mystery. The Earth itself follows a 584-million-mile path around the sun each year. We're all defined by movement.

THE DEEP KNOWLEDGE OF BIRDS

Spiritual teachers in many traditions have looked to birds and their migratory flight patterns as a source of mystical insight. Cranes, geese, swallows, and terns have often been viewed as sacred, along with ravens, owls, and hawks. Winged beings, at home in the element of air, symbolize height, loftiness of spirit, access to the angelic. Medieval alchemists considered the language of the birds the most sublime of all, conveying a perfect knowledge. Ancient Egyptians thought that hieroglyphic writing was based on "the alphabet of the birds." In Icelandic lore, one learned to comprehend avian speech by tasting dragon's blood.[13]

Birds are mediators between heaven and earth, often appearing in folklore as the messengers of the gods. In the Jewish scriptures, a raven and dove offer Noah the promise of dry land after the flood. Ravens provide Elijah with food as he hides in the desert from King Ahab. Isaiah assures the exiled children of Israel that they'll soar on the wings of eagles. The bride in the Song of Songs exults at hearing the voice of the turtledove in the land, knowing the time for love has come. In the New Testament, Jesus's baptism is marked by a dove. He speaks of God's compassion for sparrows and likens himself to a hen gathering her chicks.[14]

In the folklore surrounding Francis of Assisi, birds held special prominence. A falcon on Mount Alverna regularly woke him for the night office. A nightingale joined him in a duet; they sang antiphonally like monks at choir. He preached to a congregation of doves, rooks, and jackdaws at Bevagna near Assisi. Noisy swallows (his "little sisters") obeyed his request for silence while he was preaching to the people at Aviano. At the hour of his death, his beloved larks flew in a circle overhead.[15]

In the history of symbols, birds are routinely portrayed as omens of death, embodiments of departed spirits, or symbols of transcendence and rebirth. The phoenix sets its nest afire and rises from the ashes. The pelican stabs her breast with her beak to nourish her young. Augers in ancient Rome discerned the future by analyzing the flight patterns of eagles and vultures, attending to the calls of ravens, crows, owls, and cranes. They viewed bird lore as a very *auspicious* subject (from the Latin *avis*, "bird," and *specere*, "to see").

Humans have long been intrigued by the beauty and intricacy of birdsong.[16] We're not entirely sure why birds sing. It serves a role in courtship and mating, in marking territory, in signaling alarm, and (for mockingbirds) in simply mimicking the admired skills of others. Yet birds also appear to break into song out of sheer delight. They sing even when it's dangerous to do so, revealing their location to predators. Kierkegaard observed that birds are creatures "who not only sing at their business, but whose business it is to sing."[17] Brown thrashers have an astonishing repertoire of more than a thousand songs. Blackbirds, the Vivaldis of avian songsters, warble in long, beautiful phrases. The song of the nightingale has long inspired fairy tales, operas, and books.

But of all birds, the crane—by the majesty of its size alone—inspires admiration. The red-crowned crane (*tancho tsuru*) is celebrated throughout Asia, especially in Japan. This huge white bird with black neck, black wing tips, and bright red crown is a symbol of longevity and good luck. It was believed to have a life span of a thousand years or more. Because the birds mate for life they're also a symbol of love. At traditional Japanese weddings a thousand origami paper cranes are presented to the newly married couple, wishing them a crane's lifetime of happiness. More recently we've associated the practice of origami crane-making with the story of Sadako Sasaki, a twelve-year-old

Hiroshima girl who folded a thousand cranes before dying of radiation poisoning in 1955. The crane is a worldwide emblem of hope.

A PERSIAN POET'S LONGING FOR GOD

Birds, and cranes in particular, appeared frequently in the Sufi poetry of tenth- to twelfth-century Persia. Poets from Al-Hallaj to Farid ud-Din Attar were fascinated by the Siberian white cranes that came each year to winter in northern Iran, having flown from the Ural Mountains of Siberia near the Arctic Sea. For these Sufi mystics, the birds' determination in pursuing so long a journey symbolized the soul's longing for Allah.[18]

Farid ud-Din Attar (1145–1221) was, after Rumi, perhaps the greatest of the Persian Sufi poets. He lived in the town of Nishapur, the home of Omar Khayyam, in northeastern Iran near the Afghanistan and Kazakhstan borders. He was a druggist by profession, selling aromatic essences. One day a wandering fakir walked into his shop. Looking around at its opulence, the stranger asked him, "How are you, with all of this, planning to leave?"

The question changed his life, prompting him to join the Sufi brotherhood, traveling to Mecca, Damascus, Turkistan, and India. Years later, he finally returned home to Nishapur to reopen his pharmacy and, happily, to write. The greatest of his books is *The Conference of the Birds*, a collection of stories set in 4,458 rhymed verses.[19] He organized the book within a frame narrative in which the birds of the world have gathered to seek their king. A sheik-like guide, the hoopoe bird, assures them that a glorious king—the Simorgh, the Bird of Birds—resides far away on Mount Qaf, a cosmic mountain.[20] Yet finding this king entails a perilous journey.

Even if they succeed, says the hoopoe, the grandeur of his majesty's effulgence is beyond their capacity to grasp. To gaze on his unveiled splendor will bring about their death. Seeing his face, they'll "rave and grieve and mourn their lives away," longing to be one with such astounding beauty. Rumor has it, therefore, that mirrors have been placed around the palace walls, so that admirers can safely, if indirectly, glimpse the royal magnificence. Lovers are thus kept from being destroyed by the fulfillment of their desire.[21]

The idea of meeting such a king appeals to the birds, but they offer excuses for not undertaking such a dangerous journey. The nightingale can't abandon his earthly love. The falcon resists losing his favored position at court. The owl is reluctant to relinquish his solitude. But the hoopoe urges them on, telling stories that encourage and sharpen their desire. A hundred thousand feathered pilgrims eventually set out on their quest through seven long and torturous valleys—through fear, doubt, indecision, and despair. The trip takes a lifetime, as they travel over mountains, deserts, and seas. Thousands give up along the way. Others die of thirst or drowning. Some go insane.

Those who survive are heartened by the hoopoe's stories of the grand Simorgh. These are moving accounts of spiritual longing. In one, a king is riding his horse along the seashore when he notices a child fishing. "You seem the saddest boy I've ever seen," says the monarch. The child hasn't caught any fish and is thinking of his paralyzed mother and hungry siblings back home. The royal stranger sits beside him and casts his line into the deep. They spend the day together, exchanging silences and tales, as the boy pulls in a hundred fish and more. "A splendid haul," cries the king, as he finally stands to leave. "But wait!" says the boy. Half the catch is yours! It's only fair." "Today a king has fished for you," replies his liege, laughing over his shoulder as he rides away.

> "Tomorrow's catch is mine. We won't divide
> Today's; you have it all," the king replied.
> "Tomorrow when I fish you are the prey,
> A trophy I refuse to give away."

The next day the king's words ring in the boy's ears like music, as a captain comes to fetch him—placing him, at the king's command, beside the royal throne. Courtiers murmur at the king's reckless compassion in taking in such a worthless waif. But the child sits, amazed and still.

> To every taunt the boy had one reply:
> "My sadness vanished when the king passed by."[22]

From the courtiers' point of view, the king's majesty is marred by his helplessness in the face of love. But for Attar, the sovereign's highest glory resides in this single, self-imposed weakness—his disposition to care deeply for those in severest need. That the king of glory should pass one's way and pause to love is a gift beyond belief. Yet such is the wonder of Allah, the merciful and compassionate (*al-rahman al-Rahim*), says the Sufi master. The birds listen to the story with rapt attention as they once again take to flight.

In another tale, the hoopoe speaks of an old woodcutter leading a donkey piled high with brushwood along a narrow mountain road. The wood slips and falls to the ground. As the man struggles to raise it, the incognito king passes that way and stops to help. His hands embrace the thorns; his back bends to the task. The old man mumbles thanks as the king rides on ahead to meet his waiting retinue.

The woodcutter continues down the mountain track, eventually catching up with the royal company. To his horror, he discovers who has helped him with his load. "I made a king hump wood for me," he cries in dismay. But the king smiles and offers to buy his donkey's load, letting him name a price he thinks fair. A gleam of understanding comes into the old man's eye, and he explains that such wood can't be sold cheaply. Ten bags of gold he figures to be its worth. The king's attendants laugh, saying the whole lot isn't worth two barley grains. But the woodcutter insists that a great hand has touched these thorns, bringing forth a hundred flowers—pointing to the bloodstains on the rough kindling.

> The wood itself is worthless, I agree—
> It is that touch which gives it dignity.

The woodcutter knows the worth of a king's touch. And the king, in turn, finds his boldness in love irresistible. Attar knows that Allah rewards those who come with a daring, zealous love, risking everything for their heart's desire. The king yields to an enterprising grasp when he never would have bent to an unimpassioned fealty.[23]

In the end, a mere thirty bedraggled birds make their way to the king's palace. Drawn by the "strange, magnetic force that holds God's ancient lovers to their course," they arrive with tattered, trailing wings.[24] Having passed through the valley of poverty and annihilation, they've learned that the price of entry to the royal court is nothing less than their own lives.

But then an amazing work of grace unfolds, the hinge on which the whole book hangs. The thirty exhausted birds see a door opening to the grand chamber of the king. Yet on entering, they find only a mirror. Incredulous, they stand before a monarch they never would have guessed.

> There in the Simorgh's radiant face they saw
> *Themselves* the Simorgh of the world—with awe
> They gazed, and dared at last to comprehend
> *They* were the Simorgh and the journey's end.[25]

Attar hangs the mystical insight of his poem on a Persian pun. The Farsi word for king, *simorgh*, is rooted etymologically in two separate words: *si* for "thirty" and *morgh* for "bird(s)." To their amazement, the birds have glimpsed the grandeur of the king in their deepest undivided *selves*, in what they've had to relinquish—only subsequently to receive them back again in love.

They're cast into a "blessed perplexity," unable to reconcile the difference (or *no*-difference) between themselves as thirty birds and the divine king.[26] They ask, "How is it true that 'we' is not distinguished here from 'you'?" They're astonished that what they'd longed for most had been within them all along. *They* are the king. They are God in hiding, pretending not to be himself, made one with those he loves.

The mystics of the great religions have always dreamed of union with the divine. The Upanishads speak of the atman (the soul) and Brahman (ultimate reality) becoming one. Rumi writes of the ecstatic experience of *fana*, the falling away of the ego in union with Allah. Teresa of Ávila experiences a mystical marriage with Christ as the bridegroom of her soul. The Baal Shem Tov teaches the importance of *devekut* (cleaving to God), annihilating the self in the rapture of prayer. Yet these mystics were always held in suspicion, accused of blurring the distinction between sacred and profane.

Legend has it that Attar was tried for heresy and banished, and that he was violently killed in the Mongol massacre of Nishapur in 1221. The man was a flame that burned with a wild intensity all of his life. "Birds make great sky-circles of their freedom," said Rumi two generations later. "How do they learn it? / They fall / and falling, / they're given wings."[27]

TAKING FLIGHT: THE SOUL'S JOURNEY

I sit in a stand of thick cedars along the Platte River's south channel, having slid Attar's book back into my pack. I take in the smell of harvested cornfields and cedar trees, loamy black earth and acrid river water. Tall prairie grass flutters in the distance. Wind sings in a cottonwood overhead. I ponder what the birds have been teaching me, reading this medieval text against the background of circling sandhill cranes.

I'm sensitive to the danger of anthropomorphism. I've no desire to turn these birds into metaphors of something else—spiritual gurus in feathery costumes, cast in the image of Sufi poets. They're a mystery to themselves. They teach me by their delight in community, their perseverance in flight, their passion for dance and music and the wildest places on Earth. Being who they *are* is enough. Attar's fascination with them only adds to my sense of wonder.

When I put myself in their place, I imagine a grueling, exhausting flight that ends in the recognition of a wild place as my final home. Plato said we're all on a journey back to the place from which we came. But what if, at the beginning of our lives, we were to glimpse the unfolding of the entire story? What if, all along the way, we were reminded of where we most wanted to go? Is the instinct that's driven sandhill cranes over these Nebraska wetlands for ten million years the same ravenous longing that summons me home—in a flight back to my deepest desire?

Since childhood I've been on a quest for what I've wanted to love but haven't always been able to name. It's the Jesus I encountered as a ten-year-old boy at a revival meeting in the American South. It's the *kol dmama daka*, "sound of utter silence," heard by Elijah on a rocky crag in the Sinai desert. It's the Cosmic Christ shining through the clerestory windows of the Iona Abbey. It's the Buddha nature of a cottonwood tree holding me in the embrace of its gutted core. This is my soul's hunger.

The desire has widened through the years, even as it's deepened. I need Jesus, yes, but Sufi poets and Hasidic masters as well—physicists expanding my powers of wonder through the new cosmology, kingfishers and red-winged blackbirds singing in a language I can only guess. They take me back to that empty lot in rural central Florida where a traveling evangelist raised his tent among scrub pine trees. Endings are encoded in their beginnings.

I see my path echoed in the circular migration of these majestic cranes. The element of air—and its prime teachers, the birds—has launched me on this book's trajectory. Its aim is to see the whole of creation as *itself* on pilgrimage, journeying back to God. The evolutionary process (and us with it) inescapably tilts toward Pierre Teilhard de Chardin's Omega Point.

Lured together toward that hope, we acknowledge the holy as more than simply "out there." The divine is closer than the soft down feathers over the beating heart of a sandhill crane. Nor is nature "out there," distant from us. It's what we are: a community of which we've not known we were a part. All of it joined (and being joined) in a vast ecology of the sacred, something full of environmental and sociopolitical implications.

Once I realize the close-knit relationship I share with sandhill cranes, I bear a responsibility to them. I'm obliged to care about the Platte River being siphoned off for agriculture and aggregate mining, the way in which it is threatened by development. I'm implicated in oil drilling that endangers the cranes' winter habitat in the Arctic National Wildlife Refuge. I'm invested in the loss of wetlands that support millions of migratory birds (from ducks and geese to whooping cranes) all along the central flyway of the United States.

Pseudo-Dionysius, a sixth-century mystic, spoke of God as being "carried outside of himself in the loving care he has for *everything*. He is, as it were, beguiled by goodness, by love, and by yearning and is enticed away from his transcendent dwelling place and comes to abide within all things." God remains restless until all created beings are restored to wholeness, joined in union with himself. A fifth-century Egyptian theologian, Cyril of Alexandria, put it boldly: "Deification [becoming one with the divine] is the goal of creation, and for its sake everything which came into being was created. And *everything* will be deified—God will be everything, and in everything."[28]

This was the astonishing discovery of the birds at the end of Attar's narrative: seeing the divine through the mirror of themselves. Once we glimpse this as a reality that's true not simply of us, but of the entire cosmos, we won't be able to treat the Earth in the same way as before. Given that long-range redemptive hope, says the apostle Paul, "The created world itself can hardly wait for what's coming next.[29]

Yet the Earth has to be patient, knowing the slow rate of change over time. The river that flows in this south channel of the Platte has its headwaters in the Rocky Mountains of Colorado and Wyoming, eight hundred miles west.

It runs another two hundred miles east from here before emptying into the Missouri River south of Omaha. Today its width is 20 percent of what it was a hundred years ago, but it keeps moving. It flows under a railroad bridge that once served the Burlington and Missouri River Railroad, long gone as well. Like the ruins of Fort Kearny, which the army, too, has left behind. Amidst slow but endless change, the river sweeps over these Nebraska plains, "the flat world of the ancients," as Willa Cather called it.[30]

Meanwhile, the red-capped cranes glide overhead on their journey north, between high cirrus clouds and falling cottonwood leaves tossed by the wind. They make the whole world long to fly.

THE CHILD AT PLAY, LEAVING THE NEST

Like the crane, the child's work is to leave the comfort of the nest, leaping into the nothingness beyond its rim, obeying the call of its deepest nature, and knowing itself—against all evidence—to be lighter than air.

The nest is where we all began. "When we discover a nest," says Gaston Bachelard, "it takes us back to our childhood or, rather, to *a childhood*; to the childhoods we should have had." Children at play naturally seek out hiding spots with small openings, from which they can see what is coming, what lies ahead.[31]

Gary Paul Nabhan and Stephen Trimbell explore this impulse in their book *The Geography of Childhood: Why Children Need Wild Places*. They explain that "children, when they're not told what to do, tend to go towards the shrubbery on the edge of the playground and make little nests, and burrows, and refuges . . . They're basically going through nesting behavior, and finding a very secure, small place that makes them comfortable, and keeping a lookout for wolves and other threats out beyond that nest." I suspect this is what draws my granddaughter Elizabeth (and me) to Grandfather's hollow: its nest-like quality.

While grownups are "scanning the landscape for picturesque panoramas and scenic overlooks . . . the kids are on their hands and knees, engaged with what is immediately before them . . . Adults travel by abstraction."[32] The child, even as she's venturing out from the nest, is remembering the comfort and safety of the womb. The bird's nest, after all, is shaped by the body of the mother bird. It offers "an external womb," says Rainer Maria Rilke. It protects, but doesn't isolate the nestlings from the world beyond. Hence, the bird—perhaps more than any other creature—"enjoys a very special feeling of familiarity" with the rest of creation. When it sings, "the bird does not distinguish between its heart and the world's."[33]

Of all the birds, we may admire eagles and other large raptors or the great cranes the most. We resist the littleness, the vulnerability of small birds. As if they represented something we want to have moved *beyond*. Our language discloses the way we slight these avian neighbors. If we perceive something as worthless, it's "for the birds." A person we disagree with is a "bird brain." We resent being left as a "lame duck" or considered "henpecked." We're put off, in short, by the small, lightweight, and flighty character of winged creatures—and of children. We want to be far more weighty and substantive as adults. We forget that birds were the only dinosaurs to survive, and they did so by shrinking.[34]

Similarly, we dismiss the importance of play for children and birds alike. Both are able to delight in playfulness as an end in itself. Jays and crows collect shiny objects. Gulls carry seashells aloft, dropping and catching them again in midair. Ravens repeatedly slide down a snow bank on their tails just for fun.[35]

Children are just as naturally playful, though an American Academy of Pediatrics report observes that they're playing less these days, both at school and at home. Outdoor play has suffered especially. Today you can actually be arrested for letting your kids run around the neighborhood unsupervised. Phone and computer screens replace the playground, the neighborhood park, and the nearest vacant lot that kids used to explore.[36] This is disturbing because playfulness remains intrinsic to the spiritual life. It isn't simply time out from work, says Jürgen Moltmann. "It is kingdom foreshadowing. It is a momentary escape into the future reality that God intended for us all."[37]

The Sufi poets knew the healing power of children's laughter. According to legend, when Farid ud-Din Attar was an old man he met a young boy traveling with his family on the road to Anatolia. The boy's name was Rumi. The old Sufi master laughed as he saw this "ocean" of a poet walking toward him, perceiving the greatness hidden within the child.[38] Years later Rumi may have been thinking of the old master when he spoke of a sheik who played the fool, disguising his wisdom under the impishness of a child.

A seeker came requesting the sheik's spiritual counsel one day, only to find him playing in the town square, riding his stick-horse with the neighborhood children. "Dear father, you who have become a child, tell me a secret," inquired the man.

> "Go away! This is not a day for secrets."
> "But please! Ride your horse this way, just for a minute."
> The sheik play-galloped over.
> "Speak quickly. I can't hold this one still for long.
> Whoops. Don't let him kick you. This is a wild one."

"What is this playing that you do?" asked the man. "Why do you hide your intelligence so?" The sheik laughed, saying that people were always looking to him for a wisdom they could only find in themselves. They wanted to put him in charge, when all he sought was to romp with the children to the glory of Allah. "Stay playfully childish," he advised the man, riding off with a loud whoop.[39]

Jesus suggested the same thing, saying "Unless you become like little children, you'll never enter the kingdom of heaven" (Matthew 18:3).

As a young child I had a recurring dream in which I was able to fly, soaring over the fields and marshes of central Florida where I grew up. It was a matter of lucid dreaming—as flying dreams often are.[40] I'd always begin by running across my backyard, madly flapping my arms. When I reached the place where the grass sloped down toward the lake, I'd leap up and away, suddenly becoming airborne. Wheeling over the neighborhood, as if ascending on massive, seven-foot wings, with dawn spreading out over the wetlands below, I was never so free.

"In our dreams we are able to fly," said Madeleine L'Engle, "remembering how we were meant to be."[41] The dreams are a foretaste of what we'll become. Like the birds of Attar, we end where we began in an exhausting, sometimes euphoric journey that mirrors our highest joy.

CHAPTER FOUR

WIND

BUFORD MOUNTAIN AND *THE WAY OF A PILGRIM*

"We live as feathers on the breath of God."

—Hildegard of Bingen, Letter to Odo of
Siossons[1]

"The wind is a pair of hands that encircles us . . . by the motion-filled air that hides us so well from the dark void of outer space and by the Hebrew concept of *ruach*, by the Greek *pneuma*. By the Navajo *nilch'i*, the Iroquois *Gäoh*, the Arabic *ruh*. By wind, breath, spirit. It is all, every bit of it, the same."

—Jan DeBlieu, *Wind*[2]

Having set up camp three and a half miles in from the trailhead, I'm the sole proprietor of this four-mile-long ridge on the Ozark Plateau, the only one to sing its praises, the solitary buyer and seller of its wares. I'm keeper of its silence and chosen celebrant of its Precambrian mysteries. At 1,740 feet, Buford Mountain is the third-highest peak in Missouri, which isn't much to brag about, but these St. Francois Mountains may be the oldest mountain range in North America. Igneous rock washed by ancient seas, chiseled by ice, eroded by millions of years of wind, storm, and baking sun—it's a place that knows weather.

Yesterday I came down Highway 21, passed the old General Mercantile at Caledonia (population 130), and turned onto the county road toward the trailhead south of town. It was a blustery October day as I hiked up the ridge, through yellow maples, purple asters, bright red sumacs, and dogwood trees with a few remaining russet-colored leaves. My plan was to camp on Bald

Knob, a rocky glade at the crest of the ridge, open to winds from the west. I was hoping to avoid rain, but was prepared (I thought) for wind.

This area is part of a wind corridor, known for its gusty weather patterns. If you were to draw a one-hundred-mile-wide swath of land from Oklahoma City north to St. Louis, you'd trace the path of some of the most destructive tornadoes in U.S. history. In 2011, an EF5 twister carved a mile-wide path through Joplin, Missouri, packing winds of 250 miles per hour and killing 158 people. The Tri-State Tornado of 1925, the strongest on record (with winds nearly three hundred miles per hour), passed almost directly over Buford Mountain on its way through Missouri, Illinois, and Indiana, taking 695 lives. Tornadoes here generally move from the southwest to the northeast. Even routine winds along this "tornado alley" can be high and sustained.

Wind usually dies down after sunset, but a significant low pressure system can keep gusts going all night long. I anchored my tent alongside exposed boulders on the knob overlooking Belleville Valley to the west. I ate supper without lighting my stove and read by the light of a headlamp as the wind steadily increased in strength. It was a dry wind, bringing no rain, but it was relentless.

Wind is an interesting phenomenon to gauge, both meteorologically and psychologically. The Beaufort wind scale measures the movement of air on a scale of zero to twelve. In a *light breeze* of one to three miles per hour, you hear leaves rustling on a tree and feel the air on your exposed skin. In a *strong breeze* approaching twenty-five miles per hour, whole trees are in motion and overhead wires begin to whistle. In a *gale* of thirty-nine to forty-six miles per hour, cars will veer off the road and tree branches will break. In a force-12 *hurricane* (winds above seventy-three miles per hour) trees are uprooted and there's widespread destruction.[3]

The people on the Gulf Coast of Texas felt the power of such a storm on the morning of September 8, 1900, when the Great Galveston Hurricane brought 150 miles-per-hour winds and a 15-foot storm surge, destroying the island city and killing more than 6,000 people. Tragically, the recently formed U.S. Weather Bureau had failed to issue a warning. The storm remains the greatest natural disaster in American history.[4]

Mountaintops often bear the brunt of the severest windstorms. The highest wind velocity ever measured atop a mountain was recorded on Mount Washington in New Hampshire on an April day in 1934: an astonishing 231 miles per hour. At little more than six thousand feet, Mount Washington is known as "the most dangerous small mountain in the world." Several weather patterns collide there, causing wind chill factors in winter to dip as low as minus 100 °F. The mountain has claimed 150 lives since the middle of the nineteenth century—most of them due to hypothermia.[5]

As night went on and the wind over Buford Mountain picked up, I found myself facing near gale conditions. I had to hitch multiple guy lines to secure the tent. The wind was whipping the fabric so hard I feared it would tear it to shreds. Sometime after midnight I had to break it down, cowering in my sleeping bag behind a boulder for the rest of the night. It was hard to concentrate. The wind dominated everything, seemingly shouting obscenities, threatening to rip off the top of the mountain. Even rabbits and birds sought shelter beside me on the leeward side of the rock. They were less afraid of me than of the wind. Nothing escaped its force.

Wind varies in its emotional effect on humans depending on the ions in the atmosphere. A hot, dry, dusty wind—like I experienced that night—generates *positive* ions that cause increased tension and irritability. It wore me out. Radio/TV transmitters and direct-current power lines can have a similar effect. On the other hand, waterfalls, pounding surf, and the aftermath of a thunderstorm release *negative* ions that clear away airborne particles, relieve stress, and boost energy.

The power of wind occupies the mind, colonizing the imagination like an alien force—a growing ferocity that becomes personal. "With violent air," says Gaston Bachelard, "we grasp elemental fury," the furious exercise of a *will* that's "attached to nothing."[6] It stirs a cosmic terror. Lillian Gish, in the 1927 silent film *The Wind*, portrayed a pioneer woman who was driven insane by the "demonic winds" that rushed across the West Texas plains in the great drought of 1885–1886.

Warm, dry foehn winds—like the Santa Ana in southern California—alter levels of dopamine and serotonin in the brain. When incessant, they can cause depression. From the mistrals of Provence to the siroccos of North Africa and the mariahs of Montana, winds exercise a powerful effect on human moods and behavior.

I felt all of this atop Buford Mountain that night, finding relief only as dawn finally came and the wind abated. I was able to gather scattered gear, make some breakfast, and sit in the morning sun reading the book I'd not been able to focus on the night before: *The Way of a Pilgrim*, an anonymous nineteenth-century Russian text. It's a classic work on meditation, breathing, and the Jesus Prayer.[7] I'd read it in college back in the '60s, when J. D. Salinger popularized it with his book, *Franny and Zooey*. *The Way of a Pilgrim* draws on the teachings of the *Philokalia*, a collection of the writings of Eastern Orthodox monks in the Hesychast tradition (fourth to fifteenth centuries). The Hesychasts were monastic "keepers of silence" who taught an imageless pattern of interior prayer. They employed a few repetitive words to rid themselves of language, seeking a union with the divine that was closer even than breathing.

A RUSSIAN PILGRIM AND THE WIND OF THE HEART

The unnamed itinerant in *The Way of a Pilgrim* began his travels across the Russian countryside with the intention of learning what it means to "pray without ceasing" (as urged in 1 Thessalonians 5:17). That single biblical phrase had hijacked his imagination. His goal was to live an undistracted life as wanderer, free from attachments, continually conscious of the divine presence. But what he needed was a *practice,* a method. He searched everywhere for a teacher who could guide him in a regular discipline of uninterrupted prayer.

He finally met a monk (a starets) who introduced him to the *Philokalia*; the book changed his life. After a period of initial training, he wandered over central Asia, introducing people to the practice of the Jesus Prayer as taught by the ancient monks. How do you pray without ceasing? You relearn the simplest pattern of breathing, he said. "The mysterious sighing of creation, the innate aspiration of every soul toward God, that is exactly what interior prayer is. There is no need to learn it, it is innate in every one of us!"[8]

Since the Middle Ages, Russian religious pilgrims known as *stranniki* had spent years traveling on foot from one monastic shrine to another. The writer of *The Way of a Pilgrim* was born in a village south of Moscow, with a withered arm that kept him from working. He described himself as "by calling, a homeless wanderer who roams from place to place. My worldly goods are a sack with some dried bread in it on my back, and in my breast pocket a Bible. And that is all."[9] His commitment to backpacking as a spiritual practice made him a simple ascetic as well as a prodigious walker.

His trips took him across Ukraine, from the monastery of St. Mary Magdalene in Bila Tserkva to the Holy Dormition Cathedral in Pochaev. According to legend, the Virgin Mary had appeared there, leaving her footprint on a rock. Subsequently he rambled east and west, north and south, across the Asian steppe. He trekked 3,600 miles (each way) from the Monastery of the Caves in Kiev to the tomb of St. Innocent at Irkutsk in eastern Siberia. This took him across the Volga River, the Ural Mountains, and the western steppe. He roamed another 1,200 miles from Odessa on the Black Sea to the monastery of St. Zosima on the Solovetsky Islands (near the Arctic Circle). He was one serious hiker, covering forty miles or more a day.

Along the way he found odd jobs and stayed in the homes of peasants like himself. Often he slept outside, seeking out "a wood with a thick undergrowth of bushes." Passing through Tartar villages, he'd ask now and then for a bag of dried bread or a handful of salt. At times he encountered horrendous weather. Strong bora winds came gusting down the Caucasus Mountains and across the Black Sea. Gale-force blasts from Siberia swept over central Asia, bringing heavy snow and temperatures as low as minus 50°F. Yet remaining as close to nature as possible was central to his practice, despite the bitter cold. He continually looked for an "out-of-the-way place" where he could sit and pray.[10]

"Everything drew me to love and thank God," he said, "people, trees, plants, animals. I saw them all as my kinsfolk." He was familiar with the secret language of nature, knowing that "the trees, the grass, the birds, the earth, the air . . . [all] prayed to God and sang His praise." "I came to understand what *The Philokalia* calls 'the knowledge of the speech of all creatures,' and I saw the means by which converse could be held with God's creatures."[11]

Everywhere he went, he carried with him a ragged copy of the *Philokalia* with its catalog of thirty-six Greek Orthodox saints, originally published in 1782 by the monks on Mount Athos. There he found this description of the Jesus Prayer by an eleventh-century monk, St. Symeon the New Theologian.

Sit down alone and in silence. Lower your head, shut your eyes, breathe out gently and imagine yourself looking into your own heart. Carry your mind, i.e., your thoughts, from your head to your heart. As you breathe out, say: "Lord Jesus Christ, have mercy on me." Try to put all other thoughts aside. Be calm, be patient, and repeat the process very frequently.[12]

The starets who introduced him to the practice had given him a rosary, a knotted rope to use in counting. He instructed the pilgrim to recite the prayer three thousand times a day, whether he was walking or sitting under trees in a forest. He was to continuously repeat the words, "Lord Jesus Christ, have mercy on me," breathing *in* on the first phrase and *out* on the second. Breathing in the silence of God, breathing out the cares of the day. In time, he increased the repetition to 6,000, then 12,000 times a day.[13] The prayer began to repeat itself in him, even in his dreams.

Thumbing his rosary as he walked, the uninterruptedness of prayer became the order of his daily routine, as natural as breathing. This "Prayer of the Heart" had originated with the Desert Fathers in fourth-century Egypt and was later developed by Greek monks on Mount Athos. Thirteenth- and fourteenth-century Orthodox saints like Gregory Palamas, Gregory of Sinai, and Nikiphoros the Hesychast refined it still further.[14] Their concern was to move beyond prayer as "outward chatter," allowing the mind to abandon all words and images as one's breathing carried the intellect into the heart. What the intelligence couldn't comprehend, the heart was able to love.

"Without mastering breathing nothing can be mastered," said G. I. Gurdjieff, the twentieth-century Russian-Armenian philosopher.[15] Breathing techniques in meditation have a long history, from the pranayama yoga of Patanjali to the psychosomatic techniques of the Hesychasts. Focusing on one's calm and even breathing is a powerful way of being centered, escaping the rush of contemporary life. It forms the beginning of any contemplative practice. In Sufi spirituality, the habit of repeating a short phrase in prayer is called dhikr (remembrance). Muhammad himself recommended using the phrase "There is no God but God" (*La ilaha Illalla*), reciting it over and over. Gregory of Nazianzus, a fourth-century Christian, similarly urged: "Remember God more often than you breathe."[16]

Teachers of prayer are careful to recommend a knowledgeable guide for any serious practice of meditation. Breath prayer isn't a gimmick for manipulating ritual experiences. Unsupervised techniques of rapid or forced breathing can put pressure on the heart or prove disorienting to the mind. That's why the pilgrim himself frequently sought out experienced teachers. He also regularly engaged others on his travels—befriending a blind man he met on the road, caring for a sick monk, and helping a peasant girl who'd run away from home. The guidance and community of others is essential, said Theophan the Recluse, a nineteenth-century Russian saint.[17]

FIERCENESS OF WIND, INTIMACY OF BREATH

Buford Mountain made me appreciate how much the mystery of wind and breath has absorbed the human imagination. We take air for granted, yet it captures our attention in persistent ways—from daily weather reports to respiratory problems. We attend to storm fronts, wind chill factors, and hurricanes. We watch out for chest congestion, shortness of breath, and allergies that affect our breathing.

I remember as a child sitting over a bowl of steaming water with Vicks VapoRub, my head covered with a towel. I learned early not to take my own breathing for granted, hearing the doctor tell my mother, "He's a weak child. The asthma makes him susceptible to every cold. It's hard for him to breathe." I knew the wheezing and whistling of each breath, dragged from my lungs as if with a string attached. Years later I came to appreciate Zhuangzi (Chuang Tzu's) observation that "a true sage breathes from the heels; everyone else breathes from the throat."[18] The movement of air—whether it's wind in the atmosphere or breath in our bodies—is a visceral reality. It affords an endless supply of symbolic meanings.

In sacred stories everywhere, the divine takes joy in the raucous majesty of wind. God answers Job out of the whirlwind. "The fierce breath of the divine" (the kamikaze in the Japanese Shinto tradition) brings justice in medieval tales. Aeolus, the Greek storm god, gives Odysseus a bag full of captured winds that prove impossible to contain. Jesus's disciples ask themselves, "What sort of man is this, that even the winds and the waves obey him?" (Matthew 8:27).

For Native Americans, winds are messengers of the Great Spirit. They signify the arrival of change, of new life. The Whirlwind Woman of the Arapaho and Cyclone Woman of the Shawnee possess a fierce energy. You see their swirling hair in the tendrils of a tornado on the western plains, bringing visions and spiritual gifts as well as destruction. Life is kept in motion by the stirring of the wind.

All breathing, therefore, is holy. When Jesus breathes on the disciples, they receive the Holy Spirit (John 20:22). Avalokiteshvara, the Bodhisattva of Compassion, exhales the gift of loving kindness, allowing individuals to feel each other's pain. Elijah encounters the Great Mystery, not in a "mighty wind that tore the mountains and shattered the rocks," but in "the sound of a gentle breeze" (1 Kings 19:11–12). The Russian pilgrim stands in awe at stormy winds sweeping over the steppe, but it's the rhythmic breathing of prayer that touches his heart—as if God and he were breathing each other.

In the Celtic tradition, a slight gust of air—a mischievous fairy wind (*gaoithe sidhe*)—often awakens what is stirring within. It happened to C. S. Lewis on a September night in 1931, when a sudden whirlwind on an Oxford footpath changed his life. He and his friend J. R. R. Tolkien were strolling Addison's Walk, talking about metaphor and myth. Lewis had always delighted in Norse mythology, but up until this time he'd dismissed myth (and religious faith) as no more than "lies breathed through silver." Just as Tolkien was pressing his case for divine mystery set loose in the world, a rush of air "came so suddenly on the still, warm evening and sent so many leaves pattering down that we thought it was raining. We held our breath," said Lewis, caught up in the ecstasy of the moment. He later confessed that his readiness to believe stemmed from this experience.[19]

The movement of air is a mystery, whether we feel it in our bodies or trace it on a weather map. It stirs as a dust devil rising from the Kansas plains, a "perfect storm" off the Grand Banks in the North Atlantic, a baby's first gasp for air, or an elderly woman's last breath in a nursing home. Wind arouses a sense of the ineffable. God rides a forty-knot wind across the southern Pacific, giving rise to one-hundred-foot rogue waves. But God pants just as readily in the pains of a woman giving birth. The "wind without" is as astonishing as the "wind within."

John Muir was crazy in love with storms. In a series of "stormy sermons," published between 1872 and 1878, he shared experiences of a windstorm in the Yuba River Valley, a blizzard on Mount Shasta, and a flood and earthquake in Yosemite. Only "after one has seen pines six feet in diameter bending like grasses before a mountain gale," he said, can you appreciate the "glorious perfection" of the world exactly as it *is*. Muir heard the voice of the divine in nature's onslaught of wind, in what others deplored as "the violence of her most destructive gales." Most people's God is not wild enough to exult in unruliness, he lamented. "Storms are fine speakers," but "we are poor listeners." He knew that a forest's best tutor and sustainer is wind.[20]

But a soft breeze is just as persuasive in conveying mystery. The Greeks honored all four children of the weather god Aeolus, the winds of the four cardinal directions. The west wind Zephyrus sent the gentle breezes of spring. Eurus in the east brought warmth and rain. Notus sent fog and mists from the south. Boreas was the stormy, violent wind of the north. Together they formed a medley of complementary currents, heard in the otherworldly music of the Aeolian harp. This instrument, played by natural wind moving over strings on a sounding board, was used by the Greek oracle for divination.

The Earth itself breathes in fascinating ways. The Lakota people point to Wind Cave as a sacred place in the Black Hills of South Dakota. According to tradition, the first humans emerged there from the underworld. The inhaling and exhaling of this "Sacred Breath Cave" expresses the rhythmic life-breath of the Creator, Wakan Tanka.

In 1881, two white settlers stumbled onto this enormous cave complex, hearing wind whistling from a hole in the ground. It was blowing out so forcefully that it blew their hats off. A few days later, when one of them returned, the wind was still blowing, but this time from the opposite direction. It sucked the cowboy's hat *into* the cave. A cavern this large has its own air pressure system, shifting wind direction in response to changes in the outside barometric pressure.

The mystery of "shared breath" is a profoundly intimate experience. It's what a father discovers in holding his infant child. The baby comes into the world knowing how to breathe—naturally from the diaphragm, the belly rising and falling with each breath. But the father—anxious from a day's work—pushes air in and out of his lungs with the muscles of his shoulders, neck, and rib cage. His breath is shallow, forced. Only as they rock together does he relax, breathing with the child, letting the child "breathe him."

Shared breathing is an intimate, even erotic experience. A wonderful part of working with a horse is putting your nose next to his velvet-soft nostrils and breathing deeply. It's the sweetest smell in the world. Horse whisperers blow gently into the animal's nose as a way of bonding. It's how horses themselves greet each other. It's what teenagers experience in learning to kiss. I'll never forget lying beside a brown-haired, blue-eyed girl on the grass near the lake years ago. Our lips joined, we breathed each other for what seemed an eternity that afternoon, my chest rising and falling with the air being breathed in and out of me. Fifty years later, I'm still being breathed by this woman I love.

Grandfather and I breathe each other on a late summer afternoon. I inhale the oxygen he releases from the underside of his leaves while he absorbs the carbon dioxide I exhale, feeding each other in the baffling process of photosynthesis.

God wouldn't be God without being encountered in these ways. The Spirit is "a mighty wind sweeping over the waters" (Genesis 1:2) *and* a quiet breath enlivening Ezekiel's dry bones (Ezekiel 37:9–10). If your God is only one and not the other, you may be selling the Holy One (and yourself) short. Divine love is as reckless in its passion as it is vulnerable in its longing to connect.

THE WAY OF THE WIND: LEARNING CONTEMPLATION

The trip up Buford Mountain reinforced my own need to accept the storms that come in my life and to renew the contemplative practice that keeps me centered, in tune with myself and with God.

But how do you learn to breathe calmly within as the winds of an anxious world churn without? Franny, in J. D. Salinger's *Franny and Zooey*, asks this question. She complains that everything in her life "seems so tiny and meaningless and—sad making . . . I'm just sick of ego, ego, ego. My own and everybody else's." She's taken by *The Way of a Pilgrim* with its teaching on the Jesus Prayer. As she explains to a friend:

> If you keep saying the prayer over and over again—you only have to just do it with your lips at first—then eventually what happens, the prayer becomes self-active . . . I don't know what, but something happens, and the words get synchronized with the person's heartbeats, and then you're actually praying without ceasing, which has a really tremendous, mystical effect on your whole outlook.[21]

Franny discovers that this "mystical effect" drives her to a deeper compassion for others. She begins to find Christ in the people others dismiss as repugnant. The true end of the Jesus Prayer, she learns, is to see the Christ in everyone.

But if contemplation ends in compassion, it begins with a centered focus on presence—remembering simply to breathe. It's ironic how often we "forget" to breathe, sometimes literally in moments of panic. We neglect the very discipline that gives us life. We have to go back, again and again, to the child's natural pattern of breathing.

Many of us, like the Russian pilgrim, find the silence of thick trees and mountain trails helpful in doing this. As I child I would watch the minnows swimming through the cattails in a Florida swamp, and I would breathe contentedly. "Those original solitudes, the childhood solitudes leave indelible marks," says Bachelard. "In a tranquil reverie, we follow the slope that returns us to them."[22] We remember how to breathe.

We have to keep returning to that quiet reverie. It may take the violence of a mountain wind to awaken us to the blustery distractions that keep us from what we really need. The mystics say that as we learn to silence our incessant inner dialogue, God's breath begins to play us like a musical instrument—like wind in the needles of a singing larch tree. We become Rumi's reed flute with its nine holes, blown by the breath of the Beloved.

The day after the storm on Buford Mountain, I packed up my bent tent poles and torn nylon fly, and prepared to hike back down the mountain. But before leaving Bald Knob, I climbed onto the boulder where I'd cowered the night before. It was whitened by the scat of turkey vultures, now soaring again overhead. I asked for the blessing of the place and left mine in return. Then I started down the mountain, practicing the Russian pilgrim's exercise of rhythmic breathing and walking.

Falling into a steady rhythm, I used my walking stick to count the beat. "Lord / Je-sus / Christ / *plant-the-stick*. Have mer-cy / on / me / *plant-the-stick*." One, two, three, *four*. One, two, three, *four*. I followed Gregory of Sinai's instructions in the *Philokalia*: Keeping head lowered, shoulders bent, breath slow and steady. With the pressure of the pack straps on my chest, I wasn't able to breathe in all the air I wanted, but got enough to sustain the pattern. Enough to remind me that prayer is a reminder of *need*. I depend on a breath I can't take for granted.[23]

I made use of the Jesus Prayer despite the fact that Jesus had long been a problem for me. I had disturbing memories of revival meetings, summer camps, and Youth for Christ rallies as a kid. The pietistic and judgmental Jesus I had found there didn't work for me anymore. I needed a Jesus smelling of sawdust and cedar, with weeds in his hair, a raw compassion in his eyes. He had to embrace a wider community of living things, expanding the circle of what others see as holy. Pushing out, gathering in.

Nor, in using the prayer, was I asking for "mercy" from an angry God, eager to mete out punishment. The word "mercy" in the Hebrew scriptures comes from the Hebrew word for uterus, *rachmim*. It's the motherly love of a woman treasuring the child born of her own body.

Walking downhill, for the next few hours I settled into the droning repetition of the mantra, keeping the pace as the prayer repeated itself within me. The mountain and I were learning to breathe each other. I didn't "experience" anything, as such. Yet a door opened. I found a contentment shared with the universe, like a still breeze, like cranes purring.

Yahweh gathers the wind in the hollow of his hand, says the Hebrew sage (Proverbs 30:4). Allah exhales the "breath of the Merciful," the *nafas al rahman* (God's *womb* breath), and black mud assumes human form (Quran 15:28–29). Every time we release the whirlwind of our inner thoughts, the breath flows freely again.

PRAYER, LIKE BREATHING, IS AN END IN ITSELF

We shouldn't think of prayer as a technique with guaranteed results. If our purpose is to *get* something, to add another accomplishment to our spiritual repertoire, to acquire a reputation as a meditative master, the practice is sure to fail. Praying, like breathing, is its own end. It's a matter of yielding to the wind that simply longs to breathe us.

A Tibetan teaching story tells of a man who met a famous lama passing through his village and decided to devote his life to enlightenment. He asked the lama what he should do to achieve a state of continual conscious awareness. The holy man, sensing his sincerity, gave him a special prayer to chant, saying that if he practiced this every day—coordinating the chanting with his breathing—he'd surely find what he desired.

The man determined to achieve an awakened mind. He went to a cave to meditate, devoting himself with all of his concentration to the prayer he'd been given. But nothing happened. For twenty years he stayed at his work, doing everything he'd been told. Yet enlightenment eluded him.

When the lama finally came through the village again, the man rushed to see him. "What's the problem here?" he asked. "I'm still not enlightened. I've been doing exactly what you told me to do." "Oh, I forget," replied the lama. "What did I say?" The man repeated the chant he'd prescribed. "I'm afraid I told you the wrong thing," the holy man responded. "That won't help at all. I'm sorry, there's nothing I can do for you. It's too late to start over; you'll never be enlightened now."

The man walked away overcome with frustration, anger, and despair. Not knowing what else to do, he went back out of habit to his cave. Thinking, "Well, there's nothing left now, and I've gotten used to it anyway." So he crossed his legs, closed his eyes, and began to pray as usual, *this* time without any hope of attaining enlightenment. And immediately his eyes were opened, piercing through the veil. At last he understood that it was his *grasping* for enlightenment that had kept him from achieving it all along. In the silence, thought he heard the lama's distant laughter drifting toward him on a high mountain wind.

The Tibetan villager learned that the path to wisdom required calming the restless wind of desire, returning to the quiet breath of the child. It's not what we force, but what we *allow* that finally sets us free.

When we grasp this, as experienced sailors do in sailing "close to the wind," we realize—to our surprise—that a blustery, contrary wind can actually be a gift. You initially feel helpless against it, in the same way you resist the tempests that come head-on in your life. But old sea dogs assure us that if you set your sail at a twenty-two-degree angle to the opposing wind, it pulls you *into* itself, helping rather than hindering. With sails close-hauled, a sailboat heads into the wind, moving faster than it does even with the wind at its back. Tacking at such an angle, the sail (like an airplane wing) receives a "lift," a forward thrust that pushes it swiftly through the water.

There's a correlate to the spiritual life here. Yielding to what seems a contrary wind can be an aid in moving toward one's goal. A gale isn't necessarily the threat that it seems. In a forest, wind makes the trees stronger and more limber, disperses seeds over long distances, and facilitates the migration of birds and insects. A persistent wind removes noxious air, creates sand dunes, and influences ocean currents.

When a gale rises we're tempted to hold our breath in anxiety, resisting the gusty onslaught. Yet courageous souls cry out, "You've nothing to fear! Stay close-hauled. Let the wind fill your sails." On the night the children of Israel escaped from slavery, God sent a strong "east wind" coming *against* them as they walked out of Egypt toward freedom, toward the Sinai. It was harsh, blowing in their faces, retarding their progress. But by dawn they saw that it had driven back the waves of the Red Sea, letting them cross on dry land. The unfavorable wind had been a gift all along. "I bore you on eagles' wings," God said to Moses, "and brought you to myself" (Exodus 19:4).

Such is the mystery of wind. "It blows where it wills," said Jesus to Nicodemus. "You hear its sound, but you can't tell where it comes from or where it's going. So it is with everyone born of the Spirit" (John 3:8).

CHAPTER FIVE

TREES

A COTTONWOOD TREE IN A CITY PARK AND
HILDEGARD OF BINGEN

"Before we were human, we were intimate with trees."
—Michael Perlman, *The Power of Trees*[1]

"The tree is a fire-bearer . . . A flame that burns in the innermost being of the tree, where all the promise of flamboyant life resides."
—Gaston Bachelard, *The Flame of a Candle*[2]

Climbing seventy feet up can be as taxing (and exhilarating) as hiking seven miles in from the trailhead. I know it in my bones, as I collapse into the hammock near the top of the tall cottonwood tree a hundred yards from my home. I haven't gone far on this particular "backpacking" trip. But going up is another way of going in.

Since reading Richard Preston's *The Wild Trees*, with its stories of tree climbers ascending the canopies of three-hundred-foot redwoods, I've wanted to climb a tree with ropes.[3] Not a redwood, of course—just the tree that I love. I've long dreamt of spending the night in Grandfather's branches.

Knowing nothing about double-rope tree-climbing techniques, I found an arborist and climbing teacher in St. Louis who works extensively with high school and college groups, a man of enormous patience and skill. We made an initial training climb together in a nearby forest, enough to show me how difficult the project would be. Then a few weeks later, on a perfect spring afternoon with a clear night ahead, we started up Grandfather.

I wore the necessary helmet, gloves, and seat harness to which assorted carabiners and connectors were attached. I'd been told that the half-inch, sixteen-strand braided polyester rope, looped over one of the tree's highest limbs, could hold a five-thousand-pound pickup truck. But I had misgivings. There's no safe or easy way up a ninety-foot tree for a seventy-year-old man.

Using what's called a Blake's hitch (a friction knot) to slide up the rope, holding my weight as I rested between efforts, I gradually inched my way up—extending one leg in a foot loop as I rose a little higher each time. It was an exhausting, leg-pushing, knot-sliding, arm-pulling business. Nor did it help to have learned that ropes can "melt" when you apply too much friction (as in sliding down too quickly on the descent). This can raise the rope's temperature to 400 °F, where the fibers begin to change from a solid to a liquid state. Not a nice thought.

What seemed an hour later I made it up to the hammock my guide had strung with nylon webbing to the limbs below the canopy. I was physically wasted, but also elated. Previously I'd known Grandfather only from ground level. Now I was connected in an altogether different way. Suspended in air, surrounded by flowering red catkins, I felt his life surging around me. His blossoms were pumping out pollen carried by the wind to female trees nearby.

My allergies were overwhelmed by all this cottonwood testosterone. I kept sneezing throughout the night, my eyes watering and nose running. But it was wonderful. I took in the sights and sounds of the St. Louis neighborhood as night came on—baseball practice ending, hip-hop music drifting up from a car radio, the laughter of men drinking beer, the gradual quieting of traffic, silence finally settling over the city. A three-quarter moon passed slowly overhead. I was forced to sleep on my back so as to remain hooked onto the rope above, and that made a few things difficult—like peeing into an old canteen when necessary. But nothing diminished the ecstatic experience of sleeping in the arms of a grandfather. I never felt safer in my life.

OUR COMPULSION TO CLIMB

How do you explain the urge of a seventy-year-old man to climb a hundred-year-old tree? My relationship with Grandfather has been a mystery for a long time. Through the years we've shared the vulnerability that aging friends know well. We've worried over wood rot, pondered the hopes and fears of retirement, kept an eye out for approaching storms. Each of us had reached the point of our normal life expectancy. Yet there we were: one of us scarred by lightning, fire, wind, and ice, still casting pollen to the wind. The other exhausted by a gallant effort to resist gravity, sneezing and weeping through the night with a euphoric joy.

The evolutionary memory of climbing trees is lodged deep within us. It's the child's urge to ascend, scrambling beyond the reach of adults. It's the allure of verticality. Trees invite us to the challenge of the perpendicular. Lodgepole pines, rising like arrows in a Wyoming wilderness, just do it with an exclamation point.

We knew the call of the canopy even before we were human. Three million years ago, our hominid ancestor "Lucy" (*Australopithecus afarensis*) was scaling thorn trees in a river gorge in Ethiopia. Exercising her prehensile thumbs, developing motor skills in judging height and distance, evading predators from below, she succumbed to the appeal of trunks and branches, taking pleasure in all things tall. Our collective unconscious remembers when climbing was as easy for us as walking.

Tree climbing has long been a sacred ritual. Among the Sarawak of Malaysia the third and highest degree of shamanic initiation involved a tree climb, symbolizing ascent to the sky and return to earth. The thirteenth-century Persian Sufi Qutb ud-din Haydar was frequently seen in the tops of trees.[4]

Yet for most of us climbing remains a forgotten childhood joy. We've lost the young child's fondness for towering limbs. We may remember our parents lifting us into high branches, our faces plunging into flowering plum tree blossoms. We recall the rope swing hanging from a maple tree in the backyard and the makeshift tree house we built with neighborhood kids. But we've ceased to heed the call of our wooden grandfathers and grandmothers, saying: "Come on up. Crawl into my lap. Let me hold you."

Much of my delight in climbing Grandfather was how each of us seemed to grow younger in the process. The higher I ascended, the farther back I went into my life—and his. From my perch beneath his canopy, I could imagine myself as a child looking fifteen feet up into the top of a tree that was only three or four years old, a young boy lying under a young tree, the two entranced by each other.

When I was growing up in Florida, there was a banyan tree outside my bedroom window. Banyan trees beg to be climbed, lowering roots everywhere from their limbs in order to make the effort easier. Some trees exult in having climbers. Grandfather's lowest branch, for example, had tempted me for years. A few years before my rope climb I'd initially succumbed to his allure, making my first effort at free climbing a cottonwood tree. I'd been able to scramble up the thick folds of his trunk, reaching his first limb twelve feet off the ground.

As I sat on the branch, overjoyed at having made it up into his arms, a passing teenager asked if I needed help. "Should I call the fire department?" he inquired facetiously. "No, thank you very much," I replied, resisting the temptation to add, "you little snot." Why should he think it so weird to find a fully grown man sitting in a tree?

Another time, on a backpacking trip in the Ozarks, I'd fallen asleep one afternoon in the limbs of an old red cedar. I'd climbed about twenty feet up, lodging myself tightly in its branches. After journaling there for a while, I yielded sleepily to the image of the tree's sap and my blood flowing into and through each other—the two of us merging as one. I was startled awake by a bird landing near my arm.

Human beings, like birds, hanker for a place where earth and sky are joined. Trees invite us to a height that's grounded in roots. They dance in the wind because they're anchored to the earth. All trees, to that extent, are "inverted" trees, their massive root system mirroring an expansive canopy above. In climbing up we're also reaching down.

THE INNER LIFE OF A COTTONWOOD TREE

Grandfather is first of all a tree. I may speak of him as a spiritual guide or an emblem of hallowed things, but his singularity as a "tree" eludes my every effort to turn him into a symbol of anything else. Novelist John Fowles, in his book *The Tree*, admits the inadequacy of most of our language about trees. Since Linnaeus, whose system of binomial nomenclature gave us their Latin names, we've locked them into fixed categories. We speak scientifically, economically, aesthetically, and religiously about what they *represent*—what their uses are to us. We assign trees a market value, turning them into furniture and magazines, weaving them into poetry and song. Yet none of this captures the mystery of the tree itself.

Standing beside a weathered oak on a Devon hillside, Fowles acknowledges, "I sit in the namelessness, the green phosphorus of the tree, surrounded by impenetrable misappellations." A tree can't be known "through surrogate and replica, through selected image, gardened word, through other eyes and minds." It can't be known through anyone else's description of it. You encounter a tree's "inalienable otherness" through direct experience alone.[5] That begins with submitting yourself to the intricacies of the individual tree's life.

I gaze at the rotting wood in Grandfather's cavity knowing there's more here than meets the eye. Beneath the decay, the tree is skillfully sealing himself off from his wound, creating a barrier zone around the injury. It's an area rich in auxin, a plant hormone that fosters cell growth and development. For years now, a healthy callus tissue (called "woundwood") has been growing around the edges of the scar, forming two columnar growths on either side, strengthening the trunk at its weakest point. Trees have a phenomenal ability to heal themselves.

The growing, living part of any tree lies just beneath its bark, a one- to three-inch layer of incessant activity. This is the sapwood. It contains the phloem, vascular tissue that transports nutrients up and down the tree. The xylem, a little further inside, consists of tiny tubes through which water is sucked up into the limbs by evaporation from the leaves. Between these two you find the cambium, a thin but vital layer that produces new cells for phloem and xylem alike. Deeper inside is the tree's dead heartwood. Its annual "rings" are the dried remains of xylem layers no longer conveying water.

The magical process that drives the tree's continued growth, of course, is photosynthesis. We had to memorize the chemical reaction in high school biology:

$$6\,CO_2 + 6\,H_2O \rightarrow \text{Sunlight \& Chlorophyll} \rightarrow C_6H_{12}O_6\,(\text{Glucose}) + 6\,O_2$$

Trees are masters of the color green, using chlorophyll pigment to manufacture their lifeblood. They come in all shades of green—olive, teal, jade, shamrock, chartreuse, emerald, forest green. Environmental biologist Robin Kimmerer confesses to "full-blown chlorophyll envy," marveling at a tree's ability to shimmer at a meadow's edge, mysteriously turning light into sugar.[6] In feeding themselves, trees support human life, producing up to 30 percent of the oxygen in our atmosphere.

So there's nothing obscure or mystical about the fact that Grandfather and I "breathe" each other. It's science. He absorbs my carbon dioxide even as I inhale his oxygen. Yet the exchange fills me with wonder, suggesting an intimacy known only by lovers.

The tree's love affair with light is yet another mystery. Grandfather extends his branches in every direction so as to reach the greatest possible sunlight. Heliotropism is a tree's capacity to move toward the sun. Darwin was enthralled by how plants and trees bend toward light as they grow. In his last book, *The Power of Movement in Plants*, he noticed how the tip of a new shoot turns in an oscillating spiral, probing for optimal light. There are photoreceptor cells inside the leaves that communicate with a motor organ at the base of the stem, allowing the foliage to bend.[7]

Right now Grandfather is shorn of leaves. They turned yellow back in late September. Cooler weather signaled his need to produce abscisic acid, making his leaves fall, triggering dormancy, and increasing resistance to internal freezing during the months to come. Through the winter he's been hibernating like a bear. But with the coming of early spring he began counting, taking note of the days above 68 °F. Having now reached the necessary threshold, he's wide awake, ready to leaf out. Dark red catkins dangle from his limbs like kitten tails.[8]

Grandfather is a broadleaf angiosperm—different from the evergreen conifers that make up the great boreal forests of the north. In a month, his waxy, heart-shaped leaves—connected to their branches by flat, highly flexible stems—will be shaking wildly in the wind.

Meanwhile, underground there's a whole other domain of this cottonwood's life. Huge lateral roots extend out beyond the tree's drip line. Some of them are more than a foot in diameter, rising even above ground level. From these lateral roots, thousands of feeder roots descend into the surrounding soil. In a tree this size, roots can reach out seventy feet or more in every direction—making Grandfather's root system nearly twice as wide as he is tall. Deeper taproots help to anchor and support the tree. But the important work happens within a few feet of the surface, where the feeder roots absorb food and water.

This is where yet another mystery unfolds. Microscopic fungal cells are attached to each of the feeder roots, linked to the tree in a symbiotic relationship. These *mycorrhizal* (Greek meaning "fungus + roots") fungi feed on carbohydrates extracted from the tree's roots. In exchange, they extend millions of hair-like tentacles into the soil, absorbing water, minerals, and nitrogen—feeding them directly into the tree. You can find eight miles of them in a single cubic inch of dirt. They eat rocks, turning them into topsoil.[9]

Scientists are finding that trees communicate with each other through this underground fungal network. It allows them to share food and water with adjacent trees, nursing their sick neighbors as may be needed. It even functions as an Internet cable, warning other trees of danger (the coming of bark beetles or leaf rust) by sending electrical signals across this fungal grid. Trees are social beings.[10]

In short, Grandfather manages to thrive through a combination of sophisticated chemical engineering, self-healing networks, cooperation with others, and the tree's own vibrant will to live. He possesses a quality of awareness and persistence that can't be measured. It's no wonder that people have long attributed a bewitching, even hallowed, quality to the life of trees.

SACRED TREES

"Forests are immediately sacred," says Bachelard.[11] In the world of myth, trees are mediators of a higher consciousness (above their branches) and a darker unconscious (beneath their roots). According to Scandinavian lore, the roots of the world tree (an ash named Yggdrasil) reached into the netherworld below, even as its limbs stretched into the world of the gods above.

The *Bhagavad Gita* describes the *asvattha* (the sacred fig or Bodhi tree) under which the Buddha received enlightenment as having roots anchored in the sky, with branches growing down into the earth. This inverted tree appears repeatedly in religious symbolism, from the Zohar of the medieval Kabbalists to Christian mystics like Hadewijch and John Ruysbroeck. It's quintessentially the tree of life.[12]

Carl Jung was fascinated by the association of trees with heights and depths, pointing to the soul work that a forest invites. He spoke of the forest in fairy tales as "dark and impenetrable to the eye, like deep water and the sea . . . the container of the unknown and the mysterious. It is an appropriate symbol for the unconscious." The Swiss psychiatrist also knew that "trees have individuality." A tree is "a symbol of personality . . . a prototype of the self." He noticed that when patients approached change or breakthrough in therapy they often received symbols of the tree (in their dreams or elsewhere). They experienced themselves as "taking root" or "branching out." Going down, in the alchemical work of the soul, is but another way of going up. [13]

Trees fill the pages of classic spiritual texts. The Christian Bible begins with the Tree of Life and ends with the Tree of Paradise in the New Jerusalem, its leaves meant for the healing of the nations. Trees in scripture are frequently connected with significant moments in the spiritual life. Abraham and Sarah are camped under an oak at Mamre when they receive the promise of a child—new life breaking into their world. The exiled children of Israel wrestle with despair as they hang their harps on the willows of Babylon. Nathaniel experiences a call to discipleship standing under a fig tree where Jesus first sees him. God proclaims in Hosea 14:8, "I am (like) an evergreen cypress; your fruitfulness comes from me."

In his vision of paradise, Muhammad noticed on the outskirts of heaven a great plum tree under whose shade a horseman could ride for a hundred years. The Buddha went through 150 incarnations before being born as the historical figure we know; in forty-three of those he was a tree. The Moluccan people of Indonesia said the first humans came from a bamboo tree, its stalk splitting in two to form a man and a woman. The ancient Celts regarded a host of trees as sacred—the oak, willow, ash, hawthorn, holly, hazel, and others. They developed a tree alphabet—attributing magical powers to its runic, tree-shaped letters.[14]

Yet a forest is also dark and forbidding. Trees are symbols of the unconscious, often associated with nature's shadowy powers. Dante knew there's a dangerous quality to any murky wood. In medieval Britain, willows were considered "sinister, for they had a habit of uprooting themselves on a dark night and following a solitary traveler, muttering."[15]

Sadly, there were Christian saints who, fearing that trees could harbor evil powers, called for the destruction of sacred groves used in pagan rites. Martin of Tours chopped down a great pine revered by the Druids in fourth-century Gaul. Boniface similarly axed an oak dedicated to the god Thor in eighth-century Germany.

But for every saint who hacked down a tree, there were three others who honored them as giving glory to God. St. Bavo and St. Gerlach lived in hollow oak trees, turning them into tiny chapels. When St. Gudula died in eleventh-century Brabant, she was buried under a poplar tree where she'd gone every day to pray. People swore that the tree burst into leaf on that cold January morning.[16]

How, then, do I think of Grandfather as *sacred*? His immensity awakens a space within me. There's the radiance that he brandishes in the top of his branches at sunset. There's the wound in his side that draws people to him. There's the generosity he extends to red-tailed hawks and squirrels, caterpillars and aphids, mosses and fungi, even plants sprouting from debris in the hollows of his limbs. He's home to many; not least to me. If *relationship* lies at the core of the divine being, Grandfather offers an image of what Christians find in the Holy Trinity.

So can I speak of having a spiritual encounter with a tree? Pope Francis defines a "religious experience" as "the astonishment of meeting someone who is waiting for you."[17] This happens for me on late summer afternoons as I wander over to see Grandfather. His leaves shimmer in the lateral light, dancing in place like an impressionist painting come to life. I know I'm *welcomed*. I don't need a mystical vision or a voice from the sky to affirm it.

HILDEGARD OF BINGEN AND THE WONDER OF GREEN

For my understanding of the tree's significance I am indebted to one of the first women to be taken seriously as a prophet and visionary in the history of Christian spirituality. Hildegard of Bingen (1098–1179) wasn't formally made a saint and doctor of the church until 2012, but she's been Christianity's *greenest* saint. This medieval German nun was an herbalist and botanist of no little skill, a physician schooled in alternative medicine, a brilliant musician and visionary artist, and a poet attuned to the rich fecundity of the natural world.

Hildegard was the tenth child in a family of the German nobility. Her parents "tithed" her to the church (and the religious life) when she was eight years old. She was taken under the wing of a Benedictine sister at Disibodenberg, a town on the Nahe River south of where it flows into the Rhine. There in the Palatinate Forest of central Germany, she gathered herbs, cultivated vines with the sisters, and played her zither while walking under the trees.

She insisted that one's spiritual life is stunted if it's only an *indoor* phenomenon. "Holy people draw to themselves all that is earthly," she wrote.[18] With dirt under her fingernails, she pored over medieval manuscripts and composed new antiphons for use in worship. Forty years later, as abbess of her community, she moved downstream to a new monastery at Rupertsberg near Bingen on the Rhine. There she became a preacher of great renown and the author of six books.

Hildegard lived in multiple worlds. By the age of three, she began receiving visions. She didn't experience these in a trance-like state, but with her eyes wide open, as if overlapping spheres of reality came together for her. The visions were frequently connected with migraine headaches, accompanied by dazzling flashes of light.[19] She subsequently struggled to express, through painting and writing, the "great things of wonder" that came to her.

The visions were cosmic as well as divine, involving trees, animals, flowers, winds, and angelic figures, often arranged in mandala-like patterns. She was reluctant at first to speak of her experience, but her confidant Bernard of Clairvaux encouraged her, even interceding on her behalf with the pope. Five spiritual themes emerge out of these visionary encounters, all of them grounded in the lush landscape of the Rhine.

1. *The Radiant Goodness of All Beings.* "There is no creature without some kind of radiance," Hildegard observed, "whether it be greenness, seeds, buds, or another kind of beauty. Otherwise, it would not be a creature at all."[20] The splendor of light was a central metaphor in her thought, a divine luminescence filling the earth.

The creatures emerge from God as sparks of light, she taught. "All the living sparks are rays of his splendor." She'd heard God say, "I, the highest and fiery power, have kindled every spark of life . . . I flame above the beauty of the meadows, I gleam in the waters, and I burn in the sun, the moon and the stars . . . For all life lights up out of me."[21]

The same idea was also emerging in Jewish mystical (Kabbalistic) thought at the time, culminating a few years later in the *Zohar* (*The Book of Splendor/Radiance*). In the teachings of Kabbalah, the vessels containing God's Shekinah glory were said to have shattered at creation, dispersing divine sparks that lie hidden within all things. The healing of the world (*tikkun olam*) requires the recovery of these shards of light.[22]

Hildegard affirmed that at creation God "was rapturously happy in what he had made!"[23] She speaks of original sin as a failure on the part of Adam and Eve to take a similar pleasure in the amazing world they'd been given. In one of her drawings, Adam is presented with a lovely white flower, and he merely sniffs at it, refusing to touch or taste its radiant beauty. This was his first way of disappointing God, says Hildegard. She defines original sin, in effect, as a *lack* of sensuality, a failure in taking pleasure. She knew creation was meant to be savored. [24]

She would have noticed that in the Genesis account there's a difference between God's way of describing the trees in the garden of Eden and how the humans perceive them after talking with the serpent. Genesis 2:9 says, "The Lord God made all kinds of trees grow out of the ground—trees that were (1) pleasing to the eye and (2) good for food." God mentions *beauty* first and then *utility*. But Eve and her husband reverse the order in Genesis 3:6. There they observe "that the tree was (1) good for food and (2) pleasing to the eye." It's a telling difference. Trees are God's way of pointing us to beauty. We turn them into consumer goods and salable commodities.

2. *The Nurturing Life of* Viriditas. As artist and mystic, Hildegard was captivated by the color green. She looked to the Holy Spirit as "the source of earth's lush greening." To grow in the spiritual life was to increase in one's capacity for greenness. Weaving together botanical, spiritual, and gendered variations on the Latin word for "green" (*viridus*), she celebrated the virgin (*virgo*) Mary as a leafy twig (*virga*) and Jesus as a flowering tree where the birds of heaven nest. She viewed moral courage (*virtus*) and manliness (*virilis*) as chlorophyll-like virtues expected of women and men alike.[25]

You see this verdant intensity in one of her songs for Mary, O *Viridissima Virga*:

> O branch of freshest green,
> O hail! Within the windy gusts of saints
> upon a quest you swayed and sprouted forth.
> When it was time, you blossomed in your boughs—
> "Hail, Hail!" you heard, for in you seeped the sunlight's warmth
> like balsam's sweet perfume.
> For in you bloomed
> so beautiful a flow'r, whose fragrance wakened

all the spices from their dried-out stupor.
They all appeared in full viridity.
Then rained the heavens dew upon the grass
And all the earth was cheered.[26]

For this exuberant nun, the soul was the life force (*viriditas*) of the body, infusing greenness into all its branches, like the sap in a tree.[27] It's not surprising that images of the Green Man were flourishing in Hildegard's time. Stone masons decorated churches, cathedrals, and abbeys with figures full of leafy hair, foliage growing out of their mouths. They symbolized the life-giving breath of the spirit even in appropriating pagan motifs.

3. *The Healing Power of Trees and Herbs.* The Abbess of Bingen spent much of her free time combing the forests around her monastery, gathering herbs and exploring their medicinal uses. She discussed their curative powers in her book *Causes and Cures.* For dimness of the eyes, she suggested a salve made from apple leaves taken in the spring when fresh and healthy, "like young girls before they have borne children." Peach bark, she found, was good for skin infections and headaches. Aspen leaves helped to heal babies' skin rashes.[28]

Her visionary encounters enriched her botanical studies. The Sybil of the Rhine, as she came to be called, received a "secret language" (*lingua ignota*) that she used in naming the attributes of various plants. She delved into the *secreta Dei*, the divine secrets hidden within the natural world.[29] "For there are concealed in all of nature—in the animals, reptiles, birds and fishes as well as in the plants and fruit trees—certain hidden mysteries of God which no human being and no other creature can know or feel unless this is especially granted by God."[30]

Mother Hildegard looked on trees in particular as teachers of holy things. She saw a tree's intelligence (*intellectus*) in the green of its branches and leaves, its will (*volunta*) in its blossoming, its spirit (*animus*) in its preparation of fruit, and its reason (*ratio*) in spreading out into full maturity.[31] In the wind at dusk, trees whispered to her of God.

4. *Praise as the Proper Response of Creation.* Music was one of Hildegard's great loves, another gift coming to her from the natural world. She perceived the cosmos as a well-tuned musical instrument, creation as "a single hymn in praise of God."[32] "Each element has its proper tone, its own timbre, the

elementary sound of the order of God's creation . . . as if issuing from so many harps and lyres."[33] On a starlit night, she strained to grasp the music of the spheres, knowing that "in its revolving the firmament emits marvelous sounds, which we nevertheless cannot hear because of its great height and expanse."[34] Her *Symphonia*, with more than seventy songs of her composition, was rich in earthy imagery and liturgical adventurousness.

Hildegard of Bingen understood the world as giving praise to God in all of its diversity—in flowers, birdsong, singing brooks, even the barking of dogs. She loved dogs, knowing that "the devil hates them because of the faithfulness they show to people."[35] "Underneath all the texts, all the sacred psalms and canticles," she exclaimed, "these watery varieties of sounds and silences, terrifying, mysterious, whirling and sometimes gestating and gentle must somehow be felt in the pulse, ebb, and flow of the music that sings in me."[36]

5. The Hard Voice of Mistress Prophecy. This brilliant German nun had a habit of dismissing herself as a "poor little female," an "unworthy servant girl." Modesty was a necessity for any talented medieval woman. But she was bold in speaking truth to power when integrity required it, and she got away with it. She didn't hesitate to confront emperors, popes, and men of religious standing. She wrote to Pope Anastasius IV, "You, Rome, are just lying there like someone waiting to die . . . You have no burning love of justice." To Emperor Frederick Barbarossa, she declared, "You may be King, but my mystical insight shows me very clearly that you are behaving like a child—even worse, in fact: like a fool." Another pope, Eugenius III, eventually complained, "Who is this woman who rises out of the wilderness like a column of smoke from burning spices?"[37]

For her part, Hildegard lamented living in what she called a "womanish age" (*muliebre tempus*). She grumbled that men had become "so lax, weak, and sensual—in a word, effeminate—that God had to confound them by making women virile."[38] Hence her appeal to "Mistress Prophecy," who had spoken unflinchingly through the Hebrew prophets. This feminine embodiment of God's prophetic spirit unavoidably "appears with a certain hardness," she explained. "Like the rigidity of marble. She flatters no one, for she is subject to the inflowing of the Holy Spirit . . . She yields to no human being."[39] No more could Hildegard stifle the voice of the spirit rising within her.

In her righteous anger she gave explicit voice to a beleaguered Earth as well. She heard its elements lamenting, "We cannot move and finish our journey as determined by our Master, for men subvert us with their crooked ways . . . We stink with pestilence and hunger after justice.'"[40] This was a tall tree of a woman, exuding a greening, life-giving energy that couldn't help but captivate the people of her time.

She has prompted me to listen more carefully to the teaching and healing properties of my own leafy mentor. I've found an old recipe for making a cottonwood leaf bud salve, for instance. You gather the extra buds that fall in early spring, soak them for a year in olive oil, and then mix the filtered solution with beeswax. The resulting cottonwood oil or Balm of Gilead is an ointment rich in salicin and populin—pain relievers and anti-inflammatories akin to aspirin. Good for burns, swollen arthritic joints, and sore muscles. Grandfather, in short, heals me in more ways than one. Hildegard would be pleased!

TWO STORIES, TWO TREES

Two stories are helpful in thinking about our different ways of relating to trees and how they might serve as teachers. The first is a favorite children's book, Shel Silverstein's *The Giving Tree*. It tells of an apple tree who delights in a little boy's climbing her limbs and eating her apples. "Come, boy, swing from my branches and play!" she cries whenever she sees him.

As the boy gets older—in adolescence—he needs money, and she invites him to take her apples to sell. Later in adulthood, he requires a house, so she allows him to cut her branches to build a home. By middle age, he wants only to escape, sailing away in a boat. She then gives him her trunk to carve into a canoe. In the end, nothing is left but a stump. But the boy (now an old man) needs only a "quiet place to sit and rest." The tree takes joy, at last, in providing even that. Through the four stages of his life the boy remains dependent on a tree that never stops giving.

The tale serves as a curious commentary on how we treat trees, how men expect women to cater to them, and how (in helping others) we compulsively need to be needed.[41] This story requires another narrative as a balance and corrective, another way of thinking about our care for others, our forest management, and our expectations surrounding gender.

The second tale comes from Zhuangzi (Chuang Tzu), a fourth-century BCE Chinese Taoist sage.[42] One spring, as peach blossoms filled the valley below with a spray of white fragrance, an ancient sage wandered the heights of Shang. He noticed a huge tree on a hillside where all other trees had been chopped down. The others had been cut to build a palace for the emperor's many wives. This remaining tree was so enormous that the horses drawing a hundred chariots could be sheltered under its shade. It was amazing that it had never been felled! He marveled at how much timber it must contain.

But as he looked up into its branches, he noticed how they were all twisted and crooked, growing in every direction. None were straight enough to be cut into rafters or beams. He broke off a twig and tasted the sap, finding it bitter. The tree would be useless for tapping, producing no syrup of any worth. The leaves, as he crumbled them, gave off an offensive odor. They broke too easily to be woven into mats or braided into baskets. They wouldn't even make good mulch! The roots, moreover, were so gnarled that you'd never be able to carve a bowl or fashion a fine decorative box out of them.

"This, indeed," said Zhuangzi, "is a tree good for nothing! That's why it has reached such a great old age. The cinnamon tree can be eaten; so it is cut down. The varnish tree is useful and, therefore, incisions are made in it. We all know the advantage of being useful, but only this tree knows the advantage of being *useless*!"

The Taoist master sat in the shade of that great tree for the rest of the day, as a light wind drifted up from the valley below. He breathed the scent of distant peach blossoms and sat in studied silence, contemplating his own uselessness. He stopped making judgments about the tree's worth, its market value. He sat instead in its welcoming shadow, realizing that his own worth had nothing to do with what he was able to produce.

***

What, then, is the final measure of a tree? An ancient Zen koan asks, "From seed to full blossom, when is a tree most perfect?" A tree's perfection has no beginning or end. It exists always in the now. The glory of a tree is this morning's leafy radiance, this afternoon's capture of light, tonight's exhilaration of height. Central to both stories is the tree's quiet invitation to companionship—to a presence shared in the moment. Trees return us to the immediacy of a child's experience of the world. They call us back to a playful imagination, to a time before we had schedules to keep, to an awe we can remember in looking up.

"I pity the man who cannot fall in love with a tree," wrote Vicesimus Knox, an eighteenth-century Anglican headmaster. "If you don't love trees, you don't love God," added St. Nikephoros of Chios.[43] Loving a tree is a process fostered over time. It demands a longing for heights, a slowing down of one's life, and a release of the fear of being anchored to a single place. "Emancipation from the bondage of the soil is no freedom for the tree," wrote Rabindranath Tagore.[44] Nor is it for us. Only as we delight in the tree's dark, rooted mystery can we grasp the wisdom hidden beneath its brown or gray bark, within its color green. Only then do we begin to see the tree as a carrier of light.

Visiting Grandfather at the end of a day, I marvel at how he and the other trees hold the last rays of the sun in the height of their branches. A rising wall of flame moves slowly into the treetops. A burning bush in an urban park. On the evening of my climb last March, as I breathlessly crawled into the hammock in Grandfather's upper arms, I realized the mystery was happening again, but this time with myself at its heart. The tree and I were surrounded by golden light, sharing a radiance held for a moment in the high limbs and then as quickly released. It was a world briefly transfigured, including myself in its amazement.

FIRE: The Adolescent

"Praised be You, my Lord, through Brother Fire,
through whom You light the night,
and he is beautiful and playful and robust and strong."

—Francis of Assisi, "Canticle of the
Creatures"[1]

Moving clockwise around the wheel, we arrive next at the south quadrant—the stage of the adolescent, a creature of fire. Young people (in the 10- to 24-year-old age group) push the edges of all that is wild, burning like a star, rising on the tip of a flame. He builds a tower to express his self-identity. She battles obstacles with a keen *warrior* energy. They sense the call of mystery and heroic adventure.[2]

As they anticipate leaving their family of origin, they work at fitting into a larger social configuration. They fall in love, finding themselves overwhelmed by a passion that's both sexual and spiritual. They're drawn to a higher vision, though not yet knowing what that is. Entering into a desert of desire—burning, burning, as T. S. Eliot said in his "Fire Sermon"—they're invited to recognize the cravings that don't serve them, being emptied of what keeps them from the One Great Longing.[3] Nature archetypes offering assistance in this quadrant are wildfire, stars, and deserts. This is the season of summer. The color is red, the color of blood, vitality.

Fire is hypnotic. "The fire confined to a fireplace was no doubt for man the first object of reveries . . . the invitation to repose," says Gaston Bachelard.[4] But the blaze that brings calm can also destroy. We're drawn to the ephemeral leaping of its flames, the dread of its power to consume. Fire symbolizes transformation. It occasions the purification of metals as well as the soul. The first thing we learn about fire is that we mustn't touch it.[5] It's an energy as dangerous as it is metamorphic. Yet we can't resist its allure.

Part of the attraction of fire is that it lies largely beyond our control. Even Elijah couldn't guarantee another feat like what he accomplished on Mount Carmel. "God doesn't necessarily throw down fire where we build the altar."[6] None of the four elements of the universe are subject to human mastery.

The fifth-century BCE Greek philosopher Empedocles was the first to propose the idea of four primeval elements. Fire was the one that fascinated him most. He viewed it as the fundamental principle of all living things. He ended his life by throwing himself over the flaming lip of Mount Etna in his native Sicily. His longing was to merge with fire, with "the pure element of the Volcano." Like the mesmerized moth, the adolescent in each of us is attracted to all that burns brightly.

The next three chapters lead us into the wonder, the illuminating power, and the hazard of flame, the fire that demands our constant yielding to change. "Deep in the wintry parts of our minds, we know that there is no such thing as a work-free transformation," says Clarissa Pinkola Estés. "We know that we will have to burn to the ground in one way or another, and then sit right in the ashes of who we once thought we were and go on from there."[7]

CHAPTER SIX

WILDFIRE

NORTH LARAMIE RIVER TRAIL AND CATHERINE OF SIENA

"Fire . . . It shines in Paradise. It burns in Hell. It is gentleness and torture. It is cookery and it is apocalypse."

—Gaston Bachelard, *The Psychoanalysis of Fire*[8]

"Since my house burned down
I now have an unobstructed view
of the rising moon."

—Seventeenth-century haiku by
Mizuta Masahide[9]

It was the first time I'd hiked a forest path through miles of fire-scorched trees. Blackened skeletons were left standing on one burnt hillside after another. I was walking through a section of Medicine Bow National Forest south of Laramie Peak in eastern Wyoming. It was the summer of 1996. A lightning strike in July had touched off a seven-thousand-acre fire, racing through trees left dead by years of drought and a mountain pine beetle epidemic.

There were charred stumps, naked tree trunks, and fallen limbs every-where. Yet new pioneer species were thriving. I was amazed at how quickly the forest had begun to repair itself. People said that within a week or two fireweed had already begun to sprout up—red flowering plants seen all over the West. They thrive in areas that have been cleared by fire.

I hadn't noticed a marker for the trailhead, but presumed I was hiking the North Laramie River trail, hoping to make my way down to the river where the fire hadn't reached. I'd been told the trail led to the ruins of the old Bullock family homestead, an abandoned cluster of cabins and barns dating back to 1915. During the Depression era, it was developed into a rustic resort known as Rainbow's End—a beautiful place for imagining yourself back on the Wyoming frontier. But the cindered path I walked kept following the ridge instead. Eventually it gave out altogether. I ended up having to bushwhack my way down toward the river several miles upstream from the old homestead.

Leaving the burnt forest, I descended into a narrow ravine, lowering myself down a rocky slope filled with prickly pear cactus––the kind of place where Wyoming's prairie rattlesnakes love to nest. Fortunately, I saw no snakes, but a few hundred feet from the bottom the going got steep and treacherous. At one point I faced a twelve-foot drop to a ledge below. A good rule of thumb is that you don't go down what you can't imagine yourself coming back up. So I was about to turn around, when I noticed the side rails of a weathered, makeshift ladder over to the side. A *ladder* in the middle of nowhere! God knows how old it was. But it proved an unexpected stairway to paradise.

I camped that night down by the river, in as beautiful and pristine a place as I could imagine. There were tall green grasses, foot-long rainbow trout swimming in the river's water, birds twittering in the rushes, the smell of ponderosa pine nearby. It was the exact opposite of what I'd been walking through all afternoon. After a supper of fried potatoes, beef jerky, and dried fruit—topped off with a little of Mr. Jameson's Irish whiskey—I gave my-self to the gratitude of being alone in wilderness. I watched pink and purple clouds slowly give way to night.

WILDERNESS AND FIRE'S DOUBLE EDGE

The contrast between the burnt ridge above and the lush river valley below was stunning— vividly illustrating the awful effects of fire on a vulnerable ecosystem. Over the last forty years, the number of large fires in the eleven Western states has increased dramatically.[10] There have been huge "megafires" making the seven-thousand-acre burn of 1996 look like a minor brushfire. Take the Yellowstone fires of 1988, on the other side of the state. Almost eight hundred thousand acres burned, more than a third of Yellowstone National Park. Nine thousand firefighters had to be brought in to fight the blaze. The event resulted in a major change in the National Park Service's long-standing fire management policy, which was to suppress fires in every way possible.

This strategy had been in place since the Big Blowup of 1910. The second largest wildfire in American history, it had burned more than three million acres in Idaho, Montana, and Washington—an area roughly the size of Connecticut.[11] Putting the fear of God into everyone, this fire shaped the newly established U.S. Forest Service. Instead of allowing fires to burn as a normal part of nature, the approach was to battle every wildfire in an all-out effort to protect forest land. Nobody wanted a recurrence of what happened in the summer of 1910.[12]

What followed was a decades-long buildup of fallen trees and heavy underbrush, turning wilderness timberland into a matchbox waiting to be struck. Lightning set the dry, dead branches of Yellowstone ablaze in 1988, a fiery year in which 72,000 fires were reported across the United States. It was a portent of things to come.

Yet fire, we've come to know, is a gift as well as a curse. Within a few months of the Yellowstone burns, the land was in bloom again. Increased sunlight on the forest floor and mineral nutrients left in the ashes brought wildflowers in a riot of color, along with grasses, green moss, and sagebrush. Berry bushes were sprouting in new meadows. Lodgepole pine trees actually benefitted from the fire. They need temperatures of 150 °F in order for their cones to open and seeds to drop. They were back in full force . . . along with aspens, the preferred grazing food for elk, helping to restore the animal herds.

Fire, says forest biologist Robin Wall Kimmerer, works as "a paintbrush on the landscape. Touch it here in a small dab and you've made a green meadow for elk; a light scatter there burns off the brush so the oaks make more acorns . . . Draw the firebrush along the creek and the next spring it's a thick stand of yellow willows."[13] What is this mystery of fire as killer and as life-bringer? What are we watching as we gaze into its glittering flames?

Sitting beside the river that night, I thought about the impact of fire on the land, the vulnerability of so many things in a wilderness landscape. On my way down to the river that afternoon, I'd disturbed a bird that was sitting on a pair of eggs lying on a flat stone. A brown bird with white stripes around its neck, it was a killdeer, I think. She flew to a nearby rock where she began making strange movements, breaking into the "broken wing act" that killdeer are known for. I was struck by the vulnerability of her two gray-speckled eggs lying without a nest on the bare ground.

Life is insistent, even in places where it's safer to lay eggs on the open earth. Despite all the dangers, through her ingenuity and loyalty, the bird brought her young into an unprotected world. The fire had raged, but life went on.

As night settled, I thought back on the sporadic wildfires—the burned-over districts—of my own life. Most of us can remember times of exuberant, uncontrolled adolescent energy. We recklessly threw ourselves into excessive commitments—trying to prove things to ourselves, seeking an identity, looking for love in all the wrong places. For the most part, these were legitimate first-half-of-life concerns. But they sometimes play themselves out in our experience long after their time should have passed. We find ourselves, like Augustine, looking back on charred forests of our own. Lamenting his misspent adolescence, in his autobiography the Bishop of Hippo confessed, "I arrived at Carthage, where the din of scandalous love-affairs raged cauldron-like around me."[14]

It proved hard for Augustine to acknowledge the value of his earlier mistakes, but he did come to appreciate the importance of desire in the spiritual life. By the time he wrote his *Confessions*, he could speak of Christ in a language of passionate yearning: "He peeps through the trellis of our flesh, and coaxes us, and enkindles our love until we run after him, allured by his fragrance."[15]

The awakening of desire, occurring sometimes very early in our lives, doesn't have to be a cause for lament. It often flashes with innocent delight. My wife and I were seven and eight years old when we first met. Our families were attending a Wednesday night church dinner, where Patricia accidentally broke my mother's water pitcher. It was a fortuitous mishap. I remember a few years later our playing house with her younger siblings in their back yard. We'd cut a door in an empty cardboard refrigerator box. She played the mother and I (as father) had to leave for work every day . . . saying goodbye to the kids and kissing her as I left. As I remember, I had to leave for work several times that afternoon.

It was my first kiss. Looking back now on fifty years of marriage with that same woman—fifty years of hard work, mixed faithfulness, and continued joy—I wonder at the enduring (if sometimes flickering) flame of desire that was sparked so early. I'm grateful for all of it, for how it mirrors my spiritual journey.

Wendell Berry speaks of his inability to separate his love of the Earth from his vows of marriage. For him the two slide together as part of a single membership. When we stay at our commitments long enough, he says, we find to our amazement that "what we have chosen and what we desire are the same."[16] The fire of excitement gets banked into the embers of a persistent love. New life keeps flourishing amidst the old burn.

FIRE AS REALITY AND SYMBOL

What is fire? Scientists explain it as "a self-sustaining, high temperature oxidation reaction."[17] It's a triangular combination of fuel, heat, and oxygen. When you hold a match under a piece of wood, the heat releases molecules of carbon gas from the wood surface. When these reach an ignition temperature, they join with oxygen in the air and burst into flame. The fire then gives off heat energy, carbon dioxide, and water vapor. If it's a wood fire, it produces a yellow or orange flame. Since the fuel isn't entirely combustible, some is left over as smoke and ash. The flame on a gas stove, by contrast, burns a bright blue, as almost everything is consumed.

To stop a fire you have to remove one of the three parts of the triangle. You can put water on it to reduce the heat. You can smother it to remove the oxygen. You can pull things out of its way to reduce the fuel. But this isn't always easy. A smoldering coal seam fire has burned continuously for six thousand years at Mount Wingen (the "Burning Mountain") north of Sydney, Australia. Some fires are hard to light; others are hard to extinguish.

What fire awakens in the human psyche is another matter altogether. Our use of fire goes back a million years to when *Homo erectus* began keeping fires for warmth, cooking, and protection. Ever since, we've walked a fine line between our need for fire and our impulse to resist it. Our lives wouldn't be possible without fire-making. We depend on asbestos-clad workers tapping slag from the bottom of a blast furnace, processing molten iron. These are the fire-eaters of an industrial society. We need the steel they produce.

But we also depend on those who serve as smoke jumpers—hotshot crews of elite firefighters assigned to the hottest part of a forest fire. They parachute into a blaze with ninety pounds of gear . . . parachutes, puncture-proof Kevlar suits, chain saws, shovels, and fire shelters. We depend on those who sustain the fires *and* those who put them out. Both may carry Catherine of Siena medals in their pockets. This fourteenth-century mystic is the patron saint of firefighters and fire protection, as well as a doctor of the church.

Fire, says Bachelard, is both a domestic element (symbolic of warmth, love, and the hearth) and an unruly element (wild, threatening, attacking from without). Either way, we're fascinated by its dominant color of red. Color psychologists tell us that the color red exerts a profound influence on our moods, perceptions, and actions. Red grabs your attention. It raises the pulse rate. Almost universally, it means stop, danger, hot.

But it also suggests vivacity and the life-giving quality of blood. Neanderthal shamans used red ocher in consecrating Paleolithic burial sites. We don't know why. Red seems to linger in the human imagination, pervading the dawn and dusk of each new day. It's the longest wavelength of light, the highest shade on the arc of the rainbow.

In religious symbolism, fire signifies the transformative power of the divine and the flaming passion of human desire. Both can be as dangerous as they are life-changing. In the Hebrew scriptures, fire is often associated with a call to action, a summons to a new identity, an awakening of desire. Moses experiences the call of Yahweh through a burning bush. Jeremiah describes God's word as "a burning fire shut up in his bones." An angel touches Isaiah's lips with a flaming coal, giving him the power of speech. Elijah calls down the *aish shamayim* (fire from heaven), defeating the prophets of Baal on Mount Carmel.

In the New Testament, Jesus says, "I've come to set the world on fire, and how I wish it were already kindled!" The Holy Spirit arrives with cloven tongues of flame on the Day of Pentecost.[18] Two centuries later a Christian bishop in Italy—St. Elmo—would narrowly escape being struck by lightning. He became the patron saint of sailors, protecting them with St. Elmo's fire, a meteorological phenomenon in which a bright ball of blue light appears on the top of ships' masts in a thunderstorm.

Fire is a sacred symbol in every spiritual tradition. Agni, the Hindu god of fire, points to the divine spark hidden within all beings. Vesta was the Roman goddess of the hearth, keeper of the sacred fire on Mount Olympus. In ancient Persia Zoroastrians welcomed Atar (the blazing fire of creation) in their temple rituals. The Buddha's "Fire Sermon" warned his disciples against the fiery cravings of a sensuous life.

In alchemy, fire is the catalyst for change, the phoenix rising from the ashes. The Irish St. Bridget evoked earlier associations with the Celtic goddess of the hearth. The nuns in the monastery she founded at Kildare kept a fire going for a thousand years. In medieval cathedrals, the feast of Pentecost was originally celebrated by dropping flaming bits of straw from the Holy Ghost hole in the ceiling above the nave. They later found it safer to drop red rose petals instead.

The Talmud contains my favorite image of fire as a divine mystery. The rabbis used it to symbolize the fervent praise of God. They spoke of a river of fire, the River Rigyon, flowing from under heaven's throne. The stream springs from the perspiration of the angels who support the throne and burn themselves out each day in singing God's glory. At night they sink back into the flames, exhausted, as fresh ones arise from the fire to sing anew. The splendor of the divine evokes a passion too intense to endure longer than a single day.[19]

The fervency of fire—in all that it represents—captures the imagination. It "suggests the desire to change, to speed up the passage of time, to bring all of life to its conclusion," says Bachelard. "Through fire everything changes. When we want everything to be changed we call on fire."[20] That's what makes it such a fitting image for the enormous social, emotional, and physical changes of adolescence.

Today we take adolescence as a normal (exuberant and tempest-tossed) stage of life in human development. But during the Dark Ages in Europe, life expectancy was diminished to thirty years or less. By the age of twelve, children were plunged directly into adult life. But as economic conditions improved through the medieval period, bringing a longer lifespan, families were able to provide their teenagers with a few years to think, to question, and to develop a sense of individual identity.[21] Adolescence, therefore, is (at most) an early modern development. Catherine of Siena was one of the beneficiaries of this social change.

CATHERINE OF SIENA AS FIERY SAINT

Caterina di Benincasa (1347–1380) was born in Siena, Italy, a town surrounded by olive groves, sheep pastures, and vineyards, fifty miles south of Florence. She was the twenty-fourth of twenty-five children born to a prosperous wool dyer and his wife. As a child, she helped to keep fires burning under vats of colored dyes filled with skeins of wool. She also spent time in the Gothic cathedral up the hill from the family home, drawn to the red stained-glass windows and the flame of God's presence in the sanctuary lamp.

Red was her favorite color: the red-tiled roofs and towers of Siena, the red bougainvillea blossoms of Tuscany, the red wine of Christ's blood in the chalice at Mass. Her renowned asceticism didn't keep her from delighting in the Earth's beauty. "All the way to heaven is heaven," she exclaimed.[22]

This was a woman consumed by the fiery presence of the divine in the world around her. Catherine's short life was marked by an excess of adolescent exuberance. Dying at the age of thirty-three, she had never outgrown it. She did nothing by halves. She spoke of a "fire of holy desire" continually burning within her. Fire was her favorite element—full of life, intensity, brilliance, death, and danger. She knew God above everything else to be a fire of love. This is what set her aflame. "If you are what you should be," she wrote to a friend, "you will set the world on fire."[23]

Catherine was a bright and imaginative child, headstrong and independent. She received her first vision at the age of six. She talked with Christ and the saints (especially Mary Magdalene), who were as familiar to her as neighborhood visitors dropping in to chat with her father, Jacopo. A year later she made a vow of virginity, promising herself in marriage to God. For the next thirteen years she explored the inner life, maintaining a contemplative practice. When she wasn't cleaning house or helping in the kitchen, she stayed in a small cell that she'd been given under the stairs.

The woman was falling madly in love with God. She wanted nothing less than to "become" God, in fact, to disappear into that which she desired. She yearned for union with the glorious King that the thirty birds had encountered in Farid ud-Din Attar's Sufi poem. For her, physical reality (even her own body) largely got in the way. It wasn't a matter of self-hatred. Catherine knew she was attractive. Having pondered her reflection in the town fountain where she went to fetch water each day, she later wrote to a friend that we ought to be able to see God within us, "just as when we look into a fountain, and see our image, we take pleasure in it and love ourselves."[24]

But having betrothed herself to Christ, she resisted her family's efforts to marry her off. At the age of fifteen she cut off her hair in order to discourage suitors. Three years later she joined a group of women known as the Mantellate, a Third Order Dominican community. These were mostly widows, wearing the black and white Dominican habit. They lived in their own homes, serving the poor and sick under the direction of the friars.

Catherine continued to live a life of solitude in her family home until she was twenty-one, when she had the defining experience of her adolescent years—a mystical vision of being espoused to Christ as her bridegroom. She heard Jesus saying to her, "My most beloved daughter, you know that the bride adorns herself when she goes before the bridegroom. She wears the color ruby-red to please her spouse. I want you to do the same." She asked, "Who is this bride you seek?" "She is *another me*," answered Christ, "made so by the affection of love."[25]

The experience was life-changing. Having devoted thirteen years of her life to an inner world, she gave the next thirteen years to the outer world. Plunging into the streets with her white veil and black cape, she gathered food and clothes for beggars, visited the sick, served lepers, cancer patients, and those dying of the plague.[26] The reclusive Emily Dickinson became a mystic-driven Florence Nightingale.

By her late twenties, Catherine was exerting an international influence—seeking peace among warring factions in Italy, urging the pope to return to Rome from his exile in Avignon, and trying to end the Great Schism as multiple popes were claiming the papal throne. In a time of social, political, and ecclesiastical chaos, her fiery spirit was irresistible. She possessed an infectious, charismatic spirit that captivated others. Priests and nuns, popes and noblemen spoke of her as their spiritual mother, "Mamma Caterina." She was an earth mother, a hearth keeper in a world of turmoil.

Her courage in speaking to people of authority was legendary, recalling Hildegard of Bingen before her. To a bishop who refused to address scandals in the church, she wrote, "No more silence! I'm seeing the world going to ruin because people like you aren't speaking out!" In a letter to the pope, she warned, "Don't make it necessary for me to complain about you to Christ crucified." She was just as bold in her pastoral and healing work. To a beloved friar who seemed near death, she exclaimed, "I command you in the name of Our Lord Jesus Christ, do not die." He promptly obeyed, recovering to resume his work.[27]

Hers was the kind of fierce honesty you look for in a spiritual director. One who's willing to confront you when necessary, pointing out when your need for approval is getting in the way . . . when you've gotten absorbed in too damn many things again. The fiery saint spoke God's "gentle first truth" with an unflinching boldness. Preaching in town squares as she traveled, she drew large crowds. "No halfheartedness made its home in Catherine," says one of her biographers. "She wasn't a woman who could measure out her life in teaspoons."[28]

Though she lacked formal education, Catherine became the first woman in Italy to write and be published in the vernacular. The one book she left was her *Dialogue*, an intimate conversation between God and herself. God was, for her, a "fire surpassing every fire," a fire of love engulfing the soul.[29]

She grasped at every image she could find to speak of this love, describing the body of Christ as a "bridge" leading the soul to God by three distinct steps. Unconcerned about mixing her metaphors, she offered a comparison to a little child running to its mother, wanting to clamber up her body to be as close to her as possible. The child first clings to the mother's feet, not wanting to let her go, then scrambles up to her side and nurses at her breast. Finally the child crawls up to her shoulders to be kissed by her lips. These are the three stairs on the bridge: the feet, side, and mouth of Christ.[30] They lead the soul to God's infinite love.

Such images are the mystic's wild effort to say what finally can't be put into words. What is God's love? Catherine asked. It's an all-consuming fire, a mother's yearning for an infant child, Christ's suffering body bridging heaven and earth. She knew in the end that "love transforms one into what one loves."[31] Fire turns the soul into flame.

"In your nature, eternal God, I come to know my own nature," Catherine prayed. "And what is that? *Fire* is my nature, because you are nothing but a fire of love." Within that fire, she could proclaim, "I become another *you*."[32] This was Catherine's greatest love—a longing for nothing less than perfect union with God.

A SPIRITUALITY OF FIRE

Hotshot crews working wildfires in the West sometimes witness a rare phenomenon known as "superheating." This happens when rising temperatures from an approaching fire drive resinous vapors out of pinyon pines and juniper trees on a distant slope. It's like gas left on in an unlit oven. All that's needed is a spark to send everything up.[33] Intense human desire has a similar effect. Yielding to a dangerous temptation or falling in love with God can (in either case) be as traumatic and life-changing as a hillside exploding into flames.

The worst sinners and the greatest saints share a significant trait: They throw themselves unreservedly into what they love. It's why God delights in them both. "You can't become one with the fire if you don't throw yourself into it wholeheartedly, holding nothing back," Catherine wrote to an abbot in France.[34] Let everything go up in flames.

Catherine used the image of fire in her analysis of holy desire, her sharing in Christ's suffering, and the purifying effect of tears.

1. Fire as Holy Desire. "O Fire of Love," she addressed God. "What drove you to be so mad with love [for us] as you are?"[35] She pointed to God's infinite fiery desire as the source of her own desire. She wouldn't have this yearning if it hadn't first been planted within her by God's own yearning. "I am fire and you are the sparks," God told her.[36]

Catherine relished the story of the two disciples who met the resurrected Christ on the Emmaus road, afterward asking, "Didn't our hearts burn within us as he talked with us on the way?" (Luke 24:32). She was fascinated by a moth dancing around a candle flame. To borrow the words of Goethe, she felt compelled "to praise what is truly alive, what longs to be burned to death." A "desire for a higher love-making" swept her upward.[37]

The Christian church has too often been wary of desire, particularly erotic desire, making passion itself the root of all evil. When this happens, says Richard Rohr, the church starts to think its primary work is sin management rather than spiritual transformation. We lose something visceral in the process. "The flame is in some way a naked animality," said Novalis, "a kind of excessive animal. It is glutton par excellence."[38] According to Catherine, the soul's infinite desire for God (its ravenous hunger) is the only infinite thing it can offer to an infinite God.[39]

2. *The Fire of Suffering.*   On the other hand, Catherine's ascetic practices—especially with respect to food—were widely known in her day.[40] She slept on a wooden board, praying through most of the night. Throughout her life she survived on a little bread, uncooked vegetables, and water. Today we'd be tempted to diagnose her as anorexic. By the age of thirty-three when she died, she was reportedly living on nothing but the host she received at Mass. Her life was lived out in a fiery blaze of reckless longing.

We shouldn't be too quick to dismiss Catherine's embrace of suffering as a dualistic rejection of the body or a self-hatred rooted in the misogyny of her time. Recent studies of medieval women mystics argue that food, eating, and fasting were ways of identifying with the humanity of Jesus, sharing in his suffering, giving oneself as food for others, and in the process realizing a deeper union with God.[41] Catherine continually provided sustenance for those in need while enduring the fire of abstinence herself. She savored the image of Christ as bread baked in an oven, kneaded into the dough of the Holy Trinity even as the faithful are kneaded and baked into him.[42] Identifying with Christ, she in turn became bread baked for others.

3. *Fire as Purification.*   Watching the fires burning under her father's dye vats, Catherine knew as a child that green wood has to weep before it burns. The soul on its way to God, she learned, does the same thing—expressing and releasing its longings by means of tears. There are wounds that have to be cauterized by fire, she observed.[43]

Disordered desire is always a problem. The soul can't help but love. "She [the soul] always wants to love something because love is the stuff she is made of." But while the love of God is the only love that satisfies, the soul imagines herself gratified by things that dazzle the eye.[44] To be cleansed of these lesser desires, she moves through various stages of tears. There are egocentric tears of frustrated desire and self-pity, tears of sincere repentance, tears of sympathetic concern for others, genuine tears of longing for God, and "tears of fire" that arise out of the depths of the soul when ordinary tears have long dried up.[45] To pass through the flames—indeed, to *give* oneself to Fire—is the soul's chief aim.

BEFRIENDING THE FIRE

Norman Maclean, who grew up on the northern plains of Montana, wrote of his fascination with recurring wildfires in his last book, *Young Men and Fire*.[46] His story begins on the afternoon of August 5, 1949. Fifteen young men—smokejumpers for the U.S. Forest Service—were about to leap out of a C-47 flying over Mann Gulch just up from the Missouri River in the Rocky Mountains of western Montana. They were between seventeen and twenty-three years old, crack firefighters knowing exactly what they were doing.

It looked like a regular ground fire from the sky. They'd get to it fast, dig a fire line around it, and be out by ten the next morning. That was their usual pattern in working fires. But something unexpected happened that day after they got on the ground. The wind changed direction and the fire went up into the crown of the trees. A crown fire moves much faster, roaring through timber, beginning to sound like a railroad train, becoming a monster as fires in the mountains sometimes do.

The worst thing that can happen in a forest fire is when it turns into a blowup. That's when a crown fire starts explosively throwing out fiery branches in advance of itself, starting spot fires up ahead. When this happens, a convection effect sucks oxygen into the space between the fires, drawing everything up into an inferno—throwing flames two hundred feet high, reaching temperatures of two thousand degrees.

On that day in August, the firefighters suddenly saw something like that roaring toward them as they raced up the ridge toward safety. It was almost a hundred degrees that day already, the hottest on record. They were running up a seventy-six-degree slope over thick dry grass, slippery as hell. They got within two hundred yards of the ridge, but the fire was only fifty yards behind them and coming fast.

That's when Wagner Dodge, the foreman of the crew, did something un-heard of. Running out in front of his men, he took a match and lit a fire in the dry grass in front of him. As this new fire quickly burned up the slope, he yelled at the others to jump into its burning ashes with him. They thought he was crazy, maybe trying to commit suicide. So they raced on up toward the ridge as he lay down in the hot ashes, covering his face with a wet handkerchief.[47]

The fire caught thirteen of the others; they died on that August 5, 1949. Dodge survived, however, as the main fire swept around his burned-out circle. He was left breathing what little air there still was close to the ground. Who would have thought of escaping a monster by burning a hole in the fire and lying down in it?

Our natural inclination—whether in wilderness or in the spiritual life—is to flee from the fire, to avoid the painful experiences that come in our lives. Yet God's way, Catherine of Siena knew, isn't *around* the wilderness, but *through* it. Not in escaping the fire, but in lying down in it.

"I have called you by name, you are mine," God told the prophet Isaiah. "When you pass through the waters, I will be with you; and through the rivers, they shall not overwhelm you; when you walk through fire you shall not be burned; and the flame shall not consume you. For I am the Lord your God" (Isaiah 43:1–3).

The one fire of which Isaiah (and Catherine) had no fear was the fire of love. It may devour, it may refine; but it always transforms. Its goal in overtaking dead wood is to transmute it into the splendor of flame. This is a transformation in which the tree itself delights. I suspect Grandfather knew something of this on the day the flames swept up the east side of his trunk. In the minutes before the firemen arrived and before the blaze reached into his higher branches, he must have experienced a terror mixed with awe—being transformed into a fiery beauty even in facing his own death.

Might he have apprehended the words of Mechthild of Magdeburg in that moment, "Lie down in the fire, and see and taste the flowing Godhead in your being"?[48] I can imagine Catherine of Siena asking, "Was he—were WE—made for anything less?"

CHAPTER SEVEN

STARS

CAHOKIA MOUNDS AND ORIGEN
OF ALEXANDRIA

"The nitrogen in our DNA, the calcium in our teeth, the iron in our blood, the carbon in our apple pies were made in the interiors of collapsing stars. We are made of starstuff."

—Carl Sagan, *Cosmos*[1]

"Astronomy may justly be called the alphabet of theology."
—John Calvin, *Commentary on Jeremiah*[2]

The weather wasn't promising. But the winter solstice comes only once a year and I'd packed for the trip. I was going to spend the night on Monk's Mound at one of the largest and oldest sacred places in North America. The Cahokia Mounds Historic Site lies on the bottomland of the Mississippi River north of East St. Louis, off Interstate 70. On the edge of immense urban poverty and untreated Superfund sites, it's a place older than Chartres Cathedral. Most people drive by it without ever noticing.

The Mississippian peoples who lived there between 800 and 1400 CE were as creative and mysterious as their contemporaries—the Anasazi in the Four Corners region of the Southwest. They were astute astronomers, building the most advanced earthen and stone structures of their time, establishing great economic and cultural centers reaching out in every direction. Cahokia was the Chaco Canyon of the Midwest.

I'd come to participate in an astronomical event that annually captivated twelfth-century Mississippian scientists and shamans. At a time when Bernard of Clairvaux was taking medieval French spirituality to its heights, Cahokia's thirty thousand inhabitants were building ceremonial mounds and circular wood-henges as a way of measuring the path of the sun, moon, and stars across the sky. On the night of the winter solstice, along a southeast-to-northwest axis, they watched the Winter Hexagon passing overhead (a pattern including Orion's brightest stars as well as the Pleiades cluster). A few hours later they'd welcome the rising of the sun on the morning of the shortest day of the year. I wanted to be part of that.

I spent my first day there hiking the 10-mile trail of the park, winding through the dozens of mounds still found on its 2,200-acre tract. On a cold, cloudy day before Christmas, I had the place to myself. Wandering through swamp marshes and game trails, I surprised four does and a five-point buck under one of the large red oaks. Trying to forget the railroad tracks and interstate highway nearby, I could almost imagine what it had been like to be there a thousand years ago.

I sat that afternoon atop Mound 72, a burial site from which archaeologists have learned much about the people who lived in this place. Gazing into the bare limbs of a tall sycamore nearby, I could sense the presence of the old ones. I imagined priests leading the royal family through the trees, bearing the dead king on a litter. Proceeding on a straight line south from the Great Mound where the royal ceremonial house stood, they placed the king on a bed of twenty thousand marine-shell beads arranged in the shape of a huge falcon.

He was the Birdman King of the Sky People—laid to rest near the bodies of fifty-three young women, apparently sacrificed to accompany him to the world above. Forty generations ago this was a place of brilliant artifice, built on the back-breaking work of men hauling dirt for the mounds and the expendable lives of women. Violence, it seems, has always accompanied the sacred.

As sundown approached, I made my way to the reconstructed wood-henge on the western edge of the city's east-west axis. The Cahokians used this large circle of forty-eight red cedar posts to plot the rise of the sun at the four pivotal points of the solar year. I stood at the tall center post where astronomer calendrists would have waited through the night, watching the ascent of sacred stars heralding the sun. The next morning the solar deity, as promised, would ascend directly over the post marking the winter solstice.

This is a haunting place, a vortex of the imagination—like England's Stonehenge or Wyoming's Bighorn Medicine Wheel. People are lured here for many reasons. While I stood that evening in the wood-henge circle, two middle-aged couples entered and gathering around the post marking the winter solstice with crystals in their hands. They told me they were adherents of a spiritual teacher in the United Kingdom named Solara An-Ra, a woman who channels messages from Pleiadian star beings. Later, at midnight, I found a young man doing Tai Chi all alone on top of the tallest mound. I almost expected to see a pith-helmeted archaeologist emerge from a hidden tunnel with a trowel in his hand.

What draws people to this place with its unique connection to the mystery of sky? I asked the question that night with Origen of Alexandria in mind. He was a third-century Christian theologian and dazzling thinker, fascinated by the early Greek notion that the stars were living beings. We aren't alone in the universe, said Origen. We share in a spiritual community where falling stars and the stellar glory of distant nebulae are full of moral insight. Origen was variously perceived as a heretic, a glittering eccentric, and the greatest theologian of the early church. Some might say that all of us "crazies" were there that night—each of us beguiled by the wonder of the stars.

The weather remained unpredictable as I made my way, loaded with gear, up the hundred-foot height of Monks Mound. It's the tallest of the mounds, named after a handful of Trappist monks who established a mission there in the nineteenth century. Measuring 1,000 feet long and 770 feet wide, it's larger at its base than the Great Pyramid of Egypt, and must have taken more than 150 years to build. In its day, it would have looked out over a highly developed civilization with commerce reaching out thousands of miles in every direction, astronomer shamans maintaining spiritual continuity with the heavens, and farmers growing corn, squash, and beans on incredibly fertile land.

I carried with me two sleeping bags, a tarp, flashlight, star charts, and an iPhone star app—hoping for a few hours of clear sky before rain and snow moved in from the west. I chose a spot on the northwest top of the mound, at the corner of what would have been the king's ceremonial house. A few of the clouds started to clear away after midnight. Despite the distant lights of the city of St. Louis, I could see the stars I'd been looking for. Rigel, Aldebaran, Capella, Pollux, and the major and minor dog stars—all passing overhead (see Figure 7.1). These form the Winter Hexagon, what I like to think of as the jeweled face of God. The Pleiades hang like a cluster of flowers on the right

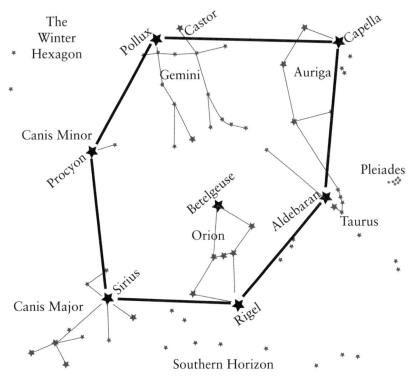

The Winter Hexagon

Castor

Pollux

Capella

Gemini

Auriga

Canis Minor

Procyon

Pleiades

Betelgeuse

Aldebaran

Taurus

Orion

Canis Major

Sirius

Rigel

Southern Horizon

Figure 7.1 The Winter Hexagon and the Pleiades.

side of the face. Who wouldn't be tempted to view these sparkling embers as pulsing with life? They include seven of the brightest stars in the entire sky.

I spent the night suspended in a world where life's meaning is linked to the movement of celestial bodies. Going back in time, I was part of a sacred landscape where great rivers converge (the Missouri and the Mississippi), where floods replicate a primeval cycle of life and death, where earthquakes (from the nearby New Madras fault) remind people of the fragility of the cosmos.

But as night wore on, strengthening winds brought clouds from the west, and I was soon wrestling with cold, wet weather. The sound of light rain falling on a tarp overhead can be the height of pleasure—if you're warm and dry. But as water seeps into the edges of your sleeping bag, as snow drifts onto your face and cold settles in, you're tempted to abort the mission. Just before dawn I finally did so, declaring my authentic Cahokia experience to have reached its limit. In the wintry drizzle, I trudged back to the wood-henge to observe the solstice sunrise on my star app. It rose where it should have been, right over the southeast post, despite my witnessing it in digital form. Soaked and chilled, I stopped on the way home for coffee and eggs at Denny's, chagrined by my faint-hearted embrace of a sacred astronomy.

FINDING A MANAGEABLE UNIVERSE IN THE VASTNESS OF SPACE

We have always sought a way to feel at home in a universe of far-flung stars. The immensity of the cosmos is overwhelming. Our planet glides through space on one of a dozen rotating arms revolving around the nucleus of the Milky Way galaxy. Our sun takes 220 million years to make a complete revolution around the massive black hole at the galaxy's core. It's made only twenty-five such trips since the sun and the Earth were born. Multiply this by the two hundred billion other galaxies in the universe—some of them spiral, some elliptical or irregular—and you have a truly inconceivable immensity.[3] The light reaching us from the most distant stars (up to ten billion light years away) began its journey before the Earth even existed.

So what *are* these astounding sources of light we refer to as stars? Astrophysicists describe them as massive balls of hydrogen and helium with nuclear fusion at their core, scattered throughout space. There are more than a billion trillion stars in the observable universe, a number beyond comprehension. Moreover, they've all originated—according to prevailing opinion—from a single point with the Big Bang 13.8 billion years ago. They continue speeding outward to this day.

Stars come in different sizes, degrees of brightness, and color. Some are blue giants, extremely hot and luminous. Red stars are cooler, nearing the end of their life, often condensing into white dwarfs. A few burst into astonishing supernovas, exploding in their death. Others eventually tumble into themselves because of gravitational collapse, becoming black holes. That's where space shrinks and time strangely stops. The mind goes numb even as the imagination takes wing in marveling at such a world.

Who isn't awestruck by the Hubble Space Telescope photographs of star farms—distant nebulae where new stars are born? These soaring columns of interstellar clouds are filled with dust, hydrogen, helium, and other ionized gases, bathed in the scorching ultraviolet light of infant stars.[4] The Crab Nebula in the constellation Taurus is one of them, resulting from an eleventh-century supernova that may have deeply affected the Cahokia community. Through the centuries, skywatchers and poets have been dumbfounded by the exploding deaths of old stars, the churning births of new ones.

How do lonely humans beings find a home in the vastness of the cosmos? How do we make it habitable, imagining a place where we seem to fit? One way, as evidenced by the early Cahokians, is to study the sky with great care, penetrating its daunting depths. We've learned to read the heavens like a map, finding our way as we travel by night. We've observed the turning of the seasons, remembering when to plant, when to reap. We attend to the reassuring presence of familiar stars.

The sun, moon, and planets all move along the same horizontal plane from our perspective on Earth, what we call the ecliptic. The Babylonians identified particular constellations lying along this plane, telling stories about each of them. These configurations, used by ancient sailors and astrologers alike, coalesced into the twelve signs of the zodiac. They became familiar patterns aligned with the fluctuations and hopes of human life.

Other skywatchers have made the universe friendlier by imagining the heavenly bodies as possessing a life of their own, similar to ours. In Carl Sagan's movie *Contact*, astronomer Ellie Arroway (played by Jodie Foster) makes contact with an extraterrestrial being from the star Vega. "You're an interesting species," he tells her. "You feel so lost, so cut off, so alone, only you're not. See, in all our searching, the only thing we've found that makes the emptiness bearable is each other." Stories of stars as animate and of human contact with star-beings are ancient and enduring.

In the Hebrew scriptures, Yahweh counted the stars, giving names to each one (Psalm 147:4). When God called to them, they responded, saying, "Here we are! . . . shining with gladness for the one who made them" (Baruch 3:34). These were celestial beings capable of uttering praise, the morning stars singing together (Psalm 19:1–3; Job 38:7). The prophet Isaiah spoke of a particularly willful star—Lucifer, the Day Star, the shining one—who "made himself like the Most High" and fell from heaven (Isaiah 14:12–15).

Plato similarly looked on the stars as living, spiritual creatures. Our souls came from them, he said, and will eventually return there. Given this kinship with the sky, we use astronomy, poetry, and music in an effort to achieve reunification.[5] Even Thomas Aquinas argued that "the luminaries of heaven are living beings," quoting Origen as support.[6]

The Cahokians created a habitable cosmos by perceiving the stars as the living source of their cultural and religious life. They built more than a hundred mounds and five wood-henges in order to carefully measure solstices, equinoxes, and star risings. They monitored the ascent of celestial objects like Venus and the star cluster we know as the Pleiades.[7] If the stars were alive, they knew they weren't alone.

Prehistoric sites are admittedly difficult to interpret. The Mississippians left no written texts. But between what archaeologists have found and what we learn from the oral traditions of native peoples descending from the Cahokians, we can put together an approximation of their celestial geography. The Osage Indians of Missouri, Oklahoma, and Kansas, for example, trace their ancestral roots to the Mississippi Valley. Their creation myth explains how they came to be known as the Sky People.[8]

By their account, the ancestors of the Osage originally came to Earth from the Pleiades, the Seven Sisters in the winter sky, located on the shoulder of Taurus the Bull. They landed as eagles in a red oak tree near the Great River, scattering acorns everywhere. Two stone tablets found at or near Cahokia picture a birdman figure (a man with a beaked nose and wings) resembling the burial cape of the Birdman King in Mound 72. On one of these tablets the figure has the six prominent stars of the Pleiades on his chest, arranged exactly as they appear in the sky.[9] The people of Cahokia may literally have traced their source to this realm in the heavens.

We know that they configured their city according to a sacred geography. Sky dwellers (priests and ceremonial leaders) lived north of the line marking the sun's daily path. Earth dwellers (administrators and officials) lived south of that line. Monks Mound and the largest wood-henge lay to the north, while burial and utility mounds were built to the south—holding pots, axe heads, and hammered copper sheets. For these early Mississippians, the Sky World was as vibrant and alive as anything on Earth. It pulsed with an ever-changing mystery of continuity and surprise, light and dark, male and female energies.

In the middle of the eleventh century the city of Cahokia suddenly burst into larger life, increasing in size and influence along the Mississippi Valley. Some archaeologists suggest this had to do with the exploding death of a great star in the constellation Taurus in the summer of 1054. This supernova observed in Europe as well as the Americas—one of the few such documented sightings we've had over the past two thousand years—lingered as a brilliant display in the night sky for weeks, appearing in the heavens very close to the Pleiades. Who knows how visionaries among the Children of the Star Cluster might have interpreted its significance?

THE STARS AND MYTHOLOGY

Stars have been a source of wonderment for as long as human beings have slept under a night sky. They awaken a yearning in the soul, an impulse to the contemplative life. The Online Etymology Dictionary suggests that our word "consider" comes from the Latin word *considerare*—literally, to think "*with* the stars" (*con-sideris*). Similarly, our word "desire" suggests a wanting that comes "*from* the stars" (*de-sideris*). "The sky is the daily bread of the eyes," wrote Emerson. Our imagination feeds on it. Mary Oliver remembers spending the night in a forest alone, experiencing "nothing between me and the white fire of the stars but my thoughts." "By morning," she reflects, "I had vanished at least a dozen times into something better."[10]

The stars do this for us. They sing; we listen. Early Greek philosophers imagined a music of the spheres—a *musica universalis*—produced by the heavenly bodies. The sun, moon, planets, and stars, said Pythagoras, all emit their own unique hum, an orbital resonance based on the mathematical harmony of their movements. Number, motion, harmonics, mystery: These are the rhetoric of the stars.[11] No wonder the ancients viewed them as gods and goddesses passing through the night.

The Egyptian goddess Sothis (with her dog star Sirius) occasioned the yearly flooding of the Nile. The Aztec "Lords of the Night" were nine star deities governing the annual calendar. In the Hindu tradition, Indra's jeweled net of glistening stars portrayed a cosmos where everything coheres. Even the Virgin Mary became Stella Maris, the Star of the Sea, and medieval seafarers used her North Star for navigation.

Especially important for Cahokian cosmology were the mythic stories associated with Venus and the Pleiades star cluster. They were the ones I most wanted to observe on my night atop Monks Mound. The Mississippians—like their contemporaries the Mayans in the Yucatán Peninsula and the Anasazi of Chaco Canyon—paid special attention to the planet Venus, known as both the Morning and Evening Star. In their mythology, the Morning Star was a masculine deity, the Sun-Carrier or Thunderbird. The Evening Star was a goddess connected with the Corn Mother.[12] The two divine beings were permeating mysteries, evidenced in a single heavenly body.

Venus is far brighter than any of the other planets or stars. You can see it in broad daylight by the naked eye. The planet appears to rise in the eastern sky before sunrise and linger after the setting sun in the west, depending on the time of the year and its orbit around the sun. I spotted Venus in the western sky on the night of the solstice, even as the Pleiades were rising on the opposite side of the ecliptic in the east. The Cahokians would have been struck by the correspondence of these descending and ascending figures as they canvassed the sky every year on that night. Did they imagine Venus, the Corn Mother, dying in the west as the seven daughters rose through the night to herald the coming of the Sun Father?

The Pleiades form the brightest open cluster in the sky, full of hot blue stars. Only six are usually visible to the unaided eye, but the constellation contains hundreds. The ones we see are grouped together in the shape of a tiny dipper. Few stars have evoked as many stories as these.

The Pleiades were the seven daughters of Atlas and Pleione in Greek mythology. Orion the hunter fancied them as he wandered the slopes of Mount Parnassus one day. For seven years he gave chase, until Zeus rescued the girls by turning them into doves soaring among the stars. Orion continues stalking them in the night sky.

In the Lakota version, the girls were tracked by a giant bear. As they prayed to the Great Spirit, the rock on which they stood began to rise, becoming Devils Tower (Bear Lodge) in the Black Hills of northeast Wyoming. The bear left his claw marks on the side of this nine-hundred-foot tall volcanic core, but the girls escaped into the sky as the Pleiades. The Lakota people consider the Winter Hexagon (the expanse of stars in the Sacred Hoop) to be a mirror image of the Black Hills.[13] All of it sacred.

For Tennyson, the Pleiades glittered "like a swarm of fire-flies tangled in a silver braid."[14] Yahweh thundered out of the whirlwind, asking Job, "Can you bind the chains of the Pleiades or loosen Orion's belt" (Job 38:3, 31). Who can comprehend the enigma of the stars?

I crawled into my two sleeping bags that cold night on Monks Mound, thinking of the Pleiades, the red oak I'd seen on the trail that afternoon, and the whimsical idea of eagles landing there in a mythic past. My mind wandered to notions of time travel, worm holes, and distant galaxies. I thought of people on this mound gazing on this same night sky a thousand years in the past—and forty generations in the future. I even imagined those in the years to come contemplating a colony they'd just established on a planet circling Alcyone, the brightest star in the Pleiades cluster. In my dream, the Mississippian myth would have come full circle—people traveling from the stars to the Earth and back again.

ORIGEN AND THE STARS

These are speculative musings that might have intrigued Origen of Alexandria (185–254). This early Christian theologian creatively engaged the thought of his time, becoming a fascinating—and controversial—model for those who succeeded him.[15]

He lived in Alexandria on the Nile, one of the great intellectual and cultural centers of the Roman Empire. It was famous for its library (the largest in the world, with half a million papyrus scrolls), its Pharos lighthouse (one of the seven wonders of the ancient world), and its colorful tales of Antony and Cleopatra. Alexandria was a large and beautiful city, attracting scholars, scientists, philosophers, mathematicians, and artists. Everything flourished there—Neoplatonic philosophy, rabbinic learning, Gnostic thought, Egyptian mystery religions.[16]

Origen was born to Christian parents during a time of religious persecution. When he was seventeen, Roman authorities arrested and executed his father, Leonides. The son was left obsessed by martyrdom for the rest of his life. Fortunately, he could support his mother and six siblings by teaching, having previously received an excellent education. He soon took over the small Christian academy that had been established in Alexandria.

The young Origen had a voracious mind, devouring books and attending every lecture he could. He wrote some two thousand works, keeping seven stenographers busy taking dictation. His best-known book, *On First Principles*, was the first Christian effort to write a systematic theology. Two things stand out about him: his wide-ranging thought, incorporating the philosophy of his time, and his fiery desire for union with the Logos, the all-encompassing "Word" of divine love.

A modern scholar of Origen describes him as a man of "spirit and fire"—mesmerized by the light of flaming stars, drawn as a mystic to the blazing Eros of God's glory.[17] As a boy he'd been tempted to follow his father into the fiery death of martyrdom.

I am reminded of the movie *Backdraft*, in which Donald Sutherland plays the role of a pyromaniac captivated by the experience of a firefighter (played by Kurt Russell) who as a child had witnessed his dad's death by fire. "You watched him dance with the animal," the Sutherland character exults. "You saw your dad burn! . . . Did the fire *look* at you? . . . It *did*! Our worlds aren't that far apart are they?"

Fire reveals the face of death, appealing to the dark shadow as well as the bright light within us. Those who set fires and those who put them out are both transfixed by its burning. Origen knew this. Fire may have taken his father, but he trusted in a God who danced in flames.[18]

Throughout his life, Origen remained an impulsive, spirited man. To his later regret, as a youth he castrated himself, so as to focus his passion on God alone. Recklessly dismissing the authority of his bishop in Alexandria, he was exiled to Caesarea for the last twenty-five years of his life. As a trailblazing theologian he wrestled with speculative ideas, and three hundred years after his death he would be denounced (perhaps unfairly) as a heretic.[19]

Yet Origen was unparalleled as a seeker of truth, discerning the good in the wisdom of every tradition. He was a biblical theologian smitten by the power of the Word. He was a visionary who glimpsed the majesty of God in the unfolding of the cosmos. As the first Christian thinker to join the intellectual elite of his time, it's impossible to overestimate his importance for the history of Christian thought.[20]

1. The Truth-Seeker. Living at the thriving center of Platonic philosophy, Origen was thoroughly versed in the subjects Plato considered foundational to a sound education—arithmetic, geometry, music, astronomy.

His critics faulted him for depending too much on Platonic thought in articulating his Christian faith. Origen insisted that truth is the same wherever you encounter it. "If we happen to find a word of wisdom on the lips of a pagan, we should not immediately disdain the word itself because of the speaker."[21] There were ideas he rejected, yet he nonetheless gave them the credit for being philosophically discussable.

He acknowledged both the value and the peril of what he called "the gold of the Egyptians." On their flight from bondage, the Israelites had used some of the gold they received from the Egyptians to construct the tabernacle. But some found its way into the golden calf as well. Embracing foreign ideas can be helpful, Origen concluded, but also risky. So be critical, he urged, without being closed-minded. Like Abraham Heschel, he knew the danger of the mind becoming a *wall* instead of a *door* into a larger truth. He carefully labeled his speculative asides as "venturing a daring explanation" or as conjectures offered "with fear and caution."[22] This is how he prefaced what he wrote about the stars.

2. *The Biblical Theologian.* Origen was, above everything else, a student of the scriptures. His writings are saturated with biblical references. He was more bewitched by the archaic scrolls in Alexandria's great library than by the beauty of the moon over the Nile. Yet he considered pondering the wisdom of the ages as nothing compared to the contemplation of the eternal Logos in the written Word.

Origen compiled Greek and Hebrew versions of the biblical text and wrote commentaries or homilies on almost every biblical book. He explored multiple levels of the Bible's literal, figurative, and allegorical meanings. He knew that understanding the text requires a keen sensitivity to the subtleties of language. His commentary on the Song of Songs extolled erotic language as "the most appropriate way of using speech to surpass itself."[23] How else, he asked, can we describe God's intense desire for the human soul?

3. *The Visionary.* The Alexandrian theologian was also entranced by the grand sweep of God's design for the cosmos. Everything began and would end with God, he declared. In creation, the Great Mystery had brought into being a world of spiritual/rational beings (stars, angels, and human spirits) living in perfect harmony in unbounded space. They were rapt in contemplation of the divine splendor.

But God had given his creatures free will, and some exercised it in reckless ways. They became "sated" with the radiance of the Trinity, bored by God's goodness, weary of the divine beauty. Led by Lucifer, they sought a glory of their own, falling away into nothingness. To keep them from sinking any further, God created a material world of bodies (a second creation) to serve as a safety net.[24] There—in the world that we know—they could ponder their rebellion and hopefully return to the splendor they'd spurned. Hence, the materiality of the universe, in Origen's deeply Platonic way of thinking, was a second thought on God's part.

For Origen, the stars were an all-important part of this story. They, too, had sinned. (He read in Job 25:5 that they were "not pure in God's sight.") Nonetheless, they were endowed with superior faculties, and Christ died for them as well as for human beings. Even now they do penance for their sins, he affirmed, by shining to God's glory. Moving across the sky with a "majestic order and plan," they repent of their sins by helpfully marking the times and seasons for people on Earth.[25]

All this, of course, is a grand, Platonic stretch of the imagination. Yet his work serves to remind us that we're more closely related to the rest of the universe than we've thought. We share a common destiny. Contemplating the heavens, Origen asked how the great cosmic story might someday end. In the same way as it began, he concluded. "The end is always like the beginning."[26] God will be all in all, with everything finally restored to its original union with the divine (1 Corinthians 15:23–28). The stars will eventually be brought back into perfect harmony, shining yet again in boundless praise. Even Lucifer, in the end, will be unable to withstand God's love.[27]

Near the close of his life, Origen was imprisoned and tortured by the Romans, entering the same fire of persecution that his father had experienced before him. He died in 254 at the age of seventy. Throughout his life he'd been a star in his own right, flaming out with a spirited, if eccentric, brilliance. What he lacked in a grounded appreciation of the earth's materiality he made up for with a soaring refulgence of the spirit.

There's a grandeur—a star-like quality—in *every one* of us, he argued. "You must understand that *you* are another world in miniature, and that there is in you sun and moon and also stars . . . You to whom it is said that you are the 'light of the world.'"[28] God calls us to a spirituality of ascent, he said, reaching always for the light—for a higher place of spiritual knowledge, ascetic discipline, and mystical insight. All creatures, the stars included, are meant to shine to the glory of God.

ADOLESCENCE: ON BECOMING A STAR

There's a quest for stardom in every human soul. The nature of the adolescent is to give herself to flights of fancy, to the farthest reaches of the mind and heart. We've seen this in Origen. Early adolescence, says Bill Plotkin, is a time of creative fire. Young people are searching for a way of fitting in—and standing out. They are learning how to sparkle. In the first half of life, generally, says Richard Rohr, there's a need to feel special—receiving some degree of success and positive feedback. Otherwise, you spend the rest of your life demanding it from others.[29]

The unfulfilled teenager in each of us longs to have our worth affirmed, to shine like a star. This usually means being noticed by someone significant outside of our orbit. We hunger for a quality of "being" that comes only in "being *perceived*," says James Hillman. To be acknowledged by an authenticating outsider is to be blessed. The elder or sage discerns (and bestows) a transformative power in the very act of seeing.

The renowned Spanish bullfighter Manolete was "recognized" by his mentor José Flores ("Camará") a the age of eleven. In that moment the master perceived the student's greatness and the student discovered himself in the seeing.[30] In Origen's case, his teacher and predecessor at the Alexandrian academy, Clement of Alexandria, may have played the same role—urging his protégé to assume his office at the age of seventeen.

In Hindu spirituality, this awakening involves the taking and receiving of the darshan of another. It's the reverent noticing (and being noticed) that occurs in the presence of a sacred person or place. You may be stunned by the unclimbed splendor of Mount Machapuchare in Nepal or find yourself standing before a wise old woman who recognizes the gold within you.[31] However it happens, it's a moment of grace. Nothing will be the same as a result. It's what the adolescent lives for.

I experienced it myself for the first time at the age of eleven. I was at a Wednesday night prayer meeting in a little Evangelical church on Lake Barton Road east of Orlando. People in the congregation were giving testimonies. I suddenly stood up, having never done such a thing in my life. But I *had* to. My experience of God came tumbling out with an intensity that was overwhelming. Time stopped. Older folks marveled at how a child so young could speak with such profoundness. It was as if I'd "entered into myself" for the first time, with terror and amazement.

"Our deepest fear is that we are powerful beyond measure," says Marianne Williamson.[32] For a brief moment on that felicitous night I was a star. A handful of people in a Bible church on a country road had glimpsed the power of the Spirit––in me. It was the first time I could see something within myself worth admiring.

This is the unaccountable wonder of realizing our beauty before the gaze of the divine, knowing who we truly are. "Your light must shine before people," said Jesus, "so that they [and you] will see the good" (Matthew 5:16).

Yet there's a danger here of getting stuck at an adolescent level that requires endless recognition. Some people never outgrow the need for incessant valida-tion. They continually have to dazzle. Origen saw it in Lucifer's restless pride of place as the Bright Morning Star. Bill Plotkin and Ken Wilber warn of a sprawling adolescence in our culture today. Men in particular who become fixated as "patho-adolescents"—the ego gone wild, overgrown boys trapped in the narcissism of boundless achievement.[33]

Origen's antidote to this is to remind us that what we *are* before God is a given. It's nothing we can prove or accomplish. It's a naked accept-ance of unwarranted, unconditional love. Our splendor is but a reflection of the "true light that gives light to everyone" (John 1:9). It comes into the world as the Logos—the Word that was there from the beginning and ends there as well, welcoming us into a resplendence that even the stars can't imagine.

Frequently on cold winter nights I'll lie on the ground over at the park across from my house, looking up through Grandfather's bare branches into the jeweled face of the Winter Hexagon. I gaze at the Pleiades passing over-head and think of Origen. I marvel at myself having found a home in the cosmos at this time in my life, stretched out on the earth under these familiar stars, this beloved tree. Here I see as I'm seen. I love as I'm loved—by the Pleiades, by Grandfather, by the God I long for but cannot see. "The lover visible, the Beloved invisible, whose crazy idea was this?" asks Rumi.[34] The answer, if there is one, is hidden in the stars.

***

Through the centuries people have looked to the stars for an affirma-tion of their lives. You see it, for example in a story told in the Cursillo movement. Hundreds of years ago, in a desert community of monks in Spain, one of the brothers was sent each day to a distant city to beg. There he gathered food or money for the community and their work with the poor. The man often experienced abuse as he begged in the streets, but he did his work faithfully, recrossing the desert every evening, hot and tired. He never complained.[35]

God marveled at the monk's faithfulness and decided each evening to create a well of cold water to refresh him on his way back across the sand. The brother was astonished (and deeply grateful), but gave still greater honor to God by offering *back* the gift, not thinking himself worthy to drink. With enormous gratitude, he always passed it by. Consequently, each night as the monk lay down to sleep, he'd look up through the window of his cell and see a single star in the sky. He knew it had been put there just for him and slept with the greatest peace.

This was how the man lived out his life. As he grew older, the brothers chose a younger monk to go with him to learn how to do his work when he could no longer do it himself. The two set off for the city that day. The young monk found it hard begging, being scorned by strangers, and especially hot coming back over the desert at the end of the day. But then he saw the fountain—which hadn't been there in the morning—and he ran to it, gulping down the water with great appreciation.

Meanwhile, the old monk was torn. If he refused to drink as he usually did, and told the young monk why, the younger fellow would feel bad about his own impulsiveness, not having been as devout as the revered older monk. Then again, if he drank, he wouldn't be offering the same gift to God that he'd always been able to give through the years. Finally, he thought of the young monk and ran and drank to the glory of God.

As the two made their way home to the monastery, the old brother was more silent than usual. He feared that he'd disappointed God by what he'd done––drinking the water. But that night, as he lay down to sleep, he looked up through the window of his cell and saw the whole sky lit up with stars just for him! The shock of seeing (and being seen) was too much for the old man. They found him dead the next morning. He had slept with the greatest peace.

Had his brother monks been able to hear the words that last fell from his lips, they surely would have been the injunction from Hosea that mercy is always better than sacrifice. What you achieve by hard work or ascetic renunciation is nothing compared with what you offer in compassion. That's how you sparkle. Love alone is what shows you the face of God. It's what offers you a home in the universe. It's what makes the stars shine.

CHAPTER EIGHT

DESERTS

THE WESTERN AUSTRALIAN BUSH AND
GREGORY OF NYSSA

"Where does the desert begin? Beyond the black stump."
— Graeme Ferguson and John Chryssavgis,
The Desert Is Alive[1]

"The real desert is this: to face the real limitations of one's own existence and knowledge and not to manipulate them or disguise them. Not to embellish them with possibilities."
— Thomas Merton, *Learning to Love*[2]

The plane touched down at Kalgoorlie on the edge of the Great Victorian Desert. We were met by a tall Aussie with a shaggy beard who put our gear in the back of his ute and took us another hundred miles deeper into the bush of Western Australia. None of us had met before, but we were headed for a week of hiking at the Koora Retreat Centre near Boorabbin National Park. "Beyond the black stump," as they say.

Today Koora (Koorarawalyee) is a base camp for exploring desert spirituality and the surrounding wilderness. It is run by Anna Killigrew and her husband, Peter Harrison, both Anglican priests. A hundred years ago it was a stop on a now-abandoned railroad line connecting Perth with the goldfields discovered near Kalgoorlie in the 1890s. Before that it was a water hole on intersecting Aboriginal songlines. Indigenous Australians view the songlines as "dreaming tracks" left by creator-beings who walked the Earth at the dawn of creation. Rainbow Serpent, for example, was one who sang the rivers and mountains of northern Australia into being.

I was on my way from Melbourne to Perth to speak at a conference on spiritual direction. Getting there—crossing the continent and stopping in the heart of Western Australia—was a spiritual journey in its own right. I was exploring a landscape truly on the edge, farther out than I'd ever been before. Koora sits in an "uninhabited" wilderness; its closest human neighbors are nearly fifty miles away in every direction. On this primeval landscape, I was going back in time. Aboriginal cave art found recently in the Flinders Ranges of South Australia dates back 49,000 years. The cave art at Lascaux in France, by comparison, is less than 20,000 years old. I'd entered a world that casts long shadows—the immensity of its space and time exerting a hypnotic attraction.

Many Aboriginal Australians were originally sedentary, residing in farming communities along the coast. But those living in the arid region of the Red Centre tended to be a people in motion, following the seasons and the food supply, leaving a small footprint on the land. For them the landscape was sacred, strewn with songlines, the routes they walked as they reverenced the ancestors celebrated in the Dreamtime stories and associated with sites considered especially holy.

Indigenous folks say that when creation began in the Dreamtime, the Ancestors—Lizard, Spider, Wallaby, Old Man, and others—wandered the land, singing and summoning everything into life. That's how the world began. They left songlines wherever they walked, a trail of words and musical notes strewn across the landscape. When Aborigines go walkabout, even today, they follow these paths, ritually singing the world into being once again.

Over the past ten thousand years, says Robyn Davidson, we've experienced a transition from cultures of movement to cultures of accumulation, bringing a huge shift in Western consciousness. We've lost the ability to cope with flux, the deep sense of community, and the respect for the environment that marks a mobile people. Ironically, as nomadic cultures are disappearing, a deceptive hypermobility has emerged as the hallmark of middle-class life. We become tourists—privileged people with an almost unrestricted freedom of movement. But we *belong* nowhere.[3]

Davidson's interest in nomadic peoples began in 1977, when at the age of twenty-seven, she set off on a nine-month, 1,700-mile journey across the desert of Western Australia—with four camels and a dog. She said she needed "to rattle the foundations of habit." For her, this meant crossing a desert dotted with the humpies (huts) of Aboriginal folk, fire-colored dunes, dead trees, and broken promises—like Lake Disappointment in the Gibson Desert. It was a place of terror, beauty, solitude. "Nothing but the still, olive-green witchetty bushes, and miles of broken red rock and dust."[4]

It bothered her that "the rest of the world seemed neither to know nor care what was happening to the oldest culture in the world."[5] The outback forced her to wrestle with the tension between wandering and settling, being comfortable with uncertainty and needing the assurance of surplus, consulting guidebooks and relying on stories rising from the land.

It had a similar effect on me. There are times in your life when you have to ask: Is my real home a house, or the road? Does my life require a ride or is it a journey I have to make on foot?[6]

TRACKING AN ABORIGINAL SONGLINE

Our pattern as bushwalkers at Koora was to spend each day hiking, stopping for morning and afternoon tea when Peter, our shaggy bushman, heated water in smoke-blackened billies on an open fire. We walked on the red earth through gray-blue saltbush and spikey spinifex grass, passing an occasional water soak or dried salt lake. The colors of eucalyptus trees dotting the horizon were stunning. They come in hundreds of species—from red and orange mallee to tall salmon gums and white ghost gums, all shedding their thin bark in long ribbons. The under bark is as smooth and beautiful as a baby's skin. They are gorgeous trees.

Now and then we'd see a kangaroo or emu in the distance. I once spied a dingo, but none of the camels and brumbies (wild horses) that roam farther to the north. We walked by a rabbit-proof fence built in the nineteenth century to protect western croplands from the rabbits that had taken over in the east. It connects farther north with the one followed by Molly Craig in 1931, when she and two other Aboriginal girls escaped from an internment camp to walk 1,500 miles back home.[7]

We were accompanied on several of our hikes by an Aboriginal man from Kalgoorlie, Geoffrey Stokes—a wonderful bloke full of stories and laughter. He didn't let us forget how the blood of indigenous peoples in both of our countries has sunk deep into the land, a land he defends as an activist and minister.

It was with ambivalence that I approached the end of the week and my chance to spend two days alone in the outback. I'd hoped to walk a small stretch on one of the Aboriginal songlines: the one that passes through Koora, winding from Norseman in the southeast to the Die Hardy Range and Mount Jackson in the northwest. It eventually connects with the Seven Sisters—a vast songline that stretches across the continent.

I had no intention of role-playing an indigenous religious experience. I simply sought, in the brief time available to me, a one-on-one encounter with the land. But there I was, an ignorant whitefella—a stranger in someone else's world—having read a little about Aboriginal spirituality, engaging in yet another practice of spiritual tourism. I knew none of the songs or the languages appropriate to the songline. None of the paths are marked, of course, and I wouldn't have recognized any of the landmarks if I'd seen them. All I had was a compass bearing, no line etched in the heart by a community of memory.

The land saw through me, as it always does. With a cruel compassion it gives you exactly what you need. Being able to trust this was what got me through the next few days. I'd gathered my swag and tucker for the trip—rigging a makeshift pack with a one-person backpacking tent, a bed roll, flashlight, and snake-bite kit. Tucker consisted of a few small potatoes, bread rolls, apples, and cocoa mix. It was late autumn (mid-May) as I headed northwest from camp, walking through prickly spinifex and wattle brush. Some recent rain had turned resurrection plants from red-orange to green. The bush was thicker than I expected, with only an occasional eucalyptus rising above the head-high scrub. There was no vantage point from which to see what lay ahead.

With the coming of night, I camped by a rock outcropping near the bones of a dead emu. It was cold, the ground hard. I was in a remote Australian desert of redback spiders and fourteen species of poisonous snakes. Waking in the night, I was confused by the Southern Cross hanging upside down in the sky—until I realized it revolves around the South Pole in the same way the Big Dipper does in the north back home. Nothing felt familiar.

To ward off the cold at breakfast, I built a small fire between the rocks with dead mallee leaves and acacia twigs—cooking small potatoes in their ashes. Later I set out with a day-pack, planning to return to my tent site that night after walking as far as I could along my supposed songline track. But moving through the brush, around the deadfall of broken limbs, made it hard to follow a compass bearing. Left, then right, I plunged through a foliage of drooping acacia branches and thorns. It was a wearisome wood-brown, gray-green wilderness—set against the red, yellow earth. None of it was easy; none of it seemed sacred.

Gregory of Nyssa was my spiritual guide on this trip, a fourth-century theologian from the rugged desert terrain of Cappadocia in central Turkey. He'd been intrigued by the journey of Moses described in the book of Exodus, an interminable trek across the desert, up the mountain, and into a dark cloud—symbolic of his never-ending entry into God. His was a path never clear or safe.

Why had the desert been necessary for Moses, Gregory wondered? Because it doesn't give a damn, Ed Abbey would have replied. Its indifference is instructive. "The desert says nothing . . . [It] lies there like the bare skeleton of Being, spare, sparse, austere, utterly worthless, inviting not love but contemplation . . . Motionless and silent it evokes an elusive hint of something unknown, unknowable."[8] Most likely Gregory would have agreed.

It was hot and dry as I pushed through the same unchanging desert bush on the second day. I began doubting the wisdom of the trip and turned back at last—reversing my compass bearing, retracing the route. But even then I found nothing that looked welcoming or familiar. That's when my suspicion of being lost first emerged.

You shrug it off initially, reminding yourself just to keep compensating with the compass as you move from one side to another around obstacles in the way. You begin to scold yourself for not having planned more carefully. You move faster through the drooping wattle branches—getting scratched, drawing blood, imagining the terrain starting to turn on you. It becomes unfriendly, hostile. You feel a tinge of panic, embarrassment, chagrin turning to fear. You hold back from drinking that last pint of water. Before long your mouth feels as dry as the back of your hand. It's hard to swallow. Your tongue thickens. You enter the terror of being lost in the god-awful center of the Australian bush.

Fortunately old habits are hard to break. I made myself attend to the compass, methodically making ninety-degree angle cuts to the right or left every hundred yards or so in hope of finding something familiar. Just as the sun was setting, I finally spotted my campsite, and the world returned to normal.

I sat under the low branches of a gum tree nearby to rest in the shade and gather myself. I wondered how I could have been so stupid. Then it happened. A half-dozen pied butcherbirds suddenly flew into the tree I was leaning against, fluttering on the branches around my head. These were black and white birds singing together in a cacophony of beautiful native Australian melodies.

They seemed to be scolding and celebrating with me at the same time, as if to say, "You sad little whitefella: *These* are the songs you needed to know for this trip. It's a shame you never learned to understand and sing them for yourself. But, here, we'll do it for you!" They sang with a joyous (if reproachful) glee, as I sat there in my absolute ignorance of the Australian landscape and the language of birds. That was the point. My *unknowing* was what mattered most, my being prevented from adding yet another exotic spiritual experience to my list. I'd been moving through a sacred place without being present to it. Only after being emptied of what I *thought* I knew could a handful of birds sing the beauty of what I realized I'd never be able to understand.

This is what the desert does best—taking us to the end of ourselves, physically, culturally, spiritually. It alternately tricks and teases us into reaching for what lies beyond, for what's entirely too much for us to handle. Losing control is the *point*. You'll only be satisfied, the desert says, by what you give up trying to comprehend.

THE DESERT AS A NEGATIVE REALITY

Desert tales are perennially full of risk and extremity. In the Jewish and Christian scriptures, Abraham plunges into the desert from his home at Haran, not knowing where he's going. Moses—ever beset by frustration—leads a complaining people through the Sinai wilderness. Elijah endures a season of drought, fed by ravens in a desert waste. In the wilderness of Judea, John the Baptist survives on locusts and honey. The tempter comes to Jesus three times during his forty days in the desert.[9]

To move through the desert is to be stripped of nonessentials, then left to suck on what's left. It attracts only madmen, occasionally a prophet. The stories of early Australian desert explorers are typical. Charles Sturt was a British explorer who set out from Adelaide in 1844, searching for a vast inland sea, maybe huge forests, in the heart of the continent. He found only a rocky upland and salt pans, and lost his health in the process. That same year Ludwig Leichhardt, an intrepid German-born explorer, attempted to cross the continent from east to west. Somewhere along the way his party disappeared. Nothing was ever found of them.

Robert Burke and William Wills managed to cross the Australian desert from south to north in 1860, but died of starvation on the way back. A lack of bushcraft and refusal to accept Aboriginal advice plagued a number of these early European adventurers. There in the desert, they found only an enormous absence, a "hideous blank," empty and contemptuous.[10]

When you're accustomed to iconic British landscapes, rich in hay meadows and mountain lakes, you'll likely perceive the desert solely as a negative entity, something to be passed through as quickly as possible—a place of vacancy, abandonment. Early Australian settlers justified their occupation of the land on the grounds that it was *terra nullius* (nobody's land), discarded and uninhabited (despite the fact that when Captain Cook arrived in 1770 an estimated 750,000 Aborigines were already living there).[11]

Deserts occupy more than one-fifth of the Earth's land surface. Seventy percent of Australia is arid. With its ten great deserts, it's the driest continent on Earth. More than a billion people—one-seventh of the Earth's population—live in desert regions, but Westerners have historically treated the desert and its native peoples as nonexistent.

Feckless Australian explorers like Burke and Wills approached the desert as an irritation to be overcome, an enigma they refused to accept on its own terms. They starved on an arid land whose bounty they couldn't see. Meanwhile, the indigenous people around them lived well on the land, grinding acacia seeds and spinifex thorns into flour, eating witchetty grubs and termites. But the Europeans weren't able to see beyond their own dwindling food supplies. They complained of an interminable terrain of red rocks. The Aborigine, on the other hand, knew that "this is not a rock, it is my grandfather. This is a place where the dreaming comes up, right up from inside the ground."[12]

Those who haven't spent time in the desert may dismiss it as a negative landscape, defined by what *isn't* there. It lacks the sparkling streams of water, thick forests, and forms of habitation they expect. But people who trust the desert as home delight in its quality of lean simplicity. The desert imagination thrives on the absence of what others consider essential. It revels in negation, attending to what isn't seen, what can't be proved, what provides no comforting assurances.[13]

John Keats talked about "negative capability," an attribute he found in his favorite authors—an openness to lingering uncertainties, mysteries, doubts.[14] They found solace (even beauty) in the absence of what others tried to nail down with absolute specificity. This was just as true of Gregory of Nyssa and the new form of spirituality that emerged in fourth-century Cappadocia.

It's no accident that what we call the via negativa in Christian spirituality grew out of the dry, treeless terrain of central Anatolia. The three Cappadocian fathers—Gregory of Nyssa, his brother Basil of Caesarea, and their friend Gregory of Nazianzus—all lived within a few miles of each other. Theirs was a haunting landscape of hardened volcanic ash, strewn with reddish mushroom-like spires (fairy chimneys), and honeycombed with human-made caves and churches.

The three towns the three bishops served were located south of the Kizil ("Red") River, which runs in a wide arc through central Turkey, emptying into the Black Sea to the north. Gregory called it a "naked and mournful" land. Yet he and his brother loved it. Basil established a monastery in a remote desert canyon that he praised for its wildness. Gregory of Nazianzus was a little less convinced, complaining,

> Everything that is not rock is ravine, everything that is not ravine is brambles, and all that are not brambles are overhanging cliffs. The path climbs up in over-hang and is precipitous on all sides; it besets the spirits of the travelers and forces them into acrobatics for their own safety.[15]

Such a place was perfect, replied the two brothers, for entering into the vulnerability necessary for meeting the divine. In one of his commentaries, Gregory of Nyssa used the rugged terrain of his native Cappadocia to underscore his favorite theme: God's incomprehensible greatness. Imagine, he says, a steep crag of reddish volcanic rock out in a desert expanse. You stand atop this high ridge on the edge of a cliff, looking down on what seems a bottomless chasm below. You feel a sense of vertigo. You reach for something to hold on to, but nothing is there. Your foot begins to slip on the rock beneath you, and you're suddenly overwhelmed by a sense of dread. This, he says, is what it's like to encounter God.[16]

For Gregory, the land itself supplied the language to describe the limitless grandeur of God. "The knowledge of God is a mountain steep indeed and difficult to climb," he said. "Anyone looking down from such a high promontory into the sea below would be quite dizzy." But "dizziness" (the initial disabling of the mind) was, for him, a prerequisite for experiencing the God Moses had met on Sinai. It was also like trudging through desert sand, seemingly getting nowhere. The desert, in Gregory's thinking, was an anti-image, a metaphor suggesting the mystery of God by way of negation. Its lean emptiness was a reminder that in his effort to comprehend God's essence, "every intelligible attribute is a hindrance."[17]

This cuts to the heart of what came to be known as apophatic spirituality, the way of negation. The term derives from the Greek words *apo* ("apart from") and *phatikos* ("speech"). The apophatic way insists that there are finally no images, no language adequate for speaking of the great mystery. We're speechless in the presence of what we cannot name.

It contrasts with cataphatic spirituality, which affirms the value of analogies for talking about the divine ("*according to* the image").[18] Trying to understand Moses's encounter with God on Sinai, Gregory quickly found himself running out of words. He couldn't escape the unsettling image of the desert mountain shrouded in cloud. It was a barren landscape that suggested— negatively at least—an alternative point of departure. When language fails, geography may offer another way.

GREGORY OF NYSSA'S THEOLOGY OF DESIRE

Gregory acknowledged that "the attractiveness of the divine beauty has something terrifying about it."[19] The harsh desert landscape can be unnerving and its God even more so. But if the desert stripped him of confidence and control, it also made him susceptible to wonder. The more he sensed an "absence" in the desert, the more he longed for its underlying presence.

Gregory of Nyssa (335–395) was supremely a theologian of desire and one of the first great Christian mystical writers. Desire, he observed, usually "ceases with the possession of the desired object." But in the case of God (who is not an object, but infinite Love) the desire is endless, continually "transformed from glory to glory."[20]

Gregory came from an illustrious Christian family that included his brilliant sister Macrina as well as his more-celebrated older brother, Basil the Great. No fewer than five of the siblings became saints. Gregory initially pursued a career as a rhetorician, enchanted as he was by the power of language. He also married, but his wife died before his career as a theologian began. Basil, who was bishop of Caesarea, persuaded Gregory at the age of thirty-eight to assume the leadership of a new diocese in the nearby town of Nyssa. Gregory's writing proved formative in the development of the doctrine of the Trinity that was adopted by the Council of Constantinople in 381 CE.[21]

Three themes emerge as central to Gregory's thought: the incomprehensible wonder of God, the never-ending quality of desire that it evokes, and the nature of the spiritual journey it entails. All three are desert truths.

1. *The Divine Mystery.* Gregory argued that the Trinity is an effort to convey the mystery of the divine Eros. We shouldn't think of God's "being" as a static object (subject to proof) so much as a dynamic movement of persons dancing together in love. The impulse of the Trinity isn't to stay contained within itself, but to bubble over in an endless longing for ever more things to love.[22] A radical Arian bishop in Cappadocia named Eunomius had berated the idea of the Trinity, insisting that God's simple nature is easily conveyed to the intelligent mind.

Gregory replied that God is always *more* than we can ever name or describe. "Guessing at the Divine nature" is all we ever do. Any concept we propose may end up becoming an idol. "Any representation is nothing but an obstacle."[23] The Trinity is simply our best available effort at speaking the unspeakable. God in God's essence is unknowable.

For that matter, Gregory added, we can't really know the essence of *anything* in the world around us—not even the smallest shoot of a plant, much less God. He sounds like a quantum physicist here, insisting on the impossibility of "knowing" even the tiniest particles of matter. Scientists at the Fermi National Laboratory who study quarks can't detect them directly; they're limited to witnessing their activity, their movement, the traces they leave. They have no certainties, only evidence of flux.[24]

Yet the Nyssan theologian realized that he had to do more than affirm the absolute inaccessibility of the divine being. If God is an utterly remote, incomprehensible entity, then how can we *know* him in any sense whatever? Gregory made an important distinction between what he called God's essence and God's energies.[25] The divine *nature* is ineffable, but the divine *activity* is more readily apparent in the world. (This is similar to how we know the reality of the "other" in particle physics.) We see its activity in the playful harmony and unpredictability of the universe, with God dancing in it all. "Deity" in this sense, "is in everything, penetrating it, embracing it, and seated in it."[26]

Gregory was enthralled by the beauty of Cappadocia's coral-colored chimneys of eroded rock. But the source of this beauty lies beyond the powers of mind; his soul had to be carried—by wonder—"from the beauty which is seen to what is beyond." This is what Eunomius failed to appreciate, said Gregory. "He is like the child who would like to grab hold of a ray of the sun. He wants to understand rather than to adore." Witnessing the divine splendor in the world, our task isn't to take notes but to stand atremble.[27]

2. Endless Desire. God, therefore, is ultimately beyond knowing, but not beyond desiring. Longing is the heart's most natural path to God, said Gregory, our native response to the divine Eros. The soul, at its best, is aroused by desire for what's most worth wanting. C. S. Lewis said it well:

> God finds our desires not too strong, but too weak. We are half-hearted creatures, fooling about with drink and sex and ambition when infinite joy is offered us, like an ignorant child who wants to go on making mud pies in a slum because he cannot imagine what is meant by the offer of a holiday at the sea. We are far too easily pleased.[28]

The distinctive character of this yearning for God, however, is that it's never satisfied. God is "the-Always-Greater." One never gets enough. God is continually *more* than we can imagine. A holy dissatisfaction is the norm for the lovers of God.[29] Gregory exults in this. He knows he'll be reaching deeper into the vastness of God for the rest of eternity, without ever exhausting its grandeur. Every increase in his apprehension of the divine mystery makes him hungry for more, even as it increases his capacity to receive more. God continually enlarges the vessel into which he pours himself. "Grace endlessly creates ever new eyes to look upon ever new suns."[30]

Gregory used Paul's image of the athlete straining (Greek: *epektasis*) toward the finish line in a race, ever progressing into what remains the unreachable knowledge of God (Philippians 3:13). Imagine an exciting horse race, he says. The spectators are shouting, cheering their favorites. The charioteers are "urging the horses on while leaning forward and flailing the air with their outstretched arms."[31] Anticipation is intense, and it never ends. The closer the horses and riders get to the finish, the more their hearts swell in delight at what looms ever larger and grander ahead. Their strength multiplies in quantum leaps. They get a second, a third wind, and more. They can run forever.

Hadewijch of Brabant, the thirteenth-century mystic, expressed it perfectly:

> I swim towards the shore only to find
> that you have enlarged the sea.
> You leave me dazed with more desire
> and give me more muscle
> to swim again towards you.[32]

3. The Spiritual Life as Journey. Yet Gregory insisted that committing to a life of desire requires the discipline of a journey. It's more than being a tourist. "To be a tourist," says Don DeLillo, "is to escape accountability . . . You walk around dazed, squinting into fold-out maps." You try to duplicate the experiences of those who've been there before you. A journey involves risk. You trudge ahead without antecedents or guarantees of where you're finally going. "Walking is a virtue," says Bruce Chatwin. It commits to the trail. "Tourism is a deadly sin."[33]

Tracing the path that Moses walked, Gregory identified three stages in the progress we make on our journey into God. Moses first enters the *desert*. He sees the burning bush. What *is* this? An acacia tree backlit by the rising sun? He doesn't know. But his senses are put on alert. He pays attention. That's where you start, Gregory says. The desert forces you to depend on your senses—and also to know their limits. You're carried through a process of purgation. Only when the senses are utterly stunned by the desert's threat is the heart opened to its stillness.

On the second stage of his journey, Moses ascends the *mountain*, moving beyond the senses. His "going up" is a "going in." It involves a practice of contemplation, peering into the mirror of the soul. One who is pure in heart, says Gregory, can discern what he most desires even within himself. When Moses received the tablets of the law, he found them also inscribed on his heart. A steady increase in virtue (continuing without limit) will characterize the life of those who journey into God.[34]

Gregory insisted that a very practical virtue accompany the spiritual life. He was the first of the church fathers to take a strong position against slavery. He wrote sermons on "The Love of the Poor," addressing the needs of beggars and those banned from society because of leprosy. He supported his brother Basil's work in establishing a poorhouse and hospital, and echoed his words on the sin of failing to help the poor:

> The bread you do not use is the bread of the poor. The shoes you do not wear are the shoes of one who is barefoot. The money you keep locked away is the money of the poor. The acts of charity you do not perform are so many injustices you commit.[35]

For Gregory, the illumined heart is a heart full of compassion.

If the pilgrim (the athlete) persists through these first two stages in her journey, there is at last the possibility of moving like Moses into the *cloud* on the mountain's peak. Hiding in the cleft of the rock, she enters an impenetrably thick darkness. There she's the bride of the canticle waiting in trembling anticipation of her lover coming in the night. She experiences loving union with the one she'd sought all along. If she "sees" God, it's a "seeing that consists in not seeing." She perceives by love what she couldn't attain by knowledge. Gregory flails about for adequate language, variously describing Moses's encounter as a luminous darkness, a sober inebriation, a wounding that strangely delights.[36]

What I love about Gregory of Nyssa is his constant search for metaphors that he knows will never suffice. He loved the dry, rolling plateau of Cappadocia surrounded by extinct volcanoes, with the Kizil River running like a green thread through its russet expanse of volcanic tuff. The stream "gleams like a ribbon of gold through a deep purple robe," he exclaimed. It was a land worthy in its wildness of another Homer to sing its praises.[37] Yet he knew it was never equal to the task of conveying God's mystery.

Gregory had been profoundly influenced by Origen's Platonic theology. He echoed his mentor's notion of the final restoration of all things in the fullness of God's glory, the hope of universal salvation.[38] But Gregory was far more struck by the beauty and worth of the natural world than Origen had been. The desert pointed him to the wordless wonder of God's splendor. It suggested a language that supplanted language.

THE ADOLESCENT ON THE DESERT'S EDGE

The desert is a place of breakdown and reorientation. It forces you into the death of what you'd known and yet the faint possibility of something beyond. Bill Plotkin defines the stage of late adolescence in a similar way. This is the wanderer in the cocoon— poised on the edge of adulthood, moving past the self-absorbed indulgence of youth, opening to the call of the wild. It's a pivotal shift, renouncing the potential stagnation of the "patho-adolescent" we mentioned in the previous chapter.

None of these life stages are limited to specific decades in a person's life experience. Some people remain spiritually and emotionally fixed at early adolescence for the rest of their lives. Others find themselves going back in order to work through things they hadn't finished earlier. Life's recurring difficulties push us into what remains half-done. Sudden exposure to a particular landscape or natural archetype can do the same, awakening us to uncompleted soul work. That was my experience in the desert bush of Western Australia.

After returning from my challenging foray into the outback, I left Koora, taking the Prospector Train on to Perth on the west coast. Passing through the wheat belt and farmland of far western Australia, I came to the edge of the Indian Ocean. It was the end of the earth so far as I was concerned— farther away from home than I'd ever been. Perth is the largest remote city in the world, closer to Singapore than it is to Sydney, 2,500 miles away. Standing alone by the ocean's edge one moonless night, I listened to the waves on the sand and took stock of the path I'd taken over the past few years.

I'd been shaped as an academic for most of my life. It's part of what I bring to this work—paying attention to details, listening to the languages of others. I'm grateful for it. But after a lifetime of acquiring knowledge, I've increasingly needed to release my grip on what I'd learned. The academic runs the risk of becoming a tourist—continually gathering data, consulting guidebooks, investigating leads—without ever being *changed* by what he studies, never assuming the role of pilgrim. On one level, my curiosity in exploring a songline at Koora was symptomatic of an old pattern.

Yet the desert cut through me in ways I hadn't expected. It showed me the folly of having come with unrelated bits of knowledge, trying to twist a spiritual experience out of what I assumed I knew. The eucalyptus tree with its pied butcherbirds pointed me back to my own most important teacher—a cottonwood tree back home, a Grandfather calling me beyond anything I can put into words. He summons me to silence, to a larger community of teachers than I've been accustomed to acknowledging. At every level of our sharing, he's shrouded in darkness—an apophatic mystery in himself. Yet we keep moving ever deeper into love. If Moses found God in the cleft of a rock, for me it's been a wound in the side of a tree.

Tim Winton, one of Western Australia's finest nature writers, explores the power of a mysterious landscape and its creatures to reorient one's way of perceiving the world. He points to the desert's ability to disrupt certainties, to name folly, to insist on what can't be known. It calls you to a larger kinship, a wider allegiance. "A patriot need no longer devote himself to an abstraction like the state," he says. "Now a patriot will be as likely to revere the web of ecosystems . . . as if the *land* were kith and kin,"[39] as if trees and birds were one's extended family. I'm invited to this in a more visceral way than ever.

When the adolescent enters the cocoon, says Plotkin, she knows the journey ahead won't be easy. There will probably be no wise old woman or man to point the way. She'll have to sit in the darkness with what she doesn't know, trusting in the "not-knowing" as itself a gift. Yet a metamorphosis is underway. A greater passion awaits—a readiness to blaze new paths, to cut against the grain. She longs to be more than a tourist. Embracing the journey, she's confident of one thing only: It will be full of surprise.

***

Nikos Kazantzakis tells the story of an English monk who all of his life had dreamed of making a pilgrimage to the Holy Land.[40] There he would walk around the Holy Sepulchre three times, kneel, and come back a new man. Through the years he'd dreamed of leaving his monastery with its old yew tree in the cloister yard—making his way on foot from Canterbury to

Rome along the ancient pilgrimage route, the Via Francigena. He'd cross the rocky terrain of Greece to follow the Templar Trail through the dry expanse of Cappadocia. He'd visit cathedrals and the tombs of saints, coming at last to the old city of Jerusalem.

Through the years the monk had prepared for the trip, putting away money that he received as alms. Near the end of his life he'd finally saved enough to begin his journey. Taking his staff in hand, he opened the monastery gates and set out for the Holy City.

But no sooner had he left the cloister, than he encountered a man in rags, bent to the ground, picking herbs on the side of the path. "Where are you going, Father?" the man asked. "To the Holy Sepulchre, brother. By God's grace, I'll walk around it three times, kneel, and return home a different man." "Ah, that's wonderful! I hope you have enough money to provide for you on your way." "Yes, God be praised," said the monk. "I've been able to save thirty pounds for the trip."

The man then hesitantly responded, "Can I ask you something crazy, Father? I have a wife and hungry children at home. I'm searching everywhere for food to keep them from starving. Would you consider giving *me* your thirty pounds, walking three times around me, then kneel and go back into your monastery?" The monk thought for a long moment, scratching the ground with his staff. Then (with a divine absurdity) he took the money from his sack, gave the whole of it to the man, walked three times around him, knelt, and returned back through the gates of his monastery.

He came home a new man, of course, having recognized the beggar as Christ himself—not far away at the Holy Sepulchre, but just outside his monastery door, in a place he'd never have thought sacred. He'd discovered a great desert truth—that the holy is where you least expect it, that the *desire* for the trip is its own fulfillment, that he'd been drawn all along to transformation, not tourism. He greeted the old yew tree in the cloister yard, took a deep breath, and returned to his work.

WATER: *The Adult*

"Praised be You, my Lord, through Sister Water,
who is very useful and humble and precious and chaste."

—Francis of Assisi, "Canticle of the
Creatures"[1]

"I love all things that flow," wrote James Joyce. In *Portrait of the Artist as a Young Man*, Stephen Daedalus longs to leave the dry weeds of a religious crisis for the sea's flowing current. It's what we all hope to encounter by the time we enter adulthood—discovering the transformative power of water. "Water symbolizes the whole of potentiality," said Mircea Eliade. "It is *fons et origo*, the source of all possible existence."[2]

In this third quadrant of the wheel of transformation, we enter life's second half. Having passed through the elements of air and fire (the stages of childhood and adolescence), we now move to water and earth (the time of the adult and the elder). If the first half of life involved ascent, its second half demands descent. "Fire and wind go up," observed Dōgen, the thirteenth-century Zen master, "earth and water go down."[3] Adulthood summons us to the deep flow of creativity, the grit of hard work, the challenge of family-building. It's a time for learning how to move with grace into the fullness of one's gifts.

But it can feel like being thrown into a raging river at flood stage. We're overwhelmed by life's demands: mind-numbing work routines, mortgage payments, marriages that get frayed. We may find ourselves needing to jump off the tower we've built, realizing with Thomas Merton that the ladder of success we've been climbing has been leaning against the wrong wall all along. There's a shattering of self-confidence, a necessary fall.[4] Through all of this, we long to flow with graceful ease. Rivers, canyons, and islands are the archetypes we require. They offer the intuitive gifts of the *Magician*.[5] This is the season of autumn and the darkening shadows that follow the setting sun.

"If there is magic in this planet, it is contained in water," said Loren Eiseley.[6] The seas contain 97 percent of the water on earth. Its 3 percent of fresh water is mostly contained in ice sheets, glaciers, and deep groundwater. Water is the great teacher of change. It fills every space with liquid ease, expands into a frozen immobility, or escapes as vapor carried on the wind. In a stream it moves effortlessly, wearing down the hardest rock.

The midlife work of fulfilling career, family, and community responsibilities requires the fluidity of water and the discipline of containment. We need to channel the flow, keep the river within its banks. Amidst an ever-widening sea of anxieties, we look for an island—nurturing a center while completely surrounded by water. "Water is truly the transitory element," said Gaston Bachelard. "It is the essential, ontological metamorphosis between fire and earth."[7]

The most pressing concern about water today is its availability. Eighty-five percent of the world's population lives on the driest half of the planet; 844 million people have no access to safe drinking water.[8] Human thirst and world water stress are among the most demanding issues of our time.

CHAPTER NINE

R I V E R S

COLORADO'S LOST CREEK WILDERNESS AND TERESA OF ÁVILA

"So—this—is—a—River!"

"THE River," corrected the Rat.

"And you really live by the river? What a jolly life!"

"By it and with it and on it and in it," said the Rat. "It's brother and sister to me, and aunts, and company, and food and drink, and (naturally) washing. It's my world, and I don't want any other. What it hasn't got is not worth having, and what it doesn't know is not worth knowing."

—Kenneth Grahame, *The Wind in the Willows*[9]

"Eventually, all things merge into one, and a river runs through it . . . I am haunted by waters."

—Norman Maclean, *A River Runs Through It*[10]

I've camped for the night in the Lost Creek Wilderness of the Rocky Mountains, alongside a river that keeps appearing and disappearing. A few yards from my tent, the creek comes rushing from its cave like a wild animal springing to life, its scent filling the air. The water is cold—fresh snow-melt from the mountains above. Its "scent" is simply the smell of really clean air, generously charged with negative ions, free of airborne particles.

The stream has vanished and reappeared like this eleven times already on its way from its source above Kenosha Pass in central Colorado. It keeps erupting from the earth in a torrent of energy, splashing wildly around boulders and tall firs, only to plunge into another underground channel a mile or two further downslope.

It's actually a single river with two names. Upstream from this point it's appropriately known as Lost Creek. Downstream from here it remains above ground and is labeled Goose Creek on the map. Some rivers refuse to be managed, or even consistently named, especially when they have to maneuver terrain as wild as this.

It's a section of backcountry that's been too rugged and remote for mining or logging. The creek itself stubbornly resists all efforts to contain it. Everything remains pretty much the way God intended. As I hiked up the trail this morning, I passed the remains of log cabin bunkhouses built in 1891 for workers of the Antero and Lost Park Reservoir Company. Their hope had been to create a reservoir by damming up Lost Creek. The plan was to pump concrete into the crevices between the rocks, sealing off the stream as it moved through a narrow divide, creating a lake in the valley on the upper side. But the creek didn't like the idea. Eluding the dam builders, it went more than a hundred feet underground to find yet another way down the mountainside. The workers finally gave up in 1913. You can still see what's left of their old shaft house with rusted machinery at the crest where the dam would have stood.

The underground world in this wilderness must be as bizarre as what you see on the surface. In every direction there are bulging rock domes and knobs, towers and arches, as if a child had thought up a fantasy world where giants might live. There are boulders the size of houses, sometimes stacked three or four deep. Who knows what caverns and winding corridors lie underground? These slopes are covered by dense forests of ponderosa pine, spruce, fir, and aspen, dotted here and there with bighorn sheep. Immediately off the trail you'll find yourself in a wild tumble of fallen trees, broken rock, and uneven ground. You could easily be lost in such a place and never found again. Meanwhile, a dark river passes underfoot, indifferent to all things human.

I'll spend a couple of nights camping here at the emergence point of the creek, exploring the rose-rock splendor of the valley that was nearly flooded a century ago. I'm stretched out on its stream bank now, weary from the steep hike up from the trailhead today. At 11,000 feet I'm feeling lightheaded, breathing a third less oxygen than I'd be doing at sea level. Combined with the crisp air rushing from the creek's underground cave, the site provides a natural Rocky Mountain high. I'll sleep like a log tonight.

Setting up camp, I slip into the ritualized rubrics that are part of what I love most about backpacking as a spiritual practice. I begin by pitching the tent, locating a tree with an outstretched branch for the bear bag, remembering to put my headlamp in the tent's side pocket for waking in the night. It's all part of a formula, one that includes pumping the backpacking stove, lighting a match on a nearby rock, watching orange flames warm the stove's fuel circulating system, and waiting for the blue burn that welcomes a pot full of creek water. These are rubrics that assure safety and convenience, but also play a role in slowing me down—making me present to a liminal space that disappears as I reverse the process on breaking camp the next morning.

I'm intrigued by the thought of sleeping beside a river that keeps vanishing. It urges me to identify the places in my life where I need to be hidden from view, diving under the surface, becoming less accessible. With a happy synchronicity, I've brought along a copy of Naomi Shihab Nye's poem, "The Art of Disappearing."

She considers how one might respond to hackneyed questions at a cocktail party. "When they say Don't I know you? / say no," she advises. "If they say / We should get together / say why?" "It's not that you don't love them anymore," she clarifies. It's just that "You're trying to remember something / too important to forget. / [like] Trees."[11] Like the smell of ponderosa pine. You disappear for the sake of making the true appearances that are necessary in your life.

RIVERS OF THE EARTH, RIVERS OF THE PSYCHE

What is this puzzlement of water, and flowing water in particular? H_2O is the only compound found in nature in all three basic states—solid, liquid, and gas, continually edging toward transformation. On a typical spring day in the Lost Creek Wilderness, it may fall as sleet or snow, melt into watery sludge, then evaporate as the sun comes out again.

Water is the great solvent, dissolving more substances than any other liquid, inviting everything to the magic of flow. We depend upon it more than any other resource. Water covers 70 percent of the Earth's surface, makes up 70 percent of our bodies. Water is what we *are*.

But it's water confined by river banks that especially intrigues. Ever moving on, yet ever the same. "Dat ol' man river, said Heraclitus, he jus' keeps rollin' along . . . "[12] Such are the great rivers of the world—the Amazon, the Nile, the Tigris and Euphrates, and my favorite, the Mississippi. T. S. Eliot called it "a strong brown god—sullen, untamed and intractable."[13] Rivers are the arteries of the land, sustaining the soul of a people.

Hydrologists tell us there's more to rivers than what we see. They flow in pockets underground as well as above. This hidden area of a river's flow is its hyporheic zone, a subterranean ecosystem with its own forms of life—fungi, insects, and crustaceans that may never see the light of day.

Scientists recently discovered an underground stream flowing beneath the Mayan temple at Chichén Itzá on the Yucatán Peninsula. Even more astonishingly, they've found a huge river running directly beneath the Amazon, two and a half miles underground, emptying (like its surface twin) into the depths of the Atlantic Ocean.[14] Some rivers—like the Gascoyne in Western Australia—flow above ground for part of the year and below ground for the rest. Rivers relish mystery.

The idea of appearing and disappearing streams—retreating at times into the Earth's deep caverns—touches something just as deep in the psyche. The soul is full of unexplored rivers, gliding along in the dark.

There are creeks in the Galiuro Wilderness of southern Arizona that flow only at night. During the day the cottonwoods, willows, and mesquites along their banks function at a metabolic high, pumping water from their roots to the canopy above. "Instead of flowing along the ground, the creek is hoisted a hundred feet into the air into the leaves" of the trees. But when the sun goes down and the trees stop their work, the creek refills with rising ground water. Beetles and tiny fish appear. Fireflies gather. A river is reborn, only to disappear again when the sun rises the next morning and the trees get back to work.[15]

Rivers are vanishing today as a result of climate change and overuse. The Colorado hasn't made its way to the Sea of Cortez for years. Cracked mud flats stretch for miles through Baja California where John Wesley Powell's wild river once ran. The same may soon be true of the Yellow River in China, the Indus in Pakistan, the Murray in Australia, and the Rio Grande in the United States. The challenge they pose is profoundly ecological, even as vanishing streams and hidden water channels speak of a still deeper reality.

In Hindu thinking, the river is "a liquid form of the divine."[16] It's alive—swirling in eddies, sliding across shallow fords, bending around oxbow turns, breaking over rocks in whitewater rapids. It teaches you respect for what you see and what you don't see. Maneuvering a canoe down a class IV river, you're keenly aware that a single cubic foot of water weighs sixty-two pounds. Waves slam against the gunwales of the boat like sumo wrestlers. Water energizes and rejuvenates, but it also capsizes and engulfs.

The history of religion is filled with rivers—wild and serene, visible and invisible. The Greeks honored the River Styx, forming the boundary of the underworld, and the River Lethe where dead souls drank from the waters of oblivion. Sacred rivers of the world include the Nile, named after a goddess who sent floods each summer for the growing season. The Yangtze River flows in the wake of a mythical dragon twisting its way through the limestone gorges of western China. The Ganges emerges from an ice cave in the Himalayas—originally falling from heaven as an embodiment of the Milky Way, the Hindus say. Goddess and mother, it contains all rivers.

Wherever great waterways come together, believers revere their place of convergence. The Hindu Triveni in northern India marks the confluence of three sacred rivers. The Ganges and the Yamuna meet there, joined by a third (invisible and mythical) river—the Sarasvati, the most sacred of all. At the heart of everything holy is the conjunction of the manifest and the unmanifest.

In the Hebrew scriptures, rivers are associated with times of struggle in a person's life. The river's flow is healing, restorative. Jacob receives a new name as he wrestles with God one night on the banks of the Jabbok. The baby Moses stays alive in a basket floating on the Nile. Naaman bathes in the muddy waters of the Jordan and is cured of his leprosy. Ezekiel, forced into exile, imagines a stream flowing from under the ruins of the Temple in Jerusalem.[17]

Images of rivers serve as bookends to the biblical story of redemption. In Genesis, a river flows from the Garden of Eden and divides into four great branches that water the earth. At the end of the book of Revelation, the river of the water of life, clear as crystal, flows from the throne of God down the great street of the New Jerusalem.

"I don't find anything more appropriate to explain some spiritual experiences than water," said Teresa of Ávila. "I am so fond of this element that I've observed it more attentively than any other."[18] For her, the divine presence was alternately visible and invisible, revealed and hidden, an elusive yet ever-running river flowing through the high desert country of her life. It might go for years without breaking the surface, then erupt into effusions of indescribable joy.

Teresa is the spiritual companion I've taken along on this trip into the Lost Creek Wilderness. I love her honesty and wit, her no-nonsense approach to the religious life. She's accustomed to the underground depths of hard spiritual work. With her, I can imagine God stirring underfoot in a place like this. Clarissa Pinkola Estés speaks of the "Río Abajo Río," the river beneath the river—a source we access through intense yearning alone.[19]

TERESA OF ÁVILA AND THE WATER WITHIN

Teresa of Ávila (1515–1582) knew that people living in arid landscapes are particularly attuned to the presence (and absence) of water. She grew up in a dry land of saints and boulders northwest of Madrid. The desert, oddly enough, is the best place to study water: the place that yearns for it most. The arid terrain of Spain's central plateau is defined by the memory of rain, etched into the land at every turn. Canyons, ravines, barren flatlands, dry streambeds. A remembrance of flow lingers in the shadow of every rock. This is how a parched land knows water—achingly, desperately, with a passion bordering on dread. And it's also the only way we ever know God.

Teresa was born to a noble family in the Castilian town of Ávila overlooking the Adaja River. In its brown, almost treeless terrain—hemmed in by the jagged peaks of the Sierra de Gredos mountains—the river runs dry for several months each year. The town struggles to maintain its water supply. Teresa was deeply struck by the yearning of body and soul for water, for the flow of the spirit in the dry seasons of one's life.

But then everything fascinated her. She was charming, attractive, and outgoing, drawing people to herself (and to her faith) by her passion for God, for life. One of her biographers observed that she possessed "that mysterious quality the Spanish call *duende*, characteristic of gypsies, bullfighters, and flamenco dancers. *Duende* is raw, primitive, tempestuous energy . . . burning in the bloodstream."[20] In one of her reported visions, she saw an angel rushing toward her with a torch and a bucket of water. "Where are you going with those?" she asked. "With the water," the angel replied, "I'll put out the fires of hell and with the fire I'll burn down the mansions of heaven; then we'll see who really loves God."[21]

At the age of seven Teresa set out with her brother Rodrigo to the land of the Moors hoping to be beheaded for the sake of Christ. As a teenager she devoured tales of romantic chivalry. At the age of twenty she entered the Carmelite convent in Ávila, giving herself to the religious life. The Carmelite community included women of prominent families who led a relatively comfortable life, provided with servants and entertainments. It was easy there not to attend to the spiritual life. "I spent almost twenty years on this stormy sea," Teresa later reflected, "falling and rising, then falling again."[22]

At the age of thirty-nine she had a conversion experience, which led to a stark honesty in her conversations with God. "What a difficult thing I ask of you," she prayed,:

> that you love someone who doesn't love you, that you open to one who doesn't knock, that you give health to one who likes to be sick and goes about looking for sickness.[23]

Her blunt honesty was matched by the frank and wise counsel she offered to others. To sisters complaining of adversity she replied, "Obedience usually lessens the difficulty of things that seem impossible."[24]

A few years later she met a young Carmelite friar called John of the Cross, half her age at the time—a man who shared her passion for authenticity in the religious life. The two of them began a reform movement that rocked the order.

Like the other women saints mentioned in this book (all of them Doctors of the Church), Teresa was known for her outspokenness. She complained about "whining men." It annoyed her that, as "a poor little woman, weak and without much fortitude," she saw "men of prominence and learning making such a fuss" about God's not being there for them, not showering them with all kinds of encouragement. Quit your belly-aching, she said. Practice a little discipline of your *own*, for God's sake![25] This tough Carmelite nun had no tolerance for lazy, grumbling men. As a result, the papal nuncio once called her "a restless gadabout, a disobedient and contumacious woman who . . . taught others against the commands of St. Paul, who had forbidden women to teach."[26]

Teresa's sharp tongue and intense piety were matched by her down-to-earth practicality and humor. A sister in the community was shocked one day to find her in the convent kitchen, delightedly munching on a leg of roasted partridge. Teresa blithely responded, "Sister, there's a time for penance, and there's a time for partridge!" Her humor was legendary. "God deliver us from sour-faced saints," she's said to have quipped.[27]

This is the Teresa of Ávila whose mystical experiences of union with Christ were extraordinary, practically unmatched in the history of spirituality. Yet she struggled with prolonged periods of dryness. She knew from experience that "times of aridity teach you to be humble." They demand dogged perseverance.[28]

The Spanish nun struggled with physical illness for much of her life (spells of fainting, fever, headaches, even occasional paralysis). She wrestled with a church that was unreceptive to her spiritual experiences—priests suggesting she was entertaining heresy if not actually possessed by the devil. She wanted desperately to be liked by others and had to keep watch on her need for approval, only gradually learning to trust her own voice.

Teresa grappled with God's absence. She complained that the Holy One seemed to be hiding from her at times.[29] If you serve God for the sake of consolations alone, she told her friends, you'll be profoundly disappointed. On one occasion, facing hostility from without and abandonment from within, she grumbled to God, "If this is how you treat your friends, I know why you have so many enemies."[30] Yet all the while she kept chanting, *Nada te turbe, nada te espante.* "Nothing can trouble; nothing can frighten." Everything may be lost, but the Center still holds.

The truth that sustained her through all her trials was that God's divine life dwelt within her. "Let's not imagine that we are hollow inside," she cautioned. In her masterpiece, *The Interior Castle,* she described the soul as a spacious and beautiful place. Why live in one little corner when you have so many marvelous rooms to explore, she asked? Be expansive. Discern what lives and moves in the deep corridors of your soul. "It is foolish to think that we will enter heaven without entering into ourselves, coming to know ourselves."[31] Only there do we hear the rushing of the subterranean river of God.

FINDING WATER IN THE CHALLENGING
SEASON OF ADULTHOOD

What advice, then, does Teresa give for finding water in the dry seasons of one's life? She was forty years old when she passed through an extended period of aridity and into a new freedom. She knew she was a late bloomer, taking longer than usual to accept her calling, to identify her mission. Entering adulthood, according to Bill Plotkin, is to become an Apprentice at the Wellspring.[32] It's a time for finding and exercising your distinctive gifts, for committing to a discipline that allows your energy to flow. Only then do you become generative.

In her *Autobiography*, Teresa recounts four ways of obtaining water in irrigating the garden of one's life. These are four paths to discovering a new vitality, four stages for moving into a life of prayer.

1. The first involves the hard work of digging a well, drawing water up with a bucket—hand over hand—so as to start planting a garden. You begin a life of prayer (a budding generativity), she says, when you become conscious that nothing's growing in your life. Your desire is where you begin. You identify what you thirst for most and give yourself to it.

This beginning step has to do with articulating your longing, putting into words what summons you to life. You find a nearby tree and sit in its shade, taking stock of where you've been and where you're going. Listening to what rises from within. You write in your journal or mull over what you're reading. You ponder. It's a "discursive work of the intellect," says Teresa, this practice of mental prayer.[33] You don't expect a lot of emotional reward at this point. You just *do* it.

But you do it with high expectations nevertheless, being bold in asking God to make you into the man or woman God sees you to be. Don't think small, she urges. "You pay God a compliment by asking great things of Him." This is what you do in the first way of watering a garden. You sit there in the dry patch of dirt that your life has become. And you ask for what you want. Then you *act* on it, as if it were yours. She counseled her sisters to desire with abandon because theirs was a God who might very likely say "yes" to everything.[34]

2. Teresa's second method for finding water in an arid land is to make use of a windlass or water wheel, turning its handle to bring up water from below.

This is Archimedes's screw as a method of prayer. It's easier than digging, but it too requires a practice. The underground water supply varies with the rain or snow that the mountains draw from passing clouds. So you have to wait for the groundwater to fill. You have to exercise patience. The mountain brings water, but in its own time.

Here in a life of prayer, says Teresa, you silence the internal noise, moving beyond the words you depended upon earlier. The Desert Fathers and Mothers called it the prayer of the heart. It quiets the intellect, letting go of distractions. It makes a "contemplative sit" a part of your daily routine. This isn't a technique you employ to stop yourself from thinking; it's a gentle release of the inner chatter that gets in the way of your being present to the given moment. It pulls up the weeds that choke an interior silence.[35]

This is a habit of "thinking without thinking," said Francisco de Osuna, a sixteenth-century Spanish contemplative who influenced Teresa. Silencing words is the only way you embrace what the best of words try to express. *No pensar nada es pensarlo todo*: "Not to think anything is to think everything."[36] As you quiet the noise inside, a whole new world opens before you. You'll never be truly generative, says Teresa, until you carve out a space for silence and solitude in your life.

3. If these first two ways of finding water in the desert require effort, the next two ways involve God's work wholly apart from us, says Teresa. In her third way of watering a garden, you start seeing the fruit of contemplation. Your habit of going into the quiet each day begins to take root. It's as if a river has been redirected, brought down from the mountain through an aqueduct or diversion canal. It flows. All you do now is allow it to run.

Green buds appear. The garden prospers. You find yourself living more naturally, without striving so hard. Teresa calls it an infused contemplation, a sleep of the faculties. It radiates a contagious joy. You begin warming to who you are, reaching out more instinctively to others as well. An action rooted in freedom starts to flow out of the contemplation you've realized.

At this stage, Teresa says, you're not just Mary of Bethany, sitting passively at Jesus's feet (good as that may be). You're her sister, Martha, practicing a prayer that plays itself out in action. "Mary and Martha walk together."[37] You're becoming part of an undercurrent of vitality running through the entire cosmos, the surging river of creativity that brings every being into life. "Love alone is what gives value to all things," Teresa insists, even the smallest.

"The Lord doesn't look so much at the greatness of our works as at the love with which they are done."[38] Don't push the river; let it flow by itself.

The Castilian earth mother might ask, then: Is it time in your life to jump off the bank and into the river, giving yourself to its wildness? "Leap and the net will appear," promised Julia Cameron.[39] Stop telling yourself that it's *too late*, that creativity is a luxury for you, that you ought to be grateful for what you already have. Don't stop the flow. What the universe wants of you is what *you* want most for yourself.

What you give yourself to, Teresa goes on to add, has to be larger than what you're capable of doing. You won't be able to accomplish your mission (your way of channeling creativity) in a single lifetime. Sculptor Henry Moore put it plainly:

> The secret of life is to have a task, something you devote your entire life to, something you bring everything to, every minute of the day for your whole life. And the most important thing is—it must be something you cannot possibly do.[40]

4. Teresa's first step in watering the garden is to articulate one's desire in words. The second step is to release these words in contemplation. The third step is to enter into unselfconscious action. Her fourth step, then, is to leave the results in God's hands. What comes will come. There are no guarantees; but you might be astonished. A sudden, unexpected rain may come pouring down, saturating the ground.

Rain in a dry land brings a new world to life: wildflowers, the smell of sage, things turning green overnight. After a rainstorm, a massive cottonwood can heave a hundred gallons of water an hour up its trunk. A tall saguaro cactus can weigh up to six tons, after having absorbed water from recent rains. Its pleated sides expand like an accordion when there's a downpour, allowing it to store water for future need. From then on, it simply depends on what lies within.

This is the prayer of *union*, says Teresa, an intimate sense of being filled with the divine life pumping through your veins, coming up from your roots. At this point in your life, it's all about receptivity. You do nothing but allow the welling up of God's love. You don't dig a well in the desert, you don't wait for snow to melt on the mountain, you don't even channel water from the river. It springs up spontaneously from inside. It's been there all along. You do nothing to occasion it. You already *are* a well of living water!

Teresa concedes that moments like this don't come very often or last very long. You don't even know it's happening, in fact, because in a deep sense there's no longer any *you* there to do the knowing. You're no longer separate from the divine presence within. The rain has entered the river, and you can't tell the water of the one from the water of the other. Teresa admits that she can't articulate what happens between her and God in any of these levels of prayer. "If my way of explaining this seems crazy to Him, He is welcome to laugh at me."[41]

At this fourth stage, says Teresa, "The intellect is in awe." Meanwhile, "the will loves more than it understands." In her *Interior Castle*, she describes the seventh mansion of the soul as a spiritual betrothal and marriage—an indescribable experience of being enraptured by God's love, beyond any conscious analysis whatever.[42]

ENTERING THE FLOW

I'm back at Lost Creek now where the river emerges from underground for the last time on its way down the mountain. This is perfectly ordinary water from a Colorado stream. Yet it captivates the imagination by the way it constantly submerges and then erupts again. Is there a lesson here? Is it only as we lose (and regain) the ordinary that we're able to witness the wonder within it? Why aren't we conscious of a steady sea breeze, a wood thrush's repetitive call, a stream's voice until it *stops*, and starts again? Only *then* do we take notice, suddenly aware that presence and absence are a single reality, each disclosing the other.

I'm curious about this as a principle in the spiritual life. I want to be open to the interruptions that offer glimpses of the extraordinary within the commonplace. I want to attend to the abrupt "absence" that awakens me to a "presence" I hadn't noticed. If I can do that, I may learn to trust that the Holy is there even when there's absolutely no indication of its nearness. I might even believe that I'm carried—that I'm still in the flow—when the water goes underground.

But how can I count on this, trusting that there's always more than I initially see? Buddhist practitioners do it this way: They allow themselves to be lured by an unseen wonder, carried by habit, and sustained by story. They embrace three jewels: a vision, a discipline, and a community. The devotee first seeks refuge in the assurance of an enlightened wellspring of love undergirding the cosmos: the Buddha. She goes on to maintain a spiritual practice grounded in the teachings of a tradition: the Dharma. Finally, she connects with a company of sages whose tales of struggle continue to give hope. She's joined to a larger community of memory, a deeper field of connectedness as vast as the universe: the Sangha.

When you give yourself to a spiritual framework of this sort, the ordinariness of water (of fire, sandhill cranes, even a common tree in a city park) comes bursting into your awareness, singular and unpredictable, pulling everything into an integral whole. You find yourself wedded to the same mystery that overwhelmed Teresa of Ávila.

My relationship with Grandfather thrives as a result of our habitual, unremarkable practice of spending time together. I can't explain when or how this happened, but at some point over the years we bonded, making what initially seemed strange now perfectly natural: our *expecting* each other.

Was it the repetitive action of crossing the street each night? The inviting hollow in his side, the silence of the park after dark, the breathing I practice there, even the distant sound of owls and murmur of the wind? Whatever the combination of things, a sense of interdependence opens between us. Our level of communication and quality of awareness are transformed. "When we change the level of our awareness we attract a new reality," says Diarmuid O'Murchu.[43]

We begin to see the effect of everything on everything else. Take this Colorado mountain stream. It follows a path prescribed by gravity, a downhill charm that it can't resist. Gathering here and there in pools and shallows, it habitually seeks its next lowest turn. But the pattern of flow also depends on the position of boulders, interfering tree roots, the work of beavers, even weather conditions and the butterfly effect. Changes in one part of the system result in significant differences elsewhere.

My practice of spending time with a tree each night affects not only me, but the other people who frequent the park, the birds and animals who nest there, and the tree itself (in ways I'm not able to measure). A habit of attentive presence has a far greater effect on the world than I imagine.

Mystery. Habit. Story. These are the things that sustain us, written into the fabric of nature itself. I think of Kevin Locke, a Lakota storyteller from the Standing Rock Reservation in South Dakota. He ritually performs a sacred Hoop Dance that narrates the wonder of the world coming into being. In the dance, he uses twenty-eight hoops representing the number of days in a lunar month, the length of a woman's menstrual cycle. As he moves—twirling like a dervish—he configures the hoops into the seasons of the moon, the wings of a butterfly, the rising sun, flowing water. It's spellbinding.

He received the gift of this dance from an old Hidatsa elder from North Dakota, the last one to carry its memory. It was a tradition that had almost died out. The old man told Kevin he could teach it to him over several sessions, but he died before he was able to pass on the rest of the steps. With an amazement Kevin finds hard to contain, he affirms that the old man came to him in a series of dreams to complete the lessons.

Stories do this. They *insist* on being told, even when lost to human memory. The dance continues, despite the loss of the one who carried its power. Story and dance are held by the land, conveyed by the waters. They reside in a collective unconscious accessed by dream, ritual, and contemplative silence. *This* is the meaning and importance of the Great Conversation. The unlived parts of our spiritual lives are borne along on the waters of a disappearing stream, on the wind in a high mountain pass, on the movement of animals in a forest just beyond seeing.

There's a story about an old Hindu sannyasin who lived on the banks of the Ganges. A disciple asked him how he'd managed to be so generative throughout his life. What was the key to his success as a spiritual guide for so many people? The old man answered that all he'd done through the years had been to sit there by the river, *selling* river water. He'd taken what was altogether ordinary (what flowed in abundance) and presented it to people as a treasure they'd never seen before, something worth buying. He simply showed them what they'd always taken for granted and had never been able to celebrate as gift. That's what any of us live for—to claim as utterly wondrous what we possessed all along.

CHAPTER TEN

CANYONS

GRAND STAIRCASE-ESCALANTE WILDERNESS AND LAOZI

"May your trails be crooked, winding, lonesome, dangerous, leading to the most amazing view . . . beyond that next turning of the canyon walls."

—Edward Abbey, "Benedicto"[1]

"It is as though I am walking through the inside of an animal. It is dark, cool, and narrow with sheer sandstone walls on either side of me. I look up, a slit of sky above. Light is deceptive here. The palms of my hands search for a pulse in the rocks."

—Terry Tempest Williams, *Red: Passion and Patience in the Desert* [2]

Taking Utah Highway 12 from Bryce Canyon, we drove to the little town of Escalante, named after a Franciscan missionary who'd passed that way in the late 1700s. We wanted to pick up maps and guide books at the Escalante Outfitters store before heading down the Hole-in-the-Rock Road to the Egypt Trailhead. The hikers and climbers we met there were all talking about a guy called Aron Ralston who, two weeks earlier, had walked out of Blue John Canyon eighty miles away in Canyonlands National Park. Trapped under a dislodged boulder for five days, he had finally hacked off his right arm in order to free himself.

The story gave us pause, to say the least. But we knew we'd be exploring the less-challenging side canyons of the Escalante River as it flows toward its junction with the Colorado River fifty miles downstream. We were at Grand Staircase–Escalante National Monument, a million acres of dramatic canyon country in southern Utah. It's marked by sandstone terraces of chocolate, vermillion, white, grey, and pink cliffs exposed by the uplift of the Colorado Plateau ten million years ago. We'd be hiking a terrain Wallace Stegner thought equal to the lost grandeur of Glen Canyon, saying that its canyons were "as magically colored as shot silk."[3]

On our first night in backcountry, my friend and I camped near the head of Fence Canyon, planning to hike down to the river and on into Neon Canyon the next day. Between the unnerving energy of canyon country and the full moon rising that night, I found it hard to sleep. I was carrying a lot of inner baggage. It seems that we often inadvertently arrive at the place we need most—one that mirrors an interior landscape we're trying to navigate. I could read what was stirring within me off the shadowed walls of distant cliffs. Canyons speak with a voice millions of years old. They offer an equal measure of promise and threat. They beckon. But they also enclose, entrap.

The next morning we approached Neon from the lower entrance, wading across the Escalante and walking up the side canyon. We had no ropes, carabiners, or helmets, knowing we lacked the skillset to come in from the upper entrance. The idea of rappelling down through the ceiling of the Golden Cathedral was compelling, but we knew there were "keeper potholes" on that route—deep holes carved in the rock by flash floods, with smooth sides you can't climb out of. A canyoneering hazard we weren't up to.

The Golden Cathedral is a domed-space of red-orange rock located at the end of the lower Neon box canyon. Diffused sunlight passes through arch-shaped holes in its roof, a conduit for water rushing down from the upper canyon when it storms. The floor of the nave is a large pool of water with white sand. A hanging garden of watercress adorns the back wall. I sat for a long time in the silence of this haunting enclosure, dumbstruck by the painfully green cottonwood trees standing against bright red walls streaked with desert varnish. It's a show of beauty that plays to an empty house most of the time.

How do you handle something so exquisite when your interior terrain feels as hollow as the canyons you've been plodding? I took off by myself for a few hours that afternoon, walking back to the Escalante and downstream to the next side canyon, Ringtail—a narrow, winding slot that gets darker and narrower the farther you go, a place that chills, while it also intrigues.

Terry Tempest Williams writes of her experience in a similar slot canyon in the Needles district of Canyonlands: "In some places my hips can barely fit through. I turn sideways, my chest and back in a vise of geologic time. I stop. The silence that lives in these sacred hallways presses against me. I relax. I surrender. I close my eyes."[4] That wasn't my experience. Any sense of comfort in being held by the rock was overpowered by the fear of being encased by its walls. I didn't stay long.

I wasn't a very good companion on this trip—more silent than usual, heading off by myself at times, dealing with depression: Winston Churchill's "black dog." It's not uncommon for many of us—especially at midlife—faced with strained relationships, pressures at work, worries over adolescent children. This is the full catastrophe, in the words of Zorba the Greek. In my dreams at night, planes kept flying into the World Trade Center.

I'd come to the canyons of southern Utah hoping their emptiness might be healing—seeking the therapeutic indifference of dark-red cliffs, Wingate sandstone. I knew better than to expect anything dramatic. God had other fish to fry. I'd be on my own down there. Yet dark hollows might help me appreciate the subtlety of indirect light. Canyons have a way of doing that.

Returning the next day to the Egypt Trailhead, we set off on our most ambitious hike of the trip, modest by canyoneering standards. We scrambled down Egypt 3, a nontechnical but deep and narrow slot canyon. This three-mile-long crack in the earth is only four to five feet wide at the beginning, but narrows to less than twelve inches in places. Descending several hundred feet, you meander around curving walls, through arches, under a natural bridge, down waterfalls. You're continually tossing your pack ahead of you, sliding down slickrock, slipping sideways through narrow places, bracing your feet and back on opposing walls so as to chimney through a crack, standing on the shoulders of your partner to gain purchase on the lip of a pothole. It's like climbing down the convoluted back of a dragon's tail. You're moving through a space that should still be underwater.

I asked myself why I was doing this. What was I trying to prove—that I could endure a physical challenge (if nothing else in my life) at the time? Or was the *land* itself forcing me down into the very places I'd been scrambling through back home? Was the terrain mimicking the canyons of the soul— speaking a language heard only in the buffeting of my body, the reverberation of my dreams?

We returned to the SUV that afternoon, tired but pumped, and continued down the Hole-in-the-Rock Road toward Lake Powell. We stopped for our third night at the Redwell Trailhead. Our plan was to hike the next day into Coyote Gulch, one of the most beautiful canyons in the Four Corners region. But that night was a hard one. I'd lost my antidepressant pills in maneuvering down the slot canyon. It meant that I'd be plagued by edginess and insomnia for the rest of the trip.

But no matter what might be happening inside, you can't help falling in love with Coyote Gulch. You're amazed at what the universe has sculpted out of Navajo sandstone through the years, using only water and wind. You find that one red-rock canyon *isn't* just like another. Walking in the shallow creek that winds toward the river, we passed terraces scattered with willows, cottonwoods, and multijointed horsetail reeds. We walked through holes in canyon walls, marveling at arches looming in the distance.

Seven miles later we made it to Jacob Hamblin Arch, where we camped on a sandstone ledge a hundred feet above the creek. The canyon walls rose another two hundred feet above our campsite. We stood on the edge of a great curved arch of empty space, wrapping three hundred degrees around us. "A landscape that has to be seen to be believed," said Ed Abbey.[5]

As shadows gathered in the late afternoon, a single raven soared in the circle of the canyon rim above. Three riders on horses with two pack animals walked the bend in the creek below. A butterscotch line of light rose on the wall to the right as the sun slowly set. We celebrated with a dinner of black beans, cheese, tortillas, and hot sauce—washed down with Irish whiskey, the definition of contentment. But I spent the rest of the night transfixed by a framed circle of sky, the Big Dipper revolving around Polaris as the hours went by. I slept fitfully—wolves wandering through intermittent dreams.

Years ago, a National Geographic expedition had named the Hamblin Arch after a well-known Mormon missionary. Before that it was known as Lobo Arch. The story goes that a huge wolf was caught in a trap there. He'd pulled the steel trap out of the rock and dragged it with him for ten miles before hunters tracked him down and killed him. The shadow of his memory lingers. By the next morning I was more than ready to leave. We walked back to the SUV by way of Hurricane Wash and took the Hole-in-the-Rock Road back toward town, leaving the Grand Staircase–Escalante wilderness behind. I knew I'd been met by canyon walls, but didn't yet understand what they had to teach me.

THE DEEP KNOWLEDGE OF CANYONS

Both geologists and depth psychologists are beguiled by the mystery of ravines, arroyos, chasms, gorges. Deep ruts cut into the earth and the psyche alike. The Colorado Plateau is a section of the Earth's crust that—over the past few million years—has been lifted a mile and a quarter into the sky. Through a combination of upwarping and downcutting, it's been sliced into canyons by water erosion and plate shifting.[6] You find all kinds of canyons there: deep gorges between tall cliffs, narrow passes (or defiles) winding through mountains, dark slot canyons formed by flash floods, box canyons growing out of a spring at the base of a cliff, wide valleys opening onto wider plains.

On the seabed of the continental slope, off the northeast coast of the United States, you'll find submarine canyons carved by rivers in the last Ice Age, when the ocean was shallower. Hudson Canyon extends 450 miles into the Atlantic starting at the mouth of the Hudson River just beyond the Verrazano Narrows Bridge. On maps of the western Pacific, you'll see the Mariana Trench, the world's deepest underwater canyon. At 36,000 feet, it's seven times deeper than the Grand Canyon.

In most cases, canyons are formed by erosion—the sustained friction of water on rock operating over millions of years. Wind, falling boulders, and frost-wedging also help in creating these great troughs in the earth. But it's the serpentine movement of rivers that does the job best. The Escalante is a good example; it's been called "the crookedest river on earth." Along one section it takes thirty-five miles to cover a crow-fly distance of fourteen miles.[7]

As you watch the river winding its way past Scorpion Gulch, you notice it moving faster on the outside of each bend, cutting sharply into the sandstone wall. On the inside of the bend, the water moves more slowly—depositing sand on the terraces that build up there, leaving seeds that sprout into tamarisk and sandbar willows. This writhing action of the river produces canyons that are increasingly snake-like, bending in more and more convoluted turns.

Other canyons and valleys are formed by the slower, carving work of glaciers. You think of Yosemite or Glacier National Parks. Artists working with wood or stone describe carving as a subtractive art, the methodic removal of everything unnecessary. Sculptors, like glacial geologists, attend to what takes shape as small bits of the world disappear over time. "Perfection is finally attained not when there is no longer anything to add," says Antoine de Saint-Exupéry, "but when there is no longer anything to take away."[8] It's an important principle in the spiritual life as well: subtract whatever is superfluous.

But how do you know what to eliminate, what isn't necessary? It's a question asked by stone sculptors, saints, and canyons alike. We're told that Michelangelo initially carved small wooden models of the large marble statues he made. He'd submerge the model in a container of water, gradually dipping out the liquid as he observed which parts of the figure emerged first. Reducing the water showed him how to proceed with the reduction of the stone.[9]

As we ponder the waters that engulf our individual lives, we may understand how interior canyons have been formed there as well. Recognizing what we've had to leave behind—and what still needs to go.

Canyons invite contemplation: the wonderment of water eroding stone over thousands of years. The first time you approach the rim of the Grand Canyon—277 miles long and a mile deep—you're left speechless. The train ride through the larger and even deeper Copper Canyon in Mexico leaves you equally stunned. Yet canyons don't have to be huge to be sacred.

At Canyon de Chelly in northeast Arizona, Spider Woman sang her first weaving song—creating a web of the universe, joining all beings into one. Chaco Canyon in northwest New Mexico holds the ruins of an Anasazi civilization where rituals in its Great Kiva kept the world in harmony. Antelope Canyon north of Flagstaff is famous for its play of light on orange and purple rock, the dwelling place of the trickster Kokopelli with his flute.

In the Judeo-Christian tradition, the entire biblical story unfolds within a vast network of canyons. The geographical terrain of the Old and New Testaments is cut from north to south by the Great Rift Valley, formed long ago by a huge shift in tectonic plates. It runs from the Sea of Galilee down through the Jordan River and the Dead Sea to the Red Sea at Eilat. From the heights on either side of the Great Rift, deep wadis or gorges descend its slopes. Along the Kidron Valley, coming down through Jerusalem and the Mount of Olives, you'll find the Garden of Gethsemane and the tombs of the dead. The Wadi Qelt is another gorge sloping toward Jericho. It's said to be the setting of the Good Samaritan parable and the Valley of the Shadow of Death mentioned in the Twenty-Third Psalm.

Passing through a canyon on foot or floating its river on a raft is challenging, if not life-threatening. John Wesley Powell's expedition down the Green and Colorado Rivers in the summer of 1869 is a case in point. No account of river running surpasses Wallace Stegner's story of this one-armed Union Army officer setting out with ten men and four boats on rivers that had never been mapped. They maneuvered narrow sections of wild water, assigning them names like Desolation and Cataract canyons. They raced through a raging torrent capable of rolling boulders the size of small houses down its bed. Six of the original ten men made it through by the skin of their teeth.

A hundred years later Ed Abbey ran the same rapids, flowing with less fury then, but still bearing names like Big Drop, Satan's Gut, Capsize Rapids, and the Claw.[10] He loved it. We thrill at the idea of canyons as a test of courage, but—as mirrors of the soul—they take us places we don't want to go.

INTO THE DEPTHS: THE CALL OF THE CANYON

Canyons hold the prospect of drowning or getting lost. Old canyon rats recommend the latter. "Don't ask the way of those who know it, you might *not* get lost," they say.[11] They know that losing your way is critical if you have any hope of finding a better one. In the canyon maze you may well realize that you'd *been* lost for a long time, that this is the place to finally deal with it.

Canyons carry the soul into unfinished grief—into the pain we've stifled, the secrets we've hid, the depression we've feared. Deep chasms *know* the grinding action of stone scraped away, grain by grain, over millions of years. They're conversant with dark shadows. Their deep recesses receive direct sunlight only a few minutes each day, if ever. You don't see their beauty, in fact, *without* the shadows. Only at dawn or dusk do the badlands burst into relief, disclosing a color and contour you wouldn't otherwise notice.

Canyons are the grand opera of desert landscape—lavish productions bringing to the surface emotions that you didn't know you had. You hear the coloratura soprano of creek water echoing the runs and trills of the Queen of the Night in *The Magic Flute*. You sit in wonder at the full chorus of a flash flood careening down the ravine in the "Ride of the Valkyries." Thunderclouds sweep over the rimrock. You're moved by arias of grief with the libretto scratched in stone.

It's too much, overwhelming. But that's where I was on this trip into the Grand Staircase–Escalante Wilderness. I was dealing with two of the great traumas in my life. Since 9/11, multiple towers had been crumbling in my experience. I wanted nothing more than to follow Everett Ruess into the depths of Davis Gulch, one of the other side canyons of the Escalante. In the fall of 1934, the young cowboy poet had wandered into the desert with two burros and a few supplies. He was never seen again. Was he intending to disappear, running away from something back home? Or did an accident overtake him? We'll never know.[12]

When faced with depression, how do any of us deal with the dark place within? At first we try to laugh it off. For years I've met with a friend for coffee, sharing the assorted struggles of our lives. When one (or both) of us are down, we joke about leaving town for Valdosta in southern Georgia. There, along the Withlacoochee River, we imagine a bait house half-hidden among the cypress trees. We'll lean back at a table in the corner with a PBR in hand, listening to the old men talk about the weather. We may toss a minnow in the water, hoping for a smallmouth bass. Nothing much happens at a place like this. It's an ideal site for fantasied escape. When things get hard, we just think of moseying down to the Greyhound bus station to buy a one-way ticket to Valdosta.

Canyon country doesn't afford the luxury of that kind of fantasized avoidance. It cuts right through your illusions. You find yourself wedged between tight canyon walls, terrified by what's welling up inside. If there's grief to be owned, this is the place for it. You can't put it off. The Escalante canyons make that clear.

I was thirteen when my father ended his life with two shots in the chest, using his .38 Police Special early one morning at the bank where he served as a guard. I was an only child, with a mother who was falling apart at the time. Secrets had suddenly come tumbling out of my dad's past—stories of stolen money, changed identities, failed efforts at starting a new life. These were added to earlier skeletons having to do with rape, child abandonment, a botched abortion. Every family carries secrets, some known, some unknown. Some we unravel, others we hide.

At the time of my father's death I'd had to stifle my grief, for the sake of a shattered mom. It took me twenty years to even *begin* the work of acknowledging the loss, giving voice to the sense of betrayal that was mine.

I've seen this happen again and again on men's rites of passage, with military veterans and sons of abusive fathers grieving over what had been done to them. And over what *they* had subsequently done to others. As victims and perpetrators—having sinned and been sinned against—they had to grieve everything they'd lost, letting it go. Only then could they find the possibility of forgiving those who'd hurt them, and seeking the forgiveness of those they'd hurt themselves.

My father's abandoning me at a time when I needed him most was the worst thing that had ever happened to me. I'd been left with a mother who had no idea of how to raise a teenage son. But my delayed grieving showed me a connection now between the worst thing that was ever done to me and the worst thing I ever did, which was to betray my wife through an affair.

It was an emotional affair with another woman—a soulmate I thought could fulfill me in ways my wife had never been able to do. I use the word "affair" even though it wasn't sexual, because it was intense, concealed, and sustained over time, stealing from my relationship with my wife. When she learned of it, it brought her incredible pain, and it left me with overwhelming guilt. I'd had a part in betraying two marriages.

I've come to see that not dealing with my father's early abandonment of me had made me able to abandon others in turn. I'd learned that I couldn't count on the people who were closest to me. I had to look elsewhere for what I needed.

I'd also learned that living with secrets becomes addictive. Their toxic nature is to duplicate themselves. Old ones are passed down from one generation to the next. New ones carry a seductive quality in the intimacy they invite, the excitement they elicit, the danger of being found out that they harbor. All my life, I'd been tormented—and energized—by secrets.

The dark truth of the canyon depths, says Richard Rohr, is that if our pain isn't transformed, it will be transmitted.[13] We *will* pass on what we haven't brought to light, grieved over, and released. Yet descending into that dark place, fully acknowledging the truth, seems unbearable.

First there's the telephone call: "I've been to your office and read the journals. I *know.* We have to talk." You suddenly enter the bottomless sense of betrayal and anger on the part of the woman you love most. You know the Golden Boy's realization, after years of secrecy, of having finally screwed up, big time. You're left to wander under dark trees in the park each night, lapsing into the desolation that threatened your father's life.

It was a long road to healing—involving men's rites of passage, years of counseling, the persistent love of an amazing woman. But I came to learn that I'd not been alone in the belly of the whale, in either of those times. My father's suicide wasn't the punishment imposed by an angry God on a son's early teenage rebelliousness. The affair hadn't been met by a vengeful deity bent on punishing a man with a guilty conscience. In the canyon emptiness, where I lacked any claim to it whatever, I discovered I'd been loved all along. Over time, in fact, my wife and I both came to recognize the wound—indeed, the *sin*—as a gift, a call to the integrity and the marriage we'd always wanted.

Through all of this, I've come to understand the cross in an entirely new way. The suffering of Jesus wasn't about satisfying divine justice, appeasing a wrathful God. It was a sign of God's own radical participation in human (and other-than-human) suffering.[14] It was God saying, "You're not alone. This is where I myself dwell—in the dark, empty place. Not as a *cause* of suffering, but as a shared *presence* within it."

At times I wonder if God shares the depths of the world's pain so that *God* won't be lonely either. How does the Holy One make it through the night, after all, given the agony of all he has to bear? In the cross you don't find an "Almighty" God so much as a God who consents to being "All-vulnerable," walking alongside us, at great personal risk.

Why do I think this? Because of the witness of others who've walked this path before me. These are the sunburnt and muddy men and women who've perceived the canyon's emptiness as full of promise. When I came home from the Utah wilderness, I turned to an unlikely combination of teachers who had themselves spoken out of the depths: Jesus of Nazareth and a Chinese sage known as Laozi (Lao-tzu).[15]

Jesus walked through settlements of poor farmers suffering under Roman occupation, companioning those who'd cheated others and those who had been cheated. He modeled an emptiness (a kenosis) that made him receptive to a wellspring of love arising from within. Losing one's self (failing badly) isn't the worst thing that can happen, he taught. "Unless a grain of wheat falls into the ground and dies, it remains alone; but if it dies, it bears much fruit" (John 12:24). The real loss would be if you *never* fell and never flowered.

Laozi was a Daoist (Taoist) master who pondered the way of water in carving out a mountain ravine. The open space (the receptacle) that results may appear hollow, he said, but it's full of possibilities. Don't dread the cutting action of water on rock. Don't flee the emptiness. Let the stream do its work, welcoming the void that opens within. This is the life-giving way of the Dao.

The "empty space" between canyon walls is more than it seems. It's the creative void cut away from a block of wood by the sculptor, left as woodchips on the workshop floor. The space retains a substance of its own. Japanese artisans refer to it as *ma*, a quality that's more than an empty zone, waiting to be filled, separating one thing from another. It has its own distinct reality, holding everything together in a spacious continuum. The void isn't an empty interval between this and that. It flows between the two, joining them as one.[16]

The canyons of the Escalante taught me not to resist the empty places in my life—those that seem beyond healing. With Laozi, I learned that they're full of potentiality.

LAOZI, THE *DAO TE CHING*, AND THE CANYON VOID

We don't know if a Chinese philosopher named Laozi actually lived in the sixth century BCE. He may be a composite of several earlier teachers. His name simply means "Old Master." According to legend, he served as an archivist filing manuscripts at the court library of the Eastern Zhou dynasty in Central China, along the middle reaches of the Yellow River where water rushes through deep gorges.

Laozi resisted the political corruption of his day, deciding finally to withdraw altogether from society. He rode his water buffalo to the western frontier, where he engaged in conversation with a border guard. The man was so impressed that he asked Laozi to write out a summary of his teachings before moving on. The old master penned the *Dao Te Ching* (The Way of the Dao), then disappeared into the sunset. It's a slim volume of eighty-one "chapters," each offering a short poetic reflection on the meaning of life.

The Way of the Dao isn't a doctrine; it's a manner of life. It isn't bound to any faith tradition. You might summarize it as a book about the wisdom of canyons, teaching the receptivity of a deep ravine. It asks: How do you empty yourself of chatter, unnecessary activity, the compulsive needs of the ego? These are some of its central themes:

1. *The Inadequacy of Words.* Words often get in the way more than they help, says Laozi. The *Dao Te Ching* begins by not taking even itself too seriously. You can hear the master laughing as he writes:

> The true meaning of life can never be put into words.
> The words that you use to explain life are words—nothing more.
> Different parts of life may be given names,
> Different things in life may be named with words.
> But life remains a wordless mystery.[17]

When we're emptied of our dependence on words, we open ourselves to the sensual language of nature. We attend to what moves in, with, and around us. The Daoist masters learned to converse in the language of water tumbling down a mountain stream. In the silence of wild things, they whispered in the mother tongues of plants, minerals, and animals. "Who will prefer the jingle of jade pendants," asks Laozi, "if once he has heard stone growing in a cliff?"[18]

They scorned the self-congratulating speech of scholars. "Banish the intellectual!" urged Laozi. "Discard knowledge! We will all benefit a hundred fold."[19] In this respect Laozi was very different from his supposed contemporary, Confucius. The latter revered the trusted words of the ancients, calling people back to the authority of tradition. Laozi scoffed at the presumption of words, urging simplicity and humility. "Not-knowing is true knowledge," said the Daoist sage. "Presuming to know is a disease."[20]

Zhuangzi (Chuang Tzu), said to have been a student of Laozi, said it well:

> The point of a fish trap is the fish: once you've got the fish, you can forget the trap. The point of a rabbit snare is the rabbit: once you've got the rabbit, you can forget the snare. The point of a word is the idea: once you've got the idea, you can forget the word.
>
> How can I find someone who's forgotten words, so we can have a few words together?[21]

2. *The Way of Water.* Laozi turned to water as nature's finest teacher. It moves with ease, exerting no effort, yielding always to gravity's lure. Yet look at what the Colorado River has made of the Grand Canyon by doing nothing over the past 17 million years. "Nothing in the world is as soft and yielding as water," observed the master.[22] It locates the empty spaces between things, slipping through with a quiet grace. But over time, it cuts through the hardest rock.

The humbleness of water is its great virtue, Laozi explained. "All streams flow to the sea because it is lower than they are. Humility gives water its power." Its gift is that it "nourishes all things without trying to. It is content with the low spots that people disdain. Thus it is like the Dao."[23] There's an utter unselfconsciousness about water. It never has time to practice falling.

The Daoist principle of *wu-wei* (acting as not-acting) follows this pattern of the flowing stream. It cultivates a quiet and deliberate presence in any given moment—moving effortlessly, focused more on "allowing" than resisting.

> Acting in the Way of Nature
> Means that acting often means not acting—
> Not doing anything.
> Indeed, an empire can often be won
> By doing nothing at the right time.
> Indeed a life can often be lost
> By trying to do too much.[24]

3. *The Power of the Void.* The Daoist master knew the enormous potential of empty space. When the soul embraces "the ravine of the world," it discovers a great power. You see it in the hollow hub of a wagon wheel, says Laozi. Nothing's there, yet it holds together the spokes that give the wheel stability. The value of a clay pot similarly depends upon the hollowness within it. The usefulness of a house isn't defined by its roof and walls, but by the inner space that makes it livable.[25]

For Laozi, there's a spaciousness about the vacant canyon within the human self. There we needn't explain things, or hold resentments. We encounter the freedom of the Valley Spirit (Gu-shen), Laozi's favorite metaphor for the Dao. Give yourself, he said, to the universal river-valley, the "mysterious womb," the mother of the ten thousand things. It's the chasm carved by falling water, the inner emptiness of the Daoist holy man.[26]

Zhuangzi (Chuang-tzu) went on to describe canyons and caves—even the hollows of large trees—as the nostrils, mouths, and drinking bowls of the Dao. Wind passes through them, sighing and whistling—like "the music of earth drawn out of nothing more than holes."[27] Daoist teachers celebrated this melodious emptiness. The apostle Paul echoed this theme when he said, "I've been *emptied* with Christ and I no longer live, yet the Christ [the Dao] now lives in me" (Galatians 2:20).[28]

4. Leading Without Ego. A final dimension of the Dao is its hiddenness. The Daoist master remains largely unseen, working under the radar, passing unnoticed by others (as the best leaders do). He isn't full of himself, seeking the adulation of followers. "The Holy Man's power is immense, provided that it is kept secret." He may even appear to others to be a fool. "When the inferior man hears of the Tao, he bursts out laughing: if he did not laugh, it would not really be the Tao."[29] How, then, does one move through the world, leading others in such an unobtrusive way?

> If you trust those who follow you,
> They will trust you.
> If you say only what you mean,
> Your followers will know you mean what you say.
> If you always keep your proper task in view,
> Your followers will be able to complete your task,
> And make you proud by saying: "We did it ourselves."[30]

This is the unassuming way of the Dao, the canyon's hidden truth. Here secrecy becomes the great deliverer, serving as a rein on the ego, freeing the soul. There's a wide generosity in the mystery of the watercourse way.[31]

CANYON RUNNING AT MIDLIFE

How do we stay on course through the deepening gorge of career and family, negotiating the rapids of our midlife years? That's the hazard of life at midstream. The river gets wilder as we round the bend, anticipating steep canyon walls ahead. We fear what we may be losing.

Wallace Stegner, Ed Abbey, David Brower, and Eliot Porter all—at a midpoint in their lives— made raft trips through Glen Canyon before the Colorado River was dammed in the mid-1960s. As writers, environmentalists, and photographers, they knew that something wild and beautiful was dying in the American West, and in themselves.

Running a wild river through wilderness, says James Dickey in his novel *Deliverance*, you're damned sure gonna experience a loss of innocence, an entry into liminal space. Initial adventure yields to terror. Secrets are uncovered and hidden again. Hope seems lost. At best, you stay in the raft, put your back to the oars, and keep breathing till the white water passes.

Amid all of these challenges the temptation is to try to fill the void instead of resting within it. My wife and I learned that we can't look to another person to fulfill us, to make us whole. We can't even do that for each *other*. No human being—no number of distractions—can fill the hole. It's a necessary hollow— a true void—at the soul's center. Ultimately, it's where only God dwells.

It's there that we're loved in our naked vulnerability. Where we hear Julian of Norwich's quiet insistence that "sin is necessary." It's not our accomplishments but our failures that occasion our deepest healing. There in the bottomless void, forsaken by those who should have loved us and having forsaken those we should have loved, we find acceptance, not accusation.

In heaven, says Julian, we won't be ashamed of how we've been wounded or how we've wounded others. We'll wear our sins as a badge, because that's what *got* us there. Grace isn't won by our having done it all right, but it comes by our having failed and been forgiven.[32] I claim that for myself every night as I stand in the hollow of a tree that offers no blame. I receive it again and again—implausibly—from a loving wife, from a two-year-old granddaughter who looks at me and sees only love.

In seventeenth-century French spirituality, mystical writers used the word *anéantissement* in speaking of the uncompromising self-emptying of the soul. It was prerequisite, they said, to the free acceptance of God's love. It meant throwing oneself into the "nothingness" of God, into the empty canyon where soul and beloved are one. It's where loss strangely occasions a whole new life.[33]

***

The thought of falling into nothingness is terrifying. In the canyons ahead there are no guarantees that an arm won't be caught under the rock, that broken oars won't be washed up on the sand. The only promise is that we won't be alone.

Once in my life I had an actual experience of falling into empty space, knowing what it's like (almost) to fly. My son and I were on a Boy Scout camping trip in the St. Francois Mountains of eastern Missouri. We were angel-rappelling off a sixty-five-foot cliff into a tree-filled ravine below.

Leaning out over the edge of the cliff, spread-eagled, staring into the chasm into which I'd be falling, I was as frightened as any of the kids. In this kind of rappelling you don't face the cliff, coming down backward in a seated position. You come down face-first, arms open wide, holding in each gloved hand a rope that's been threaded through a ring on the back of your climbing harness. You initially keep your arms together in front, maintaining friction on the ropes to prevent your moving. But as you spread out your arms, embracing the canyon below, you begin to descend—the ropes slipping through your gloved hands. In and out—with arms outstretched and brought together, plunging faster, then slowing down, you swoop into the abyss. With wings beating, you know the weightless amazement of flight.

My terror was overcome by absolute wonder. I drifted as light as a feather on the wind, as wild as a raven in flight. "Whatever is fluid, soft, and yielding," said Laozi, "will overcome whatever is rigid and hard."[34] The soul learns this as readily as water, when it finally accepts the void. Borne at last on angel wings, it is surprised by love in the hollow into which it descends.

CHAPTER ELEVEN

ISLANDS

MONHEGAN ISLAND AND NIKOS KAZANTZAKIS

"I once found a list of diseases as yet unclassified by medical science, and among these there occurred the word *Islomania*, which was described as a rare but by no means unknown affliction of spirit. There are people . . . who find islands somehow irresistible. The mere knowledge that they are on an island, a little world surrounded by the sea, fills them with an indescribable intoxication. These born 'islomanes' . . . are direct descendants of the Atlanteans."

—Lawrence Durrell, *Reflections on a
Marine Venus*[1]

"Whoever comes to an isolated island, does not leave it as the same person: islands are both safe havens and dangerous areas of upheaval; safe wombs and insular alchemical vessels of transformation."

—"The Symbolism of Islands"[2]

We boarded the weekly mail boat, the *Laura B*, at Port Clyde on the Maine coast, headed for Monhegan Island. The sixty-five-foot former U.S. Army T-boat had spent the Second World War carrying troops in the Pacific. I sat with my backpack on its forward deck where twin 50-caliber machine guns were once mounted. My wife and I were spending several days on Monhegan, an island ten miles off the shore of the St. George peninsula northeast of Portland.

Captain John Smith had sailed into its harbor in 1614, learning from Abenaki and Micmac sources that its name meant "little island." Less than 2 miles long and a mile wide, its highest headland rises 165 feet above the sea. The high cliffs provide a good site for a lighthouse and fog signal station.

In the seventeenth century it was a major fishing center on the Maine coast, where cod were plentiful. Later it morphed into an artists' haven, attracting painters from the Hudson River School as well as realist landscape artists like Rockwell Kent, Edward Hopper, and the Wyeth family. Birdwatchers and wildflower enthusiasts flock to the place every year.

There are no cars. Most of the island is still wild, crisscrossed with trails leading through spruce and balsam fir trees, a few white birches. The interior is strewn with nettles, fiddlehead ferns, thick brush and fallen trees. It's a terrain where you're continually stepping over entangled tree roots. More than four hundred kinds of wildflowers have been identified on the island. This is an outpost of biodiversity that sea birds have been seeding for centuries.

Thunderous waves crash over the rocks on the island's seaward side. An old shipwreck lies off Lobster Cove to the south. Down at the harbor you can get morning coffee at the Barnacle or clam chowder for lunch at the Fish House near the beach. In the nineteenth century, seamen drank ale and played cards at Influence House, the island's oldest building. Folks complained that it was a bad influence.

I'd rented a small frame house up the hill from the harbor where we'd be staying. A rickety and weather-worn structure, it literally tilted downhill. Getting up to go to the bathroom in the night was like walking on a moving boat. My good-natured wife didn't share my appreciation of the character of the place. But it proved a good site from which to explore the rest of the island.

Islands are fascinating (and also daunting) places. On the one hand, they afford an escape from the bustle of mainland life, the romance of "getting away." A Maine island in July is idyllic. But most people wouldn't want to be living there in January. The isolation would be as unbearable as the weather. Of the 4,613 islands off the coast of Maine, only 14 are inhabited year-round. Fewer than forty-five people live year-round on Monhegan. Inveterate New England islanders speak of returning to "America" when taking a boat back to the mainland.[3] The island—any island—is another world.

Nikos Kazantzakis, the Greek novelist and author of *The Odyssey: A Modern Sequel*, was born on the island of Crete. "The island" formed the way he thought, the passion by which he lived, though he spent most of his life traveling to other places. Nourished by the fierce independence of an island community and culture, he was drawn by the lure of a wider world.

Crete was "the first bridge between Europe, Asia, and Africa," he wrote, the connecting keystone of the ancient world.[4] This was a place where Athens and Alexandria met, where Turks and Greeks clashed, where the local peasant and itinerant philosopher drank raki together in a harborside taverna. It has long exerted a centripetal and centrifugal force, pulling people into its heart, then driving them out again.

Islands do this. They symbolize the tension between the insular and the universal, the center and periphery. We crave the intimate bond of a small neighborhood, the secure world of an extended family, a close-knit community of faith. It poses a contrast to mainstream culture, where the individual is too easily lost among the masses.

Yet at the same time we chafe at the small town's narrow-mindedness, the island's limited possibilities, the community's deep suspicion of outsiders. We yearn for the anonymity of a society where options are boundless. We're pulled by all we've been taught to distrust.

Kazantzakis thrived on the antithesis of these two forces. It formed the creative edge of his work. They are contradictions that occupy many of us at multiple levels, especially at midlife. We want to belong, to succeed by the standards of the dominant society. Yet we're attracted to the unconventional identity of an island existence. Maybe, as Kazantzakis said of himself, we are "exiles who have not realized yet / that exile is a home."[5]

This has been the story of my life. Raised in the rural South with its inbred fundamentalism, I received a deep, nurturing sense of identity and community. Yet I was irked by the burden of always feeling different. In the eighth grade I had to bring a note to the gym teacher from the church pastor, excusing me from square dancing. It was against my religion, he said, a conviction I found embarrassing beyond words. I've always been torn between the margins and the center, the prophetic edge and the cultural mainstream, the security of certainty and the seduction of doubt.

Through the years, the island's continuing attraction has been its irresistible, Dionysian wildness. Things are different out there along the continental shelf. Bounded by a horizon of nothingness, the God you find on the island will be more than you expected. There's Poseidon, master of raging ocean storms; Aphrodite rising at her birth from the foamy waves; Thalassa, a primordial spirit spawning marine life in all its forms; and Yahweh measuring the sea in the hollow of his hand (Isaiah 40:12). This is a God who doesn't promise that you won't get hurt. But he certainly knows how to dance.

FROM CENTER TO EDGE

Hiking on Monhegan, my practice was to start from the center and move out to the edges. Leaving the wharf and its fishing boats behind, I'd pass through the clapboard houses of the village to the small museum of island history at the lighthouse atop the hill. These are places of a kind familiar to the people of Down East Maine—folks attentive to the movement of the tides, changes in weather, the shifting light of the sun as it rises and sets each day. They're people formed by a history of intimacy with the sea, taking pride in ancestors who survived by holding on to what they knew: family, tradition, solidarity.

From the center I followed various trails to the island's periphery, traveling back into a far deeper history. Millions of years ago, Monhegan was a huge hunk of igneous rock thrust up from the ocean floor. During the last ice age, twenty thousand years ago, it was covered with ice a mile thick. Under this weight it sank again into the sea, leaving a mountain top just above the waves. The island's rugged shore is a reminder of its tumultuous geological past.

My first morning there I took the Gull Cove Trail across the island to its windy eastern edge, through plum shrubs, wild rugosa roses, and stalks of blue lupine. At high tide I watched fifteen-foot breakers pounding the rocks. I was mesmerized by the dark blue water swelling, rolling over itself, then crashing into cascades of wild, frothy spray. It exploded in the sun like fireworks. When I returned later that afternoon, the fury had passed, leaving a cobblestone beach with tide pools full of seaweed, anemones, and snails.

The next day I trekked through Cathedral Woods, along a forested path strewn with hills and vales, carpets of green moss, relentless tree roots. It's a great place for fairies, or so the locals claim. For years they've had a tradition of building tiny "fairy houses" made of twigs, mosses, shells, and acorns—surrounded by minuscule gardens. It's a children's fantasy world. On an earlier trip to Monhegan I'd marveled at houses that were miniature masterpieces. But the desire to maintain the island's natural state has brought a crackdown on the excesses of fairy housing development projects.[6]

That afternoon I sat spellbound, watching the rock ledges off Lobster Point. Black shelves of bedrock come up for air here after being swallowed by massive breakers. Thirty feet of ocean spray bursting into the wind over and over again. Heading back home, I passed through the tall hardwoods on Black Head Trail, strewn with fir needles and cones. You readily sense the mystery contained in this 4.5-square-mile sanctuary of rock.

The longest track around the isle's perimeter is Cliff Trail. It ascends to White Head, Monhegan's highest point, midway along the island's eastern shore. That's where I decided to spend the night alone, overlooking the North Atlantic, on the far edge of the country I call home. Camping isn't allowed, but I brought no tent, no food. I simply stretched a hammock between two fir trees on the cliff's edge, watching as night descended. There are times when you have to push the edges, with or without permission.

I yielded to the sound of gulls and the echo of waves slamming on the rocks below, like distant thunder. Tree branches were dissolving into a dark Andrew Wyeth landscape. The slow departure of daylight took longer than I expected. It was almost ten when dusk finally turned to night.

Down-Easters attend carefully to the fading and returning of light in the sun's daily circuit. They distinguish nautical twilight from astronomical twilight. In the former, sailors are still able to steer by sighting the horizon; in the latter, they're obliged to navigate by means of the stars. The complete darkness that follows astronomical twilight on a summer night lasts only a few hours until astronomical dawn eventually yields to daybreak.

From my perch in the trees on White Head, I watched a full moon rising over the sea. It was reflected on the water as a bright orange strip painted across the ocean's blue-gray surface. It was the same color as the orange shore lichen I'd seen on rocks and roofs across the island. As the moon climbed the sky, it shifted from orange-yellow to white. By 3:30 a.m., dawn was already breaking again. Rocking in a sea breeze hammock under a passing moon, you haven't much time to celebrate the wild on a Maine island midsummer night.

As I lay suspended on the cliff's edge, I listened to what the island was saying, pondering how islands speak. They mumble, it seems, in multiple voices—one overlapping another. The breaking surf, the salt-filled wind, the cry of gulls: They all delight in repetition, and they require no response.

I was aware of being cut off from the mainland, enclosed by water I couldn't see across. I was almost an island to myself. Yet I was also part of an archipelago, connected to others in a vast watery immensity. I was sustained by lines attached to trees anchored in rock, held captive by a moon pulling the soul as readily as it does the tide. I wasn't alone at all. Indra's net had been cast over each of the seemingly separate pieces of the universe.

In Hindu and Buddhist teaching, Indra is a guardian deity holding the world together by means of a great fish net, like the braided cords of a hammock. At every connecting knot there's a jewel, and each jewel reflects the entirety of the net. The parts and the whole are interpenetrating, suspended together in an elegant web.[7] Everything belongs: even the mosquitoes buzzing around my head that night on the headland, the merlin falcons snatching the island's warblers out of the air, and the thirty-five ships that have been wrecked on its rocks over the years. All these, in some way, fit into a larger whole.

St. Bonaventure acknowledged this interlinking character of creation. He found the vestiges (or footprints) of the divine in every single part. He was beguiled by a God "whose center is everywhere and whose circumference is nowhere." For him, the Divine Connector was "within all things, but not enclosed; outside all things, but not excluded; above all things, but not aloof; below all things, but not debased."[8] For the great mystics, the insular and the universal, the part and the whole, are always one.

THE MEANING OF ISLANDS

But I have to resist reducing the island to a symbol of something other than what it is. I've a lot to learn from a relatively new field of research called island studies, or nissology (from the Greek word *nisos*, "island"). It explores the meaning of islands on their own terms—not simply as spiritual emblems, literary metaphors, tourist attractions, or places defined by a history of colonial conquest. Islands cover 7 percent of the Earth's land surface, are home to 10 percent of the world's population (more than 550 million people), and make up nearly a quarter of all sovereign states.[9]

Islands have long been a source of environmental knowledge, technological innovation, and alternative forms of government. Nature writer David Quammen says, "We are headed toward understanding the whole planet as a world of islands."[10] To think of the Earth as Turtle Island, after the pattern of the Iroquois, is to acknowledge the close interconnecting ties that we all share.

Yet there are distinctive aspects of island life that set it apart from mainland experience. "For island dwellers, the omnipresence of the sea intensifies the feeling of being cut off from the rest of the world."[11] Islanders are keenly aware of being different. Their insularity breeds a strong sense of resilience and versatility. Their island-hopping connections with other communities across the water make them more cross-culturally aware than a landlocked population might be. Islanders shouldn't be dismissed as a backwater people, isolated from the vitality of mainland life, reaching out only occasionally by means of a message in a bottle.[12]

It's the nature of "islandness" to raise the perennial contradictions of human experience: prison versus paradise, dependence versus self-reliance, isolation versus connectedness, leaving versus staying.[13] The stories we tell about islands offer deep disclosures of the human psyche. They awaken our profoundest hopes and fears.

We thrill at the idea of adventurers finding the skills they need to survive on desert islands. Odysseus dealt creatively with the threats he found on the island of the Cyclops. Robinson Crusoe salvaged supplies from his wrecked ship on a desolate Caribbean isle. Tom Hanks warded off despair with Wilson the volleyball in *Cast Away*.

Islands can symbolize the heart of human darkness, reminding us of what happens in isolated places when law and morality break down. Think of the schoolboys in *The Lord of the Flies* or the mutineers of the *Bounty* on Pitcairn Island. Islands have frequently served as detention centers, their watery boundaries defining some of the world's most notorious prisons: Devil's Island in French Guiana, Alcatraz in San Francisco Bay, Riker's Island in New York City's East River, Robben Island off Cape Town, South Africa. These are places of alienation, stripped of hope.

Yet islands are symbols of paradise and the highest human aspirations as well. In Greek mythology, access to the Elysian Fields came by way of the Fortunate Isles lying in the mists off the West African coast. St. Augustine thought the Garden of Eden continued to exist on a remote, inaccessible island. St. Brendan, the Celtic navigator, claimed to have discovered a thickly wooded island paradise shrouded in the fog off the western sea. These are places just beyond reach. Hy-Brasil, an island of saints and fairies west of Ireland, is only visible, they say, on a single day every seven years.

Northrup Frye referred to islands as "points of epiphany," locales where people can be free of themselves in order to find themselves.[14] They tell us who we are. We make them up even when they don't exist. Phantom islands have appeared on maps for centuries, finally to be removed because they were never found. They functioned as creative landscapes of the imagination. Seemingly real but illusive, their diaphanous character entices the soul. "Some islands are poorly moored; they are boats that drift and escape you."[15] They may be mapped, but they remain unreachable.

The island of Atlantis has drifted through the Western imagination since it first appeared in Plato's dialogues. Avalon near Glastonbury was the enchanted island of King Arthur and Morgan le Fay. Lyonesse, another island in the Arthurian legend, was home of the hero Tristan; it sank into the sea one night off the coast of Land's End, along with its 140 churches.[16] Thomas More's *Utopia* was situated on an imaginary island in the New World. Robert Louis Stevenson's fictional *Treasure Island* has entertained children of all ages for a century and a half.[17]

In the Hebrew scriptures relatively little attention was paid to islands. The people of Israel had limited experience of land surrounded by sea. Islands were associated with "the ends of the earth," with faraway places. When the prophet Isaiah proclaimed: "Sing the Lord's praise from the end of the earth . . . you islands," he was summoning the nations (the Gentiles) to the worship of Yahweh (Isaiah 42:10). The Hebrew word for "island" could also refer to "coastlands." With the coastal region of Canaan occupied by Israel's enemies (the Philistines), distant places near the sea were held in suspicion, subject to judgment.[18] In the New Testament islands assume greater significance as a result of Paul's missionary journeys and John's composition of the book of Revelation on the isle of Patmos.

You find endless references to island deities and saints in the wider history of religions. Zeus was born in a mountain cave on the island of Crete. The goddess Leto gave birth to twin deities, Artemis and Apollo, on the floating island of Delos. Druids went to the island of Anglesey off the northwest coast of Wales to complete their final training. Christian island saints include Columba of Iona, Aidan of Lindisfarne, and Michael the Archangel on Mont St. Michel in France.

Islands are disappearing today because of climate change. Small islands everywhere are at risk—islets, atolls, skerries, cays, and keys. They range from Skellig Michael off the Irish coast to island nations like Antigua in the Caribbean and Tonga in the South Pacific. "No man is an island," wrote John Donne, "if a clod be washed away by the sea, Europe [the *world*] is the less."[19] We lose more than a spot on the map; we lose part of a collective self.

KAZANTZAKIS, CRETE, AND A SPIRITUALITY OF RESISTANCE

The island of Crete with its ancient olive trees and sacred mountains has long been associated with Zeus, the high god of Olympus. You see the profile of his face on Mount Juktas overlooking Heraklion. According to legend, the monster Minotaur—half man, half bull—was confined in the labyrinth at Knossus, south of the city. The islanders affirm that St. Titus, the apostle Paul's companion, was consecrated its first bishop. But Epimenides, one of Crete's most celebrated philosopher/poets, cautioned that all Cretans are liars.[20] They're known, at the very least, for their fierce love of life, independence, and (invariably) a good story.

Once home of the great Minoan civilization, which flourished two thousand years before Christ, Crete struggled under foreign rule for hundreds of years. Resistance movements thrived under Venetian rule, the Ottoman Empire, and the Nazi occupation of the 1940s. Kazantzakis was born during one of the last Cretan revolts against the Turks. He remembered his father fighting on the streets of Herkalion where he grew up. Crete, says Kazantzakis, has always been an island aflame.[21]

Anthropologists observe that the close-knit character of island communities fosters an intense love of freedom and self-determination that, when threatened, inspires restlessness, even rebellion. The theme of personal and cosmic struggle—freedom or death!—flows through the writings of Kazantzakis. He was a Cretan, explained a friend, "and therefore a revolutionary."[22]

He is perhaps best known for his book *The Last Temptation of Christ*, made into a film by Martin Scorsese in 1988. The Orthodox and Roman Catholic churches condemned the book, and at his death Kazantzakis was denied burial in a Christian cemetery. But he was no enemy of Christianity. What he resisted was a doctrinaire religious certainty, a dualistic split between matter and spirit.

Throughout his life he embraced a lively juxtaposition of opposites, bringing together what others wanted to separate. He was a writer who knew the danger of words, a celebrant of the flesh drawn to the ascetic life of Mount Athos, a nihilist like Nietzsche who remained an intense lover of God's marvelous world.

Kazantzakis is an author who appeals to readers who need to be delivered from their conformity to shackling norms. His novels strike a rich chord when the call for wildness, passion, and resistance is strong: when you have to stop playing it safe; when you're chained to the job and its pen-pushing routine; when religion has stopped making your heart sing, reduced instead to the keeping of rules; when trusted institutions have betrayed their promise, adding to the world's suffering instead of lessening it. These are the times when Zorba and his summons to dance ring true. St. Francis then makes the almond tree bloom in winter and Manolios as Christ the Bolshevik calls the oppressed to freedom.[23]

"Resistance," said Alice Walker, "is the secret of joy."[24] Kazantzakis knew this. The desire to struggle against oppression flowed through his veins like wine. His prose may sometimes seem hackneyed. His larger-than-life characters are shadows of universal types. Contradictions and simplifications ramble through his writing. But when you need the sharp knife of decisive choice, he cuts to the heart.

Nikos Kazantzakis (1883–1957) was born of Greek and Arab ancestry. His mother was a devout Christian, his wine merchant father, a fiery agnostic. He left Crete in his early twenties, studying law at the University of Athens and then philosophy under Henri Bergson in Paris. He traveled widely in Spain, England, Russia, Egypt, Palestine, and Japan before settling on the Greek island of Aegina. As a writer he produced novels, plays, travel books, poetry, and Greek translations of Dante and Goethe. He was nominated repeatedly for the Nobel Prize.

Three themes stand out in his work: a celebration of *kefi*, the Greek passion for life that borders on madness; an intense wrestling with God rooted in the allure and distrust of religious belief; and a heroic inclusiveness that affirmed everything deeply human. He called it "the Cretan Glance." He was an earthy, impassioned writer—an embodiment of Homer's wave-washed island set in a wine-dark sea.

1. Kefi. A sense of buoyant defiance put Kazantzakis at odds with all of the establishments in his life. He challenged the intellectual academy, drinking the night away before taking his final exams at Athens. He resisted the church, saying the only sin God won't forgive is a man's refusing a woman who invites him to her bed. He shunned economic responsibility, experimenting with a hopeless ignite mining operation on the Greek coast. He challenged the political order, applauding the Russian Revolution as having given voice to the working class. He disparaged social propriety in general, celebrating earthy peasant life and writing in the common, demotic Greek of the people.

These themes are all in evidence in his best-loved novel, *Zorba the Greek*. The book juxtaposes the Boss, a repressed young Greek intellectual, with Alexis Zorba, a devil-may-care miner whose drinking, dancing, and impulsiveness exemplify the crazy abandonment of *kefi*. The word implies more than "joy"; it is spirit, folly, adrenaline, an enthusiasm that breaks into frenzy. It's Zorba tossing back a drink in a Greek taverna, then spontaneously breaking into a *zeibekiko* dance. He yields to the pulse of the bouzouki music, arms upraised, moving to the center of the room as others push back their chairs, clapping their hands in support. There's an infectious quality about his freedom. The carefree abandon of *kefi*.

Zorba sees the world afresh each day. Marveling at a lemon tree in blossom, he cries, "What is this, Boss? I swear I've never seen it before!" For him, "Everything seems to have a soul—wood, stones, the wine we drink and the earth we tread on. Everything, Boss, absolutely everything."[25]

Kazantzakis contrasts Zorba's zest for life with his own sense of himself as a writer who sits back, observing things at a distance. "You are a nanny goat," he scorned. "You feel hungry, but instead of drinking wine and eating meat and bread, you take a sheet of white paper, inscribe the words wine, meat, bread on it, and then eat the paper."[26] Nonetheless, he knew the power of words to effect change. He looked on the letters of the alphabet as more than "shameless demons." They were also his "twenty-six lead soldiers," an army raised in battle against all that threatens life.[27] He knew that words themselves could dance.

2. God-Wrestling. Kazantzakis was a spiritual rebel who remained intoxicated with God. His island experience helped to mold this second theme in his work. The divine, for him, was a "vehement chaos," a pulsing vitality like the crashing of ocean waves on shoreline rocks. On the outer islands (of Maine or the Aegean) you encounter a God not given to gentle amiability. All idols are smashed on the stone ledges beyond the shore. There you're face to face with a fierce majesty that brooks no equal. "Each man acquires the stature of the enemy with whom he wrestles," wrote Kazantzakis in his memoir, *Report to Greco*. "It pleased me, even if it meant my destruction, to wrestle with God."[28]

He knew that we must be fiercely faithful to our doubts. It's through darkness that we stumble into light, if we make it at all. God is the dark abyss with whom Jacob wrestles through the night, a mystery that can't be seen, but (paradoxically) can be touched—in water on the tongue, in the bark of a cypress tree, in the caress of a lover's fingertips. Kazantzakis esteemed Epaphus above all the other Greek gods. This was the God of touch, yearning to mix the warmth of the earth and the bodies of all living beings with his own. This is the God who came to Kazantzakis as a child. "He always came, a child like myself, and deposited his toys in my hands: sun, moon, wind. 'They're gifts,' he said, 'they're gifts. Play with them. I have lots more.'"[29]

This was also the Jesus Kazantzakis portrayed in *The Last Temptation of Christ*—the Nazarene who was tempted to give up the insanity of trying to save the world. He longed, instead, to take Mary Magdalene to his bed, to open a workshop in a distant village, and to raise his children like any ordinary man.[30] For Kazantzakis, the deepest impulse of our humanity is to embrace the flesh and subsequently turn it into spirit, to delight in the earth, seeing it transformed into light. For Jesus to be real, thought Kazantzakis, he had to wrestle with everything human.

> I knew that here on earth, for the full span of our lives, Christ was not the harbor where one casts anchor, but the harbor from which one departs, gains the offing, encounters a wild, tempestuous sea, then struggles for a lifetime to anchor in God. Christ is not the end. He is the beginning.[31]

In Jesus, and subsequently in Francis of Assisi, the Greek novelist discovered the three great gifts of God: "omnipotence without power, intoxication without wine, and life without death."[32] In a driven, tormented Jesus, he found the *élan vital* that his teacher Henri Bergson had emphasized—the creative pulse of evolutionary consciousness that drives the human spirit. But he also saw in Jesus a man staring into "the black eyes of the abyss" in the Garden of Gethsemane, wrestling with the terrifying secret that even God may not exist. There's no easy resolution to this kind of struggle. I find Kazantzakis closer to Kierkegaard's effort to continue believing while treading water over seventy thousand fathoms than to Nietzsche's despairing atheism.[33] Life and death grappled within him, but life always won.

3. *The Cretan Glance.* A last refrain in Kazantzakis's writing has to do with his philosophical embrace of opposites, something also influenced by his island experience. "Crete for me is the synthesis which I always pursue, the synthesis of Greece and the Orient."[34] To the East he gazed into the chaos of ancient mystery religions, the Shakti power of Hindu deities, the scimitar-waving ferocity of Turkish warriors. To the West he stared into the clear and distilled reason of classical Greece. How, he asked, do you peer into the abyss of the one without disintegrating? How do you honor the ordered mind of the other without becoming its slave?

He found an answer concealed in Crete's mythic past. There Theseus had overcome the terror of the Minotaur, using the thread of reason to make his way back out of the labyrinth. There the Minoan bull dancers at Knossos had leapt with thoughtful elegance on the backs of snorting, racing bulls. The Cretan glance looks both ways, joining stability and unruliness, Apollo and Dionysius, spirit and flesh. The two become one, transformed into something full of mystery.

This is the Odysseus that Kazantzakis describes in his sequel to Homer—the man who has embraced everything and become free of everything: religions, philosophies, political systems. He "has cut away all the strings."

He wants to try all the forms of life, freely, beyond plans and systems, keeping the thought of death before him as a stimulant . . . to whet his appetites in life, to make them more capable of embracing and of exhausting all things so that, when death finally came, it would find nothing to take from him, for it would find an entirely squandered Odysseus.[35]

MATURE ADULTHOOD: EMBRACING THE FULL CATASTROPHE

For Nikos Kazantzakis, the work of one's life is to reach beyond the cultural and religious mainstream, to dance with passion in the face of every trial and joy, to wrestle over the abyss with a wild and sensuous God. Only then, by embracing all of life's contradictions, do you perceive every individual piece as interconnected, woven into a whole.

Your work as a mature adult is to push enough edges—to make enough mistakes—to enter into the fullness of your strength. Your task is to integrate incongruities, to find your distinctive way of moving in the world, the island of your becoming. Bill Plotkin defines the stage of late adulthood as a time for bringing to fulfillment the gifts of one's soul work, exercising the delivery system that allows them to be shared with the world.

Ideally, at midlife you're welcoming a burgeoning diversity, a wealth of intercultural influences, emerging possibilities that challenge the tired expectations of others. You're embracing the island of the world, out there on the edge. Middle age, says David Whyte, is an illusory place between beginnings and endings. It goes on for years, it seems, and yet it barely exists. The "middle" is always a place for leaping to what is next.

Yet it's easy to be lost in its difficulties, settling for a life defined by career, institutions, conformity to the norm. Stalled in a narrow, rigid bind, you're driven by a frantic desire for what hasn't come—and *should* have come by now. The soul's most important work at such a time, says Kazantzakis, is to embrace the struggle—dancing on the edge, yielding to what is wild and unruly—until the passion is spent, the desire released. Only then do you find yourself wanting nothing more than what you already have and finding the entire world within it. Only then do you discern the interconnectedness of the whole, the secret of Kazantzakis's joie de vivre.

Tony De Mello tells a story about a temple that once stood on an island two miles out to sea.[36] It held a thousand bells—large and small, fashioned by the finest craftspeople in the world. When the trade winds blew, they rang out in a wild and reckless harmony, filling the hearts of those who heard it with a symphony of wonder and joy. People weary of their lives would come from far away to listen to the bells, to be set free from the cares that bound them.

But over the centuries the island sank into the sea, and with it the temple and the bells. Legend had it that they continued to ring in the deep sea currents and could still be heard by those who listened intently. Inspired by this tale, a despairing man traveled thousands of miles, determined to hear the bells. He sat for days on the shore, opposite the place where the temple had stood, and listened with all his might.

But he heard nothing more than the sound of the waves breaking on the shore. He tried to push through the distraction of the surf so he could hear the bells, but it wasn't possible. The clamor of the sea and its miserable waves flooded the universe.

He stayed there for weeks. When discouraged, he'd walk to a nearby village to listen to the stories of the old ones who'd heard the bells before. But then he'd despair again as he sat on the shore and heard nothing––nothing but the wretched sea.

Finally he decided to give up. Perhaps he wasn't one of those destined to hear the bells. Maybe the legend wasn't true after all. He decided to return home, admitting defeat. On his last day, he went to the beach to say farewell to the sea and sky, the wind and the coconut trees. He'd never realized how beautiful it was.

Lying there on the sand—looking up at the clouds, listening to the sea—he didn't resist the sound of the waves this time. Instead he gave himself to it—a pleasant, soothing sound it was. Soon he was lost in the repetitive voice of the sea, barely conscious of himself, so deep was the silence it produced in his heart.

Suddenly, in the depths of that emptiness, he heard it! The jingling of a tiny bell, followed by another and another. Soon every one of the temple bells was ringing out in a wild and reckless harmony, filling him with a symphony of wonder and joy, leaving him with what he'd been seeking all along. What simply *is*.

Maybe that's the secret of successfully negotiating the difficulties of life at midterm. If you would hear the bells, don't resist the sound of the waves. Give yourself to them. Life's reckless wonder lies hidden in the repetition of the ordinary.

***

"Happy is the man," said Kazantzakis, "who, before dying, has the good fortune to sail the Aegean Sea."[37] Years ago, that good fortune was mine, when my wife and I sailed to the island of Crete. We walked the Gorge of Samaria in the White Mountains, spent three glorious days in the tiny village of Chora Sfakion on the southern coast, and visited Kazantzakis's gravesite outside Heraklion. We were the only visitors that morning on the hill beyond the city walls. I placed a pebble on the raised stone that marks his grave, bearing a Greek inscription that translates as "I hope for nothing. I fear nothing. I am free." The man whose teachers included Nietzsche, the Buddha, and El Greco needed nothing more, in the end, than the scent of thyme and the rose-colored sea in the distance.

Nearby an old man who appeared to be the caretaker of the place was trimming flowers. He brought a small bouquet over to my wife and smiled. We spoke briefly; he was pleased that people had come so far to honor a writer from Crete. Later as we walked back into town, I had a strange feeling that we'd been talking to more than a rustic gardener. I suspected we'd met the poet himself, still tending the soil of his island home.

Kazantzakis was nursed, raised, and ravished by the island of Crete. With her three high summits, she was "a triple-masted schooner sailing in the foam," gleaming white, green, and rose in the morning sun. "A goodly number of pleasures have fallen to my lot in the course of a lifetime," he confessed, but none had surpassed the sight of Crete shining on the billows of the Aegean Sea.[38] The island was his teacher, lover, and antagonist. For him, it held the scent and taste of God.

EARTH: *The Elder*

"Praised be You, my Lord, through our Sister Mother Earth,
who sustains and governs us,
and who produces various fruit with colored flowers and herbs."

—Francis of Assisi, "Canticle of the
Creatures"[1]

As we move to the north quadrant of the path of transformation (on page XX), we enter the stage of elderhood. Here the soul comes into its own, grounded in the messiness of things, yet able to see with a new clarity. The crone or wise man delights in the child who is learning to fly, understands the adolescent's difficulty in controlling passion, and sympathizes with those harried souls at midlife who long to be able to flow. Yet the elders have become a people with larger allegiances. They're moving beyond the national, professional, and narrowly religious identities that may have formed them in the past.

Elders belong to the earth, honoring all the names of love. They tend the universe, offering blessing to everything wild. Theirs is a countercultural freedom, akin to mountain folk who don't mind being different in a world that passes them by. Knowing the call of the cave and its shadows, they've learned not to fear the dark. They hear the wolf's deep voice and remain fiercely committed to community.

Elders carry the energy of the King and Queen, offering wisdom and blessing to the realm.[2] They have a passion for the earth and future generations to come. Theirs is the season of winter and the color white—the color of snow and the hair of the elders.

They are firmly grounded, having sunk roots into the earth. This is the old farmer who each morning washed his hands before leaving the house, then stepped outside to pick up a handful of soil and rub it over his hands before starting to work. When his new young farmhand asked about the curious logic of this practice, he replied: "Don't you city boys understand anything? Inside the house it's dirt; outside it's earth. You take it off inside to eat and be with your family. You put it on outside to work and be with the animals."[3] The elders know the importance of being firmly grounded.

These older ones, having accepted their true office, aren't nearly as cautious as they used to be. Having spent the first half of their lives accumulating, in the second half they're now stripping away, says Joan Chittister. They're free to release the cares that had held them back in the past. They've learned what's worth fearing and what isn't. Consequently, she adds, "Old age is the time to be dangerous. Dangerously fun-loving, dangerously alive . . . This is the time to live with an edge, with strength, with abandon."[4] The true elders take great joy in this.

Yet their love of the earth makes them agitated about a throwaway culture that produces landfills without end, hazardous wastes that poison the ground, and the overuse of fertilizers and herbicides that deplete the soil. The world is a garden they cherish.

CHAPTER TWELVE

MOUNTAINS

HEMMED-IN-HOLLOW AND THE BAAL SHEM TOV

"Plants and animals change as one goes up the mountain, and so, apparently, do people."

—Diana Kappel-Smith, *Desert Time*[5]

"The true measure of a mountain's greatness is not its height but whether it is charming enough to attract dragons."

—Traditional Chinese Wisdom[6]

I was traveling into the mountains of northern Arkansas with my old friend Terry, a poet from the Arkansas Delta who reads Rilke and writes out of a landscape formed by the soybean and cotton fields of Crowley's Ridge, the music of B. B. King and Johnny Cash. We were on a mission that week in June to float the upper Buffalo River, to find the remains of a rundown theme park called Dogpatch USA, and to explore a mountain terrain where tongue-speaking members of the Assembly of God had long flourished.[7]

My personal agenda was to take a new look at a great Hasidic rebbe from within the context of a small mountainous community. I was curious as to whether the mountain confines of the American Midwest and Eastern Europe shared similar social and religious dynamics. Could the hill folk and charismatic believers of the Ozarks help me better to appreciate the Baal Shem Tov and his Jewish followers in the mountains of eighteenth-century Ukraine? To what extent did a highland topography lend itself to group solidarity, ecstatic spiritual experience, and social isolation?

In many ways, I was traveling back to my own roots on this trip. I could remember the tight-knit community of a nondenominational Bible church, as well as the stigma of being scorned as a religious fanatic from the rural South. As a youth, I'd treasured the escape afforded by palmetto swamps, the solace of scrub pines, the small wooden house my dad had built with his own hands. All of this prepared me for an encounter with the fervor of Hasidic spirituality and its unembarrassed celebration of difference.

Terry and I crossed the Missouri line into Arkansas on US 65, turning onto Highway 7 in the small town of Harrison. We were entering the green-saturated heart of the Boston Mountains, the youngest and tallest range of peaks on the Ozark Plateau. It's an enclave filled with oak-hickory-pine forests and spanned by the oldest National River in the United States. None of the summits here are much higher than 2,500 feet, but these are mountains with their own unique character, as distinctive as the people who live there.

Ozark mountain folk are strong individualists, deeply bound to a local community. They love the privacy their isolation affords. Living on small, hardscrabble farms dictated by the rough terrain, their mountain hollows foster independence. Their ancestors—largely of Scots-Irish descent—came from the Appalachians back East. These are people who value plainness, conservative in both politics and lifestyle. This makes them easy to stereotype. H. L. Mencken once jeered that "Arkansas stands for watermelons, the unshaven Arkie, the moonshiner, hogs, illiteracy, and hillbillies,"[8] an image that lingers to this day.

In 1967, a group of developers opened a theme park here called Dogpatch USA, playing on this familiar tune. They styled it as a typical Ozark village, based on Al Capp's popular comic strip *L'il Abner*. It had log cabins where Daisy Mae, Li'l Abner, and his dull-witted Pappy Yokum might have lived. You could take a railroad ride through Skunk Hollow, attend a Riverboat Music Show, and explore underground Mystic Caverns. The image of the lazy, fun-loving, banjo-playing, cousin-marrying Arkansas hick prevailed through it all. The project survived in one form or another for nearly twenty years, but eventually succumbed to the much greater success of Ozark developers to the north in Branson, Missouri.

Terry and I stopped at the weed-covered remains of the old Dogpatch site on our way to the river. Today it's just another Ozark hollow, filled with rotted buildings and corroded water slides. It's part of an economically depressed landscape characteristic of northern Arkansas in recent years. The Marble Falls Full Gospel Church stands across the road from the now-defunct park, and it's still active. The church is a quaint old building made of mortared river rocks. Here in the Bible Belt people still exercise the miraculous gifts of the Holy Spirit, sing gospel music with gusto, and exult in the power they find in the "name" of Jesus. These things bring back old memories.

On our way there, we'd noticed the predominance of charismatic religion in the town of Harrison. A town of 13,000 people, it has fifty-four churches, including eighteen Baptist and eleven Pentecostal congregations. It's also the home of Pastor Thomas Robb of the Christian Revival Center, who happens to be national director of the Ku Klux Klan. More than a hundred years ago, the town of Harrison drove out all of its African American residents. Racism and anti-Semitism continue to thrive in isolated communities in this area. On our way through town, we passed a large billboard reading. "Anti-Racist is a code word for Anti-White." Welcome to Harrison, it added, a town "with no bad neighborhoods." Perhaps alt-country singer Jim White would have considered it a good place to begin "searching for the gold tooth in God's crooked smile."[9]

Coming down from Harrison, Terry and I arrived at our river access point early on a rainy Wednesday morning. As we watched the stream rushing out from under the low-water bridge, we had second thoughts. There had been three days of rain and the river had risen two feet in the past twenty-four hours. Class II or III rapids were as much as these old boys could handle. But we tied our waterproof gear into the canoe, gritted our teeth, and headed out into the current.

It was faster even than it looked. We found ourselves taking in water at several sharp turns, holding our breath as we descended cascading rock ledges, and negotiating places with names like Killer Rock and Canoe-Wrecking Rapids. We passed waterfalls all along the banks—the pour-off of water from the bluffs above. To our amazement, the old duffers survived.

The Buffalo National River is as humbling as the wilderness through which it flows. When we canoed under five-hundred-foot-high cliffs, the mountains felt enclosing and constrictive. They shelter their own, but they don't welcome outsiders. The river seemed intent on rushing us through as quickly as possible. We had planned on three or four days, taking our time to explore numerous places along its banks. But it hustled us through in two days. We were continually maneuvering new drops and turns, unable to slow down quickly enough to beach the canoe at many of the favorable sites.

"We made it, Cap'n," Terry cried as we stopped that first night to camp at a place called Bear Creek Hollow. It was a mile down from Hemmed-In-Hollow with its stunning hike through dogwood and maple trees into the highest waterfall between the Appalachians and the Rockies. It tumbles nearly 210 feet from a limestone cliff above. We took the path to explore the falls before heading back to set up camp. Finding a spot wasn't easy. With all the gravel bars underwater, everything felt contained, hemmed-in. But we found a place to put our tents, ate a freeze-dried meal of teriyaki chicken and rice with apple crisp, and went to sleep to the sound of light rain falling.

That night I read by headlamp an old paperback I'd brought along, Martin Buber's *Tales of the Hasidim,* wondering about similarities between Hasidic Jews in the Carpathian Mountains and Pentecostal Christians in the Arkansas Ozarks. Do mountains like these exercise an isolating impulse, nurture a heightened spiritual zeal? I've never been to western Ukraine, but I have to imagine its snug valleys as similar in topography and sociology to what we'd found here.

The next day we took to the river again, hoping to stop at Indian Creek Canyon farther downstream. We came upon it too soon, however, and there was no way of doubling back. One of our guidebooks had described it as "the most picturesque area in the entire Ozark Mountain Region." A narrow, twisting canyon filled with caves and underground tunnels, it warned: "Dangerous hiking, don't go alone." That's a hard one to resist, but you always need to leave something for another trip. By nightfall we pulled into Kyle's Landing, our final stopping point. That night we slept under a clear sky, still in earshot of the water, knowing the mountains and the river had shown us their roughest and their best. We'd made it, nonetheless.

A PHENOMENOLOGY OF MOUNTAINS

Mountains cover 24 percent of the Earth's surface, accommodating 12 percent of the world's population in 120 different countries. They tend to be hotspots of cultural diversity. In the Hindu Kush of the Himalayas alone people speak more than a thousand different languages and dialects.

The world's mountains cross the globe in wide belts, or cordilleras. Two great bands of mountainous activity include the Pacific Belt in the west and the Eurasian Belt in the east. The former, known as "the rim of fire," circles the Pacific Ocean and contains most of the world's active volcanoes. The latter curves northwest from the Himalayas to the Caucasus, the Carpathians, the Alps, and the Pyrenees. Two hundred and fifty million years ago, the Ozarks were themselves part of a massive mountain chain, stretching from the Appalachians through present-day Missouri, Arkansas, and Oklahoma. But by the time the dinosaurs went extinct—65 million years ago—they had eroded to a vestige of their former selves.

The tallest mountains generally get the most attention. Fourteen of the world's peaks are more than 26,247 feet high. The region above 25,000 feet is known as a mountain's "death zone," an altitude the human body can only endure for a few days. Yet this is what attracts the most adventurous climbers. When Tenzing Norgay reached the summit of Mount Everest in 1953, he reverenced the mountain (like other Nepali sherpas) as *Chomolungma*, the "Mother Goddess of the World." By contrast, after finishing the ascent his climbing partner Edmund Hillary wisecracked to a member of the team, "Well, George, we've knocked the bastard off."[10] Some folks seem tone-deaf to mystery.

Smaller and older mountains are much more amenable to human life. They harbor the close-knit, insulated communities that interest me most: the Basques on the western edge of the Pyrenees in northern Spain; the gypsies (or Roma) in the mountains of Transylvania; the Quechua in the Andes of Ecuador and Peru; the Amish in the Piedmont region of the Appalachians; even snake-handling Pentecostals in the Smokies of eastern Tennessee. Stanchly devoted to their group identity and language, these are people often harassed by outsiders. They display a fierce devotion to the traditions that sustain them.

Mountains have been universally revered as places of divine/human encounter—from Machu Picchu in Peru and Mount Olympus in Greece to Mount Sinai in Egypt and the five sacred mountains of China. In the Bible, Abraham took his son to sacrifice him on Mount Moriah. Moses received the law on Mount Sinai. Elijah defeated the prophets of Baal on Mount Carmel. Jesus was transfigured on Mount Tabor.[11]

Mountains are places of transformation. Alchemists in the Middle Ages regarded the mountain peak as "the philosopher's oven." Carl Jung said, "The mountain . . . often has the psychological meaning of the self," summoning the soul to its inner work. The Dalai Lama suggested that "the most spiritual people on this planet live in the highest places."[12]

Indigenous people often perceive mountains as active agents—"elders" within the Earth community, personally interacting with human life. They do more than conserve rain and vegetation; they respond to those who seek their counsel. William Blake observed that "Great things are done when Men & Mountains meet. This is not done by Jostling in the Street."[13]

I experienced something of this myself a few years ago at a gathering with Bill Plotkin on the banks of the Rio Grande overlooking the Sandia Peaks north of Albuquerque. At the time I'd been doing some "father work," coming to terms with a lost dad I'd never really known. As an exercise, Bill sent us out to find something in the natural world that we could talk to and wait for a response. I wandered out among the sagebrush on the bosque, spending time with the Red Mountain, as the Santa Ana people call it. I sat for a long while looking up at the Sandia Crest, introducing myself, waiting patiently for the mountain to speak. But nothing came. I did what I'd been told to do, and the mountain didn't say a thing. Absolutely *nothing*. In frustration, I finally gave up and walked away. As I did so, I felt a resentment rising within me.

I knew I'd *been* there before. How many times in my life had I done everything right, following all the directions, but getting no response? Nothing, but silent indifference. Being *ignored*, as if I didn't count. Waiting for a reply that never came. I suddenly turned and exploded at the mountain in furious exasperation: "Fuck you . . . *Fuck* you!" And the tears came. The tears poured out and the mountain spoke at last, saying, "Your anger is welcome here. Your *anger* is welcome here."

Sometimes you wait a long time for the mountain (for anything) to speak. Only when the student is ready does the teacher come. But count on it, the encounter won't be what you expect. Henry David Thoreau learned this on his trek up Mount Katahdin in 1846. He was struck there by something "primeval, untamed, and forever untameable . . . made out of Chaos and Old Night."[14] It unhinged him completely.

Attitudes toward mountains have dramatically changed over the centuries. In the ancient world mountains were avoided, held in fear and apprehension. They weren't climbed. Since the end of the Enlightenment and the Romantic period, however, popular sentiment has changed to admiration and love. Yet ragged peaks can still trigger terror. A knife-edged crag in the wilderness of northern Maine left Thoreau grasping for words.[15]

MOUNTAINS, THE TZADDIK, AND THE HASIDIC MOVEMENT

In the early eighteenth century, the Carpathian Mountains in western Ukraine and southern Poland were the breeding ground for a new religious movement within Judaism. An obscure rabbi of humble origins captured the imagination of beleaguered Jews in scattered villages throughout the Poland-Lithuanian Commonwealth. His name was Israel ben Eliezer, but he was known as the Baal Shem Tov, "The Master of the Good Name" (1700–1760).

He lived in an apocalyptic era, full of catastrophe and dashed hopes. Half a century earlier, in 1648, a Cossack uprising had slaughtered tens of thousands of Jews living in small shtetls scattered throughout the mountains. Known as the Deluge, it was one of the bloodiest pogroms in history. The town of Medzhibozh, where the Baal Shem later took up residence, had almost been eradicated—2,500 people massacred. Pious Jews had implored the Holy One to send his Messiah, and a charismatic rabbi named Shabbetai Tzvi had stepped forward, claiming to be the promised one. The disappointment that followed his failure and the devastation of anti-Jewish violence left the faithful desperate, hungry for hope.[16]

Within this vacuum, the role of the *tzaddik* emerged among small, long-suffering Jewish communities. The tzaddik (or "righteous one") came to be recognized as a channel of divine grace, around whom the faithful (the Hasidim) gathered, benefiting from his teaching and prayers. The word "Hasid" comes from the Hebrew word *chesed*, referring to God's loving kindness for those without hope.

The Baal Shem Tov, also known as the Besht (an acronym of his title), became the most celebrated of these tzaddiks. Born to elderly parents in a small mountain village, he had been orphaned at the age of five. Taken in by the community, he gradually came to spend more and more time in the nearby forest, gathering herbs and learning the lore of the land. After he married, he and his wife lived in poverty, isolated in the Carpathian foothills. There he began retreating to a cave where he met a hidden tzaddik said to be none other than Ahijah the Shilonite, the mythical teacher of the prophet Elijah. After eighteen years of reclusive learning, at the age of thirty-six, Rabbi Israel revealed himself as the Baal Shem Tov—becoming a wandering healer, captivating storyteller, and ecstatic teacher of Torah.[17]

While his years of formation occurred in the seclusion of the mountains, the Besht's later work thrived on the steppes of western Ukraine, at Medzhibozh southeast of Kiev. As the movement expanded after his death, it spread once again into the mountains and beyond.

In the Jewish tradition at the time, the title "Baal Shem" referred to a spiritually gifted rabbi—one who allowed the four-letter name of God (YHWH) to vibrate within him as he prayed, producing the primal sound God had used in bringing creation into being. This released a healing power, occasioning miraculous answers to prayer.[18]

Hasidic Jews made their way to the Baal Shem to participate in his fervent prayers, as well as to ponder his interpretations of Torah. There they practiced ecstatic singing and dancing, breaking into jubilant melodies (*nigunim*) that employed nonsense syllables, akin to speaking in tongues. After an especially powerful teaching, the Besht might ask the faithful to place their hands on the shoulders of those next to them, forming a tight circle. As the people closed their eyes, they felt a sublime force flowing through the human ring, the divine presence moving among them.

One year, we're told, the Hasidim were dancing with the scrolls of the Torah as Reb Israel went into a trance. He entered the Garden of Eden and grasped a handful of leaves from the trees growing there. On returning, he crumbled the leaves in his fingers, filling the House of Study with the fragrance of paradise. On another mystical ascent to heaven, he asked the Messiah when he'd return to earth. "When all your teachings shall become known," he was told.[19]

The Hasidic movement attracted criticism from within Judaism itself, however. Some Talmudic scholars viewed the Hasidim as uneducated fanatics, undermining the vital importance of Torah study. The Baal Shem himself was steeped in the mysteries of Kabbalah, but wrote very little. The movement he inspired was primarily an oral phenomenon, spread by storytelling and euphoric devotion. But its effect on a Jewish community ravaged by suffering was profound.

Its subsequent influence on Western thought and culture has been enormous, inspiring theologians like Martin Buber and Abraham Heschel, artists like Marc Chagall, novelists like Elie Wiesel and Chaim Potok, leaders of Jewish renewal like Zalman Schachter-Shalomi, and even shaping klezmer music and the Yiddish theater.

THE TEACHINGS OF THE MASTER

The Baal Shem's gift was being able to express time-honored Jewish wisdom in ways that captured the popular imagination. Four themes flow from his mystical insights into the Torah, as filtered through his Carpathian Mountain experience.

1. Creation and the Shards of Light. If you had to summarize the rebbe's teachings in a single phrase, it would be these words from Isaiah 6:3: "The whole earth is full of God's glory." He knew that nature has no separate existence apart from God. In the Jewish mystical tradition of assigning numerical value to words in the Torah, the values of the words for nature (*ha-teva*) and God (*elohim*) are the same (86).[20] The Besht was intrigued by the Kabbalistic doctrine of creation as taught by Isaac Luria a century earlier. This affirmed that God, who had previously filled every existing space, contracted himself so that there would be room for the universe to exist.

This put the world at risk of falling in on itself, however. So God poured his Shekinah glory into vessels placed throughout the universe to hold everything together. These containers weren't strong enough to contain the divine light and they broke, leaving shards of light scattered throughout the world.[21]

Many rabbis saw this event as a catastrophe, requiring these shards of light to be gathered together to redeem the world (the work of *tikkun olam*, saving the Earth). But the Baal Shem saw it as a blessing, God's inadvertent way of filling the world with sanctity. No corner of the universe, he said, is without the divine presence. "He is everywhere, in every blade of grass, in every scudding cloud."[22] In his early years, Rabbi Israel was an ardent nature wanderer, walking from place to place as he preached, blessing the land as he went. He was one of many itinerant rebbes who helped to raise up the fallen sparks through their holy walking (*halikhah*).[23]

The Baal Shem taught that God had given each creature its own language for the praise of God's glory. His disciple, Dov Baer, the Maggid of Mezritch, once said of his master: "He taught me the language of birds, the great secrets of the sages, and the mystical meanings of many things." Another disciple, Reb Shlomo of Karlin, urged the faithful to learn the languages of the grasses, animals, trees, and stones in blessing God. They honored the Jewish holiday Tu B'Shevat, the New Year of the Trees, celebrated each spring when sap starts flowing in the trees again. They knew that everything sings, every species of tree with its own melody of adoration.[24]

2. *Devotional Fervor and Storytelling.* Once you're aware of the divine splendor saturating the world with light, said Rabbi Israel, you'll spontaneously give yourself to a devotion expressing itself in every aspect of your life. This entails a "cleaving of the heart" to the Lord (*devekut*, as in Deuteronomy 4:4). Whatever you're doing—whether digging potatoes, milking the cow, or lighting Shabbos candles—your thoughts never wander far from God. The Holy One becomes a powerful, immediate presence.[25]

The Hasidic rebbes found storytelling to be one of the best vehicles for conveying this sense of immediacy. In expounding biblical narratives, the storyteller was able to "make his listeners *there*," vividly re-creating the drama of the text in the weaving of the tale. When Rabbi Shmelke of Nikolsburg told the story of the crossing of the Red Sea, his listeners unconsciously lifted the hems of their kaftans to avoid the salty spray of the water rising around them.[26]

Years ago I found myself sitting on the floor of a rabbi's living room, listening to Reuven Gold, a Hasidic storyteller from Chicago. I imagined myself sitting at the feet of the Baal Shem as this large man with bushy beard, long side curls, and tears in his eyes brought to life the stories of the great rebbe.[27]

He told how the Besht and his scribe were once held captive on a desert island. The worst part of their suffering was that they'd forgotten the teachings of the Torah, everything they'd been studying for years. The rebbe asked his assistant if he could remember *anything* whatever. "Nothing," the scribe replied, "except maybe a few letters of the alphabet." "What are you waiting for, then!" cried the rebbe. "Aleph, beth, gimel, . . . daleth," the scribe hesitantly began as the master joined in. The two of them recited the first four letters of the Hebrew alphabet, over and over again, slowly at first and then more vigorously. Caught up in the power of prayer, overturning the laws of time and geography, the Baal Shem and his scribe suddenly found themselves back home in the House of Study, remembering all of the wisdom they'd lost.[28] Ardor was able to accomplish what learning could not.

3. *Contagious Joy.* In an age of despair, when cruelty seemed to have full rein, Rabbi Israel was unreservedly given to joy. He saw only good in the world. Despite the apparent "exile of God's Presence," he knew that a hidden divine force sustained everyone's existence, even in the moment when they transgressed God's will. Evil has no power, claimed the Baal Shem, apart from this underlying actuality of good.[29]

Hence, laughter should be acknowledged as the highest form of absolute trust in the goodness of God. "Weeping is very bad, for one must serve G-d in joy," said the Master of the Good Name. "If one weeps out of joy, only then is it good."[30] In the early days of the movement, the Hasidim were referred to as the *freilicheh*—the "happy ones." They affirmed joyousness as a biblical command.

When asked why the Hasidim were given to such dancing and delight, the Baal Shem replied:

> "When a person experiences the joy that he's actually a part of God, that he is bone of His bones and flesh of His flesh, so to speak, that there's nothing separating him from his Creator, then, words . . . are superfluous, because they're only garments—mere external coverings—for the feelings and thoughts within them.[31]

One *has* to dance. Centuries later, Elie Wiesel marveled at Hasidic Jews singing in the boxcars on their way to Auschwitz.

The Besht knew that even the mountains and hills burst into song, in a language he understood (Isaiah 55:12). In one story told of him, robbers were pursuing the rebbe as he walked through the wilds of the Carpathian Mountains. Coming to the edge of a cliff overlooking a deep ravine, he saw that there was no way of escape. But as he prayed, the adjoining mountain moved toward him, filling the valley between them. He walked across on level ground unharmed, as the mountains then moved apart again. The robbers were dumbfounded. "The man who looks only at himself cannot but sink into despair," said the Master, "yet as soon as he opens his eyes to the creation around him, he will know joy."[32]

4. *The Faith of the Common People.* A final theme basic to the teachings of the Baal Shem was that authentic spiritual knowledge was best found among the simple, unpretentious people of the mountain villages. These were the shoemakers, chicken farmers, tailors, and innkeepers who made up his followers. He pointed out that God had appeared to Moses in an ordinary thorn bush, set aflame in the desert. "It is in the simple folk—the 'lowly' thorn-bush," he said, "that this insatiable Divine flame is found," there in the unquenchable thirst of the humble.[33]

The Baal Shem showed the same respect for dairy farmers as he did the great rabbinical masters. He also had a special regard for those who'd sinned greatly, convinced that penitent transgressors possess a sanctity far greater than the virtuous who'd never sinned. "The most righteous men are unworthy of standing in the place occupied by repentant sinners," he claimed. "Our sages say there are two ways of serving the Creator: one is the way of the righteous, the second, the way of the *baal teshuvah*."[34] The latter is a "master of repentance," one who's exceptionally bold in seeking God's forgiveness, despite the shame of his past.

You see the master's love of simple folk in the tale of a Ukrainian peasant who came with his son for the rebbe's Yom Kippur service one year. The boy had struggled with a learning disability all his life, unable to recite any of the holy prayers. His father kept him close, lest he eat something out of ignorance on the solemn fast day. The boy had brought his flute with him, carried in his coat pocket. He was accustomed to playing it while he watched his father's sheep and goats back home. No one, of course, played music on the Day of Atonement. One didn't even touch a musical instrument.

The father was appalled when his son whispered during the afternoon *musaf* prayer that he wanted to play his flute, and he told him to be still. The child asked again later during the *minha* prayer, and his father rebuked him: "Don't even touch the thing!" Growing more agitated, the boy eventually cried out, "Whatever happens, let me play some notes on my flute!" The father was terrified and grabbed the flute in his coat pocket, holding it through the cloth so as not to defile himself or allow the boy to get to it. But during the closing *neila* prayer, the boy suddenly tore the flute from his pocket and his father's grasp, and let out a single powerful note.

Everyone gasped. The father was horrified. But the Baal Shem shouted with joy on finishing his prayer, saying that with the voice of his flute the boy had lifted up all of their prayers in a final note of praise. Unable to utter a word of prayer himself, the boy had felt the fervent entreaties of those around him burning like a fire within. So his passionate, concentrated burst on the flute had been offered up in perfect purity, carrying the prayers of all the others with it.[35]

Such was the character of the Baal Shem Tov: wonder-worker and peasant, mystic and holy fool, a teacher formed by the mountains he loved.

MOUNTAIN WISDOM AND THE ELDER'S ROLE

Elders in every society have traditionally provided the stability and perspective that mountains exemplify. Old and weathered, they constitute a continuing source of insight for the community. Thoreau thought that every college claiming to impart wisdom should be located at the base of a mountain. "Every visit to its summit would, as it were, generalize the particular information gained below, and subject it to more catholic tests." The advantage of such a location, he thought, would be "as good at least as one well-endowed professorship."[36]

"Like mountain climbers who have scaled a high peak," says Zalman Schachter-Shalomi, the spiritual elders "have achieved a vantage point in old age from which to observe the path of [their] ascent." They undertake the harvesting of their lives, appreciating the contributions they've made, discerning what remains unfinished, and passing on a legacy. Such work occupies the October years of life, he thought, from age sixty-three to seventy. It's followed by the November years (seventy to seventy-seven) when one attends to the well-being of the planet, and the December years (seventy-seven to eighty-three) when one prepares for the last creative transition into death.[37]

Reb Zalman mentions the Baal Shem Tov as having passed through each of these stages with aplomb. Surrounded by disciples at his death, he assured them: "I know clearly that I'll exit through this door and immediately enter through another door."[38] For him, a well-lived life meant transformation into ever-greater mystery.

Joanna Macy sees the elder as absorbed in "deep time work," sensitive to the sweep of the Earth's evolutionary movement from the past and into the future. She laments the fact that our culture is increasingly "cut off from nature's rhythms." We're "marooned in the present," losing our connection with ancestors and descendants alike.[39] Bill Plotkin sees the elder as linking herself to life's interconnecting web, caring for the soul of the human and other-than-human community. She "can now both hear and speak, fluently, a language older than words."[40]

My own experience in becoming a grandparent has vastly deepened my sense of investment in a world beyond myself. Because of Elizabeth, I become one of the ancestors myself, obliged to speak for a world I hope she will inherit.

Why, then, are the elders important, asks Joan Chittister? "If for no other reason than that they are really the only ones who are free to tell the truth. They have nothing to lose now: not status, not striving, not money, not power. They are meant to be the prophets of a society, its compass, its truth-tellers." We need the sage, the shaman, the tzaddik and bodhisattva. What the elder offers is a grounded wisdom, an active hope, a discernment of spirits.[41] The Baal Shem possessed them all in spades.

RETURNING TO A MOUNTAIN VILLAGE

As Terry and I left the Buffalo River and the wet, green mountains of northern Arkansas, we passed again through the small town of Harrison. It took me back again to my past. I remembered the comfort of a faithful cadre for whom the scorn of others is a confirmation of their chosen-ness. I recalled the fervid preaching of revival evangelists, the "white" and "colored" drinking fountains in downtown Orlando, tales of cross-burnings throughout central Florida, the stigma of growing up poor and uneducated. But I also pondered what the Baal Shem had reawakened within me: the hallowedness of ordinary folk, the power of storytelling, the joy of those living close to the land.

We stopped to eat at T's Barbeque Restaurant off Main Street in Harrison. We left the jeep filled with camping gear out front, thinking we'd fit in like any of the good old boys. But as orphaned sons of the rural South, we were torn. John Deere caps, Carhartt jeans, and long vowels felt comfortable. But Confederate flag patches on camo jackets were jarring.

Like J. D. Vance in his *Hillbilly Elegy*, I realized I no longer belonged to the world I'd left behind nor entirely to the one I'd adopted. For years I'd walked the corridors of a Catholic university, feeling ashamed of the down-home simplicity, the naïve but tenacious faith I'd carried from my fundamentalist past. I'd spent my first few years without indoor plumbing, growing up in a storefront church that had previously been a hardware store, going to Moody Bible Institute after high school.

Yet sitting in that small-town Arkansas diner I was just as embarrassed to admit that I'd done doctoral work in Princeton, taught with the Jesuits for years, and published books with Oxford University Press. I felt like a traitor to my roots, an outsider in *both* places! "When you go from working-class to professional-class," says Vance, "almost everything about your old life becomes unfashionable at best or unhealthy at worst."[42]

There in Harrison I was brought face to face with the ambiguities of eighteenth-century Hasidic Jews in the Carpathian Mountains and uncompromising evangelical believers in the Arkansas Ozarks. I was obliged to affirm the dignity and the radical "differentness" that characterized each of them. I too had been negotiating split worlds all of my life.

Mountains and mountain communities are places set apart. They draw people by their remoteness and height, their opportunity for escape. They cast long shadows, creating a disturbing play of light and dark—chiaroscuro. Coming to Arkansas, Terry and I were taken back to our Southern roots, to the mystique of the Ozarks, the romance of the hills, but the river had rushed us through as if we'd never belonged. We hadn't, after all, been able to return home. We couldn't identify with the racism of marginalized whites, the fervor of Pentecostal religion, the stereotype of the Dogpatch hillbilly. Though we still carried each of these inside, we realized we'd never entirely belonged anywhere. We'd lived a partitioned life, torn between who we had been and what we'd become.

How, then, do you make peace with a world (with worlds) to which you don't entirely belong? How do you make peace with *yourself*, owning the rejected parts of a past you find hard to accept? If you don't do this, these things become part of your shadow, a projection onto others of what you can't acknowledge in yourself.

It happens to me as I find myself wary of super-zealous believers, embarrassed by my family roots, blind to my white privilege. It happens to people in the Arkansas hill country, feeling left out of the cultural mainstream. Some of them drop over the edge in their embitterment, projecting onto African Americans what they hate in themselves, blaming their woes on the "government," becoming scornful and estranged. Others sink their roots into the land, loving the verdant hills of the Ozarks, finding solace in their fervent Baptist or Pentecostal faith.

Marginalized Jews in eighteenth-century Ukraine faced the same dilemma. They were drawn to a Hasidic rebbe who found joy in everything around him, discovering shards of light throughout the green mountains, discerning beauty in stark simplicity. He refused to give in to rancor, affirming hope in the midst of a desperate world. People like this are the ones most deserving of a hillbilly elegy. The salt of the earth, they invite us to the best of what we've been, to the gift of simple things.

This book is about nurturing the conversations we need to have with the others, with *all* the others: teachers we've come to honor in the natural world and other teachers we've suppressed or denied. The ones we're tempted to dismiss as ignorant or overzealous may be shadowy images of what we've hidden in ourselves all along. It took an outwardly backward Arkansas village to remind me of this once again.

HOW MOUNTAINS SPEAK

Looking back on my experience over the years in the Missouri Ozarks, I'm wondering how mountains exercise an effect on the spiritual life. It's a question I'm asking throughout this book about canyons, trees, rivers, and birds as well. How do they speak, occupying the human imagination, stirring images of depth, height, flow, and flight? They suggest more than themselves, evoking a mystery beyond our grasp. We try to understand them by telling stories, by turning them into metaphors. That's what I did in seeing the Boston Mountains of Arkansas as a mirror of my childhood home.

But we also have to let them stand as mysteries in themselves. The Zen master Dōgen argued that mountains and rivers are sutras in their own right, boldly proclaiming—in their apparent permanence and transience—simply what *is*.[43] I need to sit, at length, in the memory of those disturbing and alluring mountains along the Buffalo River, and not be so quick to identify them as an emblem of something other than what they are.

A ninth-century Chinese Buddhist master summarized the course of his life: "Before I had studied Ch'an (Zen) for thirty years, I saw mountains as mountains, and rivers as rivers. When I arrived at a more intimate knowledge, I came to the point where I saw that mountains are not mountains, and rivers are not rivers. But now that I have gotten its very substance I am at rest. I now see mountains once again as mountains, and rivers once again as rivers."[44]

We start by seeing nothing that we don't expect to see, not having paid attention to what's really there. Clueless as we are, a tree is a tree is a tree. A mountain is that tall thing on the horizon.

But as we open ourselves to what we see, we suspect a mystery lurking nearby. We look for the sacred just beyond our grasp. The religious impulse is to reduce the tree to something we can "see through," imagining a world of transitory things that point to a transcendent reality wholly apart from it. We create a dualistic universe, waiting for the mystery to break in from without.

Yet there comes a point where disillusionment sets in, where we abandon the hope of some dramatic, earth-shattering experience of the Holy. We may never speak in tongues. The Shekinah glory may never overwhelm us with light. If we can sit in that emptiness long enough (accepting the mountain as mountain), we may find another truth sneaking up on us, a growing serenity with what's simply there, with what we already have, what we've known all along: our connectedness to everything else, our utter inseparability from God.

The tree then becomes a Buddha; the mountain a shard of light. We see ourselves and the tree, ourselves and the mountain, as one. We enter a unitive consciousness, viewing each piece as part of the whole. Our relationship to everything changes. We're no longer seeing *through* things, but seeing things through. This is the work of *tikkun olam*, the healing of creation.

It's the unitive work to which I'm now called. It's something far different from the "mountain-top experience" I sought in the religious fervor of my childhood. When the Psalmist prays (Psalm 121:1–2), "I lift up my eyes to the mountains from whence my help comes . . . from the Lord, the Maker of heaven and earth," he's referring to more than a peak on the distant horizon. He's looking into the farthest depths of himself, where the Holy One dwells, where he and everything else are one.

CHAPTER THIRTEEN

CAVES

LEWIS CAVE AND IGNATIUS OF LOYOLA

"The cave you fear to enter holds the treasure you seek."

—Joseph Campbell[1]

"It is not unlike a black liquid. The darkness has a life of its own. It stalks you. It crawls and creeps around you as you move. At every opportunity it seems to sweep up and cling to your back. You actually feel it sometimes . . . unrelenting and unforgiving."

—H. Dwight Weaver, *Missouri Caves in History and Legend*[2]

Missouri caves are sealed to protect endangered gray and Indiana bats. I'd been given the combination for the padlock on the steel gate at the mouth of this particular cave, but I had a problem. If I reached around the post to lock it again after I'd gotten inside, I wouldn't be able to see the numbers when I wanted to *un*lock it on leaving. Should I lock myself in with no way of escape until my friends from the Caves and Karst Conservancy arrived the next day? Or leave it unlocked, with the possibility of someone coming in behind me during the night? Meth cookers in rural Missouri came to mind. Crazy things go through your head when you're spending a night alone in a remote cave down in the Ozarks.

Lewis Cave is in Ripley County in southwest Missouri, not far from the Arkansas line. The historic Natchitoches Trace passes nearby, a Native American trail to the Southwest used by pioneers in the nineteenth century. I'd taken Highway 160 west from Poplar Bluff, passing through the county seat of Doniphan, population 14,000. During the Civil War, the entire town, including the courthouse, had been burned to the ground by Union Army soldiers taking revenge on pro-Confederate guerrilla forces operating out of the area, hiding in nearby caves.

Located several miles north of town, Lewis Cave was one of the largest in the area. A spring-fed stream flows from it into Big Barren Creek, eventually making its way to the Mississippi River.

For thousands of years this winding passage has been carved by water eating its way through limestone. Southern Missouri has more than 6,400 caves, forming a karst geography full of mysterious sink holes and underground caverns. Folktales tell of giant cave bears lurking inside, moonshiners making illegal whiskey, counterfeiters and bandit gangs like Jesse James, even the hidden entrance to a lost silver mine. And of course, there's Tom Sawyer and Becky Thatcher lost in a dark cavern with their last candle burning out. Back in 1930, the cave's owner, James Lewis, tried to make it into a show cave, hanging a few electric lights and charging admission. Apparently it wasn't showy enough, and his project folded.

I'd arrived at the entrance of the cave that morning, having come prepared for the experience, or so I thought. I had the required three sources of light that you need for caving, a helmet, knee pads, extra clothing to keep me warm and dry. I'd been given a description of what to expect—encouraged to avoid side passages where I might get lost and to keep my head down as I crawled through narrow places. I'd been told that I'd be wading through knee-deep water several hundred feet in and to look for a notch in the rock on the other side as I crossed. I was holding my pack overhead with water nearly up to my chest before I realized I was headed in the wrong direction. Having veered off to the right, I'd followed the wrong notch. This was my first unnerving mistake.

With wet clothes, slippery shoes, and a steady underground temperature of 58 °F, I needed to find a campsite and get into dry things. Eventually I located a relatively flat place where I could lay out my pad and sleeping bag, and where water wasn't dripping continually from overhead. It was less than a thousand feet in, but I couldn't see my hand in front of my face. I would spend the night there, alone in the dark.

The cave goes back more than three thousand feet, opening into larger rooms here and there. It continues in an underwater passage even beyond that. Scuba divers are still exploring how far in it goes. The sound of moving water echoes down the corridors like distant voices. Stalactites in the shape of soda straws hang from the ceiling, now and then reaching down in long arms of wet rock, even folds of flowing drapery. Blind cave fish swim in the dark water, albino salamanders you can see right through, bats clinging to the roof. The complete absence of light was unsettling.

After initially climbing into my sleeping bag to get warm, I had fallen asleep. I woke up with no idea what time it was. You experience a strange quality of timelessness inside a cave. Without the sun as a measure, time loses its sense of passing. It's always night; you don't know when it's time to sleep or eat or stay awake.

Leaving my gear, I took off to do some exploring farther down the cave, wanting to reassure myself as to what was and wasn't there. I had to be careful on the slippery clay, especially when climbing over rocks. Most cave accidents are caused by loss of light, flash flooding, or serious injury from a fall.

All around me the cave walls sparkled in the light of my headlamp, because of dripping water or shiny mineral deposits. In the absence of all but a small circle of light you appreciate the subtlety of colors. There were multiple shades of black and gray outlining the walls and ledges. Rust-red clay lay underfoot; straw-colored sand spread over the creek bottom.

I went far enough to hear the rush of deeper water in the distance beyond a high chert bridge, then made my way back to the campsite. There I ate a meal of freeze-dried beef stroganoff and trail mix with hot chocolate. I proceeded to journal into the night (or was it day?) as I tried to deal with what had been rising within me on coming into the cave. The Psalm in the lectionary for the day, number 139, was disquietingly appropriate. "If I make my bed in the depths, You are there."

Entering the cave I knew I'd be physically safe if I took the necessary precautions. There were no monsters hiding inside. But of all the trips I've made into backcountry over the years, I had more fear in anticipating this one than any other. It wasn't just my misgivings about spending the night alone in a space five to nine feet high, nine to eighteen feet wide, and a half a mile deep. I was taking a lot of inner baggage along with me at the time as well, struggling with my faith once again. I was coming to terms with the enigmatic figure of Jesus who had haunted me all of my life. Underground, in complete darkness, is probably the *last* place you want to go to wrestle with God.

THE FEAR AND WISDOM OF THE CAVE

There are elemental landscape archetypes that reach deep into the psyche, awakening unresolved fears. We've seen it already with respect to wildfires, windstorms, canyons, and raging rivers. Tales of descending into a dark cave and finding your way out again run through the literature and folklore of many cultures—from Theseus in his labyrinth on Crete to the cave in the Misty Mountains where Bilbo Baggins found Gollum's "Precious," the ring of power. Caves evoke uncommon terror, even as they disclose an equally frightening wisdom.

Mircea Eliade observed that the cave played an important role in shamanic initiation rites. It symbolized passage into another world. For the initiated the cave became a luminous place.[3] The Yaqui Indians in the Sonoran Desert of southern Arizona tell of a sacred cave on the slopes of the Red Mountain, Sikil Kawi. It's a half-mythical place that's difficult to find. The cave's opening is no larger than that of a small fox den. You squeeze yourself into a narrow passageway between the rocks, moving into the darkness. You sit on a log to rest, but the log turns into a snake that wraps itself around you. Wherever you look, wild animals move in the shadows—old memories of things you've feared all of your life.

If you show no terror, an old man leads you into an inner cavern where any talent (any gift) you might ever have wanted can be seen hanging from the walls. You're free to choose whatever you desire. Maybe it's the gift of writing or storytelling, the talent of playing the flute or carving masks, the art of training horses or being able to make yourself invisible. You only have to know what you want, and even that knowledge can grow out of the darkness there.

When you leave, however, you pass by a pit full of rattlesnakes. In that moment, if you succumb to your fear—if you try to deny the frightening and broken places in your life—your fear will change you into one of the animals you'd seen in the cave. But if you get back to the world again (and one can never be sure)—if you carry with you the fearlessness you found as well as the gift you chose—you'll have the freedom to practice that gift with fullness for the rest of your life. According to Yaqui wisdom, appropriating your gift is a matter of handling your terror.[4]

Yet there are times when the fear of the cave can be so incapacitating that you can't imagine yourself escaping its horror. In the *Diagnostic and Statistical Manual of Mental Disorders* you find environmental phobias such as nyctophobia—an intense and unreasoning fear of the dark, often accompanied by panic attacks, breathlessness, and heart palpitations.[5] It's an unusual pathology, yet all of us react to horror stories and films about being trapped in a dark place or buried alive. We either love them as a cathartic release or avoid them in every way possible.

I remember my first exposure to Edgar Allan Poe's short story "The Cask of Amontillado." The protagonist lures his enemy into the underground catacombs of an Italian town, with the promise of a taste of rare wine. There he chains him to a niche in the wall and seals him in with brick and mortar as his victim watches in helpless horror. Audrey Hepburn, in the 1967 film *Wait Until Dark*, plays a young blind woman trying to evade a desperate killer in her darkened apartment. In the cult classic film *Night of the Living Dead* (1968), zombies attack people trapped in the dark cellar of a rural farmhouse.

Caves, in short, are places where frightening things lurk or where we try to hide from still more frightening things. In scripture, the cave is a place for confronting the terrors of death. David hides from King Saul in a cave in the wilderness of Engedi. Elijah flees from Jezebel to a cave on Mount Horeb, where he hears God's still, small voice. Jesus stands before a cave tomb, shouting "Lazarus, come forth!," and Mary and Martha's fears are transformed forever. Moses hides in the cleft of the rock, where he can glimpse God's passing without dying of the shock.[6]

Caves carry us back into deep time. At Lascaux in southern France there are cave paintings of horses and stags that are more than 17,000 years old. Gabarnmung Cave in Australia's Northern Territory has paintings more than 35,000 years old. It's a virtual Sistine Chapel covered with images of crocodiles, kangaroos, and other sacred figures from the Dreamtime.

In some cultural traditions, caves play an important role in creation stories. The Navajo in New Mexico speak of the first people (the Dineh) as emerging from underground, from a hole in the roof of the underworld. Their kivas are cave-like places dug into the earth for conducting sacred rituals. A hole in the center of the dirt floor (the *sípapu*) symbolizes the original place of emergence.

The cave is the womb of Mother Earth, a place of birth and renewal. In Plato's myth of the cave, the philosopher moves through a world of shadows into the light of reason and beauty. St. Benedict lived in a cave in the mountains southeast of Rome for three years before starting his monastic community. Muhammad, in a cave on Mount Hira, heard the voice of the Angel Gabriel reciting the words of the holy Quran. The underground chamber becomes a portal between worlds—a place of illumination where the hero finds the dragon's treasure, where new life emerges.

Caves come in all shapes and sizes, depending on how they've been formed geologically. Solution caves are carved by surface water cutting through soluble rock. Rich in carbon dioxide, the water seeps through limestone or dolomite, forming a weak carbonic acid that eats into the stone. Mammoth Cave in Kentucky is a good example. The longest cave in the world, it has 450 miles of mapped passages, winding five levels deep into the earth.

Sea caves are cut out of coastal rock by ocean waves. The world's largest, Matainaka Cave in New Zealand, is more than five thousand feet long. Glacier caves are caused by meltwater running through or under a glacier. Volcanic lava tubes are created when lava flows beneath the hardened surface of an earlier flow. A lava cave forty miles long runs beneath the slopes of Kilauea on the Big Island of Hawaii. Speleologists explore the way these caves develop, the rock formations they produce, and the creatures that live in them.

I was stunned by what we found in Lewis Cave when my caving friends arrived the next day and we ventured further into its depths. We saw fossilized rocks known as stromatolites on the cave floor, left over from the Paleozoic sea that covered southern Missouri five hundred million years ago. These are small rounded mounds built up over time from multiple layers of blue-green algae. They represent the earliest record of life on Earth. The oldest ones ever found may be more than 3.5 billion years old. There in the bowels of the Earth, where life remains utterly foreign and scarce, I encountered one of the earliest forms of life on the planet.

In the "dark night" passages of our lives, we hope to find signs of life in the cave's darkness. It can happen, if we wait long enough. Given sufficient imagination, and grace, new possibilities arise. Ignatius of Loyola learned as much at a turning point in his life, discovering unexpected gifts in an underground darkness.

Ignatius and the Cave at Manresa

Ignatius of Loyola (1491–1556) was born in northern Spain to a family of the Basque nobility. The Basques remain fierce defenders of the land they've held for thousands of years in the western Pyrenees. Basque, they claim, was the language spoken by Adam and Eve in the Garden of Eden. The devil himself studied it for seven years, but never learned more than three words.

When Ignatius was a teenager, his father sent him to the royal court in Madrid, where he flourished as a promising young knight. His friends called him Iñigo, and he was admired him for his wit and reckless exuberance. He had an eye for the ladies and a readiness to fight at the drop of a hat.[7] When the French invaded the nearby town of Pamplona in 1521, he sprang to the defense, rallying his men atop the walls. But his career as a warrior ended when a cannon ball shattered one of his legs. He walked with a limp for the rest of his life.

As he recovered from multiple surgeries, Ignatius read the lives of the saints and experienced a dramatic conversion. He envisioned himself becoming a soldier for Christ, beginning a valiant new quest by making a pilgrimage to Jerusalem, but he only got as far as the town of Manresa near Barcelona. There his illusions were shattered. Everything fell apart, and Iñigo passed through a dark night of the soul. He stayed for almost a year, living in a cave for several months. There he started to write his *Spiritual Exercises.*

From the mouth of his limestone cave near the River Cardoner, he could look back on the saw-toothed ridge of Montserrat ten miles away. That's where he'd stopped on his way there, leaving his sword and dagger behind, praying all night before the Mary altar at the Benedictine abbey on the mountain's slopes. He'd envisioned himself doing great things for God.

But in Manresa the harsh symbolic realities of the mountain, river, and cave came together for him. He'd always aspired to the mountain heights—striving to be the most impressive knight at court, the bravest soldier, and now the best of all the saints. Suddenly the grandiosity of his life—his immense capacity for self-deception—became painfully apparent. It forced him down the mountain and into the cave, facing the work of carving out the canyon of his inner life. It proved the hardest time of his life, undercutting the bedrock of everything he'd known.

For the first time he found himself alone without an admiring audience, with no one to impress by his reputation. The once-proud soldier fell into a dark depression over the hollowness of what his life had been and uncertainty as to what was coming next. The elegant courtier let his hair and fingernails grow. He begged for food in the streets and went day after day without eating. Swallowed up by a sense of desolation, he feared God could never forgive him for his sins. He was tempted to commit suicide, to throw himself into a crevasse in the depths of the cave.

But then came a breakthrough. The thirty-year-old cavalier had always been a man given to his senses: beautiful women, fine clothes, the taste of good wine, the thrill of hand-to-hand fighting. He now sensed God speaking to him through the surrounding landscape. He received a vision that he later described as the single most powerful experience of his life. It came as he sat by the river outside the cave. He was suddenly aware of being surrounded by beauty. "The eyes of his understanding began to open."[8]

Iñigo perceived the whole of creation in a new light, "seeing God in all things"—a central theme he'd develop through the rest of his life. He noticed multiple layers of wonder that he traced through the natural world, revealing God's sustaining love at every point: in the *existence* of bedrock elements like water and rock; in the flowering, animated *life* of plants; in the sensate *feeling* of which animals are capable; and finally in the sparkling *intelligence* of human beings. Each of these steps led him ultimately to an awareness of himself (and everything else) as a dwelling place of the Divine Majesty, suggesting the image and likeness of God.[9]

He also received a vision of Jesus, seeing the man of Nazareth "in all of his humanity." The God he sought had to be anchored in this-worldly sensory experience, in God become flesh. It wasn't abstract ideas about Jesus that persuaded him, but specific and earthy images of a God alive in this world. He was drawn to Jerusalem, so he could touch and see the actual places where the man had lived, this new captain now demanding his loyalty. The notion of contemplating Jesus in the physical places he'd occupied became a thread running throughout the *Exercises*.[10]

A fearless new integrity emerged out of his cave experience at Manresa, a new courage based not on Basque machismo and romantic chivalry, but on Iñigo's confidence that the world is filled with God's glory and that it dwelt in him as well.

After returning from Jerusalem, he spent the better part of a dozen years getting an education, at first learning Latin with school children in Barcelona and ending by earning a master's degree at the University of Paris. In Paris he gathered a cadre of companions who became the first members of the Society of Jesus, founded in 1540. As general of the order for the next fifteen years, Ignatius dispatched Jesuit missionaries around the world—establishing schools and colleges, meeting the needs of the poor, and adapting their vision of Christian faith to the cultures to which they came.

IGNATIAN SPIRITUALITY: IMAGINATION AND SOUL WORK

It's no accident that Iñigo began taking notes for his *Spiritual Exercises* in a cave. There in the subterranean darkness, he explored the complex of motives, attractions, and revulsions that stir in the human psyche—leading toward wholeness or disintegration. This is the basic stuff of soul work, he came to learn.

Ignatian spirituality is different from the sublime, self-emptying mysticism we've seen in Farid ud-Din Attar, Origen, or Gregory of Nyssa. Its goal is union with God in Christ, but its starting point is human experience at its grittiest depths and most dizzying heights. It dares to make a fearless inventory of what is and isn't working for us, cutting to the chase about what we finally need to do.

The Ignatian way insists that we encounter the divine mystery not only in scripture and the church, but also in the full range of human experience and the dark recesses of the natural world. He viewed the cave as an ideal place for examining the conscience, for probing the depths (and convolutions) of the human soul. As Barbara Brown Taylor says about the reasons to seek out spiritual direction: "We go to counselors when we want help getting out of caves. We go to directors when we are ready to be led farther in."[11]

Ignatius's *Exercises* are explicit directions for companioning others in the spiritual life, ideally over a thirty-day period given to reflection and prayer. He organized these exercises into four "weeks," or movements. In the first week he took his retreatant through something of his own experience in the cave, through a time of purgation and release. It begins with an awareness of

God's unconditional love and the hell of having said "no" to that again and again.[12]

He urges the retreatant to acknowledge the sin that separates her from God, how easily she shifts the blame to someone else, how her self-absorption has kept her from hearing God's voice within. During the first week, he suggests physically entering a dark place from time to time. He knew from experience that praying with the shades drawn, being "deprived of light," can be helpful in confronting the darkness inside.[13]

This led, in the second week, to a decision-making point in the retreatant's life, when she chooses between two standards, deciding who she ultimately will love. Then, in weeks three and four, Iñigo carries the retreatant into an intensive, thoroughly sensuous reading of the Gospel stories of Jesus's life, death, and resurrection.

In making the "Jesus story" your own, he explained, you have to use your imagination, inserting yourself into the context and geography of the tale, incorporating what he called the "composition of place" and use of the five senses. Take the Gospel account of the cave at Bethlehem, for instance, where a very pregnant Mary comes with her anxious husband. You smell the mustiness of the animals, noticing a pile of straw thrown onto a hayrack nearby. You picture yourself as a servant girl hiding behind the harnesses and mule blankets, ready to help if she's needed. The extent to which you make the story your own depends on your ability to perceive it as actually happening in real time and place.[14]

This profoundly incarnational character of the Gospel was of primary importance to Ignatius. The Nativity story happens to a homeless couple seeking shelter for the night in a dark cave. You have to *enter* the place, experiencing the same fear and courage felt by the characters in the tale. You share in the swings of emotion that stir in the cauldron of faith.

The founder of the Jesuits was intrigued by the fluctuation of human emotions in the progress (and regress) of the spiritual life. He thought it important to monitor the movements of consolation and desolation as they come and go. In desolation, we're turned in on ourselves, struggling with confusion, feeling a loss of energy. In consolation, by contrast, we're happily focused on things outside of ourselves, feeling joyful, inspired, alive.[15]

He cautioned that one shouldn't suppose the "normal" spiritual life to involve only the latter state. Consolation can be a form of escape as well as a gift—a starry-eyed distraction from what we most need to confront. Desolation, on the other hand, isn't necessarily bad. It may be God's way of breaking us out of patterns that no longer work. Better then, says Ignatius, to exercise a basic detachment (or indifference) to all the ups and downs of our lives.[16] Simply be *aware* of them, "discerning the spirits." Our work is to know what's going on inside, what games we're playing, how we're persistently being drawn to or away from God.

Anticipating the trip into Lewis Cave, I'd been struggling myself with a sense of desolation, fearful that the cave might reopen shadows from the past. I'd been passing through a period of wrestling with the Jesus of my childhood again—torn between memories of being loved and fears of being judged for my persistent doubts. Normally I'd have approached a trip like this with consolation, looking forward to being alone in the wilderness. But I'd been shelving this Jesus stuff for a long time.

Entering the Cave: Seeing Jesus Through Ignatian Eyes

Jesus was the principal reality in the life of Ignatius Loyola. He gave this name to the community he founded—the Company of Jesus. When I was led through the exercises several years ago, I too was intrigued by the Jesus this Spanish priest had encountered. He was significantly different from my own childhood religious experience of him. Ignatius allowed me to more fully reclaim the scriptures—this time not as a didactic text aimed at proving a theological agenda, but as a transformative story luring me into its life.

For years I'd grappled with a Jesus full of contradictions. "You can know a thing to death and be for all purposes completely ignorant of it," says John Ames, the Congregationalist pastor in Marilynne Robinson's *Gilead*.[17] I knew the old atonement theories of a punishing God—Jesus as a blood sacrifice assuaging the Father's wrath. I knew (and rankled under) the miracle stories of Jesus withering a fig tree and walking on water. I'd resisted exclusivist claims about Christ, his being the only way to God—leaving those who didn't know him condemned. Jesus, for me, was a carryover from years of suppressed fears. Yet I couldn't escape him.

"Who Is This "Jesus'?"

Who is this contradictory figure who rattles my cage and rumbles through the history of my life? Who proves an embarrassment and stumbling block to my mind, but who won't go away, this man who brings awe and tears to my eyes, who makes me want to resist authority when it's wrong, who points me to a God who works from the underside of every system of power?

Who is this Jesus? He's the disturbing teacher of the Gospels, comfortable with children and irritating to scholars, unsettling people by his enigmatic stories. He's a dancing member of the Holy Trinity, looking out from a golden Russian icon. He's the object of saccharine devotion in the Sacred Heart of Catholic spirituality, the "Jesus and me" sentimentality of evangelical piety, the unbridled passion of seventeenth-century metaphysical poets.

He's the first-century Jewish rabbi of the Jesus Seminar, calling for justice and inclusivity, making no ethereal claims about his own divinity. He's the Jesus of Jelaluddin Rumi, who wants to be born in the mystical experience of every soul. He's the Cosmic Christ who weaves his spirit through the fabric of the natural world.

This is the Jesus who lures and seduces my heart, who bugs the hell out of me, uprooting my comfortable white, straight, male, middle-class values. He roams the streets with the homeless, far from the gilded crosses of suburban sanctuaries, and he rages against those who would turn him into an other-worldly Savior, safely ascended into heaven, too distant to be real.

"Call me by *all* my names," cries Thich Nhat Hanh[18] and Jesus, as well. "I'm Warner Salmon's head of Christ," he says, "and the Piss Christ of shocking modern art. I'm Francis of Assisi's leper on the road to Perugia and Mary Oliver's snow geese announcing my participation in the family of things. I'm the blue wildebeest calf separated from its herd and the East African lion that takes it down. I'm the grieving women of the Plaza de Mayo in Argentina and the men of the military junta who've yet to learn that power is not truth. I'm the redwood trees cut down by Pacific Lumber and the out-of-work loggers whose families have to eat. I'm the young girl raped by a pirate on a boat of refugees in the South China Sea and the pirate whose heart has never known love. I'm all of these broken, vulnerable beings, yearning for the wholeness and healing of the Earth."

Who is this Jesus? I'm less concerned with *defining* him than I am with *experiencing* him. I'm more taken by his vulnerability than by his miraculous power. In the end, there's no escaping this, "Jesus, lover of my soul." "He walks with me and he talks with me and he tells me I am his own," affirming my doubts, encouraging my yearning, forbidding my indifference. I can't get away from him. Nor—at last—do I want to.[19]

Over the years, the Cosmic Christ had become more central in my thinking about God. It's what New Testament writers see Jesus to have become in his resurrection (Acts 2:36). "The radiant light of God's glory . . . sustaining the universe by God's powerful command," says Hebrews 1:3. This is a universal reality, far wider than Christianity alone—or any faith tradition. It's a Christ who "was before all things, and in him all things hold together" (Colossians 1:17). We're talking here about a Christology that's global in significance.[20]

But in appreciating an all-embracing Christ of the universe, I'd run the risk of turning Jesus into God's embarrassing stepson. I resisted a tribal, *exclusivist* Jesus who held unbelieving *sinners* in the hands of an angry God. I could *delight* in the Cosmic *Christ*. It was *Jesus* I stumbled over, that seemingly *obscure figure in first-century Palestine*.

As I thought of going into the cave—back into the shadows of the past—I feared encountering him once again. I dreaded a Jesus who sat in judgment, rebuking my departure from the straight and narrow, punishing me for my doubts. Who might I meet there in the cave's darkness? I was surprised by how much residual fear I had.

The night before I left, I went over to see Grandfather. Leaning against his trunk, I breathed into the silence between us and heard a voice speaking deep within me. It was as if Grandfather himself were saying, "You know, Belden, there's nothing for you to be afraid of going into the dark of that cave tomorrow. *Who* have you been meeting every night all these years in coming over to me—if *not* Jesus? You stand in the wound of his side every night! Touching it with your hands. My bark, his flesh. Same difference."

There it was, a tree pointing me to Jesus in a profoundly Ignatian way. A Jesus "in-wooded" in the rough grain of tree bark, the earthy smell of heartwood—standing in a city park where families walk their dogs and drug dealers pass in the night.

Here was a gritty, earthy Jesus, readily merging with an all-inclusive Cosmic Christ. The one holding together the wide expanse of space, the other suffering out of love with each individual part. I saw the two now as one: the universal and particular, both discovered in a broken tree.

Yet there was more. As I leaned into Grandfather, he went on to say, "You know what's even *more* outrageous than your finding Jesus in me? It's not your doubts about whether he's divine. It's the question—can you *imagine* this?—whether *you* are divine as well! Just like me. *Both* of us reflecting God's glory." That's what I heard the tree saying.

The next morning as I left for the cave, I went without fear. Something had shifted inside. I'd been misunderstanding this "Jesus problem" all along. It wasn't an intellectual conundrum about problematic biblical texts and doctrinal theories. It was about coming to terms with a disconnected part of *myself*—with what God had been trying to tell me for a long time.

Jesus wasn't *out there*, as part of the dualistic dichotomy I'd grown up with. He was closer, more intimate than I'd ever dreamed. I could know him as truly in a tree as in the core of my own being. A scandalous truth, you might say. Yet isn't this what Jesus prayed for his disciples (for the entire world) when he asked "that they may *all* be one, as you, Father, are in me and I in you" (John 17:21)? Isn't it what Paul affirmed when he said, "It is no longer I who live, but Christ who lives in me" (Galatians 2:20)? Isn't it what God meant to do from the very beginning—to make all things one?

In some of her workshops, psychologist Jean Houston uses an exercise called "Are You God in Hiding?" Working with more than a hundred people in a large, dimly lit ballroom, she'll ask them to close their eyes and wander slowly around the room. When they bump into another person they're to ask softly, "Are you God in hiding?" That person then responds, asking the same question, "Are *you* God in hiding?" They continue on to someone else, asking the same question over and over.

Jean has assigned the role of "God" in advance to one individual in the group. When you run into that person and, ask, "Are you God in hiding?" you get no response. He or she is silent. After receiving this silence in response to your question, *you* become God as well, remaining silent when others question you. Gradually a stillness spreads across the room. Houston says it never takes more than a few minutes for more than a hundred people to enter into complete silence, in awe at the fact that God is there, in every one of them.

Christian mystics speak of the mystery of theosis or deification, a process of entering fully into the image and likeness of God. Theologians of the Eastern Church affirm that the destiny of the Earth is to find its wholeness in God. Being *ingodded* is the hope of every created being. God wants to love each of his creatures, says Meister Eckhart, not as creatures, but *as Himself*.[21]

In the stunning Greek and Russian Orthodox icons of the Transfiguration, Jesus is lit by a transfiguring divine light, but the disciples are too (Peter, James, and John) and the entire *mountain* as well, the rocks, grass, and trees all ablaze. Here Jesus is the Cosmic Christ, the *inside* of everything. He's Hildegard's greening, life-giving spirit, Teilhard's Omega Point to which all things are drawn. This is the luminous Buddha nature of every sentient being. It's not something they have, but what they *are*. "Verily," says the Quran, "He encompasses everything!" (Surah 41:54).

The power of this realization—coming to me from Ignatius of Loyola, a cave, and a cottonwood tree—is the assurance that if I'm being transformed into love, there's no longer room for fear. What I wish for is already within me. I simply have to accept Ignatius's permission to trust my imagination, Grandfather's agency in helping me do so, and God's longing to knit all things together in love. In so doing, I enter more fully into the Great Conversation.

The Cave and the Season of the Elder

In many cultures the cave symbolizes the dwelling place of the spiritual elder or sage. In India it's the sannyasin (the holy man or woman) sitting before a sacred *dhuni* fire beneath an overhanging rock on a high mountain. Having passed through the earlier life stages of the student, householder, and forest dweller, the sannyasin is now "laying everything down" (*san-ni-asa*), releasing the concerns that have long occupied him, freed now to share with others the wisdom of that relinquishment. The crone or wise man enters a wider community, becoming a citizen of the world, urging compassion for all.[22]

Three characteristics mark the women and men who actively serve us as elders.

1. They aren't afraid of the dark. They've learned to befriend the night— knowing it calls them into the cave of contemplative practice, into the silence of themselves. They can sit without having all the answers. They can wrestle with God's absence, which sometimes proves a deeper way of discerning God's presence.

The rest of us think it's safer to stay busy, keep the lights on, turn the music up, and pretend we have all the answers. We've been taught to be wary of the silence and solitude of the cave. "Our suffering," says Barbara Taylor, "comes from our reluctance to learn to walk in the dark."[23]

Entering into their role, elders adopt a practice of retreating at times to a hermitage somewhere, maybe a cabin in the woods. They set aside a daily time for contemplative prayer in a dark nook under the staircase, a place to be still. The Russian Orthodox call it a *poustinia*, an intentional "desert place" into which one habitually withdraws.[24] For me, it's the cavity in Grandfather's side each night. (When was the last time *you* spent twenty-four hours alone and in silence?)

2. Elders also serve as trusted holders of the tradition. They stand on the shoulders of those who've come before them, knowing what's worth remembering, the stories that need to be told. Religiously speaking, this is more than a matter of simply "thinking with the church."[25] It means "wrestling" with the tradition as well—making it your own, arguing with it.

A tradition isn't a dead weight that anchors you in place. It's a pendulum, a weight in motion, swinging back into the past (for balance) and forward into the future (for what is alive and new). The elders show us how to keep grappling with what we've learned to love.

3. Finally, elders aren't afraid to speak their minds. They exercise a countercultural, prophetic role in speaking truth to power. They don't worry about what other people think. These outspoken old men and fiery women speak out of the depths of compassion for what they love. They've moved, with Ignatius, from contemplation into action, from fear into love. Such is the core of Ignatian spirituality: a life of prayer that leads to authentic change in the world.

One of a community's greatest dangers is being paralyzed by fear. It puts a stranglehold on love: building walls, withdrawing into gated communities, arming itself against every perceived enemy. Danger is real, says the sage, but fear is a choice.[26] We deal with it by entering the cave of our own terror, finding a love that's stronger than fear. It's among the hardest work we do, but it allows us to harvest the gifts of spiritual darkness identified by Barbara Taylor: "Familiarity with the divine absence, mistrust of conventional wisdom, suspicion of religious comforters, a keen awareness of the limits of all language about God."[27] In the dark place, we may have less certainty about what we've long believed. But there we unaccountably find ourselves set free from fear and made open to love. It took the voice of a tree, heard in the dark of night, to bring this home to me.

I've had it confirmed again and again in the work I do in helping to lead men's rites of passage in wilderness settings, raising up elders through the work of Illuman.org. Here men who are passing into the second half of their lives confront all the mistakes and untapped grief of their past, moving through fear into a new freedom and compassion.[28] It never fails to amaze me.

Turning Fear into Love

When my daughter was seven or eight years old, she went through a time of being afraid of the dark. One day we found a children's book in the public library: Mercer Mayer's *There's a Nightmare in My Closet*.[29] She loved it! We had to read it three times that night before going to sleep.

It's the story of a boy who's been frightened by something hiding in his bedroom closet. One night he decides to deal with the beast. Putting on his toy army helmet, he grabs his play gun and loads the cork in its muzzle. He gets into bed, pulls up the covers, and turns off the light. But he doesn't go to sleep. He's armed and ready.

Slowly the closet door opens and a huge monster creeps out. Big eyes, immense ears, a long forked tail. Suddenly the boy turns on the light. If *he'd* been afraid of the dark, the nightmare was equally frightened by the light—especially as he sees a boy with a loaded gun aimed at him. "Please, don't shoot," the nightmare pleads.

The boy is torn. He's basically a nonviolent kid, but the nightmare has scared him too many times. So he shoots him anyway. The monster begins to cry, tears rolling down his face. "You gotta stop making all that noise," the boy says. "You'll wake up mommy and daddy." But the nightmare is inconsolable.

The boy gets out of bed to calm him down, patting his hand. That helps some, but he finally has to put the nightmare in bed with him to stop him from crying. He tucks him in on one side and gets back in on the other. Just before turning off the light, he says to himself, "There may be more than one nightmare in my closet, but there's only room for two of us in bed."

He falls asleep—the boy and the nightmare snuggled contentedly in bed, a big lump and little lump lying side by side. Yet on the book's last page, you see the closet door opening once again, with another nightmare peering out.

With big eyes, immense ears, and a long forked tail, she wonders if she, too, can be loved in the same way as the first nightmare was loved.

My daughter absolutely loved that story. The next morning, she came running from her bedroom into ours, saying, "Daddy, do you know what happened last night?"

"No, what?" I asked.

"Four or five nightmares came out of my closet and got into bed with me!"

"Wow," I said, "Was there room for all of you?" "Oh, yeah!" she answered, so taken by the possibility that what had been most *terrifying* in her experience could prove the most *loving*.

Ignatius learned that in the cave. It's what a life of wilderness backpacking has tried to teach me. I keep coming back to a God before whom I'm completely undone—stripped of language, driven to awe-filled silence. But then a tree speaks in the silence of the night, reminding me that what I've feared has been longing for me all along. Who would have guessed?

CHAPTER FOURTEEN

WOLVES

GREATER YELLOWSTONE ECOSYSTEM
AND FRANCIS OF ASSISI

"We have doomed the wolf not for what it is, but for what we deliberately and mistakenly perceive it to be—the mythological epitome of a savage, ruthless killer—which is, in reality, no more than the reflected image of ourselves. We have made it the scapewolf for our own sins."

—Farley Mowat, *Never Cry Wolf*[1]

"He was mastered by the sheer surging of life, the tidal wave of being, the perfect joy of each separate muscle, joint, and sinew in that it was everything that was not death, that it was aglow and rampant, expressing itself in movement, flying exultantly under the stars."

—about Buck, leader of the wolf pack in
Jack London's *The Call of the Wild*[2]

A sign at the private road leading into DuNoir Valley, west of Dubois, Wyoming, read "Trespassers will be shot, and survivors will be shot again." We wisely avoided that route and took the next turn north onto Forest Road 513, toward the Washakie Wilderness. We were heading up behind DuNoir Valley into an area where gray wolves had settled since their reintroduction to nearby Yellowstone National Park in the 1990s.

This is rugged country. My buddy Mike and I were being led by a friend and hunting guide, Ben Verheul. He's been tracking and hunting this area since he was six years old. He's a man who loves wolves and everything wild. We were headed into the rocky terrain of Shoshone National Forest in the Absaroka Mountains, just southeast of the nation's first national park. Part of the Greater Yellowstone Ecosystem. There's *nothing* on the map for fifty square miles between Dubois and Cody up near the Montana border. It's a place for "Sasquatch research," they say—for finding six-inch-long paw prints with each toe the size of a half-dollar.

It was early September and bull elk were going into rut, a perfect time to look for wolves. When you find elk, the wolves won't be far behind, Ben had said. Nor will the grizzly bears. We saw the tracks of all three as we hiked from the high desert foothills through steep forests up toward the windswept meadows on the high ridges. Passing lodgepole pines and juniper trees, we climbed through thickets of tall spruce and occasional whitebark pines, old and twisted.

I had known all along that I'd wanted to finish this book with a trip into wolf country, thinking of Francis of Assisi, the saint who was said to have "tamed" the wolf of Gubbio in thirteenth-century Italy. We had no illusions of imitating Francis's peacemaking skill. We each wore bear canisters on our belts; Ben carried a twelve-gauge Mossberg shotgun as a last resort.

We were moving through a landscape with more top predators than anywhere I'd ever been. Grizzlies, wolves, and mountain lions abound in the area. Their presence, even when unseen, is daunting. "Among the earliest forms of human self-awareness," says David Quammen, is "the awareness of being meat." Knowing yourself as imminently edible is a visceral experience. Quammen's book *Monster of God: The Man-Eating Predator in the Jungles of History and the Mind* explores the ecological and psychic loss that humans may likely experience with the coming extinction of alpha predators—a reality he predicts by the year 2150.[3] Animals large enough to be life-threatening, he says, have been crucial to our imaginative life, if not also our survival.

We left the cabin at five that first morning, taking our time as we drove up the dirt road to stop periodically to listen for movement in the trees. Shivering in the dark, with the frost penetrating every layer of our clothes, I wondered if freezing your ass off was a necessary part of listening for wolves. I had to learn that waiting is what any kind of hunting is all about. Before long we heard a wolf howl not far away and spotted a lone coyote—a white-tan ghost—running straight toward us, away from something larger in the morning mist.

Nothing happened for another fifteen minutes. Then Ben gave one of his imitations of a wolf howl echoing off the distant cliffs. Coyote yips and more wolf cries came instantly in response. This is how it went for the next three days: animals surrounding us, but the wolves remaining elusive—heard but unseen.

The elk, on the other hand, were much less aloof. Ben was able to call them in by whacking with a stick on the limbs of a dead spruce tree, imitating the sound of an elk scraping the velvet off his antlers. There's something primitive and powerful about the clash of bone on wood, as bull elk prepare to challenge each other in battle. I marvel at how they can even walk through timber with a six-foot-wide, thirty-pound rack on their heads.

I'm equally impressed by the quiet savvy and irrepressible joy of a man like Ben. He thrives on this mountainous terrain. He's been treed and mauled by grizzly bears. He's spent winter nights on search and rescue teams with temperatures reaching forty below. ("Your spit freezes before it hits the ground.") He's a bow hunter who can shed tears over the deer he's brought down with his PSE Brute X compound bow.

On our second day in backcountry, we hiked farther up, making our way through the thick grass, elk thistle, and yellow arnica flowers of the high country. Ben had to leave us that afternoon to attend to needs back at the ranch. So Mike and I were left on our own, camping that night at ten thousand feet atop Fire Tower Meadows. It's a grassy knoll overlooking the expanse of DuNoir Valley to the east and the Grand Tetons to the west. Pinnacle Buttes—where a wooden fire lookout once stood—rises another 1,500 feet to the north. All of this is within walking distance of the Continental Divide.

We chose a campsite in a small copse of spruce and pine trees in the heart of the meadow. At the center was an old limb-twisted whitebark pine that we identified by its requisite five needles to a bunch. It's a tree I've learned to love almost as much as cottonwoods. Seventy-five percent of them have died in the Greater Yellowstone Area over the past thirty years—succumbing to bark beetles and blister rust. The oldest known whitebark pine (going strong after 1,280 years) stands in the Sawtooth Mountains of central Idaho. To sleep alongside one of these elders is a gift.

Yet we had some reservations as night came on. We'd seen a gallon-size pile of grizzly scat (and fresh tracks) a couple hundred yards from the top of the meadow as we came up. Ben figured the bear must have weighed six hundred pounds or better. We noticed that he'd dined on elk steak with huckleberry compote at his last meal. I'd picked some of the same red huckleberries myself on the way up the mountain.

We had a deep respect for the wolves, although we knew that wolf attacks on humans have been extremely rare in North America. Ben assured us, however, that grizzly bears can be shit-in-your-pants terrifying. As it happened, on walking out the next morning we stumbled onto an elk carcass stashed between fallen logs, less than three hundred yards from where we'd slept. We got out of there as fast as we could.

The night before, we sat in blissful ignorance at the top of the ridge after dinner, looking west onto the road toward Yellowstone, Brooks Lake hidden in the valley below. A red sun was setting in the west just as a red moon was rising behind us in the east. That happens on the night of a full moon, when the universe seems to fall into harmonic alignment.

A huge bull elk with full rack and a cow were watching us from a nearby rise, as other bulls were sounding off in the timber below. *Eeeuuuuh! ee-uh! ee-uh!* It's a bugling note as wild and stirring as the high-pitched moan of the wolf. What more could you ask of a Wyoming wilderness than to be sitting at the end of a day, aligned with celestial bodies, surrounded by antlered animals and lupine predators, with a massive grizzly shuffling nearby in the gathering night?

THE GIFT OF NOT SEEING

We were encircled by wolves on this trip, but never actually saw one—only their shadows moving in the dark trees. They remained a phantom presence, following our scent, observing us from a distance, never allowing themselves to be seen. They had good reason to hide.

Earlier that year a federal appeals court had lifted endangered species protection for wolves in Wyoming. We were in the newly assigned trophy game hunt area, where a limit of forty-four wolves could be harvested through the last three months of the year. All the rest of the Equality State (yep, that's Wyoming's nickname) had been designated a predator zone where any number of wolves could be shot at will. The animals were rightly afraid of being seen by humans.

Initially I was disappointed at not seeing the wolves. I knew we could have driven up the road overlooking Lamar Valley in the northeast corner of Yellowstone Park, where we could have watched the wolves through a spotting scope, not having to walk more than a few feet from the car. But we wouldn't have been nearly as close to the wolves as we were there in the depths of the Washakie Wilderness. We'd have had no more idea of their life and habitat than if we'd been watching another YouTube video on the computer back home.

Knowing the wolf is knowing where it lives, moving through its world. While I didn't see the animals, I knew they were seeing *me*. I was walking right through them. We came as no surprise. They'd heard us and smelled our scent from miles away.

It was enough, therefore, to have been a part of their territory, knowing a presence just beyond the trees. Getting there had required engagement with the entire landscape. We'd been hiking steep ridges, studying tracks, dodging spruce branches, watching the skittish flight of ravens and Clark's nutcrackers, discerning the direction of the wind as dust fell through Ben's fingers. We were moving through something we couldn't see, but nonetheless knew to be real.

Not seeing the wolf was as significant for me as Peter Matthieson's Zen-like experience of not seeing the snow leopard in the mountains of Nepal. The wolves were a humbling reminder that what I long for most I'm never able to see. Embracing what can't be seen (can't even be known) may actually be the first step in renewing the Great Conversation. We won't learn what the wolf has to teach until we've released our need to spot the beast, to lock him firmly in a niche of visual memory, imagining that having seen, we've also "trapped" what remains ultimately unknowable.

This is a caution voiced by all of the principal spiritual traditions. The great mystery is always finally beyond our seeing and knowing. We crave a glimpse of more than its shadow, but realize that the encounter would leave us gawking in speechless wonder. We long to gaze into the golden eyes of what prowls the edges of our consciousness, although we have no proof of its existence. We trace the footprints of an indescribable glory in the natural world, but can't finally name what we see.

We haven't words for what the heart longs for most. This is the insistence of the apophatic tradition in the history of Christian spirituality. Trying to speak the unspeakable, language quickly gives out. We become hopelessly incoherent, lacking words for what's too wild and wondrous to convey.

We discover an approximation of that mystery in risking ourselves to a wild and unnerving terrain, where we're viscerally aware of an unseen presence. The place—with its haunting immediacy—may be enough. The fierce landscape discloses nothing, yet hints at what looms over the rocky horizon. The Desert Fathers and Mothers learned this in the desert beyond the Nile, where the apophatic tradition first took shape. Peter Matthiessen sensed it in the high snowy world of the Himalayas, where he found the snow leopard's "terrible beauty" to be "the very stuff of human longing."[4] I've felt it myself on a number of the trips made for this book.

THE FEAR OF THE BEAST

We're captivated by what lies beyond the limits of our comprehension. It fills us with terror as well. Over the centuries the wolf's stealthy elusiveness has led us to project a sinister quality onto these extraordinary animals. Barry Lopez speaks of our "theriophobia," our irrational, deep-seated fear of the "beast."[5] It evokes an impulse to kill what we don't understand.

The truth is that Little Red Riding Hood lied. Wolves don't eat grandmas. Yet her tale, like that of the Three Little Pigs, is rooted in a long-standing hatred of an animal perceived as vicious and cunning—an evil to be eradicated. You see it on a sign in an Idaho bar: "Help Preserve Wolves, take one to a taxidermist." Or a bumper sticker on a Montana pickup: "Wolves: Smoke a Pack a Day." Or the poster in a Wyoming gun shop: "Wolves are Illegal Immigrants, Too."[6] There are few animals we loathe as much as wolves.

The history of this hatred goes back at least ten thousand years, when human beings began turning to a sedentary, agricultural life. Wild animals became enemies, killing stock and eating crops. The wolf came to symbolize the worst of nature's threats to civilized life.[7]

Through the centuries wolves haven't just been hunted. They've been persecuted and tortured: burned at the stake like witches and heretics; dragged to death behind horses; their mouths wired shut and released to starve to death. American colonists set out strychnine-laced meat for the wolf just as they gave blankets infected with smallpox to the Indians.[8] In the four hundred years between 1500 and 2000 CE wolves were driven to the edge of extinction.

In recent years, game hunting has taken to the air. In Alaska, hunters in planes or helicopters have located wolves by the radio collars placed on them by researchers, hounding them from the sky until they're exhausted, then landing and shooting them. In one case, a wolf pack near Denali that had been studied by Park Service biologists for twenty years was wiped out in a single day.[9]

Ranchers and farmers, of course, have a legitimate concern about their livestock being killed by wolves. Programs have been set up to subsidize landowners for animals taken by predators as well as to urge ways of adapting to the presence of wolves. These include monitoring grazing patterns and staying away from hot spot regions.[10]

Over the years we've gradually learned to appreciate wolves without demonizing (or romanticizing) them. By the time Aldo Leopold wrote his *Sand County Almanac,* you could discern a shift in societal perceptions of apex predators. He spoke of grieving as he knelt beside a wolf he had shot, watching "a fierce green fire dying in her eyes." He realized that "something known only to her and to the mountain" had been lost. More importantly, he noticed how the absence of wolves allowed the deer population to explode, with every edible tree stripped of its leaves.[11]

Subsequent ecologists have gone on to argue that keystone species like the wolf exert a cascading effect on the well-being of their ecosystem. Before wolves were reintroduced to Yellowstone, an overpopulation of elk had eaten willow, aspen, and cottonwood shoots down to the ground. This in turn had weakened river banks, causing erosion, and reducing the trees available for songbirds to nest. There were fewer beavers with fewer resources for building dams and creating pools for fish to thrive. Field biologists caution that multiple factors are always involved in eco-systemic change, but the reintroduction of top predators in northwest Wyoming has played a significant role in restoring ecological balance.[12]

A deeper question is how we can learn to exult in the wolf's wildness, even as we find manageable ways of living together. What does the wolf tell us about the Creator's rowdy playfulness, "sporting" with Leviathan, the primeval sea monster (Psalm 104:26)?

John Muir was one who gloried in all things wild, discovering God at the heart of what others dismissed as nature's "dark side." He reveled in the wolves' reminder of what we cannot control. On his thousand-mile walk through southern swamps to the Gulf of Mexico, Muir encountered alligators and leeches. "Fierce and cruel they appear to us," he wrote, "but beautiful in the eyes of God. They, also, are his children." The problem, as he saw it, is our "narrow, selfish, and conceitful" sympathies—thinking everything in the world should revolve around us and our safety. If there is a "divine harmony" in nature, he concluded, its goal is the good of the *whole*, not the exclusive well-being of human life alone. In the vast evolutionary process, life and death continually feed each other. We can view this as a random, senseless riot or as a sacramental mystery.[13]

The Scots mountaineer had renounced his childhood religious roots. But he didn't stop believing in what he couldn't understand. He simply learned that God was far wilder than what he'd been taught. For him, the divine exuberance wasn't confined to flower-filled meadows and nests of baby field mice. God was there also in the hailstorm flattening the meadow and the red-shouldered hawk snatching the mice in her talons. When we protect ourselves from everything wild, he said, we lose sight of a God who is both riotous in adventure and extravagant in love.

Teachers in the natural world tend to operate like Zen masters. They generally appear as gentle reminders of silent tranquility, but they're prone on occasion to break into storm, sending flash floods down the canyon, whacking you with their flat wooden stick. One way or another, they get your attention. Wolves are like that.

Our need isn't to eradicate wolves as destructive marauders, nor to tame them, turning top predators into lap dogs. Our task, instead, is to recognize them as *family*, distant relatives who rarely get together, yet recognize their importance to each other. They share a fierce commitment to the land they love and the relationships that sustain its life.

THE SCIENCE AND MYTHOLOGY OF WOLVES

Like all wild things, wolves confront us with contradictory realities. On the one hand, they're more like us than we realize. They're very sociable animals, living and working in families, joining together to protect and feed the young, sick, and old members that aren't able to fend for themselves. Wolves generally mate for life, and the pack shares a devotion to pups that are born blind and remain helpless for the first two weeks of their lives.

On the other hand, these are animals that face the stark necessities of backcountry survival. To be a wolf is to be feral. "It's standing on your prey's neck and eating while your prey watches, but not paying attention as the light fades from its eyes because if you don't eat quickly, chances are that a stronger predator will come along and either steal your food or eat you too."[14] That's the precarious character of life in the wilds. It's something you miss at the meat counter in the local grocery store.

Wolves stir a deep attraction and uneasiness within us, wandering in and out of our dreams. It's important to attend to the images they evoke for us, as well as the reality of their life in the wilds.

An adult gray wolf (*Canis lupus*) can be four to six feet long and weigh up to 175 pounds. They move in packs of six or seven, ranging across the mountain states of the American Northwest and Canada. Subspecies include the eastern timber wolf in the Great Lakes region, the Mexican wolf in the American Southwest, and the threatened red wolf in the swampland of North Carolina.

We've been taught to think of wolves as living under a strict hierarchy, ruled by an alpha male who continually fights off other wolves to maintain his position of power. This is only partially true. They live in families usually under the shared leadership of an alpha couple—mom, dad, children, and a few extended family members. Wolves are excellent fathers. They bring home food for the pups, who romp and play all over dad, greeting him with tail wagging and face licking.[15]

Yet hierarchy is important. Given the dangers of life in the wilds, wolves need to know who is in charge. The alpha male is the largest and most capable member of the group. He and the alpha female are the only ones who breed and produce pups for the pack. There's a sentinel who warns of approaching danger, and a nanny who watches the pups and guards the den. At the bottom of the hierarchy is the omega wolf. Subordinate to all the others, he diffuses tension, initiates play, and keeps things light. "Lone wolves" are very much an exception; wolves generally don't do well on their own, preferring the settled order of an established pack.[16] Family is everything.

Wolves are very territorial, hunting over a fifty-square-mile area or more. They're able to run as fast as forty miles an hour for short distances, sometimes attacking animals five times their size. Their communication skills are phenomenal. The wolf's sense of smell is a hundred times keener than ours. Using scent marks, vocalization, and body language, they continually transmit information and confirm relationships within the group. When one animal stares intently at something, the others are aware of it in an almost telepathic way.[17]

A lower-ranking male will respond to an alpha leader by crouching down, tucking his tail, and turning his gaze to the side. This might seem an act of submission to a dominant aggressor, but it's an acknowledgment of the order that keeps everyone comfortable and safe within the group. Wolves don't have to be in charge, but they want to know they can count on someone to do the job.[18] Cultivating respect and honoring family are essentials to the life of the pack.

When we look at the stories of wolves handed down from indigenous traditions and classical mythology, we find that they have been venerated as much as they've been maligned. "All stories are about wolves," says Margaret Atwood. "All worth repeating, that is. Anything else is sentimental drivel."[19]

You have the she-wolf who rescued and suckled the twins Romulus and Remus, who grew up to become the legendary founders of the city of Rome. Among the Shoshoni in northwest Wyoming the Wolf was revered as a creator god—his wisdom contrasted with his irresponsible brother, Coyote the trickster. Then there's La Loba, the wolf woman celebrated in tales from the Sonoran Desert in northern Mexico and southern Arizona. She preserves what's at risk of being lost, gathering the bones of wolves and coyotes strewn across the desert, then singing them into life again.[20]

The wolf is associated with the night. For Chinese astronomers Sirius, the Dog Star, is the Celestial Wolf, keeping watch from his vantage point on the bridge of the Milky Way. Anubis, the Egyptian god of death, had a man's body and the head of a jackal or wolf. As guardian of the night, he guided souls into the afterlife. "The hour of the wolf"—halfway between midnight and dawn, or 3 a.m.—is traditionally a bewitching hour, when more people die and more are born than at any other hour of the day. This is when the wolf is afoot, stalking the boundaries of the night.

In Norse mythology there's Fenrir, the wolf son of the god Loki. Feared by the other gods, he was kept bound with a magical chain. The Vikings revered his power, wearing wolf skins and drinking wolf blood on going into battle. In Bram Stoker's novel, the Transylvanian vampire Count Dracula could turn himself into a wolf as well as a bat. Herodotus and Virgil repeated earlier stories about the gift (or curse) of lycanthropy, the ability to physically shapeshift into a wolf.

Tales of bloodthirsty wolves are matched by other accounts of wolves adopting human children. An Irish saint named Ailbe of Emly was said to have been forsaken in the wilderness as a baby and raised by a mother wolf. Maintaining a great affection for her, he reportedly thought of himself as half human and half wolf.

Wolves never fared very well in the Bible. The prophet Ezekiel described the corrupt leaders of Jerusalem as wolves tearing their prey, shedding blood and destroying lives (22:27). Jesus warned of false prophets as ravenous wolves, disguised in sheep's clothing (Matthew 7:15). Wolves, like dogs, were marked in scripture by ceremonial impurity. Only in the utopian kingdom of the future can one imagine the wolf and the lamb living peacefully together (Isaiah 11:6).

FRANCIS OF ASSISI AND THE DAWNING OF A NEW AGE

At the dawn of the thirteenth century, a deeper way of appreciating the natural world emerged with Francis of Assisi (1181–1226).

Francesco Bernadone was born into the family of a wealthy cloth merchant in the Apennine Mountains of Umbria, one hundred miles north of Rome. As a young man, he played the role of a troubadour, party animal, and would-be knight. In his early twenties an encounter with a leper on the road to Perugia changed his life. He found Christ among the poorest of the poor and began giving away his father's cloth.

This led to a violent confrontation, with his father furiously "pouncing on Francis like a wolf on a lamb," beating him and dragging him in chains to the cellar of their home.[21] After regaining his freedom, Francis abandoned any claim to his father's wealth and placed himself under the care of the bishop of Assisi.

A band of brothers began accompanying Francis in his work with the poor. Calling themselves Franciscans, they formed an order of mendicant friars ("begging brothers") who departed from the traditional pattern of cloistered monastic life. They "gave whatever they had to the poor," Francis said, "and were content with one tunic, patched inside and out, with a cord and short trousers."[22] They wandered wherever they saw they were needed.

Francis was a short, thin man with dark hair and a sparse black beard. What attracted people to him was the man's irrepressible joy in the simplest things. He delighted in a huge old tree among the "black firs" on Mount Subasio overlooking Assisi. Birds rested on his head, shoulders, and hands as he sat outside praying. He played the role of a holy fool, sometimes preaching in his underwear. He'd use sticks to pretend he was playing the violin for the enjoyment of the stars. He'd remind the brothers to take care of Brother Ass, the body that bears them through this life and takes them to heaven, too.

On Christmas night in 1223, he asked that a straw-filled manger, with an ox and ass, be set up near the altar of the church at Greccio. People gathered by torchlight as Francis—beside himself with joy—danced around, laughing and making animal noises as he preached.[23]

Stories about this lovable, if eccentric, monk quickly spread across Europe. The times were filled with apocalyptic expectations, and many saw Francis as heralding a new spiritual awakening. A Cistercian hermit named Joachim of Fiore had recently predicted the dawning of a new age, based on his reading of the book of Revelation. He had divided history into three epochs: the age of the Father under the Old Covenant, the age of the Son under Christianity's thousand-year triumph in Europe, and a new age of the Spirit ushering in an egalitarian and utopian society. As Joachim put it, "In the first infants are taught, in the second adolescents are formed, in the third the friends are inebriated."[24]

It was easy to see Francis as the harbinger of this new age. In the simplicity of his life and depth of his compassion, people claimed to have seen Jesus. He was naïve enough to believe that Jesus actually meant for people to practice the things he had taught. Francis was perceived as the model of a new humanity, fully in tune with the natural world.

Francis widened the community of the faithful to include the entire cosmos. If Jesus said, "Foxes have dens and birds have nests, but the Son of Man has no place to lay his head," Francis welcomed foxes and birds as full-fledged members of the congregation he served. What he found in the natural world was but a wider, more universal expression of what he'd encountered in God on the cross.

Francis was recognized as a Second Jesus, a prophetic figure proclaiming the union of natural and supernatural, sacred and profane, human and more-than-human. He affirmed the hallowedness of all beings. His encounter with the wolf of Gubbio exemplifies the saint's refusal to live in a dualistic world of "us versus them." "Francis's way-of-being-with-things," says Leonardo Boff, "resulted in a total reconciliation of a man with his universe."[25]

Three stories take us into the heart of Francis's teaching. They convey the joy he found in the embrace of poverty, his inclusion of the wildest creatures in the family of God, and his radical identification with Christ near the end of his life. In each of these, he was accompanied by his confessor and closest companion, Brother Leo.

1. *The Perfect Joy of Lady Poverty.* One cold winter night Francis and Leo were trudging through the snow on their way back to the Portiuncula, the little church the friars had rebuilt with their own hands. This is "perfect joy," laughed Leo, looking forward to a warm fire and the welcoming smile of the brothers after a day of caring for the poor. Well almost, replied Francis. *Perfect* joy would be knocking on the door in a few minutes and having the brothers mistake them for thieves robbing the poor, turning them away, and forcing them to spend the night under the stars with nothing but the love of God to keep them warm. That would be perfect joy, said Francis, to share in the mistaken identity of the poor.[26]

Francis was revered (and sometimes scorned) as *il poverello*, the poor one—a man content with very little. His mission wasn't to offer charity as a friend of the poor, but to *become* poor with them, sharing in their poverty. This was more than an ascetic practice of traveling light. It was the affirmation of a universal family to which everyone belonged, where there were no outsiders, no one going without.

You can't separate Francis's view of poverty from his view of the family of all creatures. The poorer he was, the more freely he could move through the world, identifying with those sustained by what the earth supplied. In the "cosmic democracy" he envisioned, he refused "to be over things in order to be with them." Family, for Francis, was everything.[27]

2. *Encountering the Wolf of Gubbio.* One of the most popular stories about Francis didn't emerge until more than a century after his death.[28] In the legend of the wolf of Gubbio, a huge Apennine wolf had attacked the

livestock and threatened the people of a small Umbrian village. The towns-folk were unable to kill the beast and appealed to the saint for help.

Francis walked into the hills to talk with "brother wolf," scolding him for his behavior. Because of the severe winter, the wolf had been starving, but nonetheless responded to Francis by pledging nonviolence toward the people of the town. Francis, in turn, asked the people of Gubbio to pledge nonvio-lence to the wolf, promising to bring him food instead of chasing him with battle axes and pruning hooks. Incorporated into the community in this way, the animal quickly became a beloved symbol of the saint. The townspeople grieved when the wolf died a few years later.

The part of the story that intrigues me most is its description of the phys-ical exchange between Francis and the wolf. Showing deference to Francis, "the wolf gestured with its body, tail and ears, and bowed its head, showing that it fully accepted what the saint said."[29] This is the body language that a wolf typically uses in recognizing an alpha leader.

By incorporating the wolf into the human community, Francis restored the animal to the safety of the pack. Lone wolves separated from their families can be dangerous and unpredictable. They need the reassurance that an alpha superior provides. Francis wasn't trying to make the wolf more "human," but more true to its own nature. The wolf's posture, lowering his head and bowing to Francis, was an acknowledgment that he'd found a benevolent leader with his best interest at heart.

Francis reminds us that we don't have to "tame" nature, or subdue it. We make it family—incorporating it into a wider community, seeing the wildly "other" as not entirely *other* at all. The tale isn't about an "evil" wolf versus "good" people, with Francis taking sides. The real miracle is that he tames the people of Gubbio, opening them to a less dualistic way of viewing the world.

He refuses to accept a cosmos sharply divided between rich and poor; wild and domesticated; healthy, "normal" people and unclean lepers. He doesn't pit Christian crusaders against infidel sultans. For him, monks gathered for prayer and highway robbers stealing from the poor were equally children of God, disobe-dient though they might be. After all, as Gary Paul Nabhan observes, "Francesco Bernardone himself scored high on wild behavior and low on obedience."[30]

3. The Stigmata and Transitus: Union with Christ. In the last years of his life, Francis spent more and more time among the jagged rocks atop Mount

Alverna, north of Assisi, giving himself to contemplation in this wild and solitary place. In the fall of 1224, he committed to a forty-day fast there, despite being in poor health. Brother Leo and some of the other friars built a cell of tree branches for him, overlooking the surrounding wilderness. There he sat "gazing at the form of the mountain and marveling at the great chasms and openings in the massive rocks."[31] His hunger for fierce terrain increased with his hunger for God.

Feeling the need for a still wilder and more remote place to pray, he found an isolated rock shelf on a nearby cliff. With Leo's help he placed a log across the chasm ("a horrible and fearful precipice"), and Francis crossed to the other side. A few nights later, a six-winged seraph came to him there, burning the marks of the holy stigmata into his hands, feet, and side. According to the legend, the whole mountain caught fire, "illuminating all of the mountains and valleys around as if the sun shone over the land."[32]

Francis was "utterly transformed into the direct likeness of Christ Crucified."[33] It signified, for him, the identification with the poor and participation in the divine that has to mark the new humanity. In receiving the wounds of Christ, Francis experienced what we saw the exhausted and wing-beaten pilgrims in Attar's *Conference of the Birds* to have realized in meeting the Simorgh, their king. Gazing into the mirror at the fiery transformation of their own being, they saw *themselves* as divine. The birds were stunned by the depth of their participation in mystery of the holy. In the same way, Francis discovered God's deepest embrace of pain and glory within himself, in his own body—*becoming* Christ, as it were. It's what he had sought all along.

After this experience, death was for Francis but an opening into new life. He died on October 4, 1226, lying on the ground outside the Portiuncula down the hill from the town of Assisi. Every year on the vigil of that day, Franciscans commemorate his *transitus*, his "passing over" through death into life.

The saint's final days were filled with the same joy with which he'd lived. Francis completed his "Canticle of the Creatures," commemorating the praise offered to God by the elements of nature. He asked Sister Jacopa to bring some of her delicious almond cookies to be buried with him. And he died singing. A flock of larks flew overhead, whirling around the church as they continued his song.

Brother Elias, always attentive to public opinion, scolded Francis for singing, saying that it would be scandalous for people to see a saint not preparing for death in the proper sober spirit.[34] The man had known Francis for years, but sadly still missed the point. Without doubt, the *poverello* would have excused his failure, knowing that the winged and four-legged ones, that Brother Sun and Sister Moon, are so much better than humans at the simplicity of unselfconscious praise.

***

With the extraordinary vision of Francis of Assisi, this book comes full circle, returning to the end of the journey that the thirty Persian birds foreshadowed at the beginning. Like them—like the wandering Francis— the pilgrim seeks to gaze on the face of the Beloved. She yearns to glimpse what she knows has been tracking her in her dreams, prompting her lifelong yearning. The desire may have dimmed at times, but it never went out, stirred by the stories she heard along the way, by leaves swirling on the wind, fog lifting from a field.

"What we call the beginning is often the end," said T. S. Eliot. "And to make an end is to make a beginning. The end is where we start from."[35] You move through the seasons of your life—the child, the adolescent, the adult and elder—only to find yourself starting all over again. Gazing into the sky with childlike awe, you find yourself where you've always wanted to end: looking up through green branches into the very face of God. But you're now doing it with all of the *others*. You realize that each of your conversations with air, fire, water, and earth has been leading you to membership in a larger community of praise all along. You've always belonged to a wild company of saints and teachers of every sort.

Through these chapters, we've seen this hunger expressed in many forms. In Francis making his *transitus*, singing his way from death into life. In Hildegard of Bingen's vision of trees appearing in dazzling flashes of light. In Nikos Kazantzakis turning flesh into spirit, affirming the two as one, and in Gregory of Nyssa's plunging from glory to glory with ever-deepening desire. We've seen it in Farid ud-Din Attar and Teresa of Ávila finding their broken humanity made gloriously alive, in Ignatius of Loyola passing through the dark cave, and Catherine of Siena tumbling into God's fiery love.

The overwhelming "vision of God"—even for the saints—involves no "seeing" as such. There's only a luminous darkness, they'd say. Yet *being seen* is itself unbearably divine. The human soul can't abide its vulnerability to such grandeur. Stripped of words, thoughts, even consciousness, it's consumed, vanquished by an overpowering love.

In finally being seen, the saints also *see themselves* for the first time. The *visio Dei* occasions a *visio sui*. The glass through which we see darkly is a mirror as well. We know our truest, deepest selves to be nothing less than the image of the Beloved. We are wilder, more vulnerable, and more terrifyingly beautiful than we ever could have imagined. *All* of us.

THE EYES OF THE WOLF

On a cold February morning, several months after returning from Wyoming, I gazed into the golden eyes of a pair of red wolves on a Missouri hillside. They were standing under tall oak trees less than twenty yards away. The sight was electrifying, even though I was watching them from behind a double chain-link fence at the Endangered Wolf Center near Eureka, west of St. Louis.[36]

Red wolves are the world's most endangered canid, a critically threatened species. There are only thirty-eight of them left in the wild, living on the coastal marshes of the Alligator River National Wildlife Refuge in North Carolina. Slightly smaller than their gray wolf cousins, their gray-black fur has a reddish tinge. These beautiful animals once roamed the entire southeast United States.

They'll be missed when they're gone. The sea turtles along the North Carolina coast will miss them. There the wolves have kept the population of raccoons and opossums in check, keeping them from ravishing the nests of turtle eggs––in this way doing what top predators do best.

Looking into the eyes of the remnants of a vanishing species is a profoundly humbling experience. The red wolf, *Canis rufus*, has been around for two hundred thousand years. How can something that old and that feral be seriously at risk? The two wolves I saw may yet bear pups and be reintroduced to the wild as a new pack. One can only hope.

Seeing and being seen by these animals was as awkward for me as it was astonishing. The last members of a species hold a distinctive, an accusatory role. They tell us that the need to preserve wild things has never been more pressing. With Francis of Assisi, they urge us to keep as much of the "family" intact as possible. Other mammals look to us for the wisdom one should expect of an alpha leader.

"We need another and a wiser and perhaps a more mystical concept of animals," concluded Henry Beston, the early twentieth-century naturalist. "They are not brethren, they are not underlings; they are other nations, caught with ourselves in the net of life and time."[37] We need them, these other nations. We need what they show us of God's wildness, what they show us of ourselves.

Just as I was about to leave, a warning siren from the nearby town of Eureka started shrieking. It was the test of the Emergency Communications Network that sounds at 11 a.m. on the first Monday of every month. The two red wolves quickly joined in, howling together side by side, their heads raised to the sky. Mexican and maned wolves in fenced areas nearby added to the grand cacophony.

For humans the siren was a signal of fear, a reminder that we could be under threat. For the wolves it was an occasion for joyous melody—harmonizing at different pitches as wolves delight in doing. Singing chords. It was the same hair-raising sound I'd heard in the Absaroka Mountains of northwest Wyoming, but now witnessed firsthand, eye to eye, seeing and being seen.

Theirs is a voice that shouldn't be lost. I hope my granddaughter Elizabeth will still hear this glorious call of the wild when she's as old as I am—that Brother and Sister Wolf will not have vanished from the membership of the earth. Their role in conveying the mystery of a wild and exuberant God is irreplaceable. They come as close as any animal I know to suggesting what can't be seen.

CONCLUSION

TAKING THE GREAT CONVERSATION SERIOUSLY

"What a thing it is to sit absolutely alone,
in the forest, at night, cherished by this
wonderful, unintelligible, perfectly innocent speech,
the most comforting speech in the world."

—Thomas Merton, listening to the rain
outside his hermitage[1]

"Talk of mysteries! — Think of our life in nature, — daily to be
shown matter, to come in contact with it, — rocks, trees, wind on
our cheeks! The *solid* earth! the *actual* world!"

—Henry David Thoreau on the slopes of
Mount Katahdin[2]

I'm standing on the deck of a tundra buggy in the subarctic of northern Manitoba, overlooking the ice on Hudson Bay. The wind-chill factor this morning is minus 32 °F. Most of the scraggly spruce trees along the coast here have no branches on their north side, worn down by ice and wind sweeping down from the Arctic. I'm watching a polar bear grazing on kelp nearby. Weighing more than one thousand pounds, he leaves a twelve-inch footprint in the snow. These huggable-looking animals have been waiting for months for the ice to freeze so they can devour equally cuddly ringed seal pups. They're hungry enough to eat anything. Mother polar bears have to protect their young from being eaten by male polar bears. Life isn't easy in a place like this, nor is it kind.

It's easy for us to project moral judgments onto fierce landscapes. We make everything personal, as if nature were malevolent, out to *get* its creatures, including us. Exchanges of life and death within nature's Great Hoop aren't somehow vicious. (Animals need to eat.) But neither are they amicable. In a

252

wild and unruly place like Churchill, Manitoba, the Great Conversation may sound more like a barroom brawl than a mannerly drawing-room dialogue.

Each species reaches for a handhold in such an environment. Wetland grasses and sedges produce antifreeze to keep their cells alive in winter. Snow geese feed on their foliage as they nest over the summer. Arctic foxes and polar bears feed in turn on the eggs that the geese lay. Cree and Dene hunters take an occasional great white bear, the world's largest land predator, and turn the skins of foxes into clothing used for hunting. Everything eats and is eaten.

That's an important note on which to end this book, a reminder that the Great Conversation raises some hard questions. We might find some of the participants in the dialogue unsavory: bacterial decomposers, "disgusting" maggots, "heartless" predators, cancer cells. Yet they contribute, in ways we may not always like, to the balance of any ecosystem.

Theologians may find such things difficult to account for in a God-shaped universe. Some resort to simplistic theodicies that turn ferocious things into pleasantries in disguise. It's hard to rationalize a wild and rowdy world. Attempts to paint a boisterous world as "nice" are no better than efforts to tame a God who rides on the wind and laughs in the crashing thunder. In the end, we stand with the prophet Job on the edge of a harsh wilderness, knowing that a God too small could never command our praise.

The Great Conversation—like any deep exchange—involves tears, anger, and hands thrown up in despair, right alongside laughter and shouts of joy. It can't be carried on with kittens and sunflowers alone. We either embrace the entirety of an inexplicable world or we fabricate a Disney-like domain of our own making. The Great Conversation stretches us at every turn, yet it leaves us with the knowledge that we're in this together. We're part of a shared community with a growing respect for the whole. The conversation has to be as wide as the universe and as deep as the mystery of God.[3]

There are four pressing questions—scientific, philosophical, theological, and ethical—to be addressed in closing this book.

1. First, let's be honest. Can we really talk about a Great Conversation with the rest of the natural world? In speaking of my relationship with a tree, am I imagining something that doesn't exist? Or is there indeed a conversation going on out there that we all need to be a part of?

2. How do we widen our skills in listening and responding to the others? If words may be our least important means of communicating, how do we cross the borderlands of language and consciousness?

3. How do we conceive of God's role in this conversation? Where do we find God in the sometimes violent but always wild exchanges of nature, raging, exulting, dancing, weeping?

4. Once we affirm the dignity and sentience of the others, what new ways of relating to the world are demanded of us? In a time of ecological crisis, how do we stand together in a shared consciousness of the earth as a whole?

A FANCIFUL NOTION OR A TRUTH WHOSE TIME HAS COME?

The first question is how seriously we can take this idea of the Great Conversation? Is it a childish fantasy or a reality made possible by the new science and the deepening of human consciousness?

Since the Enlightenment, people in the Western world have been taught to dismiss the idea of "talking to trees" as nonsense, unless we're speaking of ancient mythology, Tolkien's Middle-earth, or children under the age of seven. We may have read about the whispering oak of Zeus at the Dodona oracle in ancient Greece, dispensing prophecy in its rustling leaves. Or Alexander the Great discovering a talking tree at the end of the earth—speaking with a male voice by day and a female voice by night. Or Muhammad's habit of preaching beside a date palm tree that wept for joy as he spoke. But we don't take these seriously.

Since the rise of anthropology as a social science in the late nineteenth century, we've learned to be suspicious of any subjective human interaction with the natural world. Early anthropologists of religion like E. B. Tylor at Oxford and James Frazer at Cambridge marveled at the childishness of "primitive" people who readily spoke to trees and attributed human traits to senseless entities in the world around them. They traced the "progress" of religious thought from lower to higher ("civilized") forms, leaving behind the naïveté of backward peoples.

Frazer was fascinated by archaic tree stories, however, gathering them in his classic study of myth and religion, *The Golden Bough*. "To the savage mind the world in general is animate," he observed.[4] His own approach was to strictly separate the conscious mind from the rest of nature, giving the authority of science to his assumption that we live in a world without companions, surrounded only by things. "The savage or barbarian has never learnt to make that rigid distinction between subjective and objective," Tylor lamented. He viewed it as a failure typical of "the lower races."[5]

We've come a long way from this reductionist, even racist, way of thinking, though its influence has been more widespread than we realize. Nineteenth-century English art critic John Ruskin coined the term "pathetic fallacy" to characterize what he saw as the gross sentimentality of Romantic poets like Blake, Wordsworth, Shelley, and Keats. They naïvely attributed emotion and sentience to inanimate nature, he said, when they wrote of a rose "weeping" in the morning dew or water "raging" in a flooded creek. In Ruskin's thinking, this revealed a "morbid state of mind, and comparatively . . . a weak one." His literary judgment parallels a more widely held suspicion that animals and (especially) plants are incapable of sensitivity or awareness.[6]

Recent developments in forestry science, religious studies, and the psychology of consciousness allow us a much more imaginative way of appreciating the mystery of trees. Plant science research is discovering astonishing things about the ability of plants to process information, attract pollinators, anticipate threats posed by insects, and orchestrate olfactory cues as part of a forest-wide warning system. We're beginning to appreciate trees and their capacity for responding to others as never before.

In evaluating claims about "plant sentience," many people recall a study in the 1960s that professed to have measured the "emotional responses" of house plants. It was based on uncorroborated polygraph tests, conducted by a former interrogator for the CIA, but it resonated with what people knew about the trees and plants they loved.[7] New studies, grounded in the work of plant biochemistry, make a strong case for plants exhibiting a degree of intelligent behavior, despite their lack of a centralized nervous system.[8]

Just as exciting are research efforts that bring together the sciences and the humanities in probing the interactions of plants and humans. John Charles Ryan, a poet/ethnographer in Australia, argues that plants are much more than passive, voiceless automatons. He calls for a new interdisciplinary field of human-plant studies (HPS) in researching the communicative life of flora.[9]

In his best-selling book, *The Hidden Life of Trees*, German forester Peter Wohlleben draws on scientific research and personal experience in portraying trees as sentient, purposeful beings living in dynamic relationship with each other. They communicate by means of a "woodwide web," sending electrical signals to neighboring trees through their roots and across fungi networks. A new field of "plant neurobiology" analyzes the cellular tissue at the tips of roots and shoots, observing how it processes information coming from various sources.[10]

British botanist Matthew Hall, in his book *Plants as Persons*, draws on contemporary plant science to argue that trees are "autonomous beings in the sense that they are sensitive, active, self-governing organisms." He questions our zoocentric (animal-centered) outlook, which largely ignores the plant kingdom except as an economic resource.[11] Forest biologists like Robin Kimmerer and Suzanne Simard speak candidly of the communicative character of plants and trees. Stephen Buhner approaches the question of plant intelligence from the angle of herbal medicine, exploring the indigenous use of sacred plants and insights gained from shamanic practice.[12]

In the field of religious studies, David Haberman's ethnographic fieldwork on tree worship in India looks at how the sacred character and "personhood" of trees is perceived through alternative cultural lenses. He argues that reverence for trees (and personal interactions with them) should be considered "a matter of cultural 'difference', not an encounter with 'the primitive mind.'" Archetypal psychologists from Carl Jung to James Hillman have asked about trees coming to us as messengers in our dreams, going beyond the tree as symbolic image to the possibility of trees actively moving in and out of our collective unconscious.[13]

Predictably, some scientists have viewed all this talk about plant sentience as a slide back into animism.[14] Admittedly, none of these approaches make a conclusive case for the possibility of people conversing with plants. But the more you learn of the new research (across so many disciplines), the less weird it sounds to talk about the intelligence of trees and our ability—on some level, at least—to communicate with them. The conversation has already moved far enough for us to be talking seriously now about the next steps in plant, animal, and human communication. We're part of a common household, needing to listen to voices other than our own.[15]

WIDENING OUR CONCEPTION
OF LANGUAGE

Poet Laureate W. S. Merwin once mused that in order to adequately describe the forests of eastern Pennsylvania where he grew up, he'd "have to speak in a forgotten language."[16] He was aware that a shift in consciousness is necessary for certain forms of communication and that it's easy to lose ancient languages we've long ceased to practice. How, then, do we speak of the languages (and shifts in consciousness) that we may need in renewing the Great Conversation?

If we were to go back to the origins of human language—some one hundred thousand to five hundred thousand years ago—we'd find patterns of speech that probably emerged as our ancestors (*Homo erectus*) began sitting together around campfires. Language would have flourished as hunters signaled each other on the African savanna and mothers tried to quiet their children in the night, perhaps echoing the sounds that came to them from the surrounding forests and grasslands.[17] Nature itself may have been the principal teacher of language.

Cultural ecologist David Abram writes of our human impulse to imitate what we hear around us. We are mockingbirds par excellence. We speak of the *buzzing* of bees, the *crack* and *rumble* of thunder, the *splashing* and *gushing* of water in a stream. Language is awash in onomatopoeia. Imitating the world around us, says Abram, "we learn our native language not mentally but bodily." Human language doesn't radically differentiate us from the rest of the natural world; it *mimics* that world in boundless ways.[18]

The myriad forms of communication that we find within any given ecosystem point to nature's inherent disposition to connect. In one way or another, everything says: "Listen. Take note. You need to hear this." We see it in the waggle dance of bees, communicating where they've last seen pollen; in the songs of humpback whales coordinating travel during annual migrations in the perfect mimicry of the eyes of owls imprinted on the wings of emperor moths, warding off potential attack from enemies. We discern it in the distinctive alarm calls of chickens, which indicate whether the threat is a raccoon or a hawk. It's there in the pheromones released by willow trees, poplars, and sugar maples as they warn each other of insect invasion.

The meaning-making activity of language emerges everywhere. Creatures have an impulse to "strut their stuff," going overboard in expressing their presence to the rest of the world. Everything is bent on communicating, and not just for purposes of reproduction and survival.

There's a profligacy about the ways creatures in the natural world seek to exert connection and allurement, as if these were ends in themselves. Blind things ten miles deep in the ocean's abyss are illuminated with some of the most lustrous colors imaginable. And for what purpose? They can't even see each other. Their beauty appears to exist for its own sake, calling attention to itself for no other reason than a celebration of wonder. Everything, it seems, cries glory.[19]

The world is a noisy playground where we all make our bids for attention. There are bullies and performance artists and those standing on the side hoping to be noticed. Everyone signals or sings, attracts or repels. The conversation never ends.

How do we as humans participate more deliberately in the exchange—finding ways of communicating more directly with the other creatures that share our world? How do we cross over the presumed void that separates us from all the others?

Creative efforts at interspecies communication have ranged from Luther Burbank talking to the plants he bred to Jim Nollman communicating with dolphins and whales through music. Then there's Buck Brannaman's phenomenal ability as a "horse whisperer" to communicate with abused animals.[20] Scientific experiments have produced some intriguing results. But they've largely operated, to my mind, in a one-sided fashion—training other animals to imitate us, teaching them to communicate on our terms.

Researchers have taught parrots and macaws to speak hundreds of human words. Animal psychologist Irene Pepperberg worked with an African gray parrot named Alex who could identify seven colors, five shapes, forty different objects, and numbers up to six, all in perfect English. When she showed him a green bottle and a green hat, asking him how they were the same, he answered "color." When she asked him how they were different, he responded "shape."[21]

Dr. Francine Patterson of the Gorilla Foundation worked for many years with Koko, a lowland African gorilla. The ape learned more than a thousand words of spoken English and could respond with an extensive use of American sign language. She could swear, gossip, rhyme, joke, and even tell fibs through signing. Putting signs together in new combinations, she identified a zebra as a "white tiger" and a ring as a "finger bracelet." When the gorilla's pet kitten died, Koko expressed profound grief through signing.[22]

These are intriguing tales, but they may say more about animals' ability to respond to verbal and nonverbal cues than our human capacity for cross-species communication. The most important work needs to be done at *our* end (as human beings). We need to develop our receptivity to other voices, resisting the impulse to connect exclusively on our own terms. The point isn't just to crack the code of other creatures' languages (reducing them to what we can understand), but to make ourselves open to what's already coming to us in ways we've not yet learned to receive.

Philosopher biologist Donna Haraway invites us to begin by thinking about the companion species we know best. In 2017, there were 85 million U.S. households with pets, providing homes to 90 million dogs and 94 million cats. Never before in modern history have pets been treated as such integral members of the family. Yet Haraway says we haven't paid enough attention to how we interact with them, how we affect each other's lives. We're inextricably involved in a web of interspecies dependencies, but we've hardly begun to explore how we relate even to the closest of these.[23]

In my apprenticeship with Grandfather, I'm starting to notice that our connecting with one another requires me to exercise an expanded awareness of everything that's going on around and between us. I have to be open to a field of multiple exchanges occurring at the same time. Philosopher Charles Taylor reminds us that language is a web. It is "present as a whole in any one of its parts. To speak is to touch a bit of the web, and this is to make the whole resonate."[24]

When I'm over at the park at night I'm simultaneously deploying at least three levels of consciousness. First, I'm obliged to use my street smarts, to remain keenly aware of what's going on in the park around me. I notice the pedestrians passing through and cars that may be stopping for drug pickups. I stay alert for any feelings of uneasiness that arise. Second, I'm attentive to Grandfather himself—to the wind in his leaves, the stillness to which he invites me, the smell of his decaying heartwood. I sink into his hollow, listening, waiting. I share with him how my day has gone—going over my examen, reflecting on what I've needed to appreciate or release from the day that's passed. We settle into each other.

Finally, I enter a contemplative silence, letting go of my thoughts and moving into an interior emptiness. This is the altered state of consciousness encountered by anyone practicing meditation. It may not be as deep as what I can achieve in a context without distractions, but the subtle interchange of these three kinds of awareness is very suggestive.

My imagination is put on alert and yet left open. Things wander into my awareness unexpectedly. The juxtaposition of edginess and contemplative stillness, sensory input and potential danger, makes for a creative mix, occasioning an experience I'm not able to name. I wonder if that isn't true of most spiritual encounters.

In "talking to a tree," I'm hearing no spoken utterance. What we experience together is largely nonverbal, received bodily. It's more of a shared "presence" than anything decipherable in language. It's untranslatable, unquantifiable. Grandfather wanders in and out of my imagination, as if my human capacity for invention were an open book on which others could also write. Increasingly I think of the imagination as a "cooperative venture" over which the ego has no exclusive control.[25]

Rupert Sheldrake's notion of morphic resonance may even apply here. He speaks of "telepathy-type interconnections between organisms," observing that a pattern of shared events or behaviors can facilitate the subsequent occurrence of similar patterns across a wider morphogenetic field.[26] Every night now for more than six years, I've been walking over to the park to spend time with a tree. What begins to happen after the 2,100th time of that recurring pattern? Out of a long-standing habit might another reality begin to take shape? Not only might the tree and I stop thinking of each other as "different," but the idea of "tree companioning" may start to make sense to a wider number of people in the neighborhood. Indeed, everything within the park's ecosystem might begin to be affected by a new pattern of growing interconnectedness.

It makes me wonder how often other sentient beings may be "thinking themselves" within us. We encounter ideas that seemingly come from within the surrounding landscape. We find ourselves in a story we didn't know we were part of—meeting neighbors, even kin, we didn't know we had. Ovid, in his *Metamorphoses*, gave us stories of humans, animals, and plants continually being transformed into and out of each other. Love was most often the driving force behind the transformation.[27]

Temple Grandin notes that "people with Asperger's or dyslexia are often good with animals because their thinking is more sensory-based than word-based." Such people think in pictures, sounds, touch sensations, smells, and tastes. When they read (or feel) the subtle changes in a horse's movements and breathing, they're meeting the animal on the common ground of a shared world of sensory perception.[28] This grants the animal a foothold for connecting across species boundaries. When entered into over a long period of time, an animal-human relationship of this sort begins to seem uncanny.

My own sensory practice of meeting nightly with Grandfather—sustained over many years now—explains my falling in love with this tree and my imagining the possibility of our crossing over the boundaries that separate us as species. "Respect for plants is the precondition for their speaking," says one plant specialist.[29] I know that to be true. Love inevitably finds a way to express itself, even across the barriers that divide those who are radically different. We see it in the classic myths—from Cupid and Psyche to Beauty and the Beast, from Peter Jackson's *King Kong* to Guillermo Del Toro's *The Shape of Water*. Love alone is what allows the *other* (the "monster," the alien) to speak, to be fully disclosed, to love in return.

But isn't all this only your imagination?" I hear that old academic voice muttering in my head at times. Trees can't listen to a story told in the woods. You only *imagine* Grandfather welcoming you on a winter night. The constellations, disappearing streams, and winding canyons that wander through this book aren't really alive, reaching out, teaching, connecting. You're making all of this up.

I take comfort in knowing that Ignatius of Loyola would be appalled at the thought of dismissing the imagination as a vehicle of genuine spiritual insight. "*It's only your imagination?*" How else does God lay hold of the human heart, Iñigo would ask. To denigrate our creative, sensory intelligence is to strip us of part of what makes us fully human. And, we should listen to the increasing number of plant scientists, forest ecologists, poets, and environmental activists who keep pushing out the edges of a more communicative world. They realize that the future of our planet depends upon our moving beyond a narrow, anthropocentric worldview.

We're just beginning to explore the nature and reach of language as it involves the rest of the creatures with whom we share the Earth. Who knows where it yet may take us? Who, for that matter, would want to live in a world wholly stripped of mystery, where humans sadly speak only to each other, a world *without* a Great Conversation?

HOW GOD ENTERS THE DIALOGUE

What is God's role in this Conversation? Is the divine mystery itself an inherently self-communicating reality, reaching out through every pore of the universe—disclosing intimacy and rowdiness at every turn? C. S. Lewis confessed that "if nature had never awakened certain longings in me, huge areas of what I mean by the love of God would never have existed."[30]

What do we make of John Muir's God of outrageous exuberance? He freely exulted in a world filled with billions of pollinators, spreading life to every new blossom, *and* in countless hordes of decomposers, eagerly feeding on death, turning it into soil. How do we comprehend a world that proclaims God's wild and reckless beauty while also raising hard questions about God's goodness and love? "On one side is radiance," observes Mary Oliver, "on another is the abyss."[31] Annie Dillard was so baffled by nature's mingling of winsome grace and horror that she walked away from words altogether, turning to painting instead.

This has been one of the great dilemmas of my life as well. On the one hand, I'm not surprised (or dismayed) by the brutishness of nature. I wouldn't want a dainty world without danger, boring me to tears. Who'd want to worship such an insipid, banal Creator? Yet there's too much suffering in the world for it to be dismissed as merely a part of God's wild adventurousness. Some things in the natural world are too malevolent to attribute to the hand of a loving God.

Darwin, for example, couldn't imagine "a beneficent and omnipotent" deity having designed an ichneumon wasp. This parasitic insect injects her eggs into the body of a living caterpillar, where they grow, eating their way from the inside out. The emerald cockroach wasp is hardly any better. It first injects venom into the brain of the cockroach it chooses as host, turning it into a zombie as eggs are deposited and eventually hatched inside its living cocoon.[32] Not to mention the postcoital murderousness of the female praying mantis.

Let's face it: The world can be horrifying at times. Annie Dillard stares at a giant water bug sucking the innards out of a motionless frog. She sees a child's face burned off in the crash of a plane, and asks: What in the world does God have in mind?[33]

Everywhere life "seethes and bubbles," says German theologian Walter Kasper. It sings, even where it is "violently devastated, throttled, gagged, and slain." The Spirit of God, he says, is at work in every niche of the natural world.[34] But how do we understand that? How does God participate in the Great Conversation?

Religious people are prone to think of God as speaking and acting from *above*—as an authoritative voice micromanaging everything that happens in the natural world. We might do better to conceive of the Divine as entering the conversation more intimately from *below*. Might God be less involved in controlling or directing than in accompanying, giving space, standing alongside, like a parent providing loving support to a growing child?

Might we find the highest expression of God's "wildness" in the reckless gamble God takes in making the world "a free partner in its own creation"? Does God largely let the world operate without direct intervention—trusting its natural powers to evolve into something as beautiful as it is complex, as interdependent as it is self-contained? "The world is in evolution," John Haught suggests, "because God is a God of persuasive rather than coercive power . . . Evolution occurs because God is more interested in adventure than in preserving the status quo."[35] In giving the world its freedom, however, God must love with God's heart in his throat at times.

An evolving creation—filled with death and predation—may have been the only way the world's beauty, diversity, and sentience could have developed as it is. God works within a broken, indeterminate system to bring wholeness out of chaos. For Christians, this involves holding God's power witnessed in a wild and wondrous world in tension with God's utter vulnerability disclosed in the cross. God is present in a world of terrifying splendor, and God is equally there in the agony of death, when hope seems altogether lost.[36]

For Abraham Heschel, these were the two poles of spirituality that formed the dialectic tension of his life, represented by his two great teachers: the Baal Shem Tov and Reb Mendl of Kotzk. The one danced in a cosmos pulsing with joy; the other bewailed a world filled with inexplicable suffering. Praise and lament walked side by side, both rabbis in love with the same God.[37]

I have to resist any theology that ignores the reality of suffering in the natural world. To associate God exclusively with goodness and light—separating the divine from everything dark—is to suggest that there are places where God cannot go. It's an idea that Psalm 139 wholly disallows: "Where can I flee from your presence?"

The Apostles' Creed goes so far as to affirm that, in Jesus, God even "descended into hell." This phrase anchors the rest of the creed in the depths of God's participation in every kind of suffering. Jesus reveals a God who empties himself of power so as to identify with those on the underside of history, the helpless who have suffered at the hands of the powerful. Yet this God reaches out as well to those who have been *abusers* of power, lost now in the darkness of self-disgust and despair. *All* of the unloved and the unlovable. God declares that no one is beyond the reach of grace.

You see this pictured in the Eastern Orthodox icons of the Harrowing of Hell. Jesus descends into hell, having experienced the oppressive power of a corrupt state, the complicity of a religious establishment, the betrayal of friends, the torture and death of the cross. Yet in the midst of that despair he discloses the supreme power of love. He breaks down the doors of hell— leaving broken hinges, latches, and keys scattered everywhere—and taking the condemned by the hand, he raises them up. This is a Jesus in defeat who claims defeat as a prize.[38]

In the icons of the transfiguration and descent into hell, we find a God who is reckless in love. We perceive a Creator who affirms the emerging novelty of an evolving universe and yet stands with the outcasts, with those discarded by a process of natural selection wending its way toward new forms of life. God is more feral and blood-spattered and pain-stricken than most Christians are ready to admit. In the cross, the divine compassion astounds us by its revelation that "love's glory has blood all over it."[39]

An evolving world, lured by God's risk-taking love, is continually drawn into greater unity, complexity, and the consciousness of its being-in-relation to everything else in the universe. Ilia Delio insists that a God intimately involved in the evolutionary process can't simply be viewed as a prime mover or distant supernatural being, but as a power of divine love pulling the world toward greater wholeness, depth, and relationality.[40]

How, then, do we conceive of God participating in the Great Conversation? From *within,* as the throbbing spirit of life, the Cosmic Christ, the Buddha nature of all things; from *below,* in the vulnerability and self-emptying of Jesus; and from *ahead,* in the lure of beauty and love that calls us forward, toward an Omega Point of increasing desire and connectedness. God isn't the *cause* of creation so much as its *goal* and lure, says John Haught.[41]

The universe hinges on hope. The world's wildness, and its conundrum of suffering, makes no sense apart from what it's becoming: a cosmos widening into deeper consciousness and greater interdependence. In the end we have to trust, with Meister Eckhart, in a God who's always giving birth—always being birthed in us, in a world bursting with ever new possibilities.[42]

This is the anticipation of theosis, or divinization, that early Christian theologians proclaimed. It's the conviction that growth in the spiritual life involves our "becoming partakers of the divine nature" (2 Peter 1:4). The disciples caught a glimpse of it in their experience of the transfiguration. They "saw" what they were becoming, what the *world* is becoming, as God's Shekinah glory fills the whole of creation. The physical world is set aglow in all its green splendor. The Cosmic Christ becomes apparent as the *inside* of *everything.*[43]

Eastern Orthodox theologians say that every created being is meant to share in the life-flow of the Trinity, the perichoresis—the weaving dance that forms the pulsing heart of God's being. This divine dance can be raucous, even dangerous. The music turns wild at times; you have to hold on tight. It persists even through unbearable grief, but the dance always weaves toward love.[44]

I encounter its mystery in a familiar cottonwood tree. His dancing, wounded body connecting me to a larger wounded community—Gaia, the endangered Earth herself—and to a God who chooses to be vulnerable as well. This is a God who sings in the timbre of wood and consents to being nailed to a tree. Split the stick and there is Jesus, said the Gospel of Thomas.[45] Lean into the tree's splintered hollow, and hope is born.

The inner language (the driving impulse) of creation is God loving God's self in every one of God's creatures. "In the end there will only be Christ loving himself," said Augustine.[46] Simeon the New Theologian stood in stark amazement as he imagined his own body awakening as the body of Christ. He moved his hand and marveled at the hand of Christ. He shifted his foot and like a flash of lightning, it was Christ's foot. Is this blasphemous, he asked? Or is it the Beloved wanting to awaken "every last part of our body" to its unmitigated radiance?[47] God chooses to dance with the hands and feet of every created being.

This, finally, is the unthinkable wonder that Attar's birds discovered at the end of their journey. It's the shocking realization that comes to Jacob after his dream of the ladder that night at Bethel: "God was in this place, and I, I did not know it" (Genesis 28:16). In the Kabbalah, the rabbis puzzled over this duplication of the first-person pronoun in the Hebrew text. But then they recalled that God's name is "I." Abraham, of course, had met God at the burning bush as the great *I AM*. Hence, when Jacob addresses God as "I" in his confession, going on to admit that he (Jacob, the *other* "I") had not been present to the place, he's stunned by the fact that he and God call themselves by the same name.

He and God are one. Had he realized this earlier, he would have recognized the presence in the place. His own "I" wouldn't have gotten in the way of the other. He would have known God by the same name that he knew himself. The realization is one that turns the mind inside out: to think that any separation between God and myself has always been an illusion. God, the human soul, and the cosmic *place* where they meet are finally inseparable. God as love is all and in all.[48]

LEARNING TO LISTEN AGAIN

How, at last, do we speak of the ethical implications of a book like this? The Great Conversation has to lead to the Great Work of addressing the environmental crisis, insists Thomas Berry. He's concerned that we've "lost our sense of courtesy toward Earth and its inhabitants, our sense of gratitude, our willingness to recognize the sacred character of habitat, our capacity for the awesome, for the numinous quality of every earthly reality."[49]

There are many excellent books on how to act in the face of the present ecological crisis—what our behavior should be in a community at risk.[50] But my concern isn't to duplicate any of these. It's to remind us that the first step in renewing any broken conversation is to begin by paying attention. *Listening* is the prerequisite first step in being ethically responsible. We have to listen carefully to those sitting across the table from us—to those who've been suffering, giving our attention in the way we'd listen at the bedside of a dying friend, or facing a person we may have hurt deeply.

Isolated individuals don't have to listen or engage. They belong only to themselves. But those who identify with a community—knowing that everything belongs—recognize the importance of listening to each member of the family: the two-legged, the four-legged, the winged, and finned; the children, adolescents, adults, and elders.

It includes even the democracy of the dead, according to G. K. Chesterton. We give voice to the ancestors, to those who've gone before us. What Christians call the Communion of Saints has become a vivid reality for me in the writing of this book, as well as *Backpacking with the Saints*. Out on the trail, I've been in regular conversation with saints and sages who've leapt into life as I've read them against the same sorts of landscapes that initially sparked their spiritual insights. They've come alive for me in a context charged by the archetypal teachers of air, fire, water, and earth.

Elizabeth Johnson says that it's high time we enlarged the traditional Christian idea of the *communio sanctorum* to "include other living creatures, ecosystems, and the whole natural world itself . . . The communion of holy people is intrinsically connected to the community of holy creation, and they stand or fall together."[51]

It's only together that we realize who we truly are. "We are a way for the cosmos to know itself," said Carl Sagan.[52] Yet the opposite is just as true. We can't know ourselves apart from the others. Indeed, if we pay careful-enough attention to this two-way process of *knowing*, we end up *loving* what we may initially have disregarded. We radically interrupt a cycle of isolation and indiscriminate use.

Listening today within the circle of the human and other-than-human community means attending to a planet under stress. The elements of nature are all speaking loudly, offering signs that we are reaching the tipping point of climate change. Something significant is happening when the sky turns black, when drought in Somalia leaves up to a million people displaced, and half of Australia's Great Barrier Reef bleaches out each year due to rising ocean temperatures.

- Uzbekistan fishermen remember when the Aral Sea in Central Asia was ten times its current size. Rusty fishing boats now stand on dry ground along its former shoreline, now fifty miles from the water's edge.

- Arctic ice melts earlier each spring and freezes later each fall. As a result, ringed seals struggle to find ice for breeding dens, and polar bears have to survive longer on stored fat reserves. Polar caps are declining at a rate of 13 percent per decade.[53]

- Prized conservation areas (and wilderness habitats) from North America to Indonesia sit atop huge mineral reserves. National parks and World Heritage Sites are more and more threatened by mining operations.

- The World Wildlife Fund reports that the illegal trade in protected wildlife continues to thrive, with elephants killed for their ivory, rhinos for their horns, tigers for their skins and bones.

For a long time, we've been canoeing down a mountain stream without any thought of the storm that's sweeping in from the distant peaks behind us. We've stopped for the night, beaching our canoe on the river's gravel bed, as high up as possible. But the rain isn't stopping and it's getting dark. Brown, churning water keeps rising in the stream. An hour ago, we placed a rock near the water's edge, but it's already underwater. The signs aren't good.

The elders have been warning us of the flood that's coming: scientists like E. O. Wilson, activists like Joanna Macy, poets like Wendell Berry. The Earth is at risk, they say, and we with it. There's no choice but to move beyond the cultural and political differences that divide us, recognizing the fragility of the ark on which we travel. Noah's boat today is the planet Earth itself.

But the elders also know that a raging river brings new life. They stand in hope at what *else* is rising around them—a wider sense of community, a growing interest in listening to the languages of the others, a readiness to learn from spiritual masters we've never taken seriously. The Great Turning has begun. The Great Conversation is resuming; it's *escalating* beyond imagination. Our choice to take part in it has never been so important.

It is time to remember our table manners. My commitment to Grandfather has made me attend more closely to how I conduct myself in the rest of my life. It drives me to recycle, compost, ride a bike, avoid using cars, sign petitions, write checks, and vote in ecologically responsible ways. It means being conscious of how I eat—giving thanks for the plants and animals that come to my table, attending to how they've been raised, thinking of the farmworkers and grocery clerks who have been part of the process.

It drives me to honor the things around me that I've considered lifeless, having taken for granted as disposable objects. I have to extend the democracy of the dead to fallen trees as their wood is fashioned into works of beauty and utility. They retain the integrity of the tree's life. I recognize it in an antique cherry rocking chair, in the mahogany bar top of an Irish pub, in the wooden choir stalls in Christ Church, Oxford. Things, too, have life.

Hafiz saw that the glory of Allah pervades *everything* that exists. It makes all things sacred and leads everything to praise.

> Because
> There is nothing
> Outside of my Master's Body
> I try
> To show reverence
> To all things.[54]

LAUGHTER AROUND THE TABLE

The sound of laughter around the table is a final requirement in renewing the Great Conversation. It signals the hope that springs from genuine community. We need more than solemn intentions. A childlike playfulness is also necessary in rejoining the dialogue, rediscovering joy in the face of wonder. I've seen it in:

- People gathered on a summer evening on Clearwater Beach in Florida, applauding yet another sunset as the deep red globe sinks into the Gulf of Mexico.

- Tears of laughter running down the faces of passengers watching dolphins and orcas leaping around the ferry as it moves through the San Juan Islands of Puget Sound.

- A handful of Chinese Christian pilgrims on the summit of Mount Sinai at sunrise, stamping their feet in the cold and singing (to my embarrassment and joy) all four verses of "How Great Thou Art."

- Two-year-old Elizabeth sitting atop the playground slide in the neighborhood park, bursting into laughter as she shouts "Hi" to the trees around her and waves to Grandfather.

We've ignored the Holy Fool's summons to laughter and play, to the child-like simplicity we knowing adults may cynically dismiss. Yet it's the well-spring of spontaneous community life. We won't be driven to save what we haven't learned to love and enjoy.

You see it in a figure like St. Anthony of Padua, one of the early Franciscans. Some of us think of him as the patron saint of lost things. But he reminds us more importantly of what's been lost to Western consciousness for centuries now: the fact that we aren't isolated individuals, but members of a vibrant, fun-loving community, much wider than we've thought.

Anthony, it seems, was a persuasive preacher.[55] He once spoke to a number of learned scholars in the town of Rimini on the Adriatic coast, northeast of Assisi. They scoffed at his unsophisticated discourse, preferring to argue over fine points of doctrine. Brother Anthony simply smiled and walked down to the shore where the Marecchia River flows into the sea. There he began talking to the fish instead.

"Since scholars refuse the word of God," he said, "here, I give it to you, my friends." It is said that a huge throng of all kinds and sizes of fishes gathered to listen. The little ones lined up near the shore, middle-sized ones behind them, and the larger fish farther back in the deeper water. They all held their heads above the waves so as to listen as carefully as they could.

Anthony preached with joyous freedom. He reminded the fish that during the flood when the other animals outside the ark were perishing, God preserved them alone without loss. He recalled that it was they who provided the tribute money when Jesus—a poor man—had nothing to pay the tax that was due to the Roman authorities (Matthew 17:24–27). It was they who kept the prophet Jonah safe for three days in the depths of the sea, before depositing him on dry land again. They, too, were chosen as food for the eternal King when the resurrected Jesus ate his first meal with the disciples that morning by the Sea of Galilee.

The fish hung on Anthony's words—opening their mouths, nodding their heads, and moving their fins in response. They were praising God in the best way they knew. When the scholars back in the city heard this, most of them scoffed, but a few came running to sit at the feet of Brother Anthony, to listen as attentively and joyfully as the fish had done.

What do we make of this story? We can write it off as a fable for children, another "fish tale." Or we can accept its invitation to laugh at ourselves, at our boorish ways of excluding others from the conversation. We can notice how the *others* have always been there in the biblical narrative, though consistently overlooked. We can accept their call to the joyous embrace of the Great Work, laughing together in the face of grim despair.

Outrageous laughter often accompanies a moment of awakening, says Thich Nhat Hanh.[56] It signals the breakthrough into any new beginning. Indeed, it's how the world came into being, according to a Jicarilla Apache narrative.[57]

The supernatural beings who created the world—the Hactcin, they say—had a prodigious sense of humor. They laughed uproariously at the odd shapes and funny behavior of the various animals and birds that they made.

When they created the first man, they howled with laughter, tears rolling down their faces as they told him to "Laugh!" as well. The man laughed, and his laughter caused the dog to jump and wag his tail. His laughter made the birds break into singing for the first time. His laughter helped to complete all that the gods had brought into being at creation.

Finally the man was caused to fall asleep, and he dreamed a creature like himself—a woman. When he awoke and found her *more* than a dream, he began to laugh, and she laughed, too. They laughed and laughed together, and that was the beginning of the world.

That's how the world must always begin anew. It's how the Great Conversation is reborn—acknowledging that we are a huge and hilarious community where laughter gives rise to magic, and magic to story, and story to hope. May it be so.

AFTERWORD

"Cottonwood" is a language I'm still struggling to acquire. I'm a slow learner. There's far more to it than figuring out grammar and syntax. I'm learning how to lean into bark, how to listen to leaves. I work at noticing the play of moonlight on branches, releasing my need to rush into anything else. But my teacher is patient, and it helps that we love each other.

There are losses involved in everything we learn. We inevitably lose a degree of effectiveness in one language as we learn yet another. Working on this book through the seventh decade of my life, I've been aware of my loosening grip on the language skills that served me so well in a teaching career. Words, after all, aren't much use in conversing with trees. I've had to develop a competence in other things.

As my ability to communicate with Grandfather slowly improves, I've noticed that the "right word" in my own language sometimes escapes me. Over breakfast at Ghost Ranch the other morning, I couldn't remember the word "asteroid" in talking about recent probes of astronomical objects making their way through the solar system. Things like that happen more often now. Is it a normal part of aging? Is my mother's Alzheimer's disease awakening in the bloodline? Or is it a natural result of my acquiring a greater proficiency in Cottonwood?

Joan Chittister debunks the notion that our mental acuity automatically weakens as we get older. It simply assumes different forms, choosing alternative priorities.[1] Losing my facility in finding the *bon mot* for every occasion that arises is no great loss. I had to play that game often enough in the academy.

Yet if it means a greater comprehension of the languages of trees, rivers, canyons, and stars, count me in. I long to be more adept at the languages of the heart, more sensitive to all that drives the Great Conversation. Out here in the red-rock canyons of the ranch, I can throw discourse to the wind. I can imagine myself as just another desert rat—an old fool talking to animals, crazy as Ed Abbey. Hearing strange voices on the distant mesa and exulting in them.

Soul work, I'm discovering, requires a forgetfulness that allows access to a deeper memory, the memory of the land itself.

This is where the Beloved hides, say Rumi and Hafiz, waiting to be found, softly whispering in the languages of trees. When I stand in the heart of a tall cottonwood, I hear the heartbeat of the Holy One, blessed be his (or her) many names. I rediscover the Jesus I'd lost. I delight in a mystery that comes breaking into my world from within, from below, from ahead. Having no fear of what may be coming next, I hear only an invitation to love.

I rest, at last, in Iñigo's prayer of utter abandonment:

> Take, Lord, and receive all my liberty,
> my memory, my understanding,
> and my entire will,
> All I have and call my own.
> You have given all to me.
> To you, Lord, I return it.
> Everything is yours; do with it what you will.
> Give me only your love and your grace,
> that is enough.[2]

NOTES

PREFACE

1. Wendell Berry, *What Are People For?* (Berkeley, CA: Counterpoint, 1990), 13.
2. Edward O. Wilson, *Consilience: The Unity of Knowledge* (New York: Vintage Books, 1998), 8.

INTRODUCTION

1. John Muir, quoted in James B. Hunt, *Restless Fires: Young John Muir's Thousand Mile Walk to the Gulf in 1867–68* (Macon, GA: Mercer University Press, 2012), 177.
2. Henry David Thoreau, *Walden* (New York: Cosimo, 2009), 171.
3. David J. Wolpe, *Floating Takes Faith: Ancient Wisdom for a Modern World* (Springfield, NJ: Behrman House, 2004), 45.
4. Ralph Waldo Emerson, *Nature and Selected Essays* (New York: Penguin Classics, 2003), 37.
5. Alexander Gilchrist, *Life of William Blake* (London: Macmillan, 1880), 1: 7. See John Philip Newell, *Christ of the Celts* (San Francisco: Jossey-Bass, 2008), 51.
6. Ilia Delio, *The Emergent Christ* (Maryknoll, NY: Orbis Books, 2011), 30; and Richard Rohr, "Jesus and Buddha: Paths to Awakening," conference with James Finley at the Center for Action and Contemplation, Albuquerque, NM, January 2008, CD.
7. Bernard McGinn, *The Flowering of Mysticism* (New York: Crossroad, 1998), 82.
8. For information on the four elements, see John Fraim, "The Place of Elements," chapter 12 in *Symbolism of Place: The Hidden Context of Communication*, at <Symbolism.org>; and Marion Grau, "Elements of

Renewal: Fourfold Wisdom," *Anglican Theological Review* 92, no. 4 (Fall 2010): 687–706.

9. *The Gift: Poems by Hafiz, the Great Sufi Master*, trans. Daniel Ladinsky (New York: Penguin Compass, 1999), 116; John Ruysbroeck, *Flowers of a Mystic Garden* (London: J. M. Watkins, 1912), 69–70; Pierre Teilhard de Chardin, *The Divine Milieu* (New York: Harper & Row, 1960); Jalaluddin Rumi, as quoted in *Rumi and His Sufi Path of Love*, eds. M. Fatih Citlak and Huseyin Bingul (Clifton, NJ: Tughra Books, 2007), 81.

10. Aldo Leopold, *A Sand County Almanac* (New York: Oxford University Press, 1949); Douglas Christie, *The Blue Sapphire of the Mind: Notes for a Contemplative Ecology* (New York: Oxford University Press, 2012); Joanna Macy and Molly Young Brown, *Coming Back to Life: Practices to Reconnect Our Lives, Our World* (Gabriola Island, BC: New Society Publishers, 1998).

11. See C. G. Jung, *The Archetypes and the Collective Unconscious*, vol. 9, *The Collected Works of C. G. Jung* (Princeton, NJ: Princeton University Press, 1981), 1; and Robert A. Johnson's *Inner Work: Using Dreams and Active Imagination for Personal Growth* (San Francisco: Harper & Row, 1986).

12. C. G. Jung, *Mysterium Coniunctionis, an Inquiry into the Separation and Synthesis of Psychic Opposites in Alchemy*, vol. 14, *The Collected Works of C. G. Jung* (Princeton, NJ: Princeton University Press, 1970), 787; and C. G. Jung, *The Symbolic Life: Miscellaneous Writings*, vol. 18, *The Collected Works of C. G. Jung* (Princeton, NJ: Princeton University Press, 1977), 292.

13. Thomas Moore, ed., *A Blue Fire: Selected Writings by James Hillman* (New York: HarperPerennial, 1991), 24.

14. Bill Plotkin, *Nature and the Human Soul* (Novato, CA: New World Library, 2007).

15. Moore, *A Blue Fire*, 121–125; and Thomas Moore, *Care of the Soul* (New York: HarperCollins, 1992), 196–203.

16. Quoted in Linnie Marsh Wolfe, *Son of the Wilderness: The Life of John Muir* (New York: Alfred A. Knopf, 1946), 144.

17. John Muir, *My First Summer in the Sierras* (Boston: Houghton Mifflin, 1911), 195–196.

18. Steven Holmes, *The Young John Muir: An Environmental Biography* (Madison: University of Wisconsin Press, 1999), 178–179.

1. Paul Tillich, *Love, Power, and Justice* (New York: Oxford University Press, 1954), 84.

2. David B. Dillard-Wright, "Thinking Across Species Boundaries: General Sociality and Embodied Meaning," *Society and Animals* 17 (2009): 68.

3. Attributed to Bhagavan Sri Ramana Maharshi (1879–1950), the Hindu sage who established an ashram at Arunachala in South India. See *Talks with Sri Ramana Maharshi, Three Volumes in One* (Tiruvannamalai, India: V. S. Ramanan, 2000), Talk 20, January 30, 1935.

4. Mary Oliver, "Wild Geese," in *Dream Work* (New York: Atlantic Monthly Press, 1986), 14.

5. Martin Buber, *I and Thou* (New York: Simon and Schuster, 1970), 57–58.

6. Quoted in Peter Tomkins and Christopher Bird, *The Secret Life of Plants* (New York: Harper & Row, 1973), ix.

7. Gaston Bachelard, *The Poetics of Reverie*, trans. Daniel Russell (New York: Orion Press, 1969), 99.

8. Thomas Berry and Thomas Clarke, *Befriending the Earth* (Mystic, CT: Twenty-Third Publications, 1991), 20 (emphasis added).

9. *The Collected Works of C. G. Jung*, eds. Gerhard Adler and R. F. C. Hull (Princeton, NJ: Princeton University Press, 1977), 18: 585. Quoted in Meredith Sabini, ed. *The Earth Has a Soul: The Nature Writings of C. G. Jung* (Berkeley, CA: North Atlantic Books, 2002), 79–80.

10. Blake to Rev. Dr. Trusler, August 23 1799, in *The Letters of William Blake*, ed. Geoffrey Keynes (New York: Macmillan, 1956), 35.

11. See Lucien Lévy-Bruhl, *How Natives Think*, trans. Lilian A. Clare (London: George Allen & Unwin, 1926).

12. "Nature cannot be regarded as something separate from ourselves or as a mere setting in which we live," urged Pope Francis. "We are part of nature, included in it and thus in constant interaction with it." *Laudato Sí: On Care for Our Common Home*, ¶ 139.

13. C. G. Jung, *Collected Works*, vol. 13, *Alchemical Studies*, trans. R. F. C. Hull (Princeton, NJ: Princeton University Press, 1967), ¶ 241.

14. Qing Li, *Shinrin Yoku: The Art of Japanaese Forest Bathing* (New York: Viking, 2018).

15. Stephen H. Buhner, *The Lost Language of Plants: The Ecological Importance of Plant Medicines to Life on Earth* (White River Junction, VT: Chelsea Green Publishing, 2002), 8; and Stephen H. Buhner, "Sacred

Plants: Native American Herbal Medicine," *Native Peoples Magazine*, January/February 2007, 68–69.

16. James J. Gibson, *The Ecological Approach to Visual Perception* (Boston: Houghton Mifflin Co., 1979), 127–143.

17. Thomas Berry, *The Great Work* (New York: Harmony/Bell Tower, 1999), 16.

18. Teilhard de Chardin, *The Future of Man* (Colorado Springs: Image Books, 2004), 117f; James Hillman, "A Psyche the Size of the Earth," in *Ecopsychology: Restoring the Earth, Healing the Mind*, eds. Theodore Roszak, Mary E. Gomes, and Allan D. Kanner (San Francisco: Sierra Club Books, 1995), xvii.

19. James Frazer, "The Soul External in Folk Tales," chapter 66 in *The Golden Bough* (New York: Macmillan, 1922). See also Steven H. Semken, *Soul External: Rediscovering the Great Blue Heron* (North Liberty, IA: Ice Cube Press, 2014), 78–87.

20. "When you love something," says Richard Rohr, "you grant it soul, you see its soul, and you let its soul touch yours. You have to love something deeply to know its soul." From *A New Cosmology: Nature as the First Bible*, Center for Action and Contemplation, Albuquerque, NM, 2009, CD.

21. See Evelyn Fox Keller, *A Feeling for the Organism: The Life and Work of Barbara McClintock* (New York: W. H. Freeman, 1983); and L. O. McMurry, *George Washington Carver: Scientist and Symbol* (New York: Oxford University Press, 1981).

22. Maurice Merleau Ponty, *Phenomenology of Perception* (New York: Routledge, 1962), 214.

23. David Wagoner, "The Silence of the Stars," in *Traveling Light: Collected and New Poems* (Champaign: University of Illinois Press, 1999), 271–272.

24. *Hildegard of Bingen: The Book of the Rewards of Life*, trans. Bruce W. Hozeski (New York: Oxford University Press, 1997), 4: 59, quoted in Heinrich Schipperges, *Hildegard of Bingen: Healing and the Nature of the Cosmos* (Princeton, NJ: Markus Weiner Publishers, 1997), 63. See also Sarah L. Higley, *Hildegard of Bingen's Unknown Language: An Edition, Translation, and Discussion* (New York: Palgrave Macmillan, 2007).

25. *Francis of Assisi: Early Documents*, vol. 1, *The Saint*, ed. Regis Armstrong, Wayne Hellmann, and William Short (New York: New City Press, 1999), 251.

26. Nachman of Breslov, *Sichoth Haran*, 163, 227, in *Rabbi Nachman's Wisdom*, ed. Rabbi Zvi Aryeh Rosenfeld (Jerusalem: Breslove Research Institute, 1984). Quoted in *Outpouring of the Soul: Rabbi Nachman's Path*

in Meditation, trans. Aryeh Kaplan (Jerusalem: Breslov Research Institute, 1980), 42.

27. Mircea Eliade, "Secret Language"—"Animal Language," in *Shamanism: Archaic Techniques of Ecstasy*, trans. Willard Trask (Princeton, NJ: Princeton University Press, 1964), 96–99.

28. George MacDonald, *Phantastes* (Grand Rapids, MI: Wm. B. Eerdmans, 1981), 13.

29. I've been given permission by native elders to tell this story. It's adapted from Frederick W. Turner's *Beyond Geography: The Western Spirit Against the Wilderness* (New York: Viking Press, 1980), 11–13.

30. *The Gift: Poems by Hafiz, the Great Sufi Master*, trans. Daniel Ladinsky (New York: Penguin Compass, 1999), 26.

CHAPTER 2

1. Alice Walker, *The Color Purple* (New York: Washington Square Press, 1983), 178–179.

2. J. R. R. Tolkien, *The Two Towers* (New York: Ballantine, 1954), 80.

3. I shared this story in an earlier book, *The Solace of Fierce Landscapes* (New York: Oxford University Press, 1998). There I referred to the place as "Upper Moss Creek," wanting to preserve its hiddenness in the wilds of the Ozarks. But there are no hidden places any more—only ones that need protection. They have to be called now by their true names.

4. Martin Buber, *I and Thou*, trans. Ronald Gregor Smith (Edinburgh: T. & T. Clark, 1950), 11; Loren Eiseley, *The Unexpected Universe* (New York: Harcourt Brace and World, 1964), 24.

5. See Joanna Macy and Molly Young Brown, *Coming Back to Life: Practices to Reconnect Our Lives, Our World* (Gabriola Island, BC: New Society Publishers, 1998).

6. He learned "to treat his thoughts, visions, and dreams like animals met in a forest, people in a room, or birds in the air—realities distinct from himself, not conjured up by his psyche." *Memories, Dreams, Reflections* (New York: Vintage Books, 1963), 183.

7. Michael Perlman, *The Power of Trees* (Dallas: Spring Publications, 1994), 130.

8. James Hillman, *Animal Dreams* (San Francisco: Chronicle Books, 1997), 37. Hillman warns of the danger of psychologizing our dreams. "In the eagerness for conceptual meanings, we ignore the actual beast" (29).

"Why do they come to us, the animals? What do they want, inhabiting our dreams? . . . What is *their* need, *their* reason for coming into our sleep?" (13).

9. David Quammen, *The Song of the Dodo* (New York: Scribner, 1997).

10. Daniel Quinn, in his book *Ishmael*, offers an intriguing analysis of modern humans as "Takers," using the world as a vast life-support system meant for their needs alone (New York: Bantam/Turner Books, 1992).

11. Derrick Jensen, *A Language Older Than Words* (White River Junction, VT: Chelsea Green, 2004), 15, 108.

12. John Burroughs, "The Art of Seeing Things," in *American Earth: Environmental Writing Since Thoreau* (New York: Library of America, 2008), 158–159.

13. Einstein to Carl Seelig, March 11, 1952; "Besten Dank für ihren Brief vom 6. März," Albert Einstein Archives at Hebrew University of Jerusalem, Online Archives 39-13.

14. Derrick Jensen, *A Language Older Than Words*, 69.

15. Christian Wiman, *My Bright Abyss: Meditation of a Modern Believer* (New York: Farrar, Straus and Giroux, 2013), 95; *Rilke's Book of Hours: Love Poems to God*, trans. Anita Barrows and Joanna Macy (New York: Riverhead Books, 2005), 171.

16. Stephen Jay Gould, "Unenchanted Evening," *Natural History,* September 1991, 14.

17. John Seed observed that in the awareness of Deep Ecology, "I am protecting the rainforest" develops into "I am part of the rainforest protecting myself. I am that part of the rainforest recently emerged into thinking." *Thinking Like a Mountain: Toward a Council of All Beings* (Philadelphia: New Society Publishers, 1988), 35–39.

18. Rilke to Magda von Hattingberg, February 17, 1914, in *Rilke and Benvenuta: An Intimate Correspondence*, trans. Joel Agee (New York: Fromm, 1987), 77–78. Cf. Gerard Manley Hopkins's notion of *inscape* (the complex of characteristics that give each thing its uniqueness, as in the graceful swerve of a particular tree's rising trunk) and *instress* (the force of being that carries this mystery into the mind of the beholder). *The Journals and Papers of Gerard Manley Hopkins* (New York: Oxford University Press, 1959), 215.

19. Thomas Berry, *The Great Work* (New York: Bell Tower, 1999), 94, 98.

20. Wendell Berry, *That Distant Land: The Collected Stories* (Washington, DC: Shoemaker & Hoard, 2004), 356. See also Berry's "The Dark Country," in *A Place in Time* (Berkeley, CA: Counterpoint, 2012), 118. His

novels *Jayber Crow* (2000) and *Hannah Coulter* (2004) are books in the Port William series.

21. Wendell Berry, *Jayber Crow* (Berkeley, CA: Counterpoint, 2000), 209.

22. Elder Frederick Evans, quoted in Edward D. and Faith Andrews, *Work and Worship: The Economic Order of the Shakers* (Greenwich, CT: New York Graphic Society, 1974), 48–49.

23. Teilhard de Chardin, *The Divine Milieu* (New York: HarperPerennial, 2001), 15, 99.

24. See his introduction to Edward D. and Faith Andrews, *Religion in Wood: A Book of Shaker Furniture* (Bloomington: Indiana University Press, 1966), xiii.

25. Edward D. and Faith Andrews, *Visions of the Heavenly Sphere: A Study in Shaker Religious Art* (Charlottesville: University Press of Virginia, 1969), 16.

26. Isak Dinesen, *Out of Africa* (New York: Vintage Books, 1972), 40–41.

27. Quoted in Georges Duplain, "On the Frontiers of Knowledge," in *C.G. Jung Speaking: Interviews and Encounters*, eds. William McGuire and R. F. C. Hull (Princeton, NJ: Princeton University Press, 1993), 420.

CHAPTER 3

1. William Wordsworth and Samuel Taylor Coleridge, *Lyrical Ballads: 1798 and 1802* (New York: Oxford University Press, 2013), 81.

2. *Francis and Clare: The Complete Works*, trans. Regis Armstrong and Ignatius Brady (New York: Paulist Press, 1982), 38–39.

3. For a discussion of Jungian archetypes, see Robert Moore and Douglas Gillette, *King, Warrior, Magician, Lover: Rediscovering the Archetypes of the Mature Masculine* (HarperSanFrancisco, 1990); and "Queen, Mother, Wise Woman and Lover: Rediscovering the Archetypes of the Mature Feminin," at Stottilien.com, February 1, 2013, <https://stottilien.com/2013/02/01/queen-mother-wise-woman-and-lover-rediscovering-the-archetypes-of-the-mature-feminine/>.

4. Gaston Bachelard, *Air and Dreams: An Essay on the Imagination of Movement*, trans. Edith R. Farrell and C. Frederick Farrell (Dallas: Dallas Institute, 1988), 63.

5. "Ambient (outdoor) air quality and health," World Health Organization website, May 2, 2018, <http://www.who.int/en/news-room/fact-sheets/detail/ambient-(outdoor)-air-quality-and-health>.

6. Mark Nepo, *Seven Thousand Ways to Listen* (New York: Atria, 2013), 95.

7. Paul A. Johnsgard, *Crane Music: A Natural History of American Cranes* (Washington, DC: Smithsonian Institution Press, 1991), 5.

8. Michael Green, *One Song: A New Illuminated Rumi* (Philadelphia: Running Press, 2005).

9. Aldo Leopold, "Marshland Elegy," 1937. Quoted in Peter Matthiessen, *The Birds of Heaven: Travels with Cranes* (New York: North Point Press, 2001).

10. Brandon Keim, "Amazing Starling Flocks Are Flying Avalanches," Wired, June 16, 2010. <http://www.wired.com/2010/06/starling-physics/>.

11. *The Masnavi*, book 4, story 2, in *Masnavi I Ma'navi: The Spiritual Couplets of Maulána Jalálu-'d-Dín Muhammad Rúmí*, trans. Edward Henry Whinfield (London: Trübner & Co., 1898).

12. Paul Johnsgard, *Sandhill and Whooping Cranes: Ancient Voices over America's Wetlands* (Lincoln: University of Nebraska Press, 2011), 10.

13. See J. E. Cirlot, *Dictionary of Symbols* (New York: Philosophical Library, 1962), 26–27.

14. Genesis 8:8–11; 1 Kings 17:6–8; Isaiah 40:31; Song of Songs 2:12; Luke 3:22; Matthew 10:29–31; and Matthew 23:37. See Debbie Blue, *Consider the Birds: A Provocative Guide to Birds of the Bible* (Nashville: Abingdon Press, 2013), 70.

15. Edward A. Armstrong, *Saint Francis: Nature Mystic* (Berkeley: University of California Press, 1973), 51–96.

16. On May 27, 1784, Mozart passed a petshop in Vienna, hearing a starling singing lines from his newly composed piano concerto. The strange encounter led to his buying the bird and it becoming his muse. See Lyanda Lynn Haupt *Mozart's Starling* (New York: Back Bay Books, 2017).

17. Charles Hartshorne, *Born to Sing: An Interpretation and World Survey of Bird Song* (Bloomington: Indiana University Press, 1992), 11; Richard J. Cannings, *An Enchantment of Birds* (Vancouver, BC: Greystone Books, 2007).

18. Al-Ghazali (1058–1111) wrote an earlier Epistle of the Birds about winged pilgrims making a long journey in search of their king. Along with Al-Hallaj, Sanai of Ghazni, and Ruzbihan Baqli, his work served as a model for Attar's work.

19. Written in 1177, the Manṭiq al-ṭayr (the "speech" of the birds) has been translated into English rhymed couplets by Afkham Darbandi and Dick Davis in Farid ud-Din Attar's *The Conference of the Birds* (New York: Penguin Books, 1984). See also Belden Lane, "In Quest of the

King: Image, Narrative, and Unitive Spirituality in a Twelfth-Century Sufi Classic," *Horizons* 14, no. 1 (Spring 1987): 39–48.

20. In the Quran, the hoopoe is the bird sent as an ambassador by Solomon to the Queen of Sheba. In the natural world, the hoopoe is a colorful, crowned bird found throughout Eurasia.

21. *Conference of the Birds*, 53–54, lines 1099–1115.

22. Ibid., 79–80, lines 1667–1691.

23. Ibid., 81–82, lines 1708–1735.

24. Ibid., 132, lines 2602–2605.

25. Ibid., 219, lines 4234–4235.

26. Lucian Stone, "Blessed Perplexity: The Topos of Hayrat in Attar's Mantiq al-tayr," in *Attar and the Persian Sufi Tradition*, eds. Leonard Lewisohn and Christopher Shackle (London: I. B. Tauris Publishers, 2006), 105.

27. *The Essential Rumi*, trans. Coleman Barks (San Francisco: Harper, 1995), 243. Rumi once said of his mentor, "Attar has traversed the seven cities of Love, We are still at the turn of one street." Quoted in Seyyed Hossein Nasr, *The Garden of Truth: The Vision and Promise of Sufism, Islam's Mystical Tradition* (New York: HarperCollins, 2008), 130.

28. *Pseudo-Dionysius: The Complete Works*, trans. Paul Rorem (New York: Paulist Press, 1987), 82 (emphasis added). Cyril of Alexandria, quoted in Rebecca Ann Parker and Rita Nakashima Brock, *Saving Paradise: How Christianity Traded Love of This World for Crucifixion and Empire* (Boston: Beacon Press, 2009), 177n14.

29. Translation from Eugene Peterson's *The Message: The Bible in Contemporary Language* (Colorado Springs: NavPress, 2002).

30. Willa Cather, "A Wagner Matinée," in *Youth and the Bright Medusa* (New York: Alfred A. Knopf, 1920), 242.

31. Gaston Bachelard, *The Poetics of Space,* trans. Maria Jolas (Boston: Beacon Press, 1994), 93. See also Mary Ann Kirkby, "Nature as Refuge in Children's Environments," *Children's Environments Quarterly* 6, no. 1 (1989): 7–12.

32. Gary Paul Nabhan and Stephen Trimbell, *The Geography of Childhood: Why Children Need Wild Places* (Boston: Beacon Press, 1995), 5. See also Nabhan and Trimble's interview on the October 6, 1995, episode of Living on Earth. Public Radio International's Environmental News Magazine, <loe.org>.

33. Rilke to Lou Andreas-Salomé, February 20, 1914, in *Rilke and Andreas-Salomé: A Love Story in Letters*, trans. Edward Snow and Michael Winkler (New York: W. W. Norton, 2006), 233.

34. Jennifer Ackerman, *The Genius of Birds* (New York: Penguin Books, 2016), 1, 9.

35. See "Do Birds Play?" on the Cornell Lab of Ornithology website, April 1, 2009, <https://www.allaboutbirds.org/do-birds-play/>.

36. Kenneth R. Ginsburg, "The Importance of Play in Promoting Healthy Child Development and Maintaining Strong Parent-Child Bonds," *Pediatrics* 119, no. 1 (January 2007): 182–191.

37. Jürgen Moltmann, *Theology of Play* (New York: Harper & Row, 1972), 2.

38. "Rumi," online article, New World Encyclopedia, <http://www.newworldencyclopedia.org/entry/Rumi#>.

39. Jelaluddin Rumi, "The Sheikh Who Played with Children," in *The Essential Rumi*, 44–46.

40. C. G. Jung, *Dreams*, trans. R. F. C. Hull (Princeton, NJ: Princeton University Press, 2010); and Jung, "The Psychology of the Child Archetype," in part 4 of *The Archetypes and the Collective Unconscious, The Collected Works of C. G. Jung*, trans. R. F.C. Hull (Princeton University Press, 1980), vol. 9, part 1, 151–181).

41. Madeleine L'Engle, *Walking on Water: Reflections on Faith and Art* (New York: North Point Press, 1980), 99.

CHAPTER 4

1. Adapted from a letter to Odo of Siossons, 1148. *Hildegard of Bingen: Selected Writings,* trans. Mark Atherton (New York: Penguin Classics, 2001), 21–22.

2. Jan DeBlieu, *Wind: How the Flow of Air Has Shaped Life, Myth, and the Land* (Boston: Mariner Books, 1998), 270–271.

3. Hurricanes are measured by using the Saffir-Simpson Hurricane wind scale, ranging from a category 1 storm (beginning at 74 miles per hour) to a category 5 storm (with winds of 157 miles per hour or higher).

4. Erik Larson, *Isaac's Storm: A Man, a Time, and the Deadliest Hurricane in History* (New York: Vintage Books, 2000).

5. The highest wind speed ever recorded was in a tornado hitting Oklahoma City on May 3, 1999. It was clocked by Doppler radar at 319 miles per hour.

6. Gaston Bachelard, *Air and Dreams: An Essay on the Imagination of Movement* (Dallas: Dallas Institute Publications, 1988), 229.

7. The original text of this work by an anonymous Russian hermit was found in a Mount Athos monastery in Greece in the nineteenth century. It was first published in 1884.

8. *The Way of a Pilgrim and The Pilgrim Continues His Way,* trans. R. M. French (New York: Seabury Press, 1965), 47. A more recent critical edition is *The Pilgrim's Tale,* trans. T. Allan Smith (New York: Paulist Press, 1999).

9. *The Way of a Pilgrim,* 1.

10. *The Way of a Pilgrim,* 140.

11. *The Way of a Pilgrim,* 106, 31–32.

12. *The Way of a Pilgrim,* 10. From *The Philokalia: The Complete Text,* trans. G.E.H. Palmer, Philip Sherrard, and Kallistos Ware (London: Faber and Faber, 1979–2007), 4: 72.

13. *The Way of a Pilgrim,* 12–14.

14. See their writings on inner prayer in *The Philokalia: The Complete Text,* 4: 64–75, 192–193, 204–206, 264–266, 331–332, 337.

15. Dennis Lewis, *The Tao of Natural Breathing* (Berkeley, CA: Rodmell Press, 2006), 19.

16. Gregory of Nazianzus, Oration 27.4. Quoted in Kallistos Ware, *The Inner Kingdom* (Crestwood, NY: St. Vladimir's Seminary Press, 2000), 67.

17. See Thomas Merton, *Contemplative Prayer* (New York: Doubleday, 1990), 19–45; and Robin Amis, ed. *The Path of Prayer: Four Sermons on Prayer* by St. Theophan the Recluse (Newbury, MA: Praxis Institute Press, 1992). For cautions about breath work, see Kallistos Ware, "Praying with the Body: The Hesychast Method and Non-Christian Parallels," *Sobernost* (incorporating *Eastern Churches Review*) 14, no. 2 (1992): 6–35.

18. *Chuang Tzu: The Inner Chapters,* trans. David Hinton (Berkeley, CA: Counterpoint, 2014), 9.

19. Walter Hooper, ed., *The Letters of C. S. Lewis to Arthur Greeves (1914–1963)* (New York: Collier Books, 1986), 421, 425.

20. Quoted in Michael Cohen, "Stormy Sermons," *Pacific Historian* 25, no. 2 (1981): 30.

21. J. D. Salinger, *Franny and Zooey* (New York: Bantum Books, 1969), 34.

22. Gaston Bachelard, *The Poetics of Reverie* (Boston: Beacon Press, 1969), 99.

23. Gregory of Sinai, "The Beginning of Watchfulness," in *The Philokalia: The Complete Text,* 4: 264–265.

CHAPTER 5

1. Michael Perlman, *The Power of Trees* (Thompson, CT: Spring Publications, 1998), 77.

2. Gaston Bachelard, *The Flame of a Candle* (Dallas: Dallas Institute Publications, 1988), 51–52.

3. Richard Preston, *The Wild Trees: A Story of Passion and Daring* (New York: Random House, 2008).

4. Mircea Eliade, *Shamanism: Archaic Techniques of Ecstasy* (Princeton, NJ: Princeton University Press, 1964), 127–127.

5. John Fowles, *The Tree* (London: Vintage Books, 2000), 90–91.

6. Robin Wall Kimmerer, *Braiding Sweetgrass* (Minneapolis: Milkweed Editions, 2013), 176.

7. Charles Darwin, *The Power of Movement in Plants* (London: John Murray, 1880). See also Dov Koller, *The Restless Plant* (Cambridge, MA: Harvard University Press, 2011).

8. Peter Wohlleben, *The Inner Life of Animals* (Vancouver, BC: Greystone Books, 2017), 90.

9. Michael Phillips, *Mychorrhizal Planet* (White River Junction, VT: Chelsea Green Publishing, 2017), 203, n.3.

10. Peter Wohlleben, *The Hidden Life of Trees* (Vancouver, BC: Greystone Books, 248–249; and Suzanne Simard, "The Networked Beauty of Forests," TED Talk, April 11, 2014.

11. Gaston Bachelard, *The Poetics of Space* (Boston: Beacon Press, 1994), 186.

12. John Borelli, "The Tree of Life in Hindu and Christian Theology," in Robert Masson, ed. *The Pedagogy of God's Image* (Chico, CA: College Theology Society, 1982), 175–184.

13. C. G. Jung, *Collected Works*, vol. 13, *Alchemical Studies* (Princeton, NJ: Princeton University Press, 1983), 193–195.

14. Quran 53:13–18. See Noble Ross Reat, "The Tree Symbol in Islam," in *Studies in Comparative Religion* 9, no. 3 (Summer 1975): 172–174; A. T. Mann, *The Sacred Language of Trees* (New York: Sterling Ethos), 71–73; Ronald B. Dixon, *Oceanic Mythology* (Boston: Marshall Jones, 1916), 168.

15. "Fairy Trees," in Katherine Mary Briggs, *An Encyclopedia of Fairies* (New York: Pantheon Books, 1976), 159.

16. Belden C. Lane, "Open the Kingdom for a Cottonwood Tree," *Christian Century* 114, no, 30 (October 29, 1997): 979–983.

17. Quoted in Carol Kelly-Gangi, ed. *Pope Francis: His Essential Wisdom* (New York: Fall River Press, 2014), 119.

18. *Meditations with Hildegard of Bingen*, ed. Gabriele Uhlein (Santa Fe, NM: Bear & Co., 1983), 64.

19. Her visions came, she said, with "a blinding light of exceptional brilliance flowing through my entire brain." See Sabina Flanagan, *Hildegard of Bingen: A visionary Life* (London: Routledge, 1989), 4.

20. *Hildegard of Bingen's Book of Divine Works* (*Liber divinorum operum*), ed. Matthew Fox (Santa Fe, NM: Bear & Co., 1987), Vision IV:11, p. 87.

21. Ibid., Vision IV:11, p. 86; I:2, pp. 8–11.

22. This Kabbalist notion reached its finest expression in the teachings of Rabbi Isaac Luria, a sixteenth-century mystic. See Lawrence Fine, *Physician of the Soul, Healer of the Cosmos: Isaac Luria and His Kabbalistic Fellowship* (Redwood City, CA: Stanford University Press, 2003).

23. Quoted in Heinrich Schipperges, *The World of Hildegard of Bingen* (Collegeville, MN: Liturgical Press, 1998), 48.

24. *Hildegard of Bingen: Scivias*, trans. Columba Hart and Jane Bishop (New York: Paulist Press, 1990), part 2.8, p. 153.

25. *Hildegard of Bingen's Book of Divine Works*, Vision X:19, p. 244.

26. "O Viridissima Virga," song 19 in Hildegard of Bingen's *Symphonia*. See Barbara Newman, ed. *Saint Hildegard of Bingen: Symphonia; A Critical Edition* (Ithaca, NY: Cornell University Press, 1998), 126. The translation is by Nathaniel M. Campbell, International Society of Hildegard von Bingen Studies. Used with permission.

27. *Hildegard of Bingen: Scivias*, part 4:25, pp. 123–124.

28. Sabina Flanagan, *Hildegard of Bingen: A Visionary Life* (London: Routledge, 1989), 81–82.

29. Hildegard of Bingen, *Liber subtilatum*, her Book on the Subtleties of the Diverse Nature of Created Things (1150). See Sarah L. Higley, *Hildegard of Bingen's Unknown Language: An Edition, Translation, and Discussion* (New York: Palgrave Macmillan, 2007), 13–34.

30. *Hildegard of Bingen's Book of Divine Works*, Vision IV:105, p. 136.

31. *Hildegard of Bingen: Scivias*, part 4:26, p. 124. In her fourth vision in the *Book of Divine Works*, she offers a mandala in which the green/brown Earth has nine trees growing from its center and six human figures engaged in cultivating the land through the changing seasons of the year.

32. *Analecta Sacra*, 352, as quoted in Schipperges, *The World of Hildegard of Bingen,* 63.

33. *Hildegard of Bingen: The Book of the Rewards of Life* (*Liber vitae meritorum*), trans. Bruce W. Hozeski (New York: Oxford University Press, 1997), 4: 59. The translation of this quote is from Heinrich Schipperges, *Hildegard of Bingen: Healing and the Nature of the Cosmos* (Princeton, NJ: Markus Weiner Publishers, 1997), 63.

34. Mark Atherton, *Hildegard of Bingen: Selected Writings* (New York: Penguin, 2005), 105. See Matthew Fox's inclusion of her songs in *Hildegard of Bingen's Book of Divine Works*, 363–393.

35. Hildegard's *Physica*, in Sabina Flanagan's *Secrets of God: Writings of Hildegard of Bingen* (Boston: Shambhala, 1996), 98.

36. Quoted in notes to *Vision: The Music of Hildegard von Bingen*, Angel Records, 1994, 4.

37. *Hildegard of Bingen: The Book of the Rewards of Life*, 3:2 and 2:38, as translated by Shipperges, *The World of Hildegard of Bingen*, 17, 20, 11.

38. Barbara Newman, *Sister of Wisdom: St. Hildegard's Theology of the Feminine* (Berkeley: University of California Press, 1987), 3.

39. *Hildegard of Bingen: The Book of the Rewards of Life*, 2:38, as translated by Shipperges, *The World of Hildegard of Bingen*, 57–59.

40. Ibid, 3:2. Quoted in Marion Grau, "Elements of Renewal: Fourfold Wisdom," *Anglican Theological Review* 92, no. 4 (Fall 2010): 704.

41. Shel Silverstein, *The Giving Tree* (New York: Harper & Row, 1964). Some critics of the book view it as a satire for adults. See Jacqueline Jackson and Carol Dell, "The Other Giving Tree," *Language Arts* 56, no. 4 (April 1979): 427–429; and Ruth Margalit, "The Giving Tree at Fifty: Sadder Than I Remembered," *New Yorker*, November 5, 2014.

42. The story is adapted from James Legge's translation in *The Texts of Taoism* (Oxford: Oxford University Press, 1891), book 4, number 7. See also Belden C. Lane, "The Tree as Giver of Life: A Metaphor in Pastoral Care," in *The Journal of Pastoral Care* 45, no. 1 (Spring 1991): 15–22.

43. *The Works of Vicesimus Knox* (London: J. Mawman, 1824), 3: 126; and Constantine Cavarnos, *The Life of St. Nikephoros of Chios*, vol. 4, *Modern Orthodox Saints* (Belmont, MA: Institute for Byzantine Studies, 1976), 30.

44. From his poem "Fireflies," in *A Tagore Reader*, ed. A. Chakravarty (Boston: Beacon Press, 1961), 340.

CHAPTER 6

1. *Francis and Clare: The Complete Works*, trans. Regis Armstrong and Ignatius Brady (New York: Paulist Press, 1982), 38–39.

2. See Stacey Couch, "Archetypes: The Warrior," March 29, 2016, < https://www.wildgratitude.com/warrior-archetype/>.

3. T. S. Eliot, *The Waste Land* (New York: W. W. Norton & Company, 2000), section 3.

4. Gaston Bachelard, *The Psychoanalysis of Fire*, trans. Alan C. M. Ross (Boston: Beacon, 1964), 14.

5. Ibid., 10.

6. I haven't been able to find the source of this quote.

7. Clarissa Pinkola Estés, *Women Who Run with the Wolves* (New York: Ballantine Books, 1996), 177.

8. Bachelard, *Psychoanalysis of Fire*, 7.

9. Mizuta Masahide, a seventeenth-century Japanese poet, wrote this after his barn burned down in 1688.

10. *The Age of Western Wildfires* (Princeton, NJ: Climate Central, September 2012), <www.climatecentral.org/wgts/wildfires/Wildfires2012.pdf>.

11. The worst fire in U.S. history was the Great Peshtigo Fire of 1871 in northern Wisconsin. It broke out on October 8, 1871, the same day as the Chicago Fire, receiving far less attention in the press as a result. It burned 3.8 million acres and killed at least 1,500 people.

12. Timothy Egan, *The Big Burn: Teddy Roosevelt and the Fire That Saved America* (New York: Houghton Mifflin, 2009).

13. Robin Wall Kimmerer, *Braiding Sweetgrass: Indigenous Wisdom, Scientific Knowledge and the Teachings of Plants* (Minneapolis: Milkweed Editions, 2015), 363.

14. Augustine, *Confessions*, 3:1, in Maria Boulding, trans. *The Confessions: Saint Augustine* (New York: Vintage Books, 1997), 37

15. *Confessions*, 13:18, Ibid., 317.

16. Wendell Berry, *The Art of the Commonplace: The Agrarian Essays* (Berkeley, CA: Counterpoint, 2002), 117–118.

17. Hazel Rossotti, *Fire* (New York: Oxford University Press, 1993), 5.

18. See Exodus 3:2; Jeremiah 20:9; Isaiah 6:6; Luke 12:49; Acts 2:3; Hebrews 12:29.

19. Howard Schwartz, *Tree of Souls: The Mythology of Judaism* (New York: Oxford University Press, 2004), 158–159. See also Carl-Martin Edsman, "Fire" in *The Encyclopedia of Religion*, ed. Mircea Eliade (New York: Macmillan, 1978), 5: 340–346.

20. Bachelard, *Psychoanalysis of Fire*, 16, 57.

21. Philip Katz, "Adolescence, Authority, and Change," in *Annals of the American Society for Adolescent Psychiatry*, vol. 21, *Adolescent Psychiatry*, ed. Lois L. Flahrety and Harvey A. Horowitz (New York: Routledge, 1997), 49.

22. Dorothy Day attributed this quote to Catherine of Siena in her book *On Pilgrimage* (New York: Catholic Worker Books, 1948), 161.

23. Letter T368 in *The Letters of Catherine of Siena*, trans. Suzanne Noffke (Tempe: Arizona Center for Medieval and Renaissance Studies, 2008), 4: 320.

24. Letter T318, quoted in Suzanne Noffke, *Catherine of Siena: Vision Through a Distant Eye* (Collegeville, MN: Liturgical Press, 1996), 168.

25. Letter T54 in *Letters of Catherine of Siena*, 2: 274; Letter T215 in *Letters of Catherine of Siena*, 3: 10, quoted in Giuliana Cavallini, *Things Visible and Invisible: Images in the Spirituality of Catherine of Siena*, trans. Mary Jeremiah (New York: Alba House, 1996), 103 (emphasis added).

26. The Black Death struck the cities of Tuscany in the spring of 1348, a year after Catherine's birth. Fifty-two thousand people died in Siena alone, more than half the population. Ten of her siblings died while they were still young. She remembered people frantically lighting fires to purify the air in their homes and burning incense to invoke God's protection. Don Brophy, *Catherine of Siena: A Passionate Life* (New York: Blue Books, 2010), 10–11.

27. Letters T16 and T255 in *Letters of Catherine of Siena*, 2: 117, 193; and Sigrid Undset, *Catherine of Siena* (New York: Sheed and Ward, 1954), 149.

28. Mary Ann Fatula, *Catherine of Siena's Way* (Wilmington, DE: Michael Glazier, 1987), 19.

29. *Catherine of Siena: The Dialogue*, trans. Suzanne Noffke (New York: Paulist Press, 1980), 273. Hereafter referred to as *Dialogue*, with page numbers from this translation.

30. Ibid., 64–160, 179–180.

31. Ibid., 115–116.

32. Prayer 12 in *The Prayers of Catherine of Siena*, trans. Suzanne Noffke (San Jose, CA: Authors Choice Press, 2001), 90.

33. Sebastian Junger, *Fire* (New York: W. W. Norton, 2001), 49.

34. Letter T109 in *Letters of Catherine of Siena*, 1: 266–267.

35. Prayer 10 in *Prayers of Catherine of Siena*, 79.

36. Letter T70, in *Letters of Catherine of Siena*, 1: 42.

37. Johann Wolfgang von Goethe, "The Holy Longing," trans. Robert Bly in *News of the Universe: Poems of Twofold Consciousness* (San Francisco: Sierra Club Books, 1980), 70.

38. Quoted in Bachelard, *The Flame of a Candle* (Dallas: Dallas Institute Publications, 1988), 44.

39. *Dialogue*, 170.

40. Her excesses were real, though probably exaggerated by her confessor and biographer Raymond of Capua so as to fit a medieval model of female suffering. Caroline Walker Bynum, *Holy Feast and Holy Fast: The Religious Significance of Food to Medieval Women* (Berkeley: University of California Press, 1987), 166.

41. Bynum, *Holy Feast and Holy Fast*, 165–218. Rudolf Bell, in his book *Holy Anorexia* (Chicago: University of Chicago Press, 1987), argues that the religious life gave medieval women more of a degree of autonomy over their bodies than they might otherwise have known (55). See also Maiju Lehmijoki-Gardner, "Denial as Action—Penance and Its Place in the Life of Catherine of Siena," in *A Companion to Catherine of Siena*, ed. Carolyn Muessig, George Ferzoco, and Beverly Mayne Kienzle (Leiden: Brill, 2012), 126.
42. Prayer 14 in *Prayers of Catherine of Siena*, 122–123.
43. *Dialogue*, 179; Letter T291 in *Letters of Catherine of Siena*, 3: 152.
44. *Dialogue*, 98, 103–104.
45. Ibid., 161–183.
46. Norman Mclean, *Young Men and Fire* (Chicago: University of Chicago Press, 1993).
47. Dodge made use of what's called an "escape fire." Another last-ditch effort employed by firefighters in a blaze (if they have time) is to dig a hole and climb inside a flame-reflecting fire shelter carried in their pack. Old firefighters, however, speak of "FEAR fires," an acronym for one's most natural response to a wall of flame heading your way: Fuck Everything and Run. Philip Connors, *Fire Season: Field Notes from a Wilderness Lookout* (New York: HarperCollins, 2011), 146.
48. See *The Revelations of Mechthild of Magdeburg*, trans. Lucy Menzies (London: Longmans, Green, 1953), 194.

CHAPTER 7

1. From "Episode 1: The Shores of the Cosmic Ocean" of the television series *Cosmos*, broadcast in 1980.
2. John Calvin, *Commentaries on the Book of the Prophet Jeremiah*, trans. John Owen (Grand Rapids, MI: Baker Book House, 2005), 9: 2, 8.
3. This number is a recent estimate from the Hubble Space Telescope's Ultra-Deep Field studies undertaken by NASA. See Marina Koren, "The Universe Just Got 10 Times More Interesting," *Atlantic*, October 14, 2016. See also Judy Connato, *Radical Amazement: Contemplative Lessons from Black Holes, Supernovas, and Other Wonders of the Universe* (Notre Dame, IN: Sorin Books, 2006).
4. See "Hubble: Pillars of Creation are also Pillars of Destruction," NASA Science Newsletter, January 7, 2015, <science.nasa.gov>.

5. Plato, *Timaeus*, trans. Donald J. Zeyl (Indianapolis: Hackett Publishing, 2000), section 38c–40d. See Richard L. Poss, "Plato's *Timaeus* and the Inner Life of Stars," at the website of the Astronomical Observatory of Palermo, Italy, <www.astropa.unipa.it>.

6. "It would seem that the lights of heaven are living beings. For the nobler a body is, the more nobly it should be adorned." *The Summa Theologica of Thomas Aquinas*, trans. Fathers of the English Dominican Province (London: R. & T. Washbourne, 1912), 524. Cf. Hildegard of Bingen's hymn to the stars, "O choruscans lux stellarum," in *Hildegard of Bingen: Symphonia: A Critical Edition*, trans. Barbara Newman (Ithaca, NY: Cornell University Press, 1998), 254.

7. Timothy R. Pauketat, *Cahokia: America's Great City on the Mississippi* (New York: Viking, 2009), 1–2; and Biloine Whiting Young and Melvin J. Fowler, *Cahokia, the Great Native American Metropolis* (Champaign: University of Illinois Press, 1999).

8. The Dhegihan Sioux language group comprises the Osage, Omaha, Ponca, Kansa, and Quapaw tribes, all having their geographical roots in the Ohio and Mississippi valleys. They also share the Classic Braden art style found at Cahokia and preserve legends of flying creatures associated with the stars. The Osage call themselves the Children of the Middle Waters, the river and the sky forming their home. See James R. Duncan, "The Cosmology of the Osage: The Star People and Their Universe," in *Visualizing the Sacred: Cosmic Visions, Regionalism, and the Art of the Mississippian World*, ed. George E. Lankford, F. Kent Reilly III, and James F. Garber (Austin: University of Texas Press, 2011), 18–33.

9. For the creation story of the Osage, see John Joseph Matthews, *The Osages: Children of the Middle Waters* (Norman: University of Oklahoma Press, 1981), 9–11. The stone artifact with the star configuration, known as the Kassly-Schaefer tablet, was found a few miles from Cahokia at Valmeye, Illinois. See the online article (with images) by Elizabeth Agnes Kassly on "The Prehistoric Birdman Tablets of Illinois," <https://arrowheads.com/www/index.php/other-stones-and-artifacts/640-the-prehistoric-birdman-tablets-of-illinois>.

10. *Ralph Waldo Emerson, Journals and Miscellaneous Notebooks, 1841–43* (Cambridge, MA: Harvard University Press, 1960), 403; Mary Oliver, *Twelve Moons* (New York: Back Bay Books, 1979), 3.

11. Joscelyn Godwin, *The Harmony of the Spheres: The Pythagorean Tradition in Music* (Rochester, VT: Inner Traditions/Bear & Company, 1992).

12. Pauketat, *Cahokia*, 101, 103, 141.

13. Ronald Goodman, *Lakota Star Knowledge: Studies in Lakota Stellar Theology* (Rosebud, SD: Sinte Gleska University, 1992).

14. Alfred Lord Tennyson, "Locksley Hall," in *Selected Poems* (New York: Penguin, 2007), 51–62.

15. Hans Urs von Balthasar argues that "Origen was as towering a figure as Augustine and Aquinas." See his preface to *Origen: An Exhortation to Martyrdom, Prayer, First Principles, Prologue to the Commentary on the Song of Songs, Homily XXVII on Numbers*, trans. Rowan Greer (New York: Paulist Press, 1979), xi.

16. Theodore Vrettos, *Alexandria: City of the Western Mind* (New York: Free Press, 2001).

17. Hans Urs von Balthasar, ed. *Origen: Spirit & Fire: A Thematic Anthology of His Writings* (Washington, DC: Catholic University of America Press, 1984).

18. In the first chapter of his systematic theology, Origen introduces God as "a consuming fire." Origen, *On First Principles*, trans. G. W. Butterworth (New York: Harper & Row, 1966), 7.

19. Origen's self-mutilation was based on his strangely literal interpretation of Matthew 19:12, where Jesus spoke of those making themselves eunuchs for the sake of the kingdom. In 553 CE, the Second Council of Constantinople condemned his ideas on the preexistence of souls and universal salvation, largely based on what others had said in his name.

20. Balthasar, *Origen: Spirit & Fire*, 1.

21. Origen, *On First Principles*, xvi.

22. *On First Principles*, 56, 61. See also Origen's letter to his student Gregory Thaumaturgus, trans. Allan Menzies, in *The Ante-Nicene Fathers*, vol. 9 (Buffalo, NY: Christian Literature Publishing Co., 1896). Abraham Heschel, *Who Is Man?* (Redwood City, CA: Stanford University Press, 1965), 84.

23. Bernard McGinn, *The Foundations of Mysticism* ((New York: Crossroad, 1991), 118. See Origen, *The Song of Songs, Commentary and Homilies*, trans. R. P. Lawson (Westminster, MD: Newman Press, 1957) and Origen's *On First Principles*, 275–282.

24. *On First Principles*, 40–43, 125–126. See Panagiotis Tzamalikos, *Origen: Cosmology and Ontology of Time* (Leiden: Brill, 2006), 79.

25. Origen wrote in his commentary on John 1:35 that "It would indeed be absurd to say that [Jesus] tasted death for human sins and not for any other being apart from man who had fallen into sin, such as the stars." *Commentary on the Gospel According to John*, books 1–10 (Washington, DC: Catholic University of America, 1989). Quoted in Alan Scott, *Origen*

and the Life of the Stars: A History of an Idea (Oxford: Clarendon Press, 1991), 141. See also *On First Principles*, 59–63.

26. *On First Principles*, 53. See Henry Crouzel, *Origen*, trans. A. S. Worrall (San Francisco: Harper & Row, 1989), 205.

27. *On First Principles*, 52–58; Scott, *Origen and the Life of the Stars*, 146. This notion of a final restoration (*apokatastasis*) of all things in Christ was much more prevalent in Eastern Christianity than in the Western tradition.

28. Origen, *Homilies on Leviticus*, trans. Gary Wayne Barkley, *The Fathers of the Church* (Washington, DC: Catholic University of America, 1990), 83: 92 (emphasis added).

29. Richard Rohr, "The Two Halves of Life," *Radical Grace* 23, no. 4 (October–December 2010).

30. James Hillman, "'Esse Is Percipi': To Be Is to Be Perceived," in *The Soul's Code* (New York: Random House, 1996), 113–127.

31. See Diana L. Eck, *Darśan: Seeing the Divine Image in India* (New York: Columbia University Press, 1996).

32. Marianne Williamson, *A Return to Love: Reflections on the Principles of "A Course in Miracles"* (New York: HarperCollins, 1992), 190–191.

33. Bill Plotkin, *Nature and the Human Soul*, 9–10, 224–226. This is Plotkin's stage three and Ken Wilber's success-driven stage of the achiever (orange level).

34. Quoted in Imam Jamal Rahman, *Spiritual Gems of Islam* (Woodstock, VT: Skylight Paths, 2013), 15.

35. This story comes to me out of the oral tradition, originating (I'm told) in the Cursillo movement in Spain.

CHAPTER 8

1. Graeme Ferguson and John Chryssavgis, *The Desert Is Alive: Dimensions of Australian Spirituality* (Melbourne: Joint Board of Christian Education, 1990), 36.

2. Thomas Merton, *The Journals of Thomas Merton*, vol. 6, *Learning To Love: Exploring Solitude and Freedom* (New York: HarperCollins, 2010), 309.

3. Robyn Davidson, "No Fixed Address: Nomads and the Fate of the Planet," *Quarterly Essay* 24 (November 2006): 1–53.

4. Robyn Davidson, *Tracks* (New York: Vintage Books, 2014), 226, 80.

5. Ibid., 121.

6. Bruce Chatwin, *What Am I Doing Here?* (New York: Viking, 1988), 273.

7. The story is told in a 2002 Australian film, based on Doris Pilkington's book *Follow the Rabbit-Proof Fence* (Brisbane: University of Queensland Press, 1996).

8. Edward Abbey, *Desert Solitaire* (New York: Ballantine Books, 1968), 270–271.

9. See Genesis 12:1; Hebrews 11:8; Exodus 17:16; I Kings 17:1–6; Matthew 3:1–6; Matthew 4:1–11.

10. Roslynn D. Haynes, *Seeking the Centre: The Australian Desert in Literature, Art and Film* (Cambridge, UK: Cambridge University Press, 1999), 14.

11. Sven Lindqvist, *Terra Nullius: A Journey Through No One's Land* (New York: New Press, 2007).

12. From George Tinamin's poem, "One Land, One Law, One People," in *Spirit Song: A Collection of Aboriginal Poetry* (Norwood, South Australia: Omnibus, 1993).

13. The desert, as "a negative landscape, is the 'realm of abstraction' located outside the sphere of existence and susceptible only to things transcendent." J. E. Cirlot, *Dictionary of Symbols* (London: Routledge, 1971), 79.

14. Keats to his brothers George and Thomas, December 21, 1817, in *The Letters of John Keats*, ed. H. E. Rollins (Cambridge, UK: Cambridge University Press, 1958), 1: 193–194.

15. Gregory of Nazianzus to Basil, letter 4, in *The Fathers Speak: St. Basil the Great, St. Gregory of Nazianzus, St. Gregory of Nyssa*, ed. George A. Barrois (Crestwood, NY: St. Vladimir's Seminary Press, 1986), 19.

16. From his "Commentary on Ecclesiastes," quoted in *From Glory to Glory: Texts from Gregory of Nyssa's Mystical Writings*, ed. Jean Danielou (Crestwood, NY: St. Vladimir's Seminary Press, 1979), 42.

17. Gregory of Nyssa, *The Life of Moses*, trans. Abraham J. Malherbe and Everett Ferguson (New York: Paulist Press, 1978), 93; Homily 6 on the Beatitudes, quoted in *From Glory to Glory*, 43; and "Commentary on the Canticle," quoted in *From Glory to Glory*, 202.

18. You find the cataphatic tradition in the earthy imagery of Franciscan and Ignatian spiritualities and the apopahatic tradition in the dark silence of Carmelite and Quaker spiritual practice. See Belden C. Lane, *The Solace of Fierce Landscapes: Exploring Desert and Mountain Spirituality* (New York: Oxford University Press, 2007), 104–107.

19. "Commentary on the Canticle," quoted in *From Glory to Glory*, 206.

20. From his "Commentary on Ecclesiastes and On Perfection," quoted in *From Glory to Glory*, 49, 52.

21. Anthony Meredith, *The Cappadocians* (Crestwood, NY: St. Vladimir's Seminary Press, 1995).

22. Morwenna Ludlow, *Gregory of Nyssa: Ancient and (Post)modern* (Oxford: Oxford University Press, 2007).

23. *Life of Moses*, 96; and "Commentary on the Canticle," in *From Glory to Glory*, 31–32.

24. Gregory's *Contra Eunomium*, quoted in Hans Urs von Balthasar, *Presence and Thought: Essay on the Religious Thought of Gregory of Nyssa* (San Francisco: Ignatius Press, 1995), 92–93.

25. Gregory wrote in his sermons on the Beatitudes that "he who is invisible in his nature becomes visible in his activities." *Gregory of Nyssa's Works*, ed. Werner Jaeger (Leiden: Brill, 1964), 7: 2, 25–27. This distinction between the divine essence and energies was developed further by St. Gregory of Palamas in fourteenth-century Greece.

26. Gregory of Nyssa, "The Great Catechism," in *Dogmatic Treatises*, ed. Philip Schaff, Nicene and Post-Nicene Fathers, Second Series (New York: Cosimo Classics, 2007), vol. 5, chapter 25.

27. *Life of Moses*, 114; *Contra Eunomium*, quoted in *Presence and Thought*, 92.

28. C. S. Lewis, *The Weight of Glory and Other Addresses* (New York: HarperCollins, 1976), 26.

29. Martin Laird, "The Fountain of His Lips: Desire and Divine Union in Gregory of Nyssa's Homilies on the Song of Songs," *Spiritus* 7, no. 1 (Spring 2007): 42.

30. Gregory, "On the Soul and the Resurrection," in *Ascetical Works*, trans. Virginia Woods Callaban (Washington, DC: Catholic University of America Press, 1967), 195–274; Jean Danielou's introduction to *From Glory to Glory*, 64.

31. *Life of Moses*, 29; and "Commentary on the Canticle," quoted in *From Glory to Glory*, 62, 211–213.

32. Quoted in Mary T. Malone, "Women's Christian Heritage: Challenges of an Alternative Story," 2007 Glasmacher Lecture at Saint Paul University, Ottawa, Canada.

33. Don DeLillo, *The Names* (New York: Vintage Books, 1989), 43; and Bruce Chatwin, *What Am I Doing Here?* (New York: Penguin Books, 1990), 139.

34. *Life of Moses*, 110–111, 30–31.

35. Gregory's *Homilies on Ecclesiastes,* quoted in John Francis Maxwell, *Slavery and the Catholic Church* (London: Barry Rose Publishers, 1975), 32–33; his "On the Love of the Poor" found in *The Hungry Are Dying: Beggars and Bishops in Roman Cappadocia* (New York: Oxford University Press, 2001); and Basil's Homily on Luke 12:18, quoted in C. Paul Schroeder, ed. *On Social Justice: St. Basil the Great* (Crestwood, NY: St. Vladimir's Seminary, 2009), 70.

36. *Life of Moses,* 95; *From Glory to Glory,* 23–46.

37. From Gregory's Letter 15, quoted in Robert Payne, *The Holy Fire* (Crestwood, NY: St. Vladimir's Seminary Press, 1980), 142.

38. Morwenna Ludlow, *Universal Salvation: Eschatology in the Thought of Gregory of Nyssa and Karl Rahner* (New York: Oxford University Press, 2000).

39. Tim Winton, *Island Home: A Landscape Memoir* (New York: Penguin Books, 2015), 29.

40. Adapted from Nikos Kazantzakis, *The Greek Passion* (New York: Simon and Schuster, 1954), 229.

CHAPTER 9

1. *Francis and Clare: The Complete Works,* trans. Regis Armstrong and Ignatius Brady (New York: Paulist Press, 1982), 38–39.

2. Mircea Eliade, *Patterns in Comparative Religion* (New York: Meridian Books, 1963), 188.

3. Dōgen, "Mountains and Rivers Sutra," in *Treasury of the Dharma Eye,* Book 29, trans. Carl Beilefeldt, in Michael Charles Tobias and Harold Drasdo, eds., *The Mountain Spirit* (Woodstock, NY: Overlook Press, 1979), 46.

4. Richard Rohr, *Falling Upward: A Spirituality for the Two Halves of Life* (San Francisco: Jossey Bass, 2013).

5. See Scott Jeffrey, "The Magician Archetype: The Knower and Creator of Worlds," at < https://scottjeffrey.com/magician-archetype/>.

6. Loren Eiseley, *The Immense Journey* (New York: Vintage Books, 1959), 15.

7. Gaston Bachelard, *Water and Dreams* (Dallas: Dallas Institute of Humanities and Culture, 1982), 6.

8. World Health Organization report on Drinking-water, February 7, 2018, <http://www.who.int/news-room/fact-sheets/detail/drinking-water>.

9. Rat and Mole's conversation in Kenneth Grahame, *The Wind in the Willows* (New York: Charles Scribner's Sons, 1922), 9–10.

10. Norman Maclean, *A River Runs Through It* (Chicago: University of Chicago Press, 1976), 104.

11. Naomi Shihab Nye, *Words Under the Words: Selected Poems* (Portland, OR: Eighth Mountain Press, 1995), 29.

12. Edward Abbey, *Down the River* (New York: Penguin Books, 1982), 3.

13. From T. S. Eliot's "Four Quartets" in *The Complete Poems and Plays, 1909-1950* (New York: Harcourt, Brace and World, 1971), 130.

14. "Brazilian scientists find signs of 3,700-mile-long river flowing far under Amazon River," *Washington Post*, August 27, 2011.

15. Craig Childs, *The Secret Knowledge of Water* (Boston: Little, Brown, and Co., 2000), 146–147.

16. Diana Eck, "Rivers," in *The Encyclopedia of Religion*, ed. Mircea Eliade (New York: Macmillan, 1993), 11: 426.

17. See Genesis 32:22-32; Exodus 2:1–10; II Kings 5:1–18; and Ezekiel 47:1–12.

18. *The Collected Works of St. Teresa of Avila*, vol. 2, *The Interior Castle*, trans. Kieran Kavanaugh and Otilio Rodriguez (Washington, DC: ICS Publications, 2012), 323.

19. Clarissa Pinkola Estés, *Women Who Run with the Wolves* (New York: Random House, 1992), 30.

20. Tessa Bielecki, *Holy Daring* (Rockport, MA: Element Inc., 1994), 11.

21. Teresa may have taken this story from Rabi'a of Basra, the eighth-century Persian mystic widely respected in the Spanish Muslim community. See Charles Upton, ed. *Doorkeeper of the Heart: Versions of Rabi'a* (New York: Pir Publications, 2004).

22. Quoted in Cathleen Medwick, *Teresa of Avila: The Progress of a Soul* (New York: Image Books, 2001), 37.

23. *Collected Works*, 1: 451. The courage of prayer, Teresa said, is "to betray the king and know that he knows it and yet never leave his presence." *Collected Works*, 1: 95.

24. *Collected Works*, 2: 281.

25. *Collected Works*, 1: 117.

26. Quoted in Alison Weber, *Teresa of Avila and the Rhetoric of Femininity* (Princeton, NJ: Princeton University Press, 1990), 3–4.

27. This quote may be legendary, but Teresa did say, "A sad nun is a bad nun . . . I am more afraid of one unhappy sister than a crowd of evil

spirits." James Martin, *Between Heaven and Mirth* (New York: HarperOne, 2012), 69.

28. *Interior Castle*, with commentary by Dennis Billy (Notre Dame, IN: Ava Maria Press, 2007), 79. Cf. chapter 8 of *Collected Works*, vol. 2.

29. *Collected Works*, 1: 327.

30. Quoted in Robert Ellsberg, *All Saints* (New York: Crossroad, 1999), 450.

31. *Collected Works*, 2: 144, 291, 303.

32. Bill Plotkin, *Nature and the Human Soul* (Novato, CA: New World Library, 2008), 301–346.

33. *Collected Works*, 1: 115.

34. Teresa continually encouraged a "holy daring" in the practice of prayer and the life of faith. See *Collected Works*, 2: 98; and Elizabeth Dreyer, *Accidental Theologians: Four Women Who Shaped Christianity* (Cincinnati: Franciscan Media, 2014), 90.

35. *Collected Works*, 1: 137.

36. *Francisco de Osuna: The Third Spiritual Alphabet*, trans. Mary Giles (New York: Paulist Press, 1981); and Peter Tyler, *Teresa of Avila: Doctor of the Soul* (London: Bloomsbury, 2013), 48–49.

37. "The virtues are now stronger than in the previous prayer of quiet. The soul . . . begins to perform great deeds." *Collected Works*, 1: 153. In this stage the will is occupied with God, leaving the heart and mind "free for business and works of service of God." *Collected Works*, 1: 426.

38. *Collected Works*, 1: 448, and 2: 450.

39. Julia Cameron, *The Artist's Way* (New York: Penguin Putnam, 2002), 2.

40. Henry Moore, quoted in Donald Hall, *Life Work* (Boston: Beacon Press, 2003), 54.

41. *The Life of Saint Teresa of Ávila by Herself*, trans. J. M Cohen (New York: Penguin, 1988), 80.

42. *Collected Works*, 1: 426, 250–252.

43. Diarmuid O'Murchu, *Quantum Theology: Spiritual Implications of the New Physics* (New York: Crossroad, 2004).

CHAPTER 10

1. Edward Abbey, *Desert Solitaire* (Tucson: University of Arizona Press, 1988), preface.

2. Terry Tempest Williams, *Red: Passion and Patience in the Desert* (New York: Vintage Books, 2002), 196–197.

3. Wallace Stegner, *The Sound of Mountain Water* (Garden City, NY: Doubleday, 1969), quoted in Ann Ronald, ed. *Words for the Wild* (New York: Random House, 1987), 257.

4. Terry Tempest Williams, *Desert Quartet: An Erotic Landscape* (New York: Pantheon Books, 1995), 9–10.

5. Edward Abbey, *The Journey Home* (New York: Dutton, 1977), 86.

6. Thomas Lowe Fleischner, *Singing Stone: A Natural History of the Escalante Canyons* (Salt Lake City: University of Utah Press, 1999), 41.

7. Ibid., 8.

8. Antoine de Saint Exupéry, *Wind, Sand, and Stars*, trans. Lewis Galantiere (New York: Harcourt Brace Javanovich, 1967), 41. See also Eric Fisher, "Naked Architecture: Addition Through Subtraction," at <fisherarch.com/wp-content/uploads/2016/07/SubtractionLR.pdf>.

9. Michelangelo's biographer Giorgio Vasari revealed this in his *The Lives of the Artists* (Oxford: Oxford University Press, 1991), 414f. Originally published in 1550.

10. Wallace Stegner, *Beyond the Hundredth Meridian: John Wesley Powell and the Second Opening of the West* (New York: Penguin Books, 1992); and Edward Abbey, *Down the River* (New York: Dutton, 1982), 47.

11. Walter Salles, in Anthony and Ben Holden, eds. *Poems That Make Grown Men Cry* (New York: Simon and Schuster, 2014), 58.

12. Fleischner, *Singing Stone*, 99.

13. Richard Rohr, *Things Hidden: Scripture as Spirituality* (London: SPCK Publishing, 2016), 25–26.

14. Elizabeth Johnson, in her book *Creation and the Cross* (Maryknoll, NY: Orbis Books, 2018), soundly criticizes Anselm's idea of Jesus's death as offering "satisfaction" to an offended deity. She proposes instead a biblical "theology of accompaniment," perceiving God as standing in solidarity with Jesus on the cross, with those everywhere who endure unbearable suffering (110–111).

15. In the modern Pinyin system for transliterating Mandarin Chinese, Lao-tzu becomes Laozi, Tao/Taoist become Dao/Daoist, and Chuang-tzu becomes Zhuangzi.

16. Alan Fletcher, *The Art of Looking Sideways* (London: Phaidon, 2001), 370.

17. Bennett B. Sims, trans., *Lao-tzu and the Tao Te Ching* (New York: F. Watts, 1971), chapter 1.

18. "Tao Te Ching," chapter 31, in Witter Bynner, trans. *The Chinese Translations* (New York: Farrar, Straus and Giroux, 1978), 369.

19. Stephen Mitchell, trans., *Tao Te Ching* (New York: Harper & Row, 1988), chapter 19.

20. Ibid., chapter 71.

21. *Chuang Tzu: The Inner Chapters*, trans. David Hinton (Berkeley, CA: Counterpoint, 2014), 11.

22. Ibid., chapter 78. See also Alan Watts, *Tao: The Watercourse Way* (New York: Pantheon Books, 1975).

23. *Tao Te Ching*, chapters 66 and 8.

24. Ibid., chapter 48.

25. Ibid., chapter 11. The masters tell of a Daoist butcher who cut meat for years without ever having to sharpen his blade. His cleaver simply sought out the empty spaces between sinew and bone in carving an ox, the joints flying apart with ease. *The Complete Works of Chuang Tzu*, trans. Burton Watson (New York: Columbia University Press, 1900), 50–55.

26. Max Kaltenmark, *Lao Tzu and Taoism* (Stanford, CA: Stanford University Press, 1969), 34.

27. *Chuang Tzu: Mystic, Moralist, and Social Reformer*, trans. Herbert A. Giles (London: Bernard Quaritch, 1889), 13.

28. I want to avoid any simplistic conflating of Daoist thinking and Pauline theology. Laozi had no interest in a transcendent or personal God. Yet the New Testament notion of kenosis, the Zen conception of *sunyatta*, and the Daoist image of Gu-shen share a great deal in common.

29. Max Kaltenmark, *Lao Tzu and Taoism*, trans. Roger Greaves (Stanford, CA: Stanford University Press, 1969), 99, 68; and *Tao Te Ching*, chapter 41.

30. *Lao-tzu and the Tao Te Ching*, chapter 17.

31. It's expressed in the *shan shui* (literally "mountain-water") style of Chinese landscape painting. Here towering cliffs represent the bright, dry, masculine energy of *yang*, rising above a winding river valley embodying the dark, moist, feminine power of *yin*. Where the two meet, they disclose the qi (chi, or life force) of the entire scene. The canyon walls contain (and yield to) the flowing creek.

32. *Julian of Norwich: Showings*, trans. Edmund Colledge and James Walsh (New York: Paulist Press, 1978), 154–155. "As sin is punished here with sorrow and penance, in contrary fashion it will be rewarded in heaven . . . There the tokens of sin are turned into honours."

33. French cardinal Pierre de Bérulle wrote, "We are a nothingness (*anéantissement*) which tends towards nothingness, which seeks out nothingness, which busies itself with nothingness, and which finally ruins itself

and destroys itself in nothingness." From the letters of Pierre de Bérulle, translated in *Christian Mysticism and Incarnational Theology: Between Transcendence and Immanence*, eds. Louise Nelstrop and Simon D. Podmore (New York: Routledge, 2016), 85.

34. "Tao Te Ching," chapter 78, in John Heider, trans., *The Tao of Leadership: Lao Tzu's Tao Te Ching for a New Age* (Palm Beach, FL: Green Dragon Books, 2015), 155.

CHAPTER 11

1. Lawrence Durrell, *Reflections on a Marine Venus: A Companion to the Landscape of Rhodes* (London: Faber and Faber, 1960), 15.

2. "The Symbolism of Islands," *symbolreader* (blog), January 19, 2014, <https://symbolreader.net/2014/01/19/the-symbolism-of-islands/>.

3. Bill Robinson, *Islands* (New York: Dodd, Mead, 1985), 4.

4. Nikos Kazantzakis, *Report to Greco*, trans. P. A. Bien (New York: Bantam Books, 1966), 142.

5. Ibid., 346.

6. Maureen Heffernan, *Fairy Houses of the Maine Coast* (Rockport, ME: Down East Books, 2010).

7. Jon Kabat-Zinn, "Indra's Net at Work," in *The Psychology of Awakening*, eds. Gay Watson, Stephen Batchelor, and Guy Claxton (York Beach, ME: Samuel Weiser Inc., 2000), 225. A seventh-century Buddhist teacher, Fasang, wrote a text, *On the Golden Lion,* in an effort to explain Indra's net. He described the universe as a golden lion, with another golden lion in every single hair of its fur. A fractal mystery repeated over and over again.

8. *Bonaventure: The Soul's Journey into God*, trans. Ewert Cousins (New York: Paulist Press, 1978), 100–101.

9. Pete Hay, "A Phenomenology of Islands," *Island Studies Journal* 1, no. 1 (2006): 19–42; Godfrey Baldacchino, "Studying Islands: On Whose Terms?" *Island Studies Journal* 3, no. 1 (2008): 37–56; and Grant McCall, "Nissology: A Proposal for Consideration," *Journal of the Pacific Society* 17, nos. 2–3 (October 1994): 1–7.

10. David Quammen, *The Song of the Dodo: Island Biogeography in an Age of Extinction* (London: Hutchinson, 1996), 130.

11. Francoise Péron, "The Contemporary Lure of the Island," *Tijdschrift voor Economische en Sociale Geografie* 95, no. 3 (2004): 326–339.

12. J. E. Terrell, "Islands in the River of Time," in *Islands of the World VIII International Conference "Changing Islands—Changing Worlds": Proceedings* (Kinman Island, Taiwan: 2004), 11.

13. Laurie Brinklow, "The Proliferation of Island Studies," *Griffith Review* 34 (October 2011), <https://griffithreview.com/articles/the-proliferation-of-island-studies/>.

14. Northrup Frye, *Anatomy of Criticism* (Princeton, NJ: Princeton University Press, 1957), 203–206.

15. Francois Taglioni, "Insularity, Political Status, and Small Insular Spaces," *Shima* 5, no. 2 (2011): 45–67.

16. L. Sprague de Camp, *Lost Continents: The Atlantis Theme in History, Science, and Literature* (Mineola, NY: Dover Publications, 1970).

17. Stephanos Stephanides and Susan Bassnett, "Islands, Literature, and Cultural Translatability," in *Poésie et Insularité*, the 2008 issue of *Transtext(es) Transcultures: Journal of Global Cultural Studies*, 5–21.

18. See Ezekiel 26:15–18; Isaiah 40:15–17; and Isaiah 59:18.

19. John Donne, *Devotions on Emergent Occasions* (New York: Oxford University Press, 1975), Meditation 17.

20. In Titus 1:12 the apostle Paul echoed this theme that Cretans are "liars, evil beasts, and lazy gluttons."

21. *Report to Greco*, 75.

22. Hay, "A Phenomenology of Islands," 23. Quote from Helen Kazantzakis, *Nikos Kazantzakis: A Biography* (New York: Simon and Schuster, 1968), 41.

23. See Kazantzakis's novels *Saint Francis* (1954) and *The Greek Passion* (1962).

24. Alice Walker, *Possessing the Secret of Joy* (New York: Harcourt Brace Jovanovich, 1992), 264.

25. Nikos Kazantzakis, *Zorba the Greek*, trans. Carl Wildman (New York: Simon and Schuster, 1965), 77, 228.

26. *Report to Greco*, 180. Cf. *Zorba the Greek*, 217, 290.

27. Nikos Kazantzakis, *Saint Francis*, trans. P. A. Bien (New York: Simon and Schuster, 1962), 23; *Report to Greco*, 465.

28. *Report to Greco*, 137.

29. Ibid., 402–403, 39.

30. Nikos Kazantzakis, *The Last Temptation of Christ* (New York: Bantam Books, 1968), 3, 89. In Kazantzakis's book *Saint Francis*, Brother Leo speaks to Francis about his love of Clare, saying: "You think you loved only

her soul. But it was her body that you loved earliest of all; it was from there that you set out, got your start. Then, after struggle, struggle against the devil's snares, you were able with God's help to reach her soul. You loved that soul without ever denying her body . . . [so] not only did this carnal love for Clara not hinder you from reaching God, it actually helped you." *Saint Francis*, 21.

31. *Report to Greco*, 276.

32. *Saint Francis*, 271.

33. See Henri Bergson, *Creative Evolution* (New York: Modern Library, 1944); Nikos Kazantzakis, *Saviors of God: Spiritual Exercises*, trans. Kimon Friar (New York: Simon and Schuster, 1960), 127–131; Nikos Kazantzakis, *The Odyssey: A Modern Sequel*, trans. Kimon Friar (New York: Simon and Schuster, 1958), 588. Cf. Jerry H. Gill, "Kazantzakis and Kierkegaard: Some Comparisons and Contrasts," in Darren Middleton and Peter Bien, eds., *God's Struggler: Religion in the Writings of Nikos Kazantzakis* (Macon, GA: Mercer University Press, 1996), 169–188.

34. *The Odyssey: A Modern Sequel*, xviii–xix. See also Morton P. Levitt, *The Cretan Glance* (Columbus: Ohio State University Press, 1980), 4.

35. *The Odyssey: A Modern Sequel*, xi.

36. Adapted from Anthony de Mello, *The Song of the Bird* (Anand, India: Gujarat Shitya Prakash, 1982), 26–27.

37. *Zorba the Greek*, 16.

38. *Report to Greco*, 122.

CHAPTER 12

1. *Francis and Clare: The Complete Works*, trans. Regis Armstrong and Ignatius Brady (New York: Paulist Press, 1982), 38–39.

2. See Stacey Couch, "The Queen and King Archetype," June 27, 2017, <https://www.wildgratitude.com/king-archetype/>.

3. Jonathan Z. Smith, *Map Is Not Territory* (Chicago: University of Chicago Press, 1993), 290–291.

4. Joan Chittister, *The Gift of Years: Growing Old Gracefully* (Katonah, NY: BlueBridge, 2010).

5. Diana Kappel-Smith, *Desert Time: A Journey Through the American West* (Boston: Little, Brown & Co., 1992), 139.

6. Quoted in Casper Henderson, *The Book of Barely Imagined Beings: A 21st Century Bestiary* (Chicago: University of Chicago Press, 2013), v.

7. For poetry evoking the Arkansas landscape of Johnny Cash, Conway Twitty, and the Ozark Mountain Daredevils, see Terry Minchow-Proffitt, *Chicken Train: Poems from the Arkansas Delta* (West Union, WV: Middle Island Press, 2016).

8. H. L. Mencken, in the *American Mercury*, 1931. After Mencken went on to call Arkansas the "apex of moronia," the state legislature passed a motion to pray for his soul.

9. In the early twentieth century, "sundown towns" became notorious in the Deep South, so named because many marked their city limits with signs typically reading, "N-----, Don't Let the Sun Go Down on You in Harrison (or wherever)." Jim White is the narrator of a documentary film by Andrew Douglas, "Searching for the Wrong-Eyed Jesus," a back-roads tour of the Deep South (2005).

10. Megan Gambino, "Conquering Everest: A History of Climbing the World's Tallest Mountain," *Smithsonian*, March 1, 2008. <Smithsonianmag.com>

11. Edwin Bernbaum, *Sacred Mountains of the World* (Berkeley: University of California Press, 1998); "The Mountain," *Parabola* 13, no. 4 (November 1988); and Belden C. Lane, "The Mountain That Was God," *Christian Century* 102, no. 20 (June 5–12, 1985): 579–581. For biblical mountains, see Genesis 22:1-8; Exodus 19-24; I Kings 18:16-40; Luke 9:28-36.

12. *Archetypes and the Collective Unconscious: The Collected Works of C. G. Jung*, trans. Gerhard Adler and R. F. C. Hull (Princeton, NJ: Princeton University Press, 1970), vol. 9, part 1, 219n14; the Dalai Lama's letter to Peter Goullart, quoted in *The Essential James Hillman: A Blue Fire* (London: Routledge, 1990), 114–120.

13. *The Complete Poetry and Prose of William Blake*, ed. David V. Erdman (Berkeley: University of California Press, 2008), 511.

14. Henry D. Thoreau, *The Maine Woods* (Boston: Ticknor and Fields, 1846), 35.

15. Marjorie Hope Nicholson, *Mountain Gloom and Mountain Glory* (New York: W. W. Norton, 1963); and Robert Macfarlane, *Mountains of the Mind* (New York: Pantheon Books, 2003).

16. Chaim Potok, *Wanderings: Chaim Potok's History of the Jews* (New York: Fawcett Crest, 1978).

17. Zalman Schachter Shalomi, *Wrapped in a Holy Flame: Teachings and Tales of the Hasidic Masters* (San Francisco: Jossey-Bass, 2003); Elie Wiesel, *Souls on Fire: Portraits and Legends of Hasidic Masters* (New York: Simon and Schuster, 1982); and Moshe Rosman, *Founder of Hasidism: A Quest*

for the Historical Ba'al Shem Tov (Oxford: Littman Library of Jewish Civilization, 2013), xix.

18. Yonassan Gershom, "Shamanism in the Jewish Tradition," in Shirley Nicholson, ed. *Shamanism: An Expanded View of Reality* (Wheaton, IL: Theosophical Publishing House, 1987), 186; and Howard Schwartz, *Tree of Souls: The Mythology of Judaism* (New York: Oxford University Press, 2004), 302.

19. *Tree of Souls*, 302; and the letter from Rabbi Israel, the Baal Shem Tov, to his brother in-law, Rabbi Abraham Gershon of Kitov, in Steven T. Katz, ed. *Comparative Mysticism: An Anthology* (New York: Oxford University Press, 2013), 144–145.

20. This Kabbalistic pattern of interpreting the deeper meanings of Torah is known as "gematria." It sees Hebrew letters as corresponding to numbers, making possible a mystical geometry that discloses hidden truths in the coded biblical text.

21. Isaac Luria (1534–1572) was the father of contemporary Kabbalah. For an account of his notion of *tzimtzum* (divine contraction), see Lawrence Fine, ed. *Physician of the Soul, Healer of the Cosmos: Isaac Luria and His Kabbalistic Fellowship* (Stanford, CA: Stanford University Press, 2003).

22. Quoted in Chaim Potok, *Wanderings* (New York: Fawcett, 1987), 464.

23. Elliot R. Wolfson, "Walking as a Sacred Duty: Theological Transformation as Social Reality in Early Hasidism," in Ada Rapaport-Albert, ed. *Hasidism Reappraised* (London: Littmann Library of Jewish Civilization, 1997), 180–207.

24. Gershon Winkler, *Magic of the Ordinary: Recovering the Shamanic in Judaism* (Berkeley, CA: North Atlantic Books, 2003), 85; and Martin Buber, *Tales of the Hasidim: The Early Masters* (New York: Schocken Books, 1947), 275. See also Yitzhak Buxbaum, *A Person Is Like a Tree: A Sourcebook for Tu BeShvat* (Northvale, NJ: Jason Aronson, 2000), 14–15, 43–45, 221–222.

25. The Besht urged his people to carve out at least a single moment of thorough-going *devekut* to God in every day. "He who grasps a part of the whole, grasps the whole," he explained. Yitzhak Buxbaum, *The Light and Fire of the Baal Shem Tov* (New York: Continuum, 2006), 124.

26. Yitzhak Buxbaum, *Jewish Spiritual Practices* (Lanham, MD: Rowman & Littlefield, 2005), 149. Within the Hasidic movement, rabbis came to be known as rebbes, emphasizing the power of their spiritual insight. "A rabbi hears what you say with your mouth, a rebbe hears what you are

saying with your soul." Aron Moss at Chabad.org, <https://www.chabad.org/therebbe/article_cdo/aid/1561748/jewish/What-is-the-Difference-Between-a-Rabbi-and-a-Rebbe.htm>.

27. For stories of the Besht, see Buber's *Tales of the Hasidim*, Buxbaum's *The Light and Fire of the Baal Shem Tov*, and Jerome Mintz, *Legends of the Hasidim* (Chicago: University of Chicago Press, 1968).

28. Elie Wiesel told this story in a lecture given on the day after receiving the Nobel Peace Prize in 1986.

29. See "The Ten Principles of the Baal Shem Tov," translated by Yaacov Dovid Shulman, April 20, 2009, <https://thebenoni.wordpress.com/2009/04/20/the-ten-principles-of-the-baal-shem-tov/>.

30. Quoted in Norman Lamm, *The Religious Thought of Hasidism* (New York: Yeshiva University Press, 1999), 389.

31. Buxbaum, *The Light and Fire of the Baal Shem Tov*, 156.

32. See Elie Wiesel, *Souls on Fire* (New York: Random House, 1972), 12, 26.

33. *Thirty-Six Aphorisms of the Baal Shem Tov* (New York: Chabad Lubavitch Media Center, 2005).

34. Quoted in "Sparks of the Baal Shem Tov," Chabad House of Monroe, <http://jewishmonroe.com/page.asp?pageID=36D33E78-4F2A-4098-BCEE-6C3A92884DB4>.

35. Ellen Frankel, ed. *The Classic Tales: 4,000 Years of Jewish Lore* (Northvale, NJ: Jason Aronson, 1989), 475–477.

36. Henry David Thoreau, *A Week on the Concord and Merrimack Rivers* (Boston: Houghton Mifflin, 1906), 197.

37. Zalman Schachter-Shalomi, *From Age-ing to Sage-ing: A Revolutionary Approach to Growing Older* (New York: Time Warner Books, 1997), 2, 11. Reb Zalman divided the developing human life into twelve stages (or "months") of seven years each.

38. Buxbaum, *The Light and Fire of the Baal Shem Tov*, 345.

39. Joanna Macy, "The Greening of the Self," in *Spiritual Ecology: The Cry of the Earth*, ed. Llewellyn Vaughan-Lee (Point Reyes, CA: Golden Sufi Center, 2013), 198.

40. See Gary Z. McGee, "The Eight Soul-centric/Eco-centric Stages of Human Development," at <fractalenlightenment.com>; and Bill Plotkin, *Nature and the Human Soul* (Novato, CA: New World Library, 2008), 394.

41. Joan Chittister, *The Gift of Years: Growing Older Gracefully* (New York: BlueBridge, 2008), 123, 127.

42. J. D. Vance, *Hillbilly Elegy* (New York: HarperCollins, 2016), 207.

43. Dōgen was the thirteenth-century author of "The Mountains and Rivers Sutra." See Michael Charles Tobias and Harold Drasdo, eds. *The Mountain Spirit* (Woodstock, NY: Overlook Press, 1979), 37–49.

44. Alan Watts, *The Way of Zen* (New York: Pantheon Books, 1951), 126.

CHAPTER 13

1. Diane K. Osbon, ed. *Reflections on the Art of Living: A Joseph Campbell Companion* (New York: Harper Perennial, 1995), 13f.

2. H. Dwight Weaver, *Missouri Caves in History and Legend* (Columbia: University of Missouri Press, 2008), 119–123.

3. Mircea Eliade, *Shamanism: Archaic Techniques of Ecstasy* (Princeton, NJ: Princeton University Press, 1964), 46–49, 51.

4. Mini Valenzuela Kaczkurkin, *Yoeme: Lore of the Arizona Yaqui People* (Tucson: University of Arizona Press, 1977), 13.

5. Similar afflictions include bathophobia, the horror of falling into or being consumed by depths, and claustrophobia, a fear of being enclosed in small spaces. See *Diagnostic and Statistical Manual of Mental Disorders (DSM-5)* (Arlington, VA: American Psychiatric Publishing, 2013), section 300.29.

6. See I Samuel 24:1–22; I Kings 19:1–18; John 11:38–44; Exodus 33:12–23.

7. A friend described him as "reckless at games, in adventures with women, in brawls and deeds of arms." See Leonard von Matt and Hugo Rahner, *St. Ignatius Loyola: A Pictorial Biography* (Chicago: Henry Regnery Co., 1956), 11.

8. Ignatius Loyola, *Autobiography*, ¶ 30, in George E. Ganss, ed., *Ignatius of Loyola: The Spiritual Exercises and Selected Works* (New York: Paulist Press, 1991), 80–81.

9. See Ignatius's "Contemplation to Attain Love," a section of the exercises that he probably wrote while in Manresa. See *The Spiritual Exercises of Saint Ignatius*, trans. George E. Ganss (Chicago: Loyola Press, 1992), ¶¶ 235–236.

10. *Spiritual Exercises*, ¶¶ 47, 91, 103, 112, 192, 220.

11. Barbara Brown Taylor, *Learning to Walk in the Dark* (San Francisco: HarperOne, 2014), 129.

12. David L. Fleming, *The Spiritual Exercises of Saint Ignatius* (St. Louis, MO: Institute of Jesuit Sources, 1978), 37.

13. *Spiritual Exercises*, ¶ 79. Women such as Iñes Pascual and Juana of Austria were among Ignatius's earliest supporters and some of the first to be led

in the exercises. Katherine Marie Dyckman, Mary Garvin, and Elizabeth Liebert, *The Spiritual Exercises Reclaimed: Uncovering Liberating Possibilities for Women* (New York: Paulist Press, 2001).

14. *Spiritual Exercises*, ¶¶ 47, 110–117, 122–125. The tradition of a cave as the site of the Nativity goes back to Justin Martyr in 150 CE.

15. Ignatius's "Rules of the Discernment of Spirits," in *Spiritual Exercises*, ¶¶ 313–336. See also Margaret Silf, *The Inner Compass: An Invitation to Ignatian Spirituality* (Chicago: Loyola Press, 2007); and David Lonsdale, *Eyes to See, Ears to Hear: An Introduction to Ignatian Spirituality* (Maryknoll, NY: Orbis Books, 2000). See also <IgnationSpirituality.com>.

16. In the "Principle and Foundation" of the *Exercises*, Ignatius urges this "holy indifference." *Spiritual Exercises*, ¶ 23. He adds that consolation can be trusted when it's un-caused, not coming as a consequence of anything we've done. When it arrives of its own accord, we should "store it up" for future occasions when darkness returns. Desolation, on the other hand, can be soul-devouring, with "no beast on the earth as fierce." Meeting it requires immense courage; one shouldn't make changes in former plans when such an attack occurs. *Spiritual Exercises*, ¶¶ 318, 325, 330 (Ganss translation).

17. Marilynne Robinson, *Gilead* (New York: Farrar, Straus and Giroux, 2004), 6.

18. See Thich Nhat Hanh, *Call Me by My True Names: Collected Poems* (Berkeley, CA: Parallax Press, 1999), 72–73.

19. Adapted from my article "Who Is This Jesus?" *Sojourners* 45, no. 4 (April 2016): 34–37.

20. Teilhard de Chardin, *The Divine Milieu* (London: Collins, 1964); Ilia Delio, *The Emergent Christ* (Maryknoll, NY: Orbis Books, 2011); Matthew Fox, *The Coming of the Cosmic Christ* (San Francisco: Harper & Row, 1988); and Brian Swimme, *The Hidden Heart of the Cosmos* (Maryknoll, NY: Orbis Books, 1996).

21. Eckhart's Sermon 56 in *Meister Eckhart*, trans. Franz Pfeiffer (London: J. M. Watkins, 1947), 142. See also Vladimir Lossky, *The Mystical Theology of the Eastern Church* (Crestwood, NY: St. Vladimir's Seminary Press, 2002); and Norman Russell, *The Doctrine of Deification in the Greek Patristic Tradition* (New York: Oxford University Press, 2006).

22. Bill Plotkin describes late adulthood as the time of "The Sage in the Mountain Cave." *Nature and the Human Soul*, 411–442.

23. *Learning to Walk in the Dark*, 185.

24. Catherine de Hueck Doherty, *Poustinia: Christian Spirituality of the East for Western Man* (Notre Dame, IN: Ave Maria Press, 1975).

25. Ignatius's "Rules for Thinking with the Church," *Spiritual Exercises*, ¶¶ 352–370.

26. Spoken by General Cypher Raige, played by Will Smith, in the 2013 film *After Earth*.

27. *Learning to Walk in the Dark*, 13.

28. Illuman is a global not-for-profit organization committed to supporting men seeking to deepen their spiritual lives. It has grown out of the work of Richard Rohr at the Center for Action and Contemplation in Albuquerque. See <Illuman.org>.

29. Mercer Mayer, *There's a Nightmare in My Closet* (New York: Penguin Putnam, 1968).

CHAPTER 14

1. Farley Mowat, *Never Cry Wolf* (Boston: Little, Brown, 1963), viii.

2. Jack London, *The Call of the Wild* (New York: Grosset and Dunlap, 1903), 91.

3. David Quammen, *Monster of God: The Man-Eating Predator in the Jungles of History and the Mind* (New York: W. W. Norton, 2004), 3.

4. Peter Matthiessen, *The Snow Leopard* (New York: Viking Press, 1978).

5. Barry Lopez, *Of Wolves and Men* (New York: Scribner, 1978), 140.

6. Rick McIntyre, *War Against the Wolf* (Stillwater, MN: Voyageur Press, 1995); and Brenda Peterson, *Wolf Nation* (Boston: Da Capo Press, 2017).

7. The historical threat of wolves is documented in Jean-Marc Moriceau's "The Wolf Threat in France from the Middle Ages to the Twentieth Century." HAL Archives-Ouvertes, 2014, <https://hal.archives-ouvertes.fr/hal-01011915>.

8. Lopez, *Of Wolves and Men*, 170.

9. Peterson, *Wolf Nation*, 47.

10. Christine Peterson, "Ranchers find ways to live with wolves despite deaths of dogs, horses, cattle," *Casper Star-Tribune*, March 23, 2015; and Julie S. Thrower, "Ranching with Wolves: Reducing Conflicts Between Livestock and Wolves Through Integrated Grazing and Wolf Management Plans," *Journal of Land, Resources, & Environmental Law*, 29, no. 2 (2009): 319–360.

11. Aldo Leopold, *A Sand County Almanac* (New York: Oxford University Press, 1949), 129–133. See also Jon T. Coleman, *Vicious: Wolves and Men in America* (New Haven, CT: Yale University Press, 2004), 214–224.

12. Christina Eisenberg, *The Wolf's Tooth: Keystone Predators, Trophic Cascades, and Biodiversity* (Washington, DC: Island Press, 2011). For a critique of the trophic cascades theory, see David Quammen, *Yellowstone* (Washington, DC: National Geographic Partners, 2016), 90f.

13. John Muir, *A Thousand Mile Walk to the Gulf*, ed. William Frederick Badé (New York: Houghton Mifflin, 1916), 98–99. See also James B. Hunt, *Restless Fires: Young John Muir's Thousand-Mile Walk to the Gulf* (Macon, GA: Mercer University Press, 2013).

14. Mark Liebenow, *Mountains of Light: Seasons of Reflection in Yosemite* (Lincoln: University of Nebraska Press, 2012), 104.

15. Carl Safina, *Beyond Words: What Animals Think and Feel* (New York: Henry Holt, 2015), 141. See also Shaun Ellis, *The Man Who Lives with Wolves* (New York: Broadway Books, 2010).

16. Jim and Jamie Dutcher, *The Hidden Life of Wolves* (Washington, DC: National Geographic, 2013), 24; Temple Grandin, *Animals Make Us Human* (Boston: Houghton Mifflin Harcourt, 2009), 26.

17. Lopez, *Of Wolves and Men,* 50, 62.

18. Ibid., 44.

19. Margaret Atwood, *The Blind Assassin* (New York: Doubleday, 2000), 424.

20. Clarissa Pinkola Estes, *Women Who Run with the Wolves* (New York: Ballantine Books, 1992), 23–24.

21. Thomas of Celano's "Life of Saint Francis," in *Francis of Assisi: Early Documents*, vol. 1, *The Saint*, eds. Regis Armstrong, Wayne Hellmann, and William Short (New York: New City Press, 1999), 192.

22. "The Testament of St. Francis of Assisi," in *Francis of Assisi: Early Documents*, 1: 125.

23. Augustine Thompson, *Francis of Assisi: A New Biography* (Ithaca, NY: Cornell University Press, 2012), 108–109.

24. Quoted in Bernard McGinn, *The Growth of Mysticism* (New York: Crossroad, 1994), 339.

25. Leonardo Boff, *Francis of Assisi* (Maryknoll, NY: Orbis Books, 2006), 36.

26. "The Deeds of Blessed Francis and His Companions" in *Francis of Assisi: Early Documents*, vol. 3, *The Prophet*, 449–450.

27. Boff, *Francis of Assisi*, 35, 41. Social historian Jacques Le Goff explores his vision of a restored society in his *Saint Francis of Assisi* (London: Routledge, 2004), 77–90.

28. It appeared in *The Little Flowers of Saint Francis*, published in the late fourteenth century. See *Francis of Assisi: Early Documents*, vol. 3, *The Prophet*, 601–605. An earlier account speaks of Francis traveling with a companion (Brother Leo?) to Gubbio, where he's warned of wolves in the area. See "The Passion of San Verecondo," in *Francis of Assisi: Early Documents*, vol. 2, *The Founder*, 807.

29. *Francis of Assisi: Early Documents*, 3: 483.

30. Gary Paul Nabhan, *Songbirds, Truffles, and Wolves: An American Naturalist in Italy* (New York: Penguin Books, 1994), 139.

31. From "Considerations of the Holy Stigmata," included in *The Little Flowers of St. Francis*, ed. Raphael Brown (Garden City, NY: Hanover House, 1958), 180.

32. Ibid., 191.

33. Ibid.

34. Legend of Perugia, quoted in Boff, *Francis of Assisi*, 130.

35. T. S. Eliot, from "Four Quartets" in *The Complete Poems and Plays* (New York: Harcourt Brace Jovanovich, 1971), 144.

36. The Endangered Wolf Center, founded in 1971, has played a major role over the years in recovery plans for the Mexican wolf and red wolf.

37. Henry Beston, *The Outermost House* (1928), quoted in *The Hidden Life of Wolves*, 180.

CONCLUSION

1. *Thomas Merton, "Rain and the Rhinoceros," in *Thomas Merton: Spiritual Master: The Essential Writings*, ed. Lawrence S. Cunningham (New York: Paulist Press, 1992), 389.

2. Henry David Thoreau, *The Maine Woods* (Boston: Ticknor and Fields, 1864), 71.

3. For me, nothing expresses the mystery of suffering in nature any better than James Dickey's poem "The Heaven of Animals," in his book *The Whole Motion: Collected Poems, 1945–1992* (Middletown, CT: Wesleyan University Press, 1992), 78–79.

4. James Frazer, *The Golden Bough: A History of Myth and Religion* (London: Macmillan, 1890), 111.

5. Edward Burnett Tylor, *Religion in Primitive Culture* (New York: Harper & Brothers, 1871), 29.

6. John Ruskin, "Of the Pathetic Fallacy," in *The Genius of John Ruskin: Selections from His Writings*, ed. John D. Rosenberg (Charlottesville: University of Virginia Press, 1998), 72.

7. Peter Tompkins and Christopher Bird reported on the controversial work of Cleve Backster in *The Secret Life of Plants* (New York: Harper & Row, 1973).

8. Anthony Trewavas, *Plant Behavior and Intelligence* (Oxford: Oxford University Press, 2015); Richard Karban, *Plant Sensing and Communication* (Chicago: University of Chicago Press, 2015); and Mark C. Mescher and Consuelo M. De Moraes, "Role of plant sensory perception in plant–animal interactions," *Journal of Experimental Botany* 66, no. 2 (February 2015): 425–433.

9. John Charles Ryan, "Passive Flora? Reconsidering Nature's Agency Through Human-Plant Studies (HPS)," *Societies*, September 8, 2014. See also Monica Gagliano, John C. Ryan, and Patricia Vieira, eds. *The Language of Plants: Science, Philosophy, Literature* (Minneapolis: University of Minnesota Press, 2017).

10. Peter Wohlleben, *The Hidden Life of Trees* (Vancouver, BC: Greystone Books, 2016); and Eric D. Brenner, "Plant Neurobiology: An Integrated View of Plant Signaling," *Trends in Plant Science* 11, no. 8 (August 2006): 413–419.

11. Matthew Hall, *Plants as Persons: A Philosophical Botany* (Albany: State University of New York Press, 2011), 3–4. See also his article "Plant Autonomy and Human-Plant Ethics," *Environmental Ethics* 31 (2009): 173.

12. Stephen Buhner, *Sacred Plant Medicine* (Santa Fe, NM: Bear & Co., 2006) and *Plant Intelligence and the Imaginal Realm* (Santa Fe, NM: Bear & Co., 2014); Julia Graves, *The Language of Plants: A Guide to the Doctrine of Signatures* (Herndon, VA: Lindisfarne Books, 2012); Roger Walsh, *The World of Shamanism: New Views of an Ancient Tradition* (Woodbury, MN: Llewellyn Publications, 2007).

13. David L. Haberman, *People Trees: Worship of Trees in Northern India* (New York: Oxford University Press, 2013), 189; James Hillman, *The Dream and the Underworld* (New York: Harper & Row, 1979) and *Dream Animals* (San Francisco: Chronicle Books, 1997). The expansion of consciousness through the use of psychoactive plants is still another area of serious research. See R. Metzner, "Hallucinogenic Drugs and

Plants in Psychotherapy and Shamanism," *Journal of Psychoactive Drugs* 4 (October–December 1998): 333–341.

14. Michael Pollan surveys the case for and against plant intelligence in "The Intelligent Plant," *New Yorker*, December 23 and 30, 2013, 92–105. See also Richard Grant, "The Whispering of Trees," in *Smithsonian* 48, no. 10 (March 2018): 48–57.

15. A "Hearing Voices Movement" has emerged in recent years as we've begun defining mental illness with more sophistication. It challenges the notion that "hearing voices" is necessarily a characteristic of mental instability. "To hear voices may instead be a meaningful and understandable, although unusual, human variation." It's a caution that might be helpful in our thinking about the Great Conversation as well. See schizophrenia researchers Marius Romme and Sandra Escher, "Exploring the Meaning of Voices," in the May 15, 2011, posting of *interVoice*, the website of the International Hearing Voices Movement, <http://www.intervoiceonline.org>.

16. Quoted in Christopher Merrill, ed. *The Forgotten Language: Contemporary Poets and Nature* (Layton, UT: Gibbs Smith, 1991), opening epigraph.

17. For theories regarding the origin of language, see Celia Deane-Drummond, *The Wisdom of the Liminal: Evolution and Other Animals in Human Becoming* (Grand Rapids, MI: Eerdmans Publishing, 2014), 172–187.

18. David Abram, *The Spell of the Sensuous* (New York: Vintage Books, 1996), 75.

19. Belden C. Lane, "Biodiversity and the Holy Trinity," *America* 185, no. 20 (December 17, 2001): 7–11.

20. Peter Dreyer, *A Gardener Touched with Genius: The Life of Luther Burbank* (Berkeley: University of California Press, 1985). Nollman is a naturalist and musician who founded Interspecies Inc., exploring interspecies communication through music and art. See his book *The Man Who Talks to Whales: The Art of Interspecies Communication* (Boulder, CO: Sentient Publications, 2002). Buck Brannaman was the inspiration for Nicholas Evans's novel *The Horse Whisperer* (New York: Delacourt Press, 1995). See also Peter Wohlleben's *The Inner Life of Animals* (Vancouver, BC: Greystone Books, 2017).

21. Irene Pepperberg is a research associate and lecturer in the Department of Psychology at Harvard. See her book *Alex and Me* (New York: Harper Perennial, 2008).

22. Francine Patterson and Eugene Linden, *The Education of Koko* (New York: Henry Holt, 1988).

23. Donna J. Haraway, *Companion Species Manifesto* (Chicago: Prickly Paradigm Press, 2003) and *When Species Meet* (Minneapolis: University of Minnesota Press, 2008).

24. Charles Taylor, *Human Agency and Language* (Cambridge, UK: Cambridge University Press, 2014), 231.

25. David Abram, *Becoming Animal* (New York: Vintage Books, 2011), 169.

26. Rupert Sheldrake, *A New Science of Life: The Hypothesis of Morphic Resonance* (Los Angeles: J. P. Tarcher, 1981). See also Judy Cannato, *Field of Compassion* (Notre Dame, IN: Sorin Books, 2010).

27. Maurice Merleau-Ponty, *Phenomenology of Perception* (New York: Routledge, 1962), 214. Thomas Aquinas suggested that angels don't communicate by means of words, but by willing mental thoughts to become evident to one another. See *The Summa Theologica of Saint Thomas Aquinas*, trans. Fathers of the English Dominican Province (Chicago: Encyclopedia Britannica, 1955), 5 vols. Prima Pars, question 107.1.

28. Temple Grandin, *Animals Make Us Human* (Boston: Houghton, Mifflin, Harcourt, 2009), 123–124.

29. John C. Ryan, "In the Key of Green," in *The Language of Plants: Science, Philosophy, Literature*, 282.

30. C. S. Lewis, *The Four Loves* (Glasgow: Fount, 1987), 23–24.

31. Mary Oliver, *Long Life: Essays and Other Writings* (Cambridge, MA: Da Capo Press, 2004), 24.

32. Darwin to Asa Gray, May 22, 1860, quoted in Christopher Southgate, *The Groaning of Creation: God, Evolution, and the Problem of Evil* (Louisville, KY: Westminster John Knox Press, 2008), 10. See also Christie Wilcox, "Your Average, Everyday Zombie," *Scientific American Blogs Network*, October 31, 2011, <https://blogs.scientificamerican.com/science-sushi/everyday-zombie/>.

33. See Annie Dillard's *Pilgrim at Tinker Creek* (New York: Harper Perennial, 1998), 7–8; and *Holy the Firm* (New York: Harper & Row, 1977), 35–36.

34. Walter Kasper, *The God of Jesus Christ* (New York: Crossroad, 1984), 228; and Jürgen Moltmann, *The Crucified God: The Cross of Christ as the Foundation and Criticism of Christian Theology* (London: SCM Press, 1973), 40–41.

35. Elizabeth Johnson, *Ask the Beasts: Darwin and the God of Love* (London: Bloomsbury, 2014), 155; John F. Haught, *Responses to 101 Questions on God and Evolution* (Mahwah, NJ: Paulist Press, 2001), 136.

36. I've addressed this dilemma, with the help of Christopher Southgate's work, in my book *Ravished by Beauty* (New York: Oxford University Press, 2011), 218–222.

37. See Abraham Heschel, *A Passion for Truth* (New York: Farrar, Straus and Giroux, 1973).

38. See Cynthia Bourgeault, *The Wisdom Jesus* (Boston: Shambhala, 2008), 119–124.

39. Andrew Harvey, *The Way of Passion: A Celebration of Rumi* (New York: Tarcher/Putnam, 2000), 90.

40. See Ilia Delio, *The Unbearable Wholeness of Being: God, Evolution, and the Power of Love* (Maryknoll, NY: Orbis Books, 2013), 78. Had I read more of her work earlier, this book might have been much improved. Delio clarifies and expands Teilhard's integration of evolution and theology with remarkable insight.

41. John Haught, *God After Darwin: A Theology of Evolution* (New York: Routledge, 2007), 87.

42. Eckhart says that from all eternity God lies on a maternity bed giving birth. The essence of God is birthing. See Matthew Fox, *Breakthrough: Meister Eckhart's Creation Spirituality in New Translation* (Garden City, NY: Image Books, 1980), 93.

43. St. Athanasius taught that "God became man so that man might become God." Yet he was careful to add that we "become by grace what God is by nature." (St. Athanasius, *On the Incarnation*, trans. John Behr (Yonkers, NY: Saint Vladimir's Seminary Press, 1993), 60. Union with God doesn't erase all differences between the creature and the Creator. St. Gregory Palamas observed that we share in the energies, not in the essence, of the divine. (*The Philokalia: The Complete Text Compiled by St. Nikodimos of the Holy Mountain and St. Makarios of Corinth* (London: Faber and Faber, 1998), 4: 396–397.)

44. Verna Harrison, "*Perichoresis* in the Greek Fathers," *St. Vladimir's Theological Quarterly* 35 (1991): 53–65. See also Michael J. Christensen and Jeffery A. Wittung, eds., *Partakers of the Divine Nature: The History and Development of Deification in the Christian Traditions* (Grand Rapids, MI: BakerAcademic, 2007), 32–46; Jürgen Moltmann, *The Coming of God: Christian Eschatology* (Minneapolis: Fortress Press, 2004), 272; and Richard Rohr, *The Divine Dance* (New Kensington, PA: Whitaker House, 2016), 26–32.

45. *The Gospel of Thomas: The Hidden Sayings of Jesus*, trans. Marvin Meyer (San Francisco, CA: HarperSanFrancisco, 1992), Saying 77.

46. Augustine, *Homilies on the First Epistle of John*, trans. Boniface Ramsey (Hyde Park, NY: New City Press, 2008), Homily 10 on 1 John 5:13.

47. Simeon the New Theologian, "We Awaken in Christ's Body," in *The Enlightened Hart: An Anthology of Sacred Poetry*, trans. Stephen Mitchell (New York: HarperPerennial, 1989), 38.

48. Lawrence Kushner, *God Was in This Place & I, I Did Not Know* (Woodstock, VT: Jewish Lights Publishing, 1991), 132–133.

49. Thomas Berry, *The Dream of the Earth* (San Francisco: Sierra Club Books, 1990), 2. Berry says the Great Work of our time is "to carry out the transition from a period of human devastation of the Earth to a period when humans would be present to the planet in a mutually beneficial manner." *The Great Work: Our Way into the Future* (New York: Random House, 1999), 3.

50. See Joanna Macy and Chris Johnstone, *Active Hope* (Novato, CA: New World Library, 2012). Thomas Berry outlines the changes in language, economics, education, religion, jurisprudence, and technology that are required of us in his *Evening Thoughts: Reflecting on Earth as Sacred Community* (San Francisco: Sierra Club Books, 2006).

51. Elizabeth A. Johnson, *Friends of God and Prophets: A Feminist Theological Reading of the Communion of Saints* (New York: Continuum, 1998), 240.

52. Carl Sagan, *Cosmos: The Shores of the Cosmic Ocean*, episode 1, PBS, 1980.

53. NASA Global Climate Change website, <climate.nasa.gov>.

54. *The Gift: Poems by Hafiz*, trans. Daniel Ladinsky (New York: Penguin Compass, 1999), 173.

55. "The Little Flowers of Saint Francis," in *Francis of Assisi: Early Documents*, vol. 3, *The Prophet*, eds. Regis Armstrong, Wayne Hellmann, and William Short (New York: New City Press, 2001), 519–521.

56. Thich Nhat Hanh, *Zen Keys: A Guide to Zen Practice* (New York: Doubleday, 2005), 44.

57. Conrad Hyers, *The Comic Vision and the Christian Faith* (Cleveland: Pilgrim Press, 1981), 14–15; and Morris Edward Opler, *Myths and Tales of the Jicarilla Apache Indians* (New York: Kraus Reprint Co., 1969), 31: 406.

AFTERWORD

1. Joan Chittister, *The Gift of Years: Growing Older Gracefully* (Katonah, NY: Bluebridge, 2010).

2. Ignatius of Loyola's Suscipe Prayer, *Spiritual Exercises*, ¶ 234.

INDEX

Note: Figures, and boxes are indicated by an *f* and *b* following the paragraph number

and prey, 242

trophic cascades theory, 240

Preston, Richard, *The Wild Trees*, 82

prophecy, 94–95

  prophetic role of elders, 231

Pseudo-Dionysius, 64

Quammen, David, 40–41, 235

Quran, 221, 230, 283n20

racism, 201, 212, 213, 305n9

Ralston, Aron, 165

rappelling, 180

religious experience, 90, 215

  and disillusionment, 215

resistance, cultural, 189–93, 231

reverie, 20, 78, 99–100

Rilke, Rainer Maria, 45–47, 65–66

rivers, 151–56, 160–61, 162, 164, 178–79

  Buffalo, 201–2

  Cardoner, 222

  Colorado, 38, 154

  Escalante, 165–66, 169

  Ganges, 57, 155

  hyporheic zone, 154

  liquid form of the divine, 155

  Platte, 53–54

  in scripture, 155

  underground rivers, 151–53

Robinson, Marilynne, 226

Rohr, Richard, 5, 173

Ruess, Everett, 172

Rumi, Jelaluddin, 7, 55, 59, 62, 66–67, 78, 274, 283n27

rural folk, 210–11

Ruskin, John, 255

Russian pilgrim, 71–78. See also *Way of a Pilgrim, The*

Ruysbroeck, John, 7, 88

Ryan, John Charles, 255

sacramental mystery, 42

Sagan, Carl, 28, 115, 120, 267

Saint-Exupéry, Antoine de, 169–70

Salinger, J. D., 77–78

sannyasin, 230

Schachter-Shalomi, Zalman, 211

scholarship, xi

  beyond rational analysis, 28

  recovering scholar, 2, 145–46

self

  emptying, 178

  knowledge of, 213, 229

senses/sensuality, 10, 19

Shakers, American, 48

Sheldrake, Rupert, 260

shinrin-yoku, 21

Silverstein, Shel, *The Giving Tree*, 95

Simard, Suzanne, 256

Simorgh, 62

sin, 92, 173–74, 210, 224–25, 228, 293–94n25, 301n32

  is necessary, 179

Smith, Jonathan Z., 197–98

soul, 24, 110, 278n20

  care of the, 17–18, 24

  distinguished from spirit, 11

  entrusting one's soul in a tree, 24

  soul work, 224–26, 274

Southgate, Christopher, 316n36

spider, Spider Woman, 45, 170

spiritual direction, director, 20–21

Spiritual Exercises. See Ignatius of Loyola

spiritual life

  consolation/desolation, 225–26, 309n16

  dryness/aridity in, 157, 225–26

  not an indoor phenomenon, 91

  spiritual practice, 8–9

stages of life, 6–7, 10–12, 95, 249. *See also* adolescence; adults; childhood; elders

  returning for unfinished work, 12, 145

  second half of life, 232

stars, 3–4, 119–24. *See also* music; Winter Hexagon (the Jeweled Face)

  Cahokian astronomy, 115–16, 121–22

  Hubble Space Telescope, 119–20